The Oriental Carpet

P. R. J. FORD

The Oriental Carpet

A History and Guide to
Traditional Motifs, Patterns, and Symbols

HARRY N. ABRAMS, INC., PUBLISHERS, NEW YORK

To the three who waited

Library of Congress Cataloging in Publication Data

Ford, P. R. J.
    The oriental carpet: a history and guide to
    traditional motifs, patterns, and symbols.

    Bibliography: p. 342
    Includes index.
    1. Rugs, Oriental. I. Title.
NK2808.F65   746.7′5   80-28851
ISBN 0-8109-1405-0   AACR1

Published in 1981 by Harry N. Abrams, Incorporated, New York

Designed by Bridgewater & Grain, Brighton
Text filmset in Great Britain by Tameside
Filmsetting Limited, Ashton-under-Lyne

Printed and bound in Japan

CONTENTS

PREFACE AND ACKNOWLEDGEMENTS

This book owes its existence to four carpet dealers, without whose generosity the project would have been unthinkable. They are: Alfred Böhmler, Horst and Eva Engelhardt and Bryan M. Huffner. Mr Huffner taught me most of what I know about oriental carpets and spent many hours giving me advice and guidance on many aspects of the book. Above all, he put the vast carpet stocks of OCM (London) Ltd at my disposal for the many photographic sessions needed to provide the illustrations. Herr and Frau Engelhardt were associated with my project from the beginning and lent me a very large number of outstanding photographs first published in their splendid exhibition catalogues 'Naturperlen' and 'Teppiche, die Bilder des Orients' (Carl Winter Universitätsverlag, Heidelberg). Herr Böhmler, although not involved with the book until a fairly late stage, came to my aid with a further large collection of photographs at a critical moment and gave very generous assistance in respect of several items I particularly wanted to include but could not find elsewhere.

In expressing my thanks to these four I should not like to forget the many friends, museums and other organizations throughout the world who have provided photographs for use as illustrations and who are named individually in the list of photographic sources overleaf; and those who have helped by filling in the many detailed gaps in my knowledge. In particular my thanks are due to R. D. Parsons for frequent advice on the important Afghan and Beluch sections of the book; to H. G. Cros for guidance on the Hamadan area; to Roland Malek-Karam in respect of the Bakhtiari carpets; and to H. Russ, editor of the magazine *Heimtex*, for several times helping me obtain suitable illustrations.

P. R. J. FORD

SOURCES OF ILLUSTRATIONS

Except as noted below, all photographs of carpets reproduced in this volume show pieces from the stocks of OCM (London) Ltd; in addition to thanking the company for allowing special facilities for photography, the author is also grateful for permission to use the description 'Kaimuri' which is registered as a trade mark by OCM. The maps (the majority are based on the OCM map of the Orient) and line illustrations (except where otherwise indicated) were drawn by Bridgewater & Grain. The sources of the remaining illustrations are as follows:

Galerie Ammergasse, Tübingen 369; Bodleian Library, Oxford 144; Einrichtungshaus Böhmler, Munich 53, 73, 81, 85, 94, 102, 120, 164, 226, 267, 277, 287, 300, 301, 320, 322, 323, 326, 331, 353, 411, 413, 445, 457, 470, 480, 481, 497, 502, 540, 564, 568, 573, 581, 594, 596, 598, 632, 633, 635, 648, 563, 656, 664, 671, 672, 683, 697, 706, 711, 723, 725, 726, 731, 735, 736, 748, 778, 784; British Library 607, 743;

I Introduction

INTRODUCTION

This volume is intended as a handbook on rug identification, a practical guide to the six hundred or so basic design styles most commonly found among the vast numbers of modern oriental carpets sold every year in the West. Although notes on the history of carpet design are included, the book is not intended as a survey of old and antique carpets; it is rather a survey of oriental carpets as seen from within the trade, and is intended to illustrate the types currently widely available both in the Orient and in the West and to help the buyer to narrow his choice and gauge value for money by recognizing styles and places of origin. Old and antique carpets, usually given prominence in books on carpets, in fact account for no more than a tiny fraction of total sales; they are therefore illustrated only if they are still available in the trade in large quantities, or if they throw light on designs still in use.

How to identify an oriental carpet by its design

It must be emphasized at once that in the narrow sense one cannot identify an oriental carpet simply by its design. The classical method used by experts in the carpet trade is to study the weave. To the trained eye the source of any oriental carpet can be ascertained by a quick glance at a small area of the back – even to the extent of pinpointing the precise village it came from. In practice, however, most carpet dealers will tell a carpet's origin by reference to the front – from the design and the colours. The dealer will turn to the back only for confirmation, or if the front foxes him. Thus, while the weave is the final arbiter, the usual guide is the design. The aim of this book is to place that guide in the hands of the non-specialist, whether his aim is commercial – the better to judge the value of what he buys – or intellectual, to increase his understanding and appreciation of an oriental rug. However, as in any other specialized field, a little learning is a dangerous thing, and even if one prided oneself on being able to distinguish, perhaps with the aid of this book, a genuine Persian Tabriz from a Rumanian imitation, one would be ill served if one did not also know that many a Balkan copy today is in fact of better quality than a Tabriz original. The prudent buyer – and it must be emphasized that care is always necessary when making a choice – should be advised by an expert retailer whose stocks are large enough to demonstrate all the different possibilities and whose taste and probity are beyond question. Even with such expert advice, however, the buyer will be better equipped to assess a carpet if he can distinguish a Persian original from a Rumanian copy than if he cannot.

The classification adopted here is different from that followed in most books, where the treatment is usually alphabetical or geographical, surveying the output of each place according to the characteristics of the place. Here, it is the characteristics of the design which are the key to the classification. The illustrations are grouped according to similarity of design, with the dual purpose of suggesting the complexity of the interrelationships between widely separated areas of production and of illuminating, for example, just what it is that distinguishes one village's style from another village's interpretation of the same design. In order to compare the many different designs often encountered in one centre of production, and to discover the stylistic features which unite them, the reader should make copious use of the index.

CLASSIFICATION OF ORIENTAL DESIGNS

The obvious feature that strikes most people about any given design is whether it has a medallion or not. This is, however, not a suitable starting point for categorizing designs, since the output of most places that produce carpets includes some with medallions and some without. The reader must therefore train his eye to notice the fundamental distinction that exists throughout the Orient between designs made up of rectilinear elements (with lines at 90°, 180° and 45° to each other) and those which also contain genuine curved lines. In order to avoid constant repetition of the words 'rectilinear' and 'curvilinear' the two types are generally referred to in this book as 'geometric' and 'floral', respectively. What is at the heart of the difference? Technically, it is decided by two factors: the fineness of the weave and the circumstances in which the carpet is produced. Culturally, the two types often reflect racial and religious differences, e.g. between the Turkish and Persian peoples, and within Persia the difference between country and town weaves.

FINENESS OF WEAVE

The finer the weave, the easier it becomes to produce curvilinear designs. In a typical coarse peasant weave there are simply not enough knots to enable a fine curve to be produced. By very skilful designing, however, the Rumanians manage to weave floral designs in the Persian style using only 110,000 knots/m² (about 70 knots/in.²). This is a remarkable achievement, even if one is often left with the impression that the designers have tried to incorporate more detail than the stitch will allow; certainly anything coarser than this is suitable only for geometric designs. (Chinese designs, it should be noted, are a special case, owing to the particular characteristics of Chinese art; cf. p. 313 and figs. 381 and 567.)

1, 2 The 'Shah Abbas' palmette in rectilinear and curvilinear forms; only by the use of a fine weave can the appearance of a curve be produced.

3, 4 In a carpet with, say, 65,000 knots/m² (42 knots/in²) the Persian weaver is limited to geometric forms such as the motif seen in fig. 3, but when a fine weave of, say, 260,000 knots/m² (168 knots/in.²) is used for a similar motif (fig. 4), careful plotting of the knots on graph paper makes it possible to create an impression of curved outlines.

5 Rumanian hunting design (detail): the weave used, of 110,000 knots/m² (70 knots/in.²), is really too coarse to convey clearly the amount of detail in this design, and consequently the animals have a clumsy and distorted appearance.

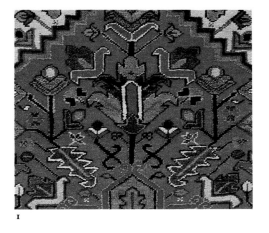

1

2

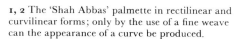

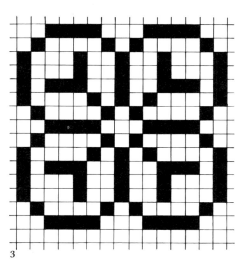

3

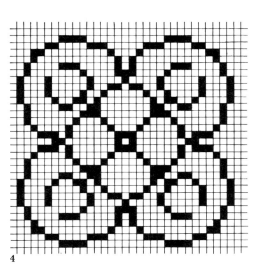

4

5

DESIGN CONDITIONS

The Rumanians run a thoroughly organized carpet-manufacturing operation (i.e. the carpets are still hand-made, but in factories or in a carefully controlled cottage industry), and this provides the clue to the second important factor. To obtain curvilinear designs one needs to set the whole pattern out on graph paper or some other design layout. This usually involves some kind of manufacturing organization, whether on the vast scale which is common in China, India and many other places, including some of the cities of Persia, with maybe thousands of weavers working for one company, or simply on the basis which is typical of provincial Persia, where one designer has only a handful of looms working for him.

The key feature in manufactured production is that the designer and the weaver are not the same person. With most nomad and village production in Persia and elsewhere, however, the weaver is also the designer. In other words, there is no design, pre-set, at all; it is created by the weaver as he (or more often she, for most carpet weaving is done by women) goes along. Under these conditions intricate floral designs are generally not possible; and even if they are technically feasible, such designs do not belong to the local tradition and hence are not produced. One may therefore make the generalization that peasant carpets are usually geometric, and manufactured or town carpets are more likely to be floral. As with all statements about oriental carpets, there are exceptions to this one, but in essence it holds true.

The reader should note the rather special use made in the trade of the word 'manufactured'. It does not in any case imply production by machines: all oriental carpets described in this book are woven entirely by hand. Only rarely, moreover, does the word imply production on hand-looms in factories. The point is simply that the word 'manufactured' refers to carpets made to order, for sale, and to designs prescribed by the manufacturer or buyer. Many people find manufactured carpets stereotyped and characterless and cling to the tribal types as being purer and more genuine: the simple, unaffected geometric designs are the symbols of a traditional culture from which Western civilization, dominated by machines, has become estranged. This view, however, disregards the fact that the highest peaks of Persian art have always been considered to include the fine carpets produced by teams of designers and skilled weavers in the Court Manufactories of the sixteenth century, whose descendants today are the artisans of the factories of Tabriz and Isfahan, Kashmir or Hereke. One may point to the incredibly fine workmanship to be found in these and many other manufactured carpets today, with their properly thought-out designs, harmonious colours and superb materials, and compare the results with some of the inferior work produced by many a latter-day nomad: one may easily confuse originality and unaffected naïveté with plain slovenliness. It will also be apparent from the pages of this book that for all the nomads' traditional methods of work, the designs themselves are often re-workings of ideas first developed by master-designers in the manufactories.

There are thus powerful arguments on both sides, and in the choice of a carpet the final arbiter can only be the buyer's individual taste. However, as one begins to delve deeper into the differences in design one notices that in the original 'heart-lands' of the oriental carpet – Turkey, Persia, the Caucasus, Turkoman Russia, Afghanistan and Sinkiang – the floral designs are produced mainly by Farsi-speaking weavers (i.e. Aryan Persians), whereas nearly all the designs woven in Turki-speaking areas are geometric. The stylistic similarities of the carpets woven by the Turki-speakers seem to reflect the common Uralic/Altaic origin of the weavers and a cultural unity which has been preserved over thousands of years despite the geographical dispersal of the people. These carpets may thus be said to reflect the spirit of the people as much as the skills of any individual. As with folk music, no one knows the origins of the art, the names of the composers and designers. It is the corporate embodiment of the people's experience that speaks to us in their works.

With the manufactured town carpets of the Aryan Persians the situation is different; they correspond to the art music of the great composers, for these 'composed' pieces show off the skill of the individual designer and weaver, though they are no less traditional for this. On a visit to Meshed the author was amazed to see that the working drawing used by the weaver was not coloured in. 'Not at all

6 Preparing a loom drawing (*naksha*) in an Indian carpet manufactory; when working on complex formal designs, the weaver depends on the graph-paper drawing as his guide.

unusual', was the comment, 'the weaver knows how to colour it – he has been making Meshed carpets for forty years.' He will have learned the traditional style as a boy and, having practised it all his life, will pass it on to his apprentices to do the same. So it is not surprising that each place of manufacture has its own 'corporate' identity which transcends the expressive intent of the individual. The experienced eye can tell a Qazi Khan from a Mahmalbaff at a glance; but one also knows that they are both Mesheds and as such are clearly distinguishable from Kashans or Kermans.

The historical differences between geometric and floral designs pose several puzzles. The 2,400-year-old Pazyryk carpet (see fig. 56) seems to be a manufactured carpet, of Persian or other Western Asian origin, employing curvilinear design techniques; however, all other known carpets made before AD 1500 are rectilinear. Only in the early sixteenth century do we see a sudden explosion of floral designs emanating from the Persian and Turkish Court Manufactories. It could be that the floral style was suppressed by the advent of Islam in the seventh century and re-emerged with a change of religious attitudes in the sixteenth; or perhaps it was suppressed in Persia by the conquest of the whole of central Asia by the Turki-speaking Turkomans and Mongols and was brought back when Shah Ismail re-established the Persian Empire. In sixteenth-century Turkey the use of ornate floral designs, in the carpets of the Court Manufactories and in other textiles, contrasted with the strict adherence to a geometric style for most other carpet designs, presents a further puzzle. There is, regrettably, not enough evidence from mediaeval Asia for any firm conclusion to be drawn.

If there is a fundamental difference between 'Persian' floral and 'Turkish' geometric attitudes to carpet design, for the purposes of this book it would be unwise to place too much emphasis on it. We are concerned with carpet design as it is today, and the gradual transformation of the carpet-producing states into 'developing' or 'developed' countries has blurred the clear-cut distinctions which the above analysis suggests. It may be noted, for example, that 'Persian' manufactured carpets will always have been made for sale, whereas the geometric tribal types, where the weaver is also the designer, will mostly have been made for the weaver's own use (again a parallel with art music as against folk music). This may have been true in years gone by, but it is certainly not the case today: thousands of tons of geometric 'tribal' rugs are produced all over the East with just as much commercial intent as is found in any organized floral-carpet industry.

So the subject raised here goes too far beyond the scope of this book to investigate. It concerns the ethnology and anthropology of Central Asia as much as the history of carpet design, and no doubt deeper questions of religion and aesthetics, too. It is

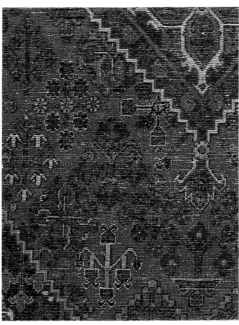

7

8

7 The back of a Joshaqan in a weave of 100,000 knots/m² (65 knots/in.²).

8 A Meimeh rug in a weave of about 320,000 knots/m² (206 knots/in.²); Meimeh traditionally weaves the geometric Joshaqan design, but the fineness of the weave leads to the introduction of curvilinear elements.

referred to because the question of whether a flower-motif in a carpet is drawn in a curvilinear or rectilinear manner has deep implications. A guide to rug recognition needs to stick to obvious technical features; but when we talk of weaving traditions let no one imagine that these represent nothing more than habitual adherence to purely arbitrary technicalities.

There are inevitably many areas where floral and geometric styles overlap. The town weavers who produce floral designs in a fine stitch clearly could also produce a geometric effect if they wanted to; and this often happens, especially in places like Qum and Tabriz where there is a tradition of being able to copy any design, whatever its origin. Thus, a Qum rug in a Caucasian design remains unmistakably a Qum, even though the design is purposely kept rectilinear in the Caucasian style, as may be seen by comparing figs. 518 and 519.

In addition, there are tribes and villages that traditionally make geometric designs, but whose weaving is very fine. All of these could successfully execute curvilinear designs; they do not, however, simply because such designs are alien to their traditions. But the fineness of their work often leads to refinement in which curvilinear elements creep in. The famous design of the village of Joshaqan is an example (fig. 7). Although this is a well-covered design including much detail, it is in essence geometric. The same design is woven in the nearby town of Meimeh, but in a very much finer stitch – perhaps 320,000 knots/m² (206 knots/in.²), as opposed to only 100,000/m² (65/in.²) in Joshaqan. Inevitably the flowers in the design shown here (fig. 8) take on a semi-curvilinear appearance. (Much of Meimeh's output is manufactured.) The basic character is still geometric and the design is classified as such in the following pages; for someone seeing this carpet for the first time it must be very much of a borderline case.

The Joshaqan/Meimeh example brings us to the third and most important area of overlapping between geometric and floral styles: that caused by the interchange of designs between different carpet-weaving areas. There are several universal designs that have been adopted by weavers and designers throughout the Orient. The process of refinement on the one hand and of stylization on the other has often transformed the design out of all recognition, as can be seen from examples of the boteh designs (figs. 9–11). The same degree of difference exists between the many versions of the 'Herati' design (figs. 12, 13). These two universal designs are treated separately in this book: but there are often cases where problems of classification occur. None of the categories (see table of contents) is fully self-contained and some cross-referring is unavoidable.

Certain other groups of designs also need separate treatment. These are: pictorial designs (which are usually curvilinear but need not be so); prayer-rug designs,

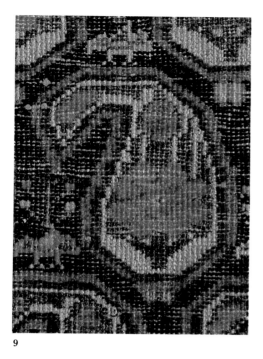

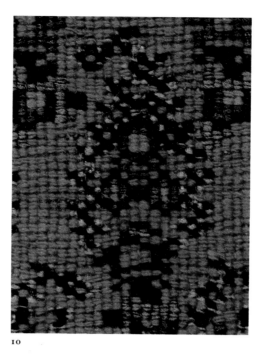

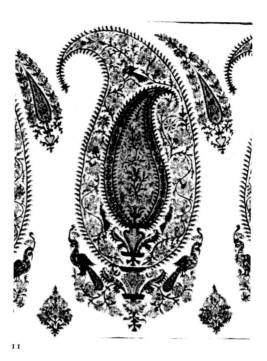

9   10   11

which were probably originally geometric but have been adopted in curvilinear form in many places; and 'garden' designs, which also exist in both geometric and floral varients. The table of contents sets out clearly the different categories into which the various designs are divided for the purpose of discussion in this book.

9–11 Boteh designs from: an old Caucasian rug; an old Serabend carpet; and a nineteenth-century Indian shawl.

Rug identification: the professional approach

If a rug's origin is not clear at a glance it must be deduced by a process of elimination, taking account of such features as the structure, the materials used, the size and shape, and the colour, as well as the design. At the most basic level there are various simple criteria, such as 'all Hamadan village rugs are single-wefted [cf. p. 256], this rug is double-wefted, therefore it is not a Hamadan'; or 'all Afghans have woollen warps, therefore this cotton-warped piece cannot be an Afghan'. Progressing from such basic rules, however, one finds that experience reveals much more subtle clues which make the detective work most rewarding. As we shall have to refer to these clues, both the basic and the subtle ones, over and over again when considering carpet designs, it will be useful to begin by listing them.

THE NATURE OF THE RUG

The vast majority of oriental rugs consist of a pile knotted into a textile backing, but the other types which should be mentioned are: *felts*, which may or may not be

12, 13 The Herati design: variant forms from Qashqai and Nain rugs.

12   13

embroidered; *pileless flat-woven fabrics*, which may also be embroidered or brocaded, and which for simplicity are known under the general name of kilims; and *weft-loop rugs*, which are primitive fabrics with a looped pile sewn into a simple flat weave. This book deals only with the designs of knotted-pile rugs.

MATERIALS USED

Most knotted rugs have a woollen pile, but the pile may also consist of other animal fibres, such as mohair, goat hair, camel hair or cow hair. Silk-pile rugs are made in some places, and artificial silk and cotton are also sometimes found. Mixtures are not uncommon – e.g. part wool, part camel hair; or part wool, part silk. The warps and wefts (see below) of pile rugs are normally wool or cotton but goat hair is also found in tribal goods, and the finest rugs sometimes have silk warps. In China and Turkey one even encounters the use of gold or silver thread as a brocade in silk-pile rugs.

It is fairly easy to distinguish silk from the artificial variety (rayon) – and both of these from wool and cotton – if one is able to put a flame to a small piece of fibre. Wool burns slowly with a bright flame, leaving a residue that smells like burnt hair; carpet silk does not burn with a flame, but simply glows and is reduced to ash; artificial silk reacts in a similar way but gives off an acrid smell; cotton (and mercerized cotton) produce a flame and leave a powdery ash smelling like burnt paper.

All these materials have both advantages and disadvantages. A silk pile gives a carpet great brilliance but generally it is not very hard-wearing. Mohair is fine, brilliant, hard-wearing if densely woven, but very expensive. Wool, when used for warps and wefts, gives a design a great fluidity and tonal warmth but can shrink or stretch very unevenly with changes in atmospheric humidity, so that woollen-warped carpets are very prone to serious distortion in shape. The two examples shown in figs. 14 and 15 illustrate typical problems that can arise with woollen warps and wefts. The extent to which these problems can be considered defects in a carpet is a difficult issue, for such distortions are inherent in the construction and may occur at any time without warning. Many carpet dealers have stretching machines which can be used to correct the faults shown, but their use carries a possible risk of damage to the carpet and there is no guarantee that the fault may not recur. Woollen fringes at the ends of the warps may be very decorative but also tend to wear out fairly quickly. Cotton is a much more stable and reliable material to use for warps and wefts, and in view of the problems with wool outlined above the reader may wonder why cotton, which is readily available throughout the Orient, is not universally used instead. In practice the rigidity which cotton imparts to the structure tends also to be transmitted to the design, with the result that cotton-warped goods almost always have a more rigid and mechanical appearance than woollen-warped ones. This point is well illustrated in figs. 16 and 17, where the greater stiffness of design evident in fig. 17 is due at least in part to the fact that present-day Kazaks have cotton warps and wefts, whereas old Kazaks were always made entirely of wool.

Structure

An oriental pile rug consists of hundreds of thousands of loops of wool individually tied by hand around the warp strings (i.e. those stretched lengthwise on the loom) and firmly anchored by the weft strings (i.e. those running crosswise), a process by which what would otherwise be simply a woven sheet or blanket is converted into the equivalent of a fleece – a conversion which has often been suggested as the motivation underlying the invention of the pile carpet thousands of years ago. It is the way the weaver arranges these three elements – knots, warp and weft – which determines the distinctive 'handwriting' in the weave by which a carpet's origin can usually be determined.

THE KNOT

Apart from the distinctive and unusual knot used in Tibet (see fig. 385), there are only two types of knot used by oriental carpet weavers: the Turkish (often loosely

14, 15 A crooked rug and one which will not lie flat.

16   17

16, 17 An old woollen-warped Kazak rug, compared with a new cotton-warped piece.

called Ghiordes), for which the abbreviation TK is used in the captions to the illustrations; and the Persian (also called Senneh – an odd misnomer since Senneh employs exclusively the Turkish knot), abbreviated here to PK. There was once a commonly held belief that weavers of Turkish origin universally use the Turkish knot while the Aryan Persians and the whole of eastern Asia use the Persian knot. There are, however, so many exceptions to this generalization that it is no longer considered helpful, and some scholars have recently abandoned the terms 'Turkish' and 'Persian' knot entirely, calling them respectively 'symmetrical' and 'asymmetrical' instead. This is no doubt appropriate in a technical sense, but the older terms seem better suited for everyday use and have been retained in this book. It remains generally true that in Turkey, western Persia and the Caucasus the Turkish knot predominates, while central and eastern Persia and all points east mainly use the Persian knot.

18 The Persian knot; the warps are shown half-staggered, as in the semi-ridged construction seen in fig. 419b.

19 The Turkish knot; the warps are shown lying side by side.

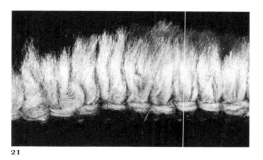

20   21

20 The Persian knot; when the fabric of a rug is opened up one has the impression of the strands of the pile arising from the side of the knot.

21 The Turkish knot: the pile threads are clearly seen to be completely encircled at the base of the knot.

Some authorities assert that the neater appearance of the Turkish knot makes for a certain 'mechanical' over-exactness and encourages the production of more angular, rectilinear designs, whereas the irregularity of the Persian knot is the linchpin of the more exciting and vibrant curvilinear designs which are what most people think of as the typical glories of Persian carpet weaving. There is no doubt an element of truth in this, but it is a sweeping generalization and one that is peppered with exceptions – it would, for example, be difficult to find anything less mechanical in appearance than a Kurdish Kakaberu rug (Turkish knot) or anything more mechanical than a Pakistani 'Bokhara' (Persian knot).

22

23

22 Mounting the warps on a roller-beam loom in India; this is one of many different types of loom used in the Orient, some being horizontal, others vertical. The most important difference in vertical looms is that in some the weaver's seat is raised at intervals as the work proceeds, while in the more advanced type both the upper and lower horizontal beams can be rotated, allowing the finished part of the carpet to be rolled around the lower beam while the weaver remains at the same level. At the beginning of the weaving process the warps are passed around a metal bar secured to the lower beam; the upper beam is rotated to put the warps under tension.

23 Each loom is equipped with an apparatus to divide the warps into two layers. On the loom shown here (at Kerman) two wooden rods are used. Alternate warp strings are attached by threads to the two rods. When one rod is pulled forward the warp strings tied to it separate from those tied to the other rod and create a 'shed', or gap. To release the shed, as is necessary in making any woven fabric, the weaver tugs the mechanism down. The white rod in the illustration is released and the brown rod is pulled forward, with the result that the layer of warps which was at the front falls back and the back layer is pulled forward.

24–28 STAGES IN RUG MAKING

24 The first step is to weave a firm kilim to secure the end of the rug; the loom shown here is a type used in India for sample trials, production looms being much larger, with several weavers sitting side by side.

25 Before the knotting begins, the weaver rolls his different-coloured yarns into balls which are hung above his head. He takes the end of one ball, ties a knot around two adjacent warp strings (one from the front layer of warps and one from the back), slides the knot down to the base of the work and cuts the thread with the heavy knife in his right hand. On the simple trial loom the loom drawing (*naksha*) lies by his side. On bigger looms the drawing is hung behind the warps for the weavers to refer to constantly.

THE WARPS AND WEFTS

The warp strings are the threads stretched by the weaver from top to bottom of the loom before weaving begins (fig. 22). In the finished carpet the warps are thus the 'spine' running from end to end. A gadget on the loom creates a 'shed' between alternate warp strings to make it easier to pass the wefts between them (fig. 23). The last few inches of warp are usually left protruding at each end, forming the fringe. In cheap mass-produced carpets the fringe is often a very rudimentary affair – an inch or two of string hanging out beyond the edge of the pile; but a weaver who takes a pride in her (or his) work will secure the pile with a kilim and go so far as to knot or plait the fringe into an intricate pattern that is both hard-wearing and decorative (see figs. 24, 46). It would be going too far to say that a weaver who takes the trouble to make a good fringe will also be certain to use only the best wool, good dyestuffs and all the other items that go to make the best rugs. A neat and well-secured kilim and fringe is only a sign, but a good sign.

The next step after the warps are mounted on the loom is to produce the kilim mentioned above. Different areas have different procedures and notable features are mentioned in the commentary on individual types, but the basic technique is for the weaver to pass a series of weft threads through the warp strings, under and over alternate strings, then back again, alternately over and under, to create a tightly woven fabric to secure the end of the rug: this is the kilim. Normally the weaver will use the same colour material for the weft in the kilim as for the warp – white cotton with white cotton, grey wool with grey wool, etc. – even though she may intend to use a different colour weft in the body of the carpet. In some places, however, the weaver typically uses a different colour weft right away, so that the kilim may be pink or light blue or red – or even black. Where this occurs we have one of the first of the more subtle clues to a carpet's origin. Once the kilim is completed, the weaver begins the pile. This starts as a ball of wool with the end hanging down over the weaver's head; she ties a Persian or Turkish knot around a pair of warp strings, then cuts the wool off with a knife. The two cut ends of the knot form the pile.

In the various different carpet types described below, the pile is always produced in this manner – thousands upon thousands of pieces of wool, each tied by hand, knot by knot, around a pair of warp strings and left hanging. Apart from cheating (e.g. tying the wool around four warps instead of two as in fig. 35), there is no short cut to avoid the painstaking work involved in this method of producing the pile of an oriental carpet. The often quite striking differences in the various ways weavers handle the warps and wefts are fairly easy for the layman to detect, and they constitute one of the most important clues in identifying a carpet's origin. Examples are shown in figs. 29–35, 39, 224, 228, 333, 342, 343, 408, 409, 503, 504, 652.

24

25

26

27

28

26 At the end of each row of knots the work is beaten tight with a heavy metal comb and the ends of the pile are cut level with a pair of shears. (After the carpet is finished a further clipping process ensures a smooth pile.)

27 After completing each row of knots, the weaver passes the weft through the shed between the warps and beats it into place with his metal comb. In a single-wefted carpet he then releases the shed and ties another row of knots. In the case of a double-wefted carpet he releases the shed and passes the weft back again in the opposite direction before tying the next row of knots.

28 When the rug is finished a further kilim is added and the end is overbound with a tight chain stitch to prevent anything coming undone. The warps are then cut at top and bottom to create the fringe. In some areas the weaving is begun tight against the bottom steel rod; when the rug is finished the warps are not cut at the bottom, the rod is simply removed, giving a fringe at the top only.

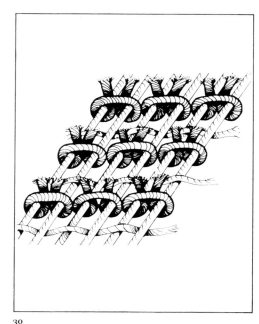

29 The back of a single-wefted carpet. The weft, covering alternate warp strings in alternate rows, is clearly visible.

30 Single-wefted structure using the Turkish knot, seen from the front.

29

30

'Single-wefted' is the description given to the structure where the weaver ties one row of knots across the whole width of the carpet, passes the weft from left to right through the shed in the warps, reverses the shed and then ties another row of knots straight away before passing the weft back again from right to left. If one turns a carpet over it is usually possible to see that there is only one weft between each row of knots, although in some very fine weaves it may be necessary to look particularly closely.

The back of the carpet is flat and if the warp is white and the weft a darkish colour (they usually are) specks of white show through in zigzag rows: the pieces of warp covered by the weft in one row show up white in the next because the weft now covers the alternate threads after the change of shed. This technique is standard in the greater Hamadan area, including the Kolyai Kurdish tribal district, in Senneh, the Karaja-Bilverdi-Barjid region, Daghestan and much of the Bakhtiari province. It may also be found in tribal rugs from many areas – although most tribal rugs are double-wefted (see below) – and in parts of India and Pakistan.

'Double-wefted' weaving involves passing the weft thread through twice between each row of knots, once in each direction with a change of warp-shed in between. Examination of the back of a carpet made by this method will show that both the warp threads on which any given knot is tied are covered by one or other of the weft threads. If the weaving is even and tight no warp threads will be visible at all (figs. 31, 32). This is the case, for example, with Chinese carpets and many fine Persian weaves. In carpets made elsewhere, however, some feature or other of the weaving technique will frequently allow parts of the warp to peep through on the back, and this contributes to the pattern of the weave which in turn helps in distinguishing one double-wefted structure from another.

A good example of this is Birjand (fig. 33). In this carpet the mass of white specks on the back makes one wonder at first if the carpet is not perhaps single-wefted. The way to be certain is to open up the pile from the front (fig. 34); by this means one can see quite clearly whether there is one weft or two. This example also reveals the cause of the white specks: the use of the *jufti* knot. This is a malpractice that is found in many parts of the Orient; the knot is tied over four warp strings instead of two (fig. 35). In extreme cases this practice can effectively spoil the carpet since it halves the pile density.

The double-wefted category also includes certain tribal goods with more than two wefts: pieces with as many as eight or nine wefts are occasionally encountered. In older goods the use of three wefts was standard in some areas, but these are still normally referred to as 'double-wefted'.

The thickness of the wefts has an important influence on the pattern of the weave. Clearly, if two wefts of equal thickness are used the effect will not be the same as if

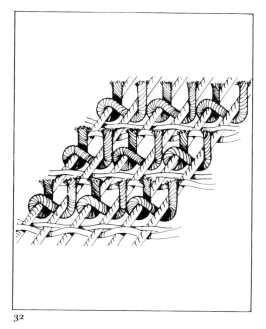

31 The back of a double-wefted Bakhtiar rug with a ridged construction (see also fig. 36). Because of the changing of the shed between the two wefts and the beating-down of the wefts with the metal comb none of the warp threads are visible. They are hidden in the fabric but their location is clearly marked by the vertical ribbing on the back of the carpet. The wefts may or may not be visible, depending on how thick they are and how tightly the carpet is woven. In peasant weaves like the one shown the wefts may be of uneven thickness so that some are more prominent than others.

32 A double-wefted structure using the Persian knot, seen from the front; when beaten down this produces a very tight fabric.

33 Detail of the back of a Birjand carpet, showing a mass of white specks.

34 Detail of a Birjand carpet showing the pile opened up.

35 The jufti knot (in India: langri). Several variant forms are found, all involving the tying of one knot on four warp strings instead of two.

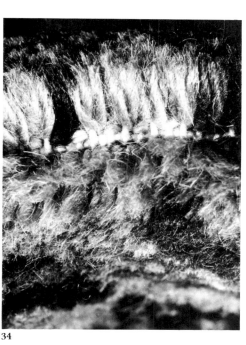

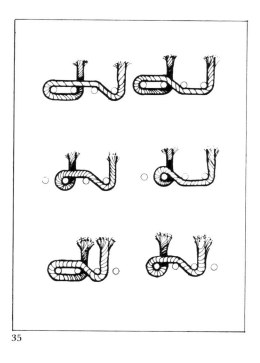

one weft is very thick and one very thin. One of the best structures is produced by using one heavy weft drawn fairly tight and a very light one inserted with less tension. This has the effect of setting alternate warps in two different planes, as fig. 36 shows.

Looking at the back of the carpet, one does not see the warps which appear in the top line of the illustration, but only those in the bottom line. These are of course covered also by the base of the knots which form the pile, so that what the eye actually registers is a series of ridges running the length of the carpet. This is the structure adopted in, for example, most of the manufactured town weaves of Persia.

One important feature here is that the knot is basically square, i.e. there are as many knots per unit of measurement in the length of the carpet as there are in the width. Usually, in fact, there are proportionally rather more knots – perhaps even up to a third more – in the length, especially in peasant weaves, such as Heriz (coarse) or Veramin (fine), but as long as the squareness of the layout of the knots is not too much distorted, the structural balance of the ridged-back technique will be maintained. A different approach to the handling of the wefts is adopted by other weavers, such as the Turkomans of central Asia (fig. 37). Here both the wefts are generally of the same weight, or if they are of different thickness they are both under

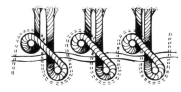

36 Construction (viewed end on) using the Turkish knot with staggered warps, one heavy and one light weft, producing a ridged or semi-ridged back; this structure is also found with the Persian knot.

37 Typical construction (viewed end on), used by the Turkomans and elsewhere, with wefts of equal weight and tension; the back shows little or no ribbing.

38 To produce the selvedge while the rug is being woven, the weaver takes the last few warps at each side, winds the wefts around them and overbinds them with a length of multiple-ply wool, usually the same colour as the outer edge of the pile.

the same tension. In this type the warps all end up in the same plane and the back is flat and smooth. This latter kind of construction does not normally feel as robust as the former.

'Double weave' is an extension of the latter technique. In a carpet with the Turkoman-type weave both halves of the back of every knot are visible, and at first glance one can be misled into thinking there are twice as many knots as there really are. By using very thin yarn and very thin wefts it is possible to pack twice as many knots into the length of the carpet as there are in the width. This heightens the illusion and makes the rug look four times as fine as the ridged-back square-knot equivalent. This is the 'trick' by which Pakistan carpets are made to look so fine, but it seems a very questionable way of putting a hard-wearing carpet together, because both the yarn and the wefts have to be flimsy in order to achieve the desired effect. A properly made square-knot carpet is a better product and will give much longer wear, even if the theoretical – or actual – knot-count is much lower. The number of knots used does not affect the basic principle. The carpet may be as fine as Sarukh or as coarse as Alti Bolagh (to quote two Afghan Turkoman examples of the ridged-back technique); it is the *relative* weight of the warps, wefts and pile that matters.

THE SELVEDGE

As weaving progresses on the loom, the side edges of the carpet are formed by the turning of the weft threads at the end of each row (fig. 38). These edges, 'selvedges' as they are called, are usually decorated and secured as the work progresses by being over-bound with coloured wool or some other material such as goat hair. Different places of production have different ways of treating the selvedge. In particular, there is a basic difference between the round, cord-like whipping commonly used (fig. 39) and a flat-woven selvedge which is used only in certain areas (fig. 40). The differences are, of course, not only fascinating in themselves; they are also useful clues to a rug's origin. In some places with a large-scale commercial production, the selvedge is not bound into the main structure during weaving but is sewn on afterwards. This is less satisfactory, but in most cases it is not considered a serious deficiency.

39 Some tribal weavers use more than one colour for the selvedge, producing a 'barber's pole' effect. This is commonly found in Qashqai rugs and those made in the Afshar area (as here).

40 Flat selvedge typical of Azerbaijan, Anatolia, many Beluch and Turkoman types and certain other origins: the weaver has used three pairs of warps for the selvedge but, instead of pulling them together, has overbound them in a flat weave. This rug is finished at the ends with a standard dark-coloured kilim and a plain fringe.

39

40

THE FRINGE

To finish off the carpet, another strip of kilim work is woven, as at the beginning, and then the warp strings at the top and bottom of the loom are cut through, thus leaving a fringe at both ends. The weaver may simply leave the fringe as it is, or perhaps knot or plait it, or decorate it in some way (figs. 41–9). In some places the decoration of the ends of the rug even includes double fringes. However, the weaver may clip the fringes to almost nothing and bind them and the kilims back behind the end of the rug. Moreover, some looms are set up in such a way that when a rug is finished the bottom cross-bar of the loom is pulled out, making it unnecessary to cut the warps; in this case there is no fringe at one end of the rug, only a flat kilim. The buyer should not imagine this is a fault – this method is a perfectly normal and reputable practice in several important weaving areas. The different ways of handling the fringes are, of course, further clues to a rug's origin.

SIZE AND SHAPE

Most oriental rugs and carpets have proportions which need no special explanation – wide runners, narrow runners, rugs 200 × 130 cm (6′ 6″ × 4′ 3″), carpets 350 × 250 cm (11′ 6″ × 8′ 3″), and so on (see also p. 29 for details of sizes and names). The interesting thing from the 'carpet detective's' point of view is that, for no obvious reason, most weaving areas make only a *very* limited range of sizes. In the case of a carpet measuring 400 × 300 cm (13′ 0″ × 10′ 0″), it cannot be an Abadeh because (apart from freaks) that size is not made in Abadeh. Equally, there are places which make exclusively – or very largely – particular unusual sizes, Kurdish rugs being a good example. Almost the whole village production of the huge Kurdish area of Persia and Turkey is in long and narrow sizes – typically 250 × 130 cm (8′ 3″ × 4′ 3″) in Persia, even longer in Turkey. In most of Persia squares and squarish shapes are less common, but again some areas specialize in them (Meshed for carpets, Sirjand for rugs, for example, and Kerman for carpets and rugs). Circles and ovals are made in quantity in China and India, but not elsewhere. A few are made in Tabriz, Kerman, Nain, as well as Turkey, but they are usually inferior in execution.

The colours

It takes a long time to acquire an eye for the typical colourings of a particular region, and this can be done only by the study of the actual rugs at first hand. The subject is so complex that a whole volume could be written on this aspect alone, and even then the reader would be given little more than a crutch on which to lean, owing to the limitations of colour printing, which can never do full justice to the subtleties of various shades. Great care has been taken with the colour illustrations in this book to try to convey the genuine colour 'flavour' of each region, but in the last resort it is simply not practicable to try to show on paper the precise characteristics of the colours and colour balance of a new Ferahan which enables one to distinguish it at a glance from a Borchalu in the same design. One has to see the actual rugs – and indeed many examples of Ferahans and Borchalus – to appreciate the difference.

However, this question of colour is crucially important; it plays a much bigger part in carpet recognition than is generally realized, and hence some time must be spent considering the subject in detail, and the many references to individual colours in the body of the book must not be overlooked.

The factors that influence the colours of an oriental rug are:

(1) the dyestuffs used;
(2) the wool or other materials used;
(3) the kind of wash the rug has received;
(4) the age and condition of the piece.

(1) DYESTUFFS

There are five rough categories into which one can divide the dyestuffs employed in carpet weaving in the Orient: (a) natural (i.e. vegetable and animal and sometimes mineral) dyes, properly used; (b) natural dyes, badly used; (c) fast synthetic dyes; (d) semi-fast synthetic dyes; and (e) fugitive synthetic dyes.

41

42

43

44

45

46

47

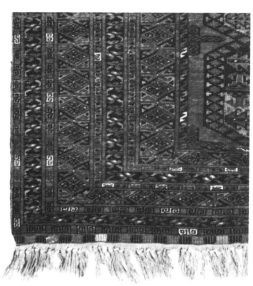

48

49

Natural dyestuffs, properly used, are unquestionably the best; they are rarely garish in themselves and usually produce subtle and harmonious combinations. They are, however, not fully fast, either to light or to washing, but produce magnificent rich glowing colours when exposed to daylight over a long period of use. It is the use of natural dyes which was the secret of the resplendent colours of antique carpets, for until about 1850 all dyestuffs used anywhere in the world were of vegetable, animal or mineral origin. Since then, synthetic dyes of one kind or another have come to dominate the carpet trade; but it is surprising how many places of production still use at least some natural dyestuffs. To name but a few examples: the best of the Kurdish villages in western Persia have traditionally used natural dyes and many still do so; a few manufacturers still use natural dyestuffs for the better grades of Kerman carpets; the best of the so-called 'Mauri' rugs from Afghanistan contain natural colours, as also do the best Heriz carpets and a particular type of runner from Meshkin in Azerbaijan; there is a small output of Mir Serabend carpets in the villages of the Arak region (western Persia), where *ronas* (madder root) is used for the ground shade; and most of the Persian tribal weaves (e.g. Afshars, Lurs, Qashqais) use at least some natural dyes. There are countless other individual cases which one comes across – often the result of above-average enterprise on the part either of some Persian businessman or master-weaver or of some European importer. Nor is the present-day use of natural dyes limited to Persia: they are found throughout the Orient from Turkey to China.

In addition, there are still large quantities of goods on the market that were made perhaps some thirty years ago in regions like Heriz, the Bakhtiari province or the Qashqai areas, which at that time used predominantly natural dyes but have since taken to using more and more synthetics in their recent production.

For the buyer, the use of natural dyestuffs is another of those signs that care has been taken over the production of a rug and provides something of a guarantee that its colours will continue to improve as the carpet ages. But, except where the rug has been woven for the weaver's own use, employing dyes derived from plants growing wild in the region of production, dyeing with natural materials on a commercial scale is both laborious and time-consuming, and thus expensive. Moreover, a weaver using the best dyes is likely also to set high standards for the other aspects of her work, which will be reflected in the even higher selling price.

Natural dyes provide many useful clues to a rug's origin. To begin with, there is a definite split between eastern Persia, where the reds are traditionally cochineal-based and thus tend towards bluish, mauve or pinkish shades, and western Persia, where the use of madder root for the principal red shades produces tones more in the brown, rust, orange or rose-brown range. There are also many clues in the subsidiary colours, like the two typical greens used by the Kurds, variants of the same two greens beloved by the Bakhtiari weavers, the famous *dughi* rose (made by softening madder red with whey or lactic acid) used in Bijars and Saruqs, or the unmistakable khaki gold used in Heriz.

How can one tell whether the colours in a carpet result from the use of natural dyestuffs? The answer is that it is not possible to do so with certainty. Nor can one for the most part rely on the assertions of carpet dealers, for natural dyestuffs increase a carpet's value and are a strong selling point, so that there is every incentive for a seller to assume a piece has natural colours unless it plainly has not. In fact, chemical tests can often establish the truth – they are carried out regularly by a few specialist carpet washers, for example – but apart from this one has, as in all matters relating to carpets, to rely on clues, experience and one's eye for colour. It should be noted that two of the most important natural colours – indigo blue and madder red – can be reproduced exactly by chemical means; for all practical purposes these two synthetics may be considered the equals of their natural counterparts.

Among the natural colours, mention should be made of the use of undyed wool. This practice is common in India for cream-ground carpets in French designs, and undyed wool is also used to great effect elsewhere. In carpets made in southern Persia and in Tibetan rugs, for example, full designs are created using only the undyed wool from black, brown, grey and white sheep, the designs often featuring a

41 Detail of an old Chinese rug showing typical rather skimpy fringe.

42 Knotted fringe on a Serabend rug.

43, 44 Typical Kurdish finish on a Bijar rug, contrasted with part of the fringe at the opposite end of the same rug. It is common practice in some areas for only one end to have a fringe.

45 Double fringe on a Beluch rug.

46 Plaited fringe on a Döşemealti rug.

47 Braided fringe on a Luri rug from Khorramabad.

48 Typical decoration on a Kala-i-Zal rug.

49 Typical decoration on a new Bokhara rug.

50 Dyeing indigo in Meimeh; photographed in March 1977.

much sought-after mottled or streaked effect that is produced by the imperfect blending of unbleached and undyed yarn.

The actual dyeing process can, of course, be badly executed with natural dyestuffs just as it can with synthetic dyes. There are plenty of carpets that have been coloured with natural dyestuffs but which are full of streaks because the dye has not penetrated the yarn properly, or that contain an excess of dye which will come out and leave marks on a fitted carpet if the rug is laid on top of it, just as there are examples in which the colours run if the carpet is washed. These defects have nothing to do with the dyestuffs themselves, only with the skill of the dyemaster. The same faults can arise with all dyes, yet with natural dyes the faults never seem to produce results that are as visually unattractive as those arising from the use of synthetic ones.

FAST SYNTHETIC DYES: This type, which is technically most perfect (and which would no doubt be a godsend in curtains on south-facing windows), is in fact the worst for oriental carpets for the very reason that the colours do not fade. However well-balanced and beautiful the colours in a new carpet, they will always get even better if they are able to mellow. The worst offender among the fast synthetic dyes is a hard orange colour used in tribal rugs in many parts of the Orient.

SEMI-FAST SYNTHETIC DYES: Happily, the vast majority of synthetic dyes used in carpet production today are only semi-fast to light and, though they may produce rather hard, even jarring shades in new goods, they will soften with age. If the article is properly made the underlying warmth and expressiveness of the colour combination will assert itself as the dyes mellow with use. The process is rather akin to the maturing of a fine red wine: a great claret when new is unpalatably harsh, and the fine bouquet and mellow flavour come only with age. Synthetic dyes rarely produce the splendid effects achieved by the use of the best natural dyes, but it is easy to over-emphasize the differences. There are many other factors to be considered in the selection of an oriental rug, and those buyers who restrict themselves to goods made only with natural dyes find themselves with a very limited choice at their disposal.

FUGITIVE SYNTHETIC DYES. The first synthetic dye to be invented, in the 1850s, was mauve. It was quickly followed by a wide range of colours which swept the Orient in the late nineteenth century and became such a menace that Persia banned their importation. These early synthetic dyes were not fast to either light or washing, and rugs dyed with them soon became two-tone beige and grey. Many old and antique rugs with practically no colour at all date from this period of fugitive dyes. To some people such rugs are beautiful simply because they are old; and they will of course fit in with any colour scheme! The ban on imports was never fully effective and was eventually lifted, and some of these same cheap fugitive dyes are still used today, especially for the mauve and orange combinations and the strident turquoise green that most Persian villagers seem to love. These dyes should be avoided if possible. One particular disadvantage is that they fade very unevenly, the tips of the pile turning grey while the rest retains its original colour, and blotches appearing where one part of the rug is exposed to more light or wear than another.

(2) MATERIALS

The second factor which affects the colours of a rug is the type of wool or other pile material employed. This is a very specialized subject, for even in an automated dyeing plant different batches of yarn will result in variations of shade even when using the same dyestuffs. The differences in the various kinds of yarn used in oriental carpets can only be fully understood and appreciated after handling thousands of carpets. When an expert touches a rug he can distinguish from its feel whether it is made from the silky yarn of Isfahan, the bristly yarn of Senneh or the soft wool of the Afshars. And when he sees a colour his vision of it is influenced by the type of yarn used – a factor which is turned to practical use in several places. It is not generally realized, for example, that the different shades of red found in Afghan carpets are often achieved simply by using the same dyestuff on different shades of yarn. This yarn/colour vision is one of the deciding factors in the recognition of Indian rugs employing Persian designs, but the secret can only be learned by the study of the rugs themselves.

(3) WASHING

An oriental carpet, when it first comes off the loom, has a very raw and crude appearance and it is universally agreed that before it can be sold in the West it needs a 'polish'. Twenty or thirty years of use in an Eastern home will do the trick: there, all the loose hairs in the wool will gradually come out and the gentle traffic of feet without shoes in a room with little or no furniture will cause the fibres to begin to glow with a natural lustre (that same sheen which is frowned upon when it develops in a businessman's suit!). However, the same effect can be achieved by a process of washing. Many techniques are used in different countries, from simply dipping the carpet in a Persian brook and hanging it in the sun to dry, to complex chemical processing carried out in modern factories in Europe or the USA.

The wash is a necessary part of the finishing process. Apart from taking off the loose fibres, cleansing excess dye and imparting sheen, it also settles the lie of the pile – thus making the design more distinct – and begins the process of mellowing and harmonizing the colours. It is this latter function which may cause problems in rug recognition because some types of washing may change the colours and indeed completely transform the appearance of the carpet. In such cases the design and the weave are a safer guide to origin than the colours, but the washed colours can also help if one remembers that – as in old carpets – it is the reds which may change most in washing. An expert washer can achieve many of the effects which would occur of themselves in the course of time – from leaving the colour bright red to toning it down through any shade from rust, rose, copper to brown, gold or beige. Dark blue also may turn brown, a change commonly found in many old rugs.

(4) AGE AND CONDITION

Unless the dyes are very fast the same colour changes that can be produced by washing will also occur naturally, through exposure of the colours to light and the friction occurring in normal wear. Since the change begins at the tips of the pile and only gradually works down to the base it is sometimes possible to get an inkling of a carpet's age by looking to see how far the fading process has gone. From the point of view of carpet recognition the colour changes caused by age must be taken into account in the same way as those caused by washing. If a Husseinabad rug is described in the following pages as 'bright red', you may nevertheless find examples which are a beautiful soft rose-pink if they are thirty years old or so. Another factor to consider is that the style of colouring – and indeed of weaving and design – employed in any given area may change considerably from one period to another. For example, the Hamadan runners of fifty years ago often had light camel-coloured grounds; today this style is unknown. Similarly, the typical weave of China in the early twentieth century was quite different from the one used now.

The question of age is a thorny problem from another point of view: that of the price. Old carpets invariably fetch higher prices in the West than new ones, partly because there is a tendency in many people's minds to assume that anything old is bound to be better than anything new; and partly because, as we have seen, age often improves the colours. Because of this well-publicized fact buyers and sellers alike are apt to exaggerate a carpet's age. In fact, it is almost impossible to assess a carpet's age accurately, unless actual evidence of the date of manufacture exists or it is of a type known to have been made only at a certain period. The main guide used by experts is the colour, but in many cases this is unreliable. A 100-year-old rug that has not been exposed to the light or to wear will look brand new, whereas a rug made with fugitive dyes and exposed to the sun will take on the appearance of an antique in only a couple of years.

In deciding what to purchase the buyer should not place too much emphasis on the tricky question of age, but should be guided only by whether he actually *likes* the colours and design; and refer to the retailer for much more important matters than the carpet's date of manufacture: its suitability for the use to which he intends to put it, and the question of which carpet represents the best value for money. This is not to say that one should not take the retailer's advice on matters of taste. On the contrary, a buyer selecting a carpet for the first time is quite likely to be attracted by some specious aspect which will later bore him. If one goes to the right kind of dealer one will encounter people whose reputation depends on the soundness of their judgement (a feature which is of course entirely absent in purchases made from the fly-by-night dealers and 'special' bargains in which the trade abounds). Serious dealers have spent their lives under the spell of the weaver's art and can help guide the customer towards the choice of a carpet which is both tasteful in its own right and suited to the buyer and the place where he intends to use it.

Values of oriental carpets

The relationship between price and value in an oriental carpet is the thorniest problem any buyer has to face, for there is only one fully valid definition: the value of a carpet is what someone is willing to pay for it. The oriental carpet is more of a work of art than any other article of everyday use; but it is also an article of greater usefulness than are the creative products of any other art form. Thus it has several 'values'; which one predominates will depend on whether the carpet in question is regarded more as a work of art or more as an article of use. The most important aspect is the carpet's aesthetic value. The opinion may have been voiced among sociologists in the Orient that it is somewhat demeaning to make carpets by hand; that, however, is a view of pure materialism. Just as every great composer can be said to have composed 'by hand', so it is the creative hand of the weaver that provides the key to the carpet's expressive power. For the Western buyer, however, many oriental carpets represent more than the artistic expression of a single individual: they embody the experience of a whole people, they are an expression of the achievements and sufferings of a different cultural tradition and, beyond that, of the aspirations of the human spirit. The desert nomad, struggling to create out of sheep's wool and goat hair the flowers in the garden that he can never have, speaks to us through his carpet (exactly as, in the context of music for example, Beethoven does, struggling with the Angel to impose his will on the recalcitrant form of the fugal Credo of the *Missa Solemnis*). This aesthetic value can never be measured in money terms at all, but it is this value which has in fact utterly confused the price relationships of different carpets.

Unlike music or paintings, however, oriental carpets also have a functional value and hence a limited life. Regrettably, many members of the public believe – and many carpet dealers encourage them to believe – that all oriental carpets will last for generations. This is quite unrealistic, not to say utter nonsense. The vast majority of oriental carpets are not designed for the kind of treatment to which we subject them and many will not stand up to heavy wear in a Western home. If one is seeking a really hard-wearing carpet one has to accept that the available choice is *very limited indeed*. Very few oriental carpets currently available will last for generations if heavy demands are made on their functional value as floor coverings. Moreover, the chances of getting a hard-wearing carpet do not increase in proportion to the amount one is prepared to pay. In the trade one often hears remarks like 'At this price I expect my carpet to be hard-wearing as well as decorative.' On reflection, however, in many cases the opposite is likely to be true, for the more people are willing to pay for the aesthetic value of a carpet the smaller will be the proportion of the price attributable to its functional value. If one attaches to a carpet's aesthetic value the kind of importance which the best examples undoubtedly deserve, one should treat whatever wearing qualities that carpet possesses as a bonus, not a prerequisite.

The third consideration is a carpet's investment value. An oriental carpet has three disadvantages as an investment. It does not pay an annual dividend – indeed its owner needs to insure it against being stolen. Secondly, as in the case of jewellery and antiques, the purchaser has to pay the retailer his profit margin and it will be some time before the investment appreciates enough in value to cover this outlay as well as yield a profit should one decide to re-sell the carpet. And thirdly, the use of a carpet as a floor covering carries the risk that it will become worn to the point where the value of the investment is impaired. Nevertheless, if the prospective buyer is properly advised and both thoughtful in making a choice and careful in the subsequent treatment of an oriental carpet, it can be among the best possible long-term investments. Almost all oriental carpet prices have risen steadily – and indeed often quite steeply – since the Second World War. As with all investments, there are many factors which influence the relative rate of increase in value between one type and another. In general, Persian carpets have risen fastest and in the long term will no doubt continue to rise, and whatever the country of origin it is wise to go for the best. Thus, if one is looking only at a carpet's investment value, a top-grade small piece is a better buy than a medium-grade large one. A further point worth remembering is that imported items like carpets have their own built-in protection against that part of a country's inflation which is attributable to devaluations of the currency. Since the Persian rial was one of the world's more stable currencies in the 1970s the prices of Persian carpets rose by 35% in France, by 45% in the U.S.A. and by a full 100% in Great Britain, purely as a result of fluctuations in those countries' currencies. Only in Germany, Switzerland, Austria and the Benelux countries were the price rises actually held back by exchange-rate movements.

In view of the three distinct aspects outlined above, the reader will now see why the price reflects only what people are willing to pay and in no way what some dealers would like to call the 'worth' of a carpet. There is no direct connection whatsoever between the 'worth', or absolute value, and the price.

Carpet sizes and names

In the technical sense, the word 'rug' as used in Great Britain indicates a piece with an area of up to about 3½ square metres (35 square ft); pieces larger than this are called carpets. In the U.S.A. this distinction is not made: all sizes are 'rugs' (the term 'carpet' is used when referring to machine-made goods). In this book the British usage is followed. Certain sizes of oriental rugs are, however, frequently referred to by their Persian or Turkish names, of which the commonest are listed in the table overleaf. Generally speaking, the sizes of Turkish types are smaller than their Persian equivalents: Turkish seççadehs, for example, often measure no more than 180 × 120 cm (6′ 0″ × 4′ 0″).

	Approximate size
pushti or *yastik*	100 × 60 cm (3′ 3″ × 2′ 0″)
zarcherek or *çerek*	130 × 80 cm (4′ 3″ × 2′ 9″)
zaronim or *namazlik*	150 × 90 cm (5′ 0″ × 3′ 0″)
mossul	200 × 100 cm (6′ 6″ × 3′ 3″)
dozar or *seççadeh*	200 × 135 cm (6′ 6″ × 4′ 6″)
long kharak	200 × 70 cm (6′ 6″ × 2′ 3″)
kelleyi	a very wide runner or long and narrow carpet, e.g. 320 × 170 cm (10′ 6″ × 5′ 6″), 500 × 200 cm (16′ 3″ × 6′ 6″) or 250 × 130 cm (8′ 3″ × 4′ 3″)

In addition, one comes across many words indicating different forms of nomad bag or tent decoration. Some of these are:

torba or *telis*: small single bag;

khourjeen: double donkey bag;

choval: single camel bag (although originally produced in pairs);

jallar or *penjerlik*: tent bag;

pushti: pillow or cushion (same word used for small rug);

asmalik or *osmolduk*: ceremonial camel trapping.

These and other terms are often seen in display windows without any further indication of origin and are mentioned here for that reason. There are almost no illustrations of these items in this book because they represent a class apart requiring very specialized treatment. The designs used in individual cases often constitute a distillation of the essential design elements in general use in the weaver's tribe. Thus while these items are completely characteristic of their place of origin in style, they are also often quite epigrammatic, not to say enigmatic, in actual design. To illustrate them in a general compendium of typical patterns such as this book would be more likely to confuse than to inform.

A note on knot-counts

Every carpet-producing region has its own method of describing the fineness of the product. In Pakistan, for example, descriptions like '9/18' are used: this refers to a double-weave structure with 9 knots per inch in the width and 18 knots per inch in the length. In Kerman they speak of '80/40'. This is not a double-weave indication: it means 80 *warps* in the width (i.e. 40 knots) and 40 *knots* in the length, measured per *gireh* (about 7 cm or 2¾ in.). In Kashmir one hears of '10/12' or '16/16'; this indicates the number of knots per inch, a straightforward system. In all systems the width is always given first. In China '90 lines' or '70 lines' refers to the number of knots per foot in the width; the length is not stated but the knot is assumed to be square. In Meshed the weavers are paid by the *moghad*, a unit of 12,000 knots, and the fineness of a carpet is calculated by the number of *moghads* per square metre; again the weave is assumed to be roughly square. The quaintest system is that used in Bhadohi in India, where figures like '5½/40' are quoted: the first figure indicates the number of scores of pairs of warps per yard in the width, the second means the number of pairs of knots per quarter-yard in the length! The UNCTAD agreement on aid for developing countries lays down classifications based on the number of knots per linear metre of warp, a system useful to no one except compilers of official statistics.

While it is fascinating to hear of all these different systems, for practical purposes the international carpet trade tends to refer to the number of knots per square metre, and this method (with approximate imperial equivalents in parentheses) has been adopted in this book. Many dealers, though, are sceptical of quoting knot-counts at all, and rightly so, since fineness of stitch is only one factor in assessing a carpet's value and in many cases not the most important one. To take an example from the figures quoted above: a 12/24 double-weave rug from Lahore in the Pakistani Punjab, with 460,000 knots/m² (about 300 knots/in.²) – and looking like double that figure – will not normally be as good as a piece made a few miles away in Amritsar, in the Indian Punjab, having a ridged-back 12/12 construction with only 230,000 knots/m² (150 knots/in.²). An above-average Meshed carpet with 200,000 knots/m² (130 knots/in.²) may easily sell for more than a 70/35 Kerman having 250,000 knots/m² (160 knots/in.²). Indeed, one of the most expensive rugs available anywhere, an antique Ning-Hsia from China, will be no less valuable for having only 40,000 knots/m² (25 knots/in.²). Fineness of weave is important if all other things are equal; but other things rarely *are* equal and the layman should beware of being deceived by so easily salable an aspect as fine weaving.

Dates and signatures in carpets

From earliest times it has been the occasional practice of oriental weavers to include the date or a signature, or even an inscription, somewhere in the carpet. One of the most famous of these, in the 'Ardebil' carpet now in the Victoria and Albert Museum, London (see p. 310), includes two lines taken from the fourteenth-century poet Hafiz, plus the date and signature of the head of the manufactory where the carpet was woven:

> *Except for thy heaven there is no refuge for me in this world*
> *Other than here there is no place for my head.*
> *Work of a servant of the court, Maqsud of Kashan, 946.*

The Western buyer may not be able to read the texts that are encountered in rugs, but for the most part they are attractive and appealing little features, often slipped in in a quite unobtrusive manner. In fig. 43, for example, it is possible to distinguish a date and a signature in the Bijar rug illustrated. Other examples are shown in figs. 51–54; in the last of these the date is given in dual form – 1333 AH and AD 1915. The rules for converting the dates of the Muslim calendar into years AD are complicated because the Muslim world has traditionally used the lunar year, which is three per cent shorter than the solar year on which the Western Gregorian calendar is based. For a quick and approximate calculation one can remember that 1400 AH is AD 1980 and work back from there, but a more accurate procedure is to deduct three per cent from the Muslim date and add 622 (the year – in the Christian calendar – of the Hegirah, Muhammad's flight from Mecca to Medina, from which date the Muslim years are calculated). This is the traditional procedure, but it applies only to rugs dated according to the lunar-year calendar. Theoretically, at least, most Muslim countries have now switched to a solar-year calendar, taking AD 622 as year 1 AH and counting the years as the same length as in the Western calendar. Under this system one simply adds 622 to the Muslim date, so that AD 1980 is 1358 AH. The new system was first introduced to the carpet-weaving world when the Russians conquered the Caucasus early in the nineteenth century. Persia switched officially on 31 March 1925. To this day, however, weavers throughout the Orient still sometimes use the old dating system. They also, being illiterate in

51 The signature of Qazi Khan, one of the best-known manufacturers of Meshed; such signatures are woven into the border at the top of almost all Meshed carpets.

52 TCCP, the initials (in the Cyrillic alphabet) of the Turkoman S.S.R., woven into a new Russian Turkoman carpet.

53 The Buddhist incantation, 'om mani padme hum', woven in Sanskrit in a Tibetan rug from Nepal.

54 Kazak rug with dual year date, 1333 in the Muslim calendar, and 1915.

many cases, frequently make mistakes in the figures they include in their carpets, so that a definite attribution of age on the basis of a date woven into a carpet must be treated with some caution.

New Chinese carpets: structural note

The vast majority of the standard new Chinese carpets produced today are in one basic style known by a wide variety of names, such as 'Tientsin', 'Super-washed', '90 lines', all of which tend to be confusing and misleading since they are used to describe a huge range of qualities: the so-called 'standard' Chinese is one of the least standardized of all the carpets of the Orient.

Among the standard types produced in large quantities the very best grade is the contract-quality super-washed close-back 90-line $\frac{5}{8}$-pile mill-spun merchandise, available only to a limited number of Western importers who place large manufacturing orders with the Chinese Government in Peking. Information about the production centres is not generally available: carpets are made in and around Peking, Tientsin and Shanghai but there are many other weaving centres over a large area of north-eastern China. Only fine mill-spun yarn is used in this super-grade, with high-quality chrome dyes and painstaking chemical washing which gives the carpets an extraordinary brilliance. The description '90-line' means that there are 90 pairs of warp strings across 12 inches of the back of the carpet, which indicates a fineness of about 90,000 knots/m² (60 knots/in.²); and '$\frac{5}{8}$-pile' means the wool on the front of the carpet is $\frac{5}{8}$ in. (16 mm) long. 'Close-back' indicates the actual warp and weft construction. As we have seen (figs. 36, 37), the warps can either lie side by side, or almost side by side, with little or no ribbing on the back, or the warps may be staggered, which gives the carpet a ridged back. The first of these constructions is common in old Chinese carpets but is not used in China today, except in the so-called 'antique finished' category (i.e. copies of old goods; cf. p. 123). The ridged back construction can have two forms, as shown in fig. 419; the tighter of the two the Chinese call 'close back'; the other is called 'open back'. In the Chinese close-back construction the warps are staggered to the extent that they lie almost vertically above one another, which produces a very tightly packed and sturdy construction. One odd result is that, since the knot is anchored to the bottom warp, it is not visible from the front, which often leads people to query whether the super-grade Chinese carpets are hand-knotted at all. In fact the new Chinese are among the technically most perfect hand-made carpets in the world. A simple sketch (fig. 55) demonstrates why the knot becomes invisible with staggered warps.

The 90-line $\frac{5}{8}$ Chinese carpet is a superb product, technically sound and made with outstanding materials. An obvious best buy? Unfortunately, not necessarily so, because throughout the Chinese trade the same or very similar descriptions are used for many different categories of goods, with very marked differences in price. Only the 'contract quality' mentioned above has the impeccable characteristics described. But there are several different grades of 90-line $\frac{5}{8}$ merchandise, all good

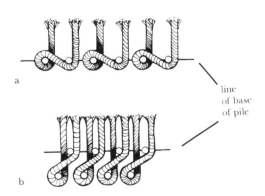

line of base of pile

55
(a) Open back, with warps side by side – knots clearly visible from above.
(b) Close back, with warps one above the other – in this case the knots are invisible from above; this effect occurs only in carpets in which the Persian knot is anchored to the lower of the two warps – if the knot is anchored to the higher warp, as in fig. 419a, it is visible from the front of the carpet, however ridged the back may be.

bargains at their respective prices, but impossible for the layman to distinguish one from another. In addition, there are also $\frac{3}{8}$ and $\frac{4}{8}$ pile goods, and even four-and-a-half eighths (how can anyone ever tell the difference between this and five-eighths of an inch in the pile of a hand-made carpet?). Variations include 70-line as well as 90-line, hand-spun as well as mill-spun yarn, unwashed goods as well as washed, open-back as well as close-back. Tufted and rubber-backed carpets are also made but these and the hand-knotted ones all have the same basic appearance and design styles. Faced with this stupefying array of essentially very similar types of goods, the buyer can do little to find out what are the best bargains among Chinese carpets; he can compare prices and qualities to some extent, but beyond that his best course is to turn to a dealer with wide-ranging stocks, or one whose reputation will guarantee good value for money, whatever the price level.

The aesthetic value of Chinese carpets is a matter of hot dispute and their investment value is low compared with other oriental carpets: the basic price has risen only slowly in recent years and in countries with a strong currency (e.g. West Germany) prices have actually fallen. However, from the purely practical point of view Chinese carpets are good value for money: soundly constructed, of outstandingly good materials and refreshingly free of those 'deliberate' mistakes, which are endearing in some Persian carpets but which in others are no more than evidence of plain shoddy workmanship.

The historical origins of carpets and carpet designs

The earliest carpets which have been preserved, those found in the Pazyryk and other tombs of the Altai region of southern Siberia, date from about 500–400 BC, but literary sources confirm that woollen rugs were in use many hundreds of years before that, although ancient writers rarely distinguished between the five different types of rug described below. Homer, writing perhaps *c.* 900–800 BC, frequently mentions the practice of drawing up a stool and spreading a rug on it for someone to sit down. The word he uses is *kivas*, which means animal fleece. This is, of course, the simplest form of early rug. But occasionally Homer uses a different word. In Book IV of the Odyssey, for example, there is a scene where Helen enters with her ladies. Adreste draws up for her a comfortable chair, while Alcippe brings 'a rug of the softest wool'. Here the word used is *tapés*, which in this context might mean a pile rug, for tapestry-woven fabrics – whichever one of the many different known techniques is employed – are not normally soft, however soft the yarn used – their construction always produces a fabric with a more or less harsh surface. A fourth possibility would be a felt rug, but the most likely meaning is the kind of looped pile rug which is made by weaving a piece of flat cloth into which woollen loops are sewn or in which some of the wefts are pulled out from the front to hang in loops, producing a kind of single-sided terry-towel fabric. This technique is used to this day for simple rugs in Tibet and was certainly used in antiquity, for a rug of this type was found in the Pazyryk tombs. These weft-loop rugs may be said to imitate the fleeces of animals and could thus well be the original form of hand-made woollen rug, the knotted rug representing a technically more advanced form developed from them.

Homer never mentions the design of the rugs or tapestries he refers to. In view of the meticulous detail of his descriptions of other visually striking pieces of craftsmanship it would seem reasonable to assume that the rugs had no design of any consequence. This would support the theory that the Achaeans' woollen rugs were weft-loop products, for a civilization as advanced as that which Homer describes would hardly have failed to take advantage of the decorative possibilities that both tapestry weaving and pile-rug knotting afford. An elaborate ancient Greek tapestry is indeed described by Ovid, in the legend of Arachne, who was turned into a spider after weaving a fabric depicting the amours of the Gods so skilfully that the Gods themselves could not surpass it. Robert Graves suggests that this legend has its origin in commercial rivalry over the flourishing woollen textile trade of the second millennium BC in south-west Anatolia, an area famous to this day for its kilims and tapestries.

The first piece of extant evidence we have of pile-rug knotting is also a carpet from the Altai mountains, illustrated in fig. 56. This remarkable fabric was excavated in 1949 from a frozen underground burial chamber at Pazyryk; now in the Hermitage Museum, Leningrad, it is universally known simply as the Pazyryk carpet. The date of the tomb can be established as fifth century BC, but the origin of the carpet is not known. The nomads who built the tomb were horsemen ranging far and wide over the steppes of central Asia. Russian archaeologists are very cautious in their identification of these people; they may have been Scythians, but the same general area seems to have been the origin of the Turkomans and of the Mongols and the Altai tribesmen are thus simply referred to as early nomads. Other items in the Pazyryk tomb come from places as far apart as China and the Black Sea; the carpet, like other figural tapestry-weave items from the Altai graves, is considered by most authorities to have come from western or southern Persia, or perhaps the Caucasus. Some scholars have asserted that the art of pile-rug knotting originated with the nomads of central Asia themselves: they sought to improve upon their flat-woven textiles by inserting tufts of pile to produce a fabric more like the fleece of an animal but more durable and more comfortable than either. Others, however, take a different view. What distinguishes a knotted-pile rug from a weft-loop pile rug is the opportunity the former offers for complicated designs. Artistically minded ladies of the western Asian leisured classes, or inventive decorative artists working in textile manufactories for the royal palaces may therefore have transformed the 'imitation-fleece' weft-loop rugs of the nomads into knotted-pile rugs, not in order to make a stronger fabric but to overcome the former's design limitations.

Another theory is that the nomads' own artistic instinct lay behind the development. For by inserting additional pile loops into a plain woven fabric it is possible to produce a thick, shaggy rug which could provide an effective floor-covering in the extremes of the central Asian climate. However, if different colours are introduced into the rug to improve its decorative quality, a long shaggy pile will be found to be unsatisfactory: to bring out the effect of the colours it is necessary to clip the pile shorter. Having done this, one needs a finer weave to hold the fabric together; but with a finer weave one can use even more elaborate patterns provided the pile is clipped shorter still. However, whether a weft-loop construction is used, or one containing separate inserted pile loops, there comes a point where clipping the pile down causes the loops to fall out unless they are secured by some form of knotting process. And thus the knotted carpet is born.

Most authorities consider it unlikely that pile rugs were first developed in the earliest civilizations of Egypt or Babylon, since the hot climate of these countries makes thick pile floor-coverings unnecessary. However, we do not know that pile rugs began their existence as floor-coverings at all. If they were used to sit or sleep on they would have been as useful in Athens as in the Altai; and if fine rugs were as highly prized then as they are now they may well have been used as wall-hangings rather than floor-coverings.

Against this must be set the archaeological evidence of Western Asia. It is beyond dispute that there was a great commercial interchange of textile products, including carpets, from about 3000 BC onwards, embracing, in the course of time, the whole of the eastern Mediterranean and Asia from Egypt and Anatolia across Mesopotamia to Persia. The most striking evidence of the use of carpets, for which the author is indebted to Dr Julian Reade of the Department of Western Asiatic Antiquities at the British Museum, comes from the royal palaces of Assyria at Nimrud, Balawat and Nineveh in the period 883–612 BC. Fig. 57 illustrates one of several stone floor-panels from these palaces, all of which are decorated with what can only be carpet patterns. The significant factor is that these panels are found only in doorways and other special situations such as the dais of the throne. Whereas the outer courtyards are paved in brick, the inner rooms have – apart from these doorway panels – plain floors of compacted mud. These must surely have been covered, not – as has sometimes been suggested – with rushes or matting, but with carpets, the designs of which are echoed in stone in areas such as doorways where woollen carpets would be impractical. Indeed, these panel patterns carved in stone are not called carpet

56 The Pazyryk carpet, 200×183 cm ($6'6'' \times 6'0''$), has 360,000 ТК/m² (232 ТК/in.²); this, the oldest known surviving knotted-pile carpet, was found in a burial mound in the Altai mountains of southern Siberia; it is now in the Hermitage Museum, Leningrad.

57 Detail of a paving slab, with carved decoration in the style of a carpet design, from the North Palace of Ashurbanipal (668–627 BC) at Nineveh. British Museum.

designs only because they look like carpets: we have the carpets themselves to prove it. Considering how few carpets and textiles are preserved from this era, it is an extraordinary coincidence that the stone panel of fig. 57 incorporates the designs of two of them: the pattern of the ground is almost identical to that of the Pazyryk carpet (fig. 56), while the inner border closely resembles that of the felt carpet in fig. 60. It has been suggested that the motif in the latter represents a lotus-bud, but in the Assyrian carvings, at least, the inner border motif has the same form as is used for the crowns of palm trees, while it is the outer border which represents the lotus, with buds and flowers alternating. However, this is a moot point, since the lotus goes through many different shapes in the course of its development, and the palmette could in any case be seen as the graphical representation of many different plant forms besides palm-crowns and lotus-buds.

What we do not know about any of the carpets referred to in the archaeological evidence is whether they were felts, flat-woven or knotted. On the evidence of the Pazyryk carpet they could easily have been knotted, for a piece as technically accomplished as this must have been preceded by a long tradition reaching back perhaps into the second millennium BC.

Whatever the origins of the craft, the Pazyryk carpet establishes that the skills were fully developed some two-and-a-half thousand years ago. But from then until the Seljuq carpets of the twelfth or thirteenth century and the Mamluk carpets of the fifteenth the only known rugs are fragments, often only a few inches long, and from sources as scattered as Cairo and Khotan in China. To trace the history of the art in detail is thus impossible. A great wealth of carpets of the sixteenth century, incorporating what seems to have been a radical change in design style, is preserved in museums, and writers have tended to trace all carpets produced since then back to this period. We must not forget, however, that the art was already two thousand years old by then, and whatever was new in 1500 had ancient antecedents. In the realm of carpet design we must look back, once again, at least as far as the Altai nomads and their Scythian contemporaries and predecessors. The leather silhouette of two stylized cockerels (fig. 58), the lotus-bud border from a felt carpet (fig. 60) and the harness-decoration of a gryphon whose tail incorporates a second head (fig. 59) all employ ideas commonly found in carpet design; while the lotus-flower palmette, perhaps the most characteristic and all-pervading single motif in sixteenth-century Persian carpets, is already present in the art of the ancient Greeks and of the Assyrians and Egyptians before them (see figs. 61 and 237).

58 Silhouettes in leather of a pair of stylized cocks, heraldically opposed, used as coffin decorations; fifth century BC, from Pazyryk. Hermitage Museum, Leningrad.

59 Double-gryphon plaque carved in wood; sixth century BC, from Tuekta, central Altai. Hermitage Museum, Leningrad.

60 Border fragment from a felt carpet, showing decoration of applied garland of flowers and lotus buds; fifth century BC, from Pazyryk. Hermitage Museum, Leningrad.

58   59

60

New oriental copies of Persian designs

No separate section of this book has been devoted to the carpets in Persian designs woven today in manufactories in India, Pakistan, Rumania, Bulgaria etc. This is because the principle involved is as old as the oriental carpet itself: time and again in the following pages examples are cited of designs from one area being copied in another. In the history of Central Asia there are frequent instances of the enforced transportation of artists from one area to a totally different cultural region to satisfy the whim of one despot or another who wished to re-create in a new part of his empire the splendours he had observed in another. Beyond this there are many examples of the spread of designs by the voluntary migration of peoples, but above all there are countless instances of straightforward copying or re-interpretation of designs from one area to another for purely commercial purposes, a process which has given rise to many magnificent carpets over many centuries. On the question of principle, then, the argument that the Indian Mir illustrated in fig. 125 is 'just a copy' does not hold water. From time immemorial it has been the practice of carpet manufactories to separate the functions of the weaver and the designer and to require the latter to re-interpret other people's ideas. If the Sheikh Safi carpet was designed in Tabriz (or wherever) in 1535, the version of it woven in Meshed in 1980 is a copy, pure and simple. The same may be said in greater or lesser degree of at least half the carpets of Persia on the market today. As noted previously, only in the case of some of the nomad and peasant weaves are *the designer and the weaver the same person.* Here the weaver will have learned the design as a young girl from her mother and will weave it from memory, adding her own embellishments and variant forms and passing it on to her own children in turn. With some of the pieces created in this manner we can speak without reservation of pure originality. But the tradition of copying designs from the town manufactories is as strong among the nomads as in the manufactories themselves. What matters is what the weaver makes of the design, to what extent she (or he) is able to imbue it with that intangible element we call individuality and originality of expression. Thus the Afshar rug of fig. 708 is a splendid piece of work, rendered in no way inferior by the fact that the design is copied from a nineteenth-century manufactured Persian town carpet, itself based on a eighteenth- or seventeenth-century French Savonnerie original.

It is over the question of expressiveness that problems arise. It is not that the Rumanian or Indian versions of traditional Persian styles are bad in principle but that they are sometimes unattractive in execution. It is partly a matter of scale. No manufacturer in the whole history of the Persian carpet ever produced anything like the quantity of goods at present being woven in the Balkan states and the Indian subcontinent: a single production unit in the Benares area may employ 5,000 weavers with an output perhaps of 100,000 m² (120,000 yds²) of carpets per annum, while the State-controlled manufactory in Rumania produces in one standard quality over 250,000 m² (300,000 yds²) per annum. This inevitably leads to a dull, mechanical repetitiveness in some of the output. But this is not the only factor: the total separation of designer and weaver may leave the latter to work in a cultural sphere which is quite alien to him, which effectively minimizes the opportunity for 'individuality and originality of expression' – or indeed of expression of any kind.

On the other hand, where these new places of origin score is in the quality of workmanship. The Indians, in particular, possess both the technical skills and the attitude of mind which are the essential foundation of outstanding handicrafts. An unstemmable fount of expressive inspiration can sometimes transcend an artist's technical deficiencies – take the composer Mussorgsky, for example – but this is rare: more often it is the fact that an artist has done the job properly, indicating that he understood what he was doing, that secures our admiration. In India – and just occasionally in Pakistan and the Balkan countries, too – one sees carpets which reveal compelling evidence that the weavers really understood what they were doing. At this point the Indian carpet begins to become an art.

On this basis, all the illustrations of Indian, Pakistani, Rumanian, Albanian, Bulgarian and Egyptian carpets have been integrated into the body of this book, just like the Persian originals, but they are listed separately on p. 348.

61 Palmette motifs as decoration on an Attic vase, *c.* 510 BC. This pattern seems to have been developed from earlier representations of opening lotus buds or the crowns of palm trees. An Assyrian version of the pattern, dating from the seventh century BC, is shown in fig. 57.

Symbolism in oriental carpet designs

In an address given in Munich and Mannheim in the autumn of 1978 Prof. Klaus Brisch of the Museum für islamische Kunst, Berlin, declared that the art of the oriental carpet is religious art. He referred to the discoveries of Dario Cabanelas who has demonstrated that the puzzle of the design of the ceiling of the Alhambra in Granada can only be understood as a depiction of the Islamic idea of Heaven, and asserted that many great classical Persian carpets must be viewed along similar lines. He also suggested that we must first understand the religion in order to understand the art. His views seemed to accord closely with those of S. V. R. Cammann, as expressed in a series of lectures (cf. index) in which he took up the cudgels against the many authorities who in the past have viewed oriental carpets solely from the aspect of their place in decorative art.

There is no reason to deny the symbolism and deeper meaning of carpet designs. We know beyond all doubt that Chinese designs are full of symbolical allusions (see p. 167); we also know that people are superstitious in every part of the world. The author was once asked 'why seek a deeper meaning in such-and-such a design? – weavers are simple folk and happy with simple explanations.' That, of course, is just the point: simple folk throughout the ages and throughout the world have relished superstition and religious symbolism. We need only look at the avid readership of the horoscope pages of popular newspapers and magazines for modern evidence of the influence of superstition. And in the era when European rulers sought to save witches' souls by burning their bodies at the stake their oriental contemporaries can certainly be credited with having ordered carpets designed specifically to express religious ideas of heaven and the after-life. Likewise, weavers who to this day clamour for a stricter institution of Islamic law in Middle Eastern countries can just as certainly be imagined weaving these 'religious' carpets and fully understanding the symbolism included in them. Any traveller to the Islamic world will encounter thousands of 'simple folk' for whom the religious concepts of the Muslim faith are very real indeed. Such people are perfectly capable of expressing their faith through the artistic medium of the carpets they weave or of interpreting it skilfully in carpets made 'to the glory of God'. The metaphysical explanations of carpet design may thus have just as much validity as the practical and straightforward ones.

There are, however, flaws in the Brisch/Cammann argument. First there is the matter of aesthetic principle: this is the suggestion that an understanding of the religious origins of the designs is necessary to an appreciation of the carpets. Although this is a romantic theory which is by now pretty well discredited, one still encounters it in countless guises in all the arts. We do not need to ask if anyone still believes they will like Mozart's music better if they know more about his life; nor need we remind ourselves that eighteenth-century composers often used in Masses and church cantatas purely secular pieces which had been written previously as parts of operas or other works. It is sufficient to draw comparisons with directly related fields of Western art, such as religious architecture. Are Protestants to be disqualified from a full appreciation of the Protestant Church of St Sebaldus in Nuremberg because it was originally built by Catholics? This magnificent edifice is an excellent example of the irrelevance of any specific sectarian beliefs to an appreciation of church architecture. It is a remarkable building since it consists of an early medieval Romanesque church completely enclosed within a later Gothic one. On entering, one finds oneself in a spacious but classically proportioned nave which brings to mind words like 'cool', 'restrained', 'devout', 'circumscribed'. Proceeding towards the altar one is embraced by a view of God or of the world dominated by order, sureness, humility, peace, respect. Suddenly one enters the choir, which is a Gothic church built over and around the Romanesque one. The roof at once appears to soar up into the sky, praising God or life with passion and exultant unrestraint, a glowing reminder of those powerful forces of human ambition which were unleashed in Europe in the twelfth century. The climax, however, comes after one has savoured this fourteenth-century Gothic explosion: on returning to the centre of the church one can see both concepts at once.

This overall effect is a truly miraculous experience, and one does not need to be a Christian to be moved by it; indeed, for many people it is not a religious experience at all but a purely artistic one. That it is also transcendental or metaphysical is certainly true, but this is saying no more than that art is expressive. The artist's view of the matter is admirably expressed by Wagner in *Die Meistersinger*. In this portrait of renaissance Nuremberg the Knight Walther, a revolutionary innovative musician, is rejected by the traditionalist composers for not keeping to the established rules. He is however persuaded by the poet Hans Sachs that it is possible to combine genius, originality and freedom of expression with formal discipline and sound technical rules, and that the resulting work will indeed be both more expressive and more enduring.

> Walther: '*How say the rules I must begin?*'
> Sachs: '*You set them yourself and then follow them*'.

This is the key to the appreciation of all art: it must obey its own rules, it must of itself express what it wants to say; only that content can be appreciated which its form communicates. If therefore one can only appreciate a carpet design by reading Prof. Cammann's lecture about it, then as art it has failed. This is the key factor in the argument about the symbolism of carpet designs. Whether weavers are superstitious or purely mercenary, whether the geometric stylization of flower forms is dictated by Islamic law or by the practical limitations of weaving without graph-paper designs, whether Bakhtiari garden designs originated in the weavers' longing for the Garden of Eden or simply because they liked flowers: all these are secondary considerations. What matters is whether the design works as a design, whether the individual weaver's expressive intent is realized, whether the content fulfills what the form promises. If one can grasp this then one need have no fear that one's own appreciation is deficient, whatever the professors may assert.

Some idea of the difficulty involved in tracing the origins of carpet designs may be derived from an essay by Heinz Baranski which appeared at the end of 1978. With reference to the Uzbek felt carpet illustrated in fig. 62 he declares that the three diamond-shaped medallions each contain four geometric motifs which probably represent 'double-headed griffins'. Since the motifs are so shaped that the background reciprocates the same form, Baranski concludes that the artist seems to have intended to 'double the power-laden and portentous bird-symbols . . . in order to strengthen their magic effect.' Maybe; or maybe not. He is no doubt right to draw our attention to the Scythians' almost exclusive preference for animal

62 A nineteenth-century Uzbek felt rug with reciprocating design motifs.

motifs in their art of 2,000–3,000 years ago, with the possibility that this dominant style of Central Asia may have had a lasting influence on the development of oriental carpet designs (this particular motif also appears frequently on early Japanese decorated mirrors). It is also worth considering the importance of ram's horn motifs as a symbol to nomadic herdsmen; and to remember the heraldic use of eagles and falcons by rulers throughout Asia and Europe. However, there is no evidence whatsoever for the specific assertions about fig. 62. On Baranski's own evidence the motifs are just as likely to be ram's horns as griffins (and why double-headed, anyway?), but above all there is nothing to suggest that this particular artist had anything other than decoration in view when he or she set out the pattern. As Baranski admits, the 'wings' of the griffins are unnaturally curled (more like ram's horns, in fact) to create the reciprocating effect. Does this not suggest we have here the work of a highly imaginative artist who, if he was depicting griffins, was perfectly happy to risk upsetting the 'magic' by bending the motif to suit his pattern, rather like a baroque composer who has a splendid tune to make a perfect fugue as the climax of a piece of sacred music. If the words do not happen to fit the tune . . . so much the worse for the words!

Pronunciation of place names

The carpet trade of China, India and Pakistan uses English for all its dealings and we are thus spared the problem of transcribing Mandarin, Hindi and Urdu names. But the other countries of the Orient use Turki or Farsi and countless dialects of these two, written in Arabic, Cyrillic or roman script. It is thus an impossible task to find a universally valid way of transcribing the names. In any case the place names are often not fixed: how one pronounces them depends on who one is and what dialect one speaks. The spellings in this book are those used in the 'Oriental Carpet Map', published by OCM (London) Ltd, except for Turkey where the names are written in roman script anyway. The only thing one needs to remember about Turkish names is that 'c' is pronounced as 'j' (as in jewel), while ç is pronounced 'ch' (as in church) and ş as 'sh' (as in short). For the rest, the Oriental Carpet Map uses the simplest possible transliteration of Farsi and Turki sounds into the roman alphabet with a plain 'q' (not followed by 'u') for the strange deep-throated 'gh' or 'kh' sound which resembles someone shaping up to make a French rolled 'r' but producing a choked 'g' instead. The vowels are all pronounced the way they are in most continental European languages, with a separate sound for each letter, and no English-style diphthongs. Thus Benares is pronounced Ben-ah-res, not Ben-airs; Mary is Mah-ree, not like the girl's name; Sirjand is Seer-jund, the first syllable not being as in 'Sir' in English; Nain is Nah-een, not rhyming with main; and Döşemealti is Dö-shay-may-ull-tee.

The difficulty with carpet names is that the distortions – caused by dialect and illiteracy – are sometimes so great that one does not even recognize which place is meant. Therefore, if a place name proves elusive, one can simply try changing some of the letters: in Persian names half the vowels are interchangeable for a start and, if that does not help, one can try swapping consonants as well. To give an idea of the possibilities, the following spellings – all appearing in authoritative publications – of an important carpet-producing village north of Isfahan provide an instructive case in point:

> Murdschekar (R. Hubel, *Ullstein Teppichbuch*); Murchehkbur (E. Girard, French economic map of Persia); Mortchekort (J. Iten-Maritz, *Enzyklopädie des Orientteppichs*, p. 222); Moutschekar (J. Iten-Maritz, op. cit., p. 81); Murcheh Khvort (*Times Atlas*); Morcha Khurt (British military 'D' survey of Asia).

The recently introduced official spellings of Chinese place names transliterated into the roman alphabet have not been adopted in this book, since they are incomprehensible to most people; they are, however, noted in the index.

II Border designs

BORDER DESIGNS

a

b

c

d

63 The basic outline of the four border types most commonly used in oriental carpets: (a) Herati border; (b) repeating rosette border; (c) cartouche border; (d) meander or scroll border.

A border consists normally of a series of strips of pattern running around the outside edge of the carpet. The centre strip is usually much wider than the others, the latter being called 'guards' and the former the 'main border'. In view of the amazing variety of designs found in the grounds of oriental carpets, it is surprising that the number of distinct border types employed is very small indeed. In fact the vast majority of all oriental carpets include some form or other of one single design (see fig. 63a); this consists of repeated flower motifs facing alternately inward and outward, and joined by diagonal lines, also alternating. The colouring of the main motifs usually alternates too. A second basic border type (fig. 63b), also quite common and having many variants, consists simply of a single repeated floral motif in alternating colours, or just two flowers alternating (perhaps with one larger than the other to provide variety and interest). A third type (fig. 63c) combines elongated medallions (usually called cartouches), placed at regular intervals in the border, with various subsidiary designs both within the cartouches and between them. A fourth layout (fig. 63d) contains a kind of meandering flower-stalk motif winding its way through the whole border, decorated with various kinds of appendages.

In the subsidiary guards – and just occasionally in the main border, too – one comes across various geometric inventions: zigzags, repeating lozenges, pyramids, interlocking and reciprocating patterns of one kind and another.

The first border type (fig. 63a) is properly called the Herati border because of its frequent use in the sixteenth- or seventeenth-century east Persian carpets. Note that the words 'Herati motif' do not refer to this border pattern but to the repeating diamond design which made up the ground of later Herat carpets (see p. 74).

As fig. 61 clearly demonstrates, the use of linked alternating palmettes as a border pattern dates from antiquity. The specific border pattern used in the classical Herati carpets seems, however, to have developed from the fusion of two strains of decorative ideas employed in the Islamic world in the fifteenth century. The first is shown in fig. 64; the tiles illustrated date from *c.* 1500, but the arabesque forms employed are much older (the pattern is used as the decorative border in illuminated manuscripts of the Koran as early as the thirteenth century; it is discernible too in fig. 743). The second and decisive element which influenced the shape of the Herati border was, however, the Chinese cloud-band pattern (see. p. 79). As with most aspects of the history of oriental carpet design, the source material is too scanty for definitive conclusions, but the internal evidence of figs. 65–8 is very strong. The cloud-band motif, shown in fig. 65, seems to have entered west Asian art with the Chinese artists established in Samarkand by the Mongol conquerors at the beginning of the fifteenth century and to have spread quite quickly throughout the Islamic world. By the sixteenth century Persian designers had adapted the Chinese form to their own uses (fig. 66); indeed, in the inner guard of the Ardebil carpet (1539) the classical Herati layout is already established (fig. 67).

The border of the Chelsea carpet (see fig. 175) illustrates in its basic layout the affinity between the cloud-band motif and the Persian-Islamic *mihrab* arch shape,

64

66

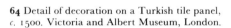

65

67

while the cloud-band itself appears as a subsidiary motif in a form resembling a ribbon tied in a bow. This joining together of the ribbon at its narrowest point is an essential step in the transition from the open cloud-band to the closed 'teapot' shape, the fusion of the Chinese and arabesque ideas. Other examples of this development may be seen in figs. 189, 696; one of the best versions, again setting the cloud-band within a *mihrab* shape, occurs in the border of one of the sixteenth-century animal carpets in Vienna (fig. 68).

Typical modern variants of the Herati border are illustrated in figs. 69–84. Various names are attached to it in the trade, such as 'samovar' or 'tortoise' border, the descriptions being derived from the shape that the principal motif assumes in certain classical Persian contexts. Its use throughout the length and breadth of Persia illustrates both the pre-eminence and the lively interchange of the ideas of the sixteenth and seventeenth century manufactories. However, figs. 69–84 also illustrate how each region develops ideas along different lines and imprints its own individual stamp on a design, whatever its origin.

64 Detail of decoration on a Turkish tile panel, *c.* 1500. Victoria and Albert Museum, London.

65 A very basic form of cloud-band border in a fifteenth-century Mamluk (Egyptian) prayer rug. Before its introduction all carpets had borders consisting of repeating geometric motifs (cf. figs. 389 and 741).

66 A more elaborate form of the cloud-band pattern in a sixteenth-century Herat carpet.

67 The cream-coloured guard of the Ardebil carpet (cf. fig. 702) reveals in embryo the typical layout of the motif used in modern carpets such as the Tabriz shown in fig. 69.

68 Corner turn in the all-over Herat piece known as the 'Emperor's Carpet', now in the Osterreichisches Museum für angewandte Kunst, Vienna.

69 The typical form of the Herati or 'samovar' border in a Tabriz carpet, photographed from the back.

70 A geometric variant used in Heriz, also photographed from the back.

71 The Saruq version is one of the most rounded and well balanced forms.

72 In Meshed the 'samovars' are turned into typical 'Shah Abbas' palmettes (cf. fig. 2).

73, 74 In Joshaqan and Meimeh the motifs take on a beetle-like appearance, while in some of the Bakhtiari villages the idea is further stylized.

75 In tribal rugs from Kurdistan only the bare essentials of the layout are preserved.

76 Some villages of the Heriz area (especially Ahar) use a more developed form of the Kurdish version shown in fig. 75. The two principal borders of the Heriz region (figs. 70 and 76) may thus be seen to be derived from the same idea.

69

70

71

72

73

74

75

76

77

77 Another famous variant is the 'wine-glass' border, seen here in a rug from Shirvan in the Caucasus, where this form is very common.

78 The 'wine-glass' variant is also used elsewhere, as in this Beluch rug.

79 As with many other designs they use, the Kurdish Kakaberu weavers transform the layout: one of the motifs is turned into a stylized peacock, but the subsidiary guard retains the same form as shown in fig. 82.

80 The fine scroll linking the principal motifs in the Herat originals is given particular prominence in Tuisarkan, where it is converted into a pattern that is easily remembered for its 'rope-loop' effect in each corner turn of the scroll and for the spiky decoration along its edge. This distinctive variant is used in several villages of the Hamadan region (see p. 289).

81 Melas and other Anatolian villages adapt the motifs while preserving the basic layout.

82 Yalameh rugs, in common with those of many other Persian origins, also use the Herati border design as the basis for subsidiary guards.

83 A similar variant is found in the guards of Mir Serabend carpets.

84 The strictest geometric form is found in Shirvan and in other Caucasian types.

78

79

80

81

82

83

84

Borders of the repeating rosette type (figs. 85–91) are found more often with geometric designs than with floral: the latter, being produced from graph-paper drawings, usually feature something more elaborate than plain alternating flowers. Repeating rosette borders may nevertheless contain a wealth of fascinating detail. In particular, the absence of a formal layout leaves the weaver considerable licence in the choice and distribution of colours, which many tribal rugs use to striking effect.

The third principal border type (figs. 92–4) is most often found in manufactured floral carpets, often in antique designs. The idea evolved in the fifteenth century from the art of miniature painting and decorative bookbinding. As a result of the superimposition of circles and polygons of different colours, compartment or cartouche patterns were produced (see figs. 743, 744). In carpet borders the cartouches may be used to contain a wide variety of subsidiary motifs.

The fourth border type, again, is more common in areas producing geometric designs (figs. 95–100). This catalogue of principal types is not exhaustive, the possibilities of geometric invention are endless and there are hundreds of individually designed borders which one may encounter from time to time.

Some examples of geometric invention and a few of the more interesting rarer border types are shown in figs. 101–10.

85 Rosette border used in Andkhoy.

86 The so-called 'Kufic' border used in a Perepedil (Shirvan) rug. Early forms of this design are discernible in fourteenth-century rugs, whose patterns are closely related to the decoration – using Kufic script – around arches in mosques of the early Mongol period (cf. fig. 616).

87 An attractive rosette border in a Shahr Babak rug. This modern Afshar rug uses the same version as is seen in old Ferahans, in the Zenjan area and elsewhere in Iran.

88 The Turkoman rosette border as seen in fig. 85 is used here in a modern Kula copy of a Qashqai design (cf. figs. 447, 448).

85

86

87

88

89 A rug from Daghestan illustrates one of the many repeating border motifs, used in the Caucasus and Anatolia, which seem to be derived from totemistic animal forms, but which may have a floral basis.

90 The treatment of the border motifs in a Yahyali rug emphasizes their possible floral origin (cf. fig. 89).

91 The main border motif of this Gebbeh rug is also found in the kilims of Quchan, in north-east Iran, and of the Afshars in the south-east of the country; it is, however, most commonly found in the Caucasus. Its use in south and east Persian goods is evidence of ethnographic links between widely dispersed tribes of Turkoman origin. The motif is also found in old Yamut Turkoman rugs (e.g. a choval in the Victoria and Albert Museum, acc. no. 311–1884).

89

90

91

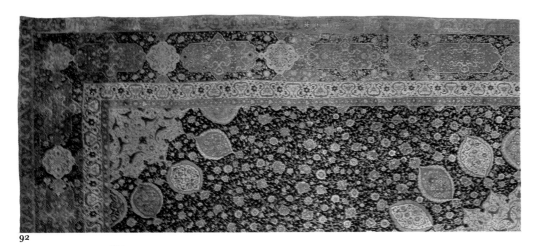

92

93

94

92 The cartouche or compartment border of the Ardebil carpet in the Victoria and Albert Museum, London.

93 The cartouche idea is much used in Qum, as seen in this detail from a silk-pile rug.

94 A Turkish rug with an inscription in the cartouche; this is a modern Hereke rug using a sixteenth-century design. Cartouches containing religious texts are often incorporated into prayer rugs, but frequently only in the upper half of the border to prevent their being defiled by being walked on.

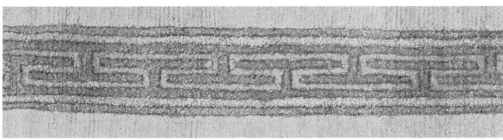

95

95 The meander border dates from ancient Greek times; much used in China, it is seen here in a Tibetan rug from Nepal.

96 The main border used in Mir Serabend carpets, known as the *shekeri* border; it is also used in some Hamadan village rugs.

97 A rather wild variant form of the meander border is found in Kurdish rugs such as Sonqurs and Bijars.

98 Kharaghan: the same version is found in some Shah Savan rugs and other products of the Hamadan region.

99 A Beluch version; in a fully curvilinear form this variant is also found in goods from central and western Iran. The layout is the same as in the border decoration of the Attic vase shown in fig. 61.

96

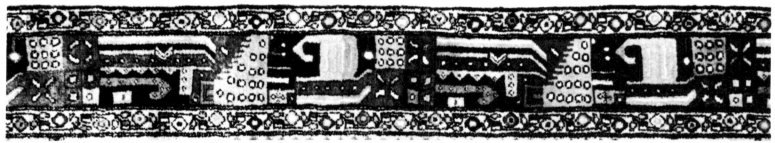

97

98

99

100 An imaginative geometric treatment of the scroll border used in the inner guard of a Sarab runner; this example also includes in the outer guard a widely used reciprocating pattern, with each half of the design interlocking with its matching, but differently coloured, counterpart. The 'fleur de lys' principal motif seems to be derived from the ancient Egyptian or Greek lotus-flower/palmette pattern, and the felicitous idea of using it in a reciprocating form also dates back to antiquity. As fig. 62 shows, the idea is used in main carpet motifs as well as in borders.

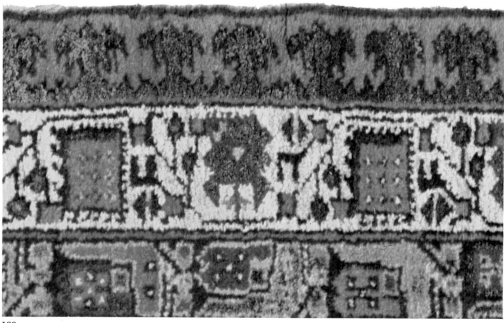

100

101

102

101 Detail of a Beluch carpet showing a riot of geometric combinations.

102 Typical Yamut border motif.

103 Bijar rose border (see also fig. 700).

104 Animal motifs in an Isfahan rug; this idea also occurs frequently in Qum goods.

105 'Tree' pattern in a Beluch rug.

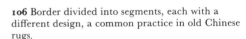

103

104

105

106 Border divided into segments, each with a different design, a common practice in old Chinese rugs.

106

107

107 A Kerman carpet in which the border breaks into the ground.

108 A Shirvan rug in which the design of both border and ground is identical.

109 A Turkish rug consisting almost entirely of border design.

110 Tibetan dragon design without border; many rugs from China and Tibet, and some from India, have no border, but this is a feature almost unknown elsewhere.

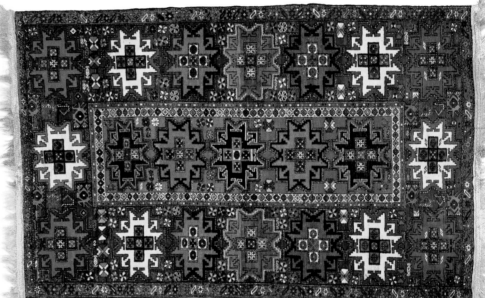

108

109

110

III Universal designs

1 THE BOTEH

111 Motif from a nineteenth-century Indian sari; note the similarity of some of the floral elaboration to the pattern seen on the Greek vase illustrated in fig. 61. Victoria and Albert Museum, London.

112 Marasali
124 × 99 cm, 140,000 TK/m²
(4′ 1″ × 3′ 3″, 90 TK/in.²).
This old prayer rug, from the Shirvan area west of Baku, shows one of the many interpretations of the boteh motif that used to be woven in the Caucasus. For notes on Caucasian botehs see p. 64.

This ancient motif constitutes a fascinating example of how one basic idea can be interpreted in an amazing variety of ways by different weavers. Its use completely transcends the geometric/floral frontiers for it is as much at home in the Turki-speaking villages of the Hamadan area as in the Farsi-speaking town of Qum. Its wide use in Turki-speaking north-west Persia suggests that the geometric forms of that area may be older and that the elaborate versions of Khorassan and of towns like Qum may represent more recent refinements. Against this must be set the facts that in Turkey the design is practically unknown, and that in India, where the design has been used for centuries, it always appear in a curvilinear form. Whatever its history, the motif offers a useful clue to a carpet's origin, for in many cases the precise shape of the motif is specific to one particular area.

The motif is basically in the shape of a pear, with the top bent over (cf. figs. 9–11). In some designs there is a little leaf or tail at the bottom; in others this tail becomes detached from the adjacent motif above and attached to the one below, in the form of a 'nose'. The motif is thus asymmetrical and it is no doubt this quality which makes it fascinating as an all-over repeating pattern – it represents a calm and restrained image without the dryness or rigid formality of plain repeating flowers. What the motif represents is one of the great mysteries of the oriental carpet. It is known always by its Persian name 'boteh', which means a cluster of leaves, or a shrub. Often this is extended to *mir-i-boteh*, which would mean 'princely plant' (note that the word *mir* in this context is not derived from the Mir Serabend – it is chance that the latter is one of the most commonly found carpets using the boteh design; see fig. 121). In the English-speaking world the boteh is usually called a pine cone. This identification is supported by the fact that the motif is sometimes shown as a pine cone or some form of fruit growing on a tree, as illustrated in fig. 113.

In Heriz carpets there is often a leaf motif in the border which looks remarkably like a boteh (fig. 114). This is perhaps pure chance but it reinforces the feeling that the origin of the motif can be traced to a plant form. Another 'fruit' version is the form found in India; this is seen in the 'carpet border' design of the inlaid *pietra dura* of Shah Jahan's palace, built *c.* 1630, in the Red Fort of Agra; there is strong Persian influence in the design of the palace. In Agra, the local explanation is that the motif represents a mango, but if one were to ask a weaver in India – where the motif is widely used in carpet design – he might call it a *suggi*, which means a female parrot. The reason for this is that the design resembles a parrot's head and beak, or even a whole parrot. Other Indian weavers call it the lichee design, but both these names seem to be cases of weavers adopting a design from an alien tradition and then reading their own meaning into it – rather as in the case of the Persian name *mahi* for the Herati design (see p. 84). These examples may serve to remind us that, as far as modern oriental carpets are concerned, the whole principle of attaching 'meaning' or 'symbolism' to the motifs is highly suspect.

In German books 'boteh' is translated to mean 'palm crown'. Attention is drawn to the immense importance of the palm tree in western and central Asia (wood, oil and dates are only three among countless products derived from palms) and to its

113 Gebbeh
173 × 114 cm, 64,000 TK/m²
(5′ 8″ × 3′ 9″, 41 TK/in.²).
Gebbehs are nomad rugs of the Shiraz region (see also figs. 478–81).

114

significance in the Jewish, Christian and Muslim religions. However, no explanation is offered for the fact that no palm tree has a top anything like the shape of the boteh as it appears in oriental carpets. Even those types of palm which have a swollen bulbous base to their stems still have a spreading and *symmetrical* tuft of fronds at the crown. Thus, from the point of view of carpet design the 'palm-crown' theory is of small interest.

A more fascinating theory is the suggestion that the forms of the motif which we know today represent stylized eyes, derived from the ancient Asian superstition of the 'evil eye'. There are many pieces of evidence of the use in antiquity of eye-motifs to ward off demons and evil spirits. Two of the best known are found in ancient Greece – the eye-motifs to be seen as decoration on many articles, from Odysseus's ship to vases of the sixth century BC, and the legend of Hera, who set the hundred eyes of Argos into the tail of the peacock to watch over her. According to the 'talisman' theory, the eye was stylized into the boteh shape very early in the history of decorative art. The boteh does not appear in known carpets as an independent design until the eighteenth century, but that the motif has an ancient pedigree is attested by the illustrations of a leather flask from Pazyryk (fifth century BC) and a stone capital from Balkh (ninth century AD). The difficulty with the 'talisman' theory is that the step from eye-motifs to boteh-shapes is not proven. It is possible to see boteh shapes in practically every curvilinear decorative figure if one tries hard enough. However, to treat every curlicue as a talisman to ward off the evil eye is not only absurd in itself, it also misses the crucial point that the greatness of great decorative artists lies in their ability to imbue old forms with new meanings.

The diversity of form which the motif evinces even in antiquity is a point taken up by S. V. R. Cammann. In a series of lectures printed in the Washington *Textile Museum Journal* in 1973 he makes out an interesting case for the religious or mythological origin of many carpet motifs. He suggests that the boteh is a form of the 'sun-bird', the allegorical creature which guards the entrance to Paradise in Islamic and pre-Islamic oriental mythology; but he goes on to stress that it is perfectly possible that the forms of the motif which we know today may have been derived from several different originals in different places. Other writers, too, have suggested an animal origin for the motif, drawing attention to the strong influence on the ancient world of the art of the Scythians, which was dominated by animal forms. Another idea sometimes put forward is that the motif represents a flame, which again may have religious significance as a symbol for immanence and eternal life. This concept can be found in the Caucasus and also among Zoroastrians, the adherents of the ancient pre-Islamic religion of Iran which was established by Zoroaster (Zarathustra) and survives today, its present headquarters being in Yezd.

None of these theories about the boteh takes account of how the motif found its way into carpet design. It does not appear in any known carpet that can be dated to much before 1800, and it seems likely that the early nineteenth-century floral textile designs of India (fig. 122) inspired the botehs of Khorassan (fig. 161) and Genje (fig. 136), Senneh (fig. 130) and Serabend (fig. 117).

114 Heriz border.

115 Decoration of applied-leather plant motifs on a leather flask from the Pazyryk tombs (fifth century BC). Hermitage Museum, Leningrad.

116 Decorated stone capital from the Nau-i-Gombad mosque, Balkh (ninth century).

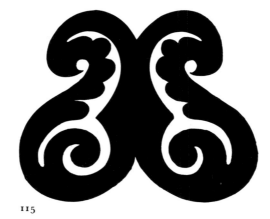

115

116

117, 118 SERABEND

The version most commonly found in carpet shops today is the Serabend or a finer type called Mir Serabend. Serabend is a region in Persia located about 2,000 m (6,500 ft) above sea-level in the mountains between Arak and Borujird. The word Serabend seems to mean a 'cold place', but there is also a river Saravand just to the north of the carpet-making area, which may perhaps be the origin of the name. For a century and a half (perhaps for many centuries) – the people in this area have woven rugs and carpets in an all-over boteh design, fairly coarse in stitch, basically rustic and rectilinear in style, and usually without pretence to elegance of colouring. Red is the most common ground colour used today, but blue and cream are also found. The Serabend is an all-over design, but a diamond-shaped medallion is sometimes found, especially in rug sizes. The knot is usually Turkish, and most sizes are made.

117 Serabend
Detail of a carpet, full size 380 × 280 cm (12′ 6″ × 9′ 3″), with all-over design; 78,000 TK/m² (50 TK/in.²).

118 Serabend rug with medallion
156 × 104 cm, 95,000 TK/m² (5′ 1″ × 3′ 5″, 61 TK/in.²).

119 Antique Serabend; detail (viewed from the back), 144,000 TK/m² (93 TK/in.²). Victoria and Albert Museum, London.

120 Malayir
208 × 136 cm, 160,000 TK/m²
(6′ 10″ × 4′ 5″, 103 TK/in.²).

121 Mir Serabend; detail of a carpet, full size
295 × 204 cm, 180,000 PK/m²
(9′ 8″ × 6′ 8″, 116 PK/in.²).

119–121 MIR SERABEND

The Serabend of course employs a fairly basic version of the motif, but at some point in the nineteenth century (possibly earlier) a finer version was created, perhaps in villages nearer to Arak, using the Persian knot. This is called the Mir Serabend (known in German-speaking countries as Saruq Mir). The reason for this choice of name is uncertain – possibly it derives from the name of the village of Mal-e-Mir in the centre of the Serabend region – and how the development of this finer version came about is shrouded in the mists of history. Some museums have pieces which seem to show the process happening, as it were. One such example is in the Victoria and Albert Museum, London (fig. 119). The piece was acquired by the museum in 1918, but must already have been quite old even then. It has much of the feel of the Serabend about it, and uses the Turkish knot, but stylistically it foreshadows the present Mir.

It is interesting to note that the boteh design is also found in the Ferahan rugs of the neighbouring Malayir/Saruq area. As our example shows, the version found in these nineteenth-century rugs can be totally different from the Serabend form in character and expression. There are other versions again, the existence of which makes one wonder whether the Mirs and the Serabends are not in fact a development one from the other, but have perhaps always co-existed, derived maybe from a common ancestor. It is perfectly conceivable that some villages of the area may have specialized in weaving fine, large pieces for the local gentry, for example, using a more elegant style than the rugs of their peasant neighbours. The source of the design may, in fact, be Indian; the bedcover shown in fig. 122 is older than any known Serabend and may have served as the basis for a carpet design, copied from it in the Arak area in the early nineteenth century.

In today's carpets the Mir can be distinguished from the Serabend not only by the knot but also by the structure; the Serabend is coarse, usually has a stiff back and a thin pile, the Mir varies from medium-coarse to quite fine, has a more flexible back and a thick, luscious pile. The colourings of the latter are usually more subtle, the best pieces having a superb rosy ground shade which results from the use of a natural dye derived from madder root. Another fine feature of the Mir Serabend is its wide border, consisting of a small main border (usually cream) surrounded by a large number of narrow guards. Indeed, the border, as is clearly seen in the illustration, can be so rich that one occasionally comes across carpets with the Mir border

120

121

that have no design at all in the ground. Like the Serabends, Mirs are also sometimes found with a diamond-shaped medallion. Persian Mirs are made in all sizes from small mats right up to large oversize carpets, and including runners and squares. There is also quite a wide range of ground shades available, including light greens and light blue, but the bulk of the production is in red or dark blue, and cream grounds are rather rare.

Another carpet of this group is the so-called 'town Serabend' – a manufactured carpet made in and around the market town of the Serabend area, Borujird. The quality is much better than that of the average Serabend and is comparable to that of the coarser Mirs, which has prompted some dealers to coin words like 'Mirabend' to suggest the superior quality.

122–125, 127 INDO-MIR

Mention must also be made of the Indo-Mir, since there is a huge production in the Mir style in India, in the Bhadohi-Mirzapur district of the state of Uttar Pradesh. Although the version of the design most commonly made there today was copied directly from a Persian original, these new Indian carpets are entirely in tune with a strong local tradition. Some authorities indeed assert that the boteh motif originated in India; whether or not this is true the pattern has certainly been used in the textile industry of Uttar Pradesh, and indeed the whole of India, for centuries. Three Indian variants are illustrated in this book: figs. 11 and 111, both

122 Indian cotton bedcover, dated 1786; textiles of this kind in both India and Persia may have been the original source of the Serabend design. Victoria and Albert Museum, London.

123 Indo-Mir
287 × 198 cm, 75,000 PK/m² (9′ 5″ × 6′ 6″, 48 PK/in.²).

122

123

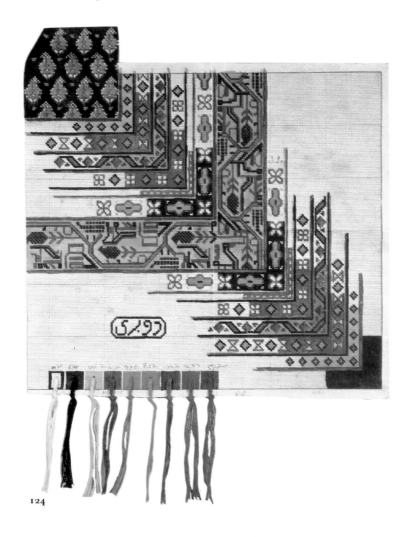

124

125

124 Loom drawing (*naksha*) for the Indo-Mir carpet shown in fig. 125.

125 Detail of Indo-Mir carpet woven from the preceding loom drawing; 190,000 PK/m² (123 PK/in.²).

126 Kerman loom drawing.

126

from southern India, and an eighteenth-century cotton bedcover, shown here, which is in a style used throughout Uttar Pradesh.

The range of Indo-Mir carpets produced in Uttar Pradesh today is very wide: the worst are cruder than the poorest Serabends, but the best are finer than any Mirs produced in Persia today. A typical *naksha*, or loom-drawing from which an Indian weaver works, is shown here together with a carpet produced from it: every knot of the repeating pattern is set out in the *naksha*, and the woollen tags attached to the code-panel at the bottom indicate which shade is to be used. Note how the essentially geometric character of the design is retained despite the fineness of the weave.

Within the Indian Mir output a much greater variety of designs is found than in Persian goods. In particular, the Indian manufacturers have appreciated the usefulness of the Mir design in producing medallion carpets, either by setting a traditional Borujird-area medallion against a Mir background, or by superimposing on an all-over Mir pattern a skeleton medallion outline of the type used in the Mesheriki Saruq illustrated in fig. 223. Indian Mirs, with or without medallion, are available in almost every conceivable size and colour.

126 KERMAN

By way of contrast with the Indian *naksha*, a Persian loom-drawing (prior to painting) is shown: this represents a boteh from a Kerman carpet made in the 1920s. Here one can see the other extreme: the motif has been subjected by master designers to the most convoluted elaboration, one boteh being placed within another and the whole consisting of a mass of finely drawn detail. Between the two extremes of the rustic Serabend and the refined Kerman lies a wide range of interpretations, geometric, floral, large- and small-scale all-over ground patterns, individual boteh

127 Indo-Mir carpet with medallion
286 × 250 cm, 190,000 PK/m²
(9′ 4″ × 8′ 2″, 123 PK/in.²).

motifs as part of a larger design, boteh motifs grouped in set patterns to form a new design, linked botehs in borders – and each one bearing the typical 'handwriting' of the style of the area or village in question. Some of the most commonly found types are illustrated on the following pages.

128 EVERU

The village of Everu, near Hamadan in north-west Persia, weaves rugs and runners of medium quality, using the small boteh design illustrated. Everu rugs are often sold as Enjilas, which description is inaccurate – Enjilas, a neighbouring village, makes pieces of a very much higher quality (see p. 96). The design layout resembles that used in the Serabend region, but the Everu rug is easily distinguished from the Serabend because the former is a single- and the latter double-wefted. The border is also quite different. Other distinguishing features are the strong deep red, rather heavy dark blue and the regrettably vicious greens and turquoise blues; Everus have fine silky wool with a quite high pile. Most rug sizes are made and also runners, but no carpets. The output in this boteh design is small, the bulk of Everu's production being woven in the Herati design (see fig. 215).

128 Everu
71 × 56 cm, 170,000 TK/m²
(2′ 4″ × 1′ 10″, 110 TK/in.²).

129

130

129 BORUJIRD

Borujird (south of Hamadan) is the market centre for the Serabend rugs, as well as for single-wefted Hamadan-type rugs in various designs, including several variants of the distinctive large boteh version illustrated. The typical features are: a single-wefted structure, coarse weave with thick grey or brown wefts, fine yarn, long pile. The rugs are often very sombre when new (over-heavy dark blue and dark red) but can be very attractive when made in softer or lighter colours. Borujirds are found only in zaronim and dozar sizes, and runners. They have much in common with the traditional old single-wefted Malayirs, a feature which is more obvious in other designs woven in this area, such as that of fig. 462.

130, 131 SENNEH, BIJAR

Senneh (properly: Sanandaj), the principal Kurdish city of Iran, uses a boteh similar in shape to the one used in Borujird, but the goods are easily distinguished from each other by the respective weaves, Senneh's being very much finer – indeed Senneh makes one of the finest single-wefted weaves anywhere in the Orient. The Kurds often use a highly-twisted yarn, which gives a knobbly appearance to the knots on the back of the rug. In the finely-woven Senneh pieces, the back of the rug feels almost like sandpaper. Pushtis, zaronims and dozars are made, plus occasional strips and carpets, the latter often being long and narrow. The colour range is extremely conservative, being largely dominated by red, blue and ivory. Many other colours occur as subsidiary shades, but usually only in very discreet quantities. The other principal Kurdish town in Iran, Bijar, does not have a design of its own

129 Borujird
215×136 cm, 78,000 TK/m²
($7'\,0'' \times 4'\,5''$, 50 TK/in.²).

130 Senneh
250×168 cm, 196,000 TK/m²
($8'\,3'' \times 5'\,8''$, 126 TK/in.²).

131 Bijar
220 × 135 cm, 180,000 TK/m²
7′ 3″ × 4′ 5″, 116 TK/in.²).

based on the boteh, but the motif often crops up as a subsidiary design element, as it does in other Kurdish rugs. The item illustrated here is not a carpet but a *vagireh*, that is a weaver's model. *Vagirehs* (also known by other terms in other areas) may be found anywhere in the Orient, but they are most common in north-west Persia and usually come from areas where there is semi-organized village manufacturing, and here they take the place of the graph-paper loom-drawings used elsewhere (see fig. 124). This Bijar *vagireh* which is very old indeed, shows a large number of design elements of a rather wild, rustic nature. There are four sets of *botehs* involving three different shapes. The largest pair are clearly meant as fruits or pine cones on the end of a branch. The others seem to have a purely abstract function as filler-elements in the design. For a general note on Bijar carpets see p. 88.

132 KAKABERU

To the south of Bijar and Senneh there is a large Kurdish area in which many designs and styles are woven, the principal markets being Sonqur and Kermanshah (see fig. 549). As in Bijars, boteh motifs occur mainly as subsidiary elements: a good example may be seen in fig. 532. The rug illustrated here, however, is one of the rarer examples of a Kurdish all-over boteh. It is only just a boteh design – in fact the design may well be a derivative of the *gol farang* (see fig. 708). The Kakaberu piece has all the unmistakable features of this tribe's work: dark, almost sombre colours, including a blue that is almost black and dark, browny red; a medium-coarse weave, but a structure as solid as a board, the kelleyi format, and, above all, a wild indomitable expressiveness highly suggestive of the rugged independence of this fierce mountain people. Kelleyis, in the size range 120–140 cm (4′ 0″–4′ 6″) wide and 230–300 cm (7′ 6″–10′ 0″) long, are the only type made.

133 SENNEH

We come now to another interpretation from Senneh; here the botehs are arranged in a set pattern to form a new, independent motif, known as *hashtguli* (i.e. eight

132 Kakaberu
261 × 132 cm, 97,000 TK/m²
(8′ 7″ × 4′ 4″, 63 TK/in.²).

133 Senneh
220 × 142 cm, 240,000 TK/m²
(7′ 3″ × 4′ 8″, 155 TK/in.²).

132

133

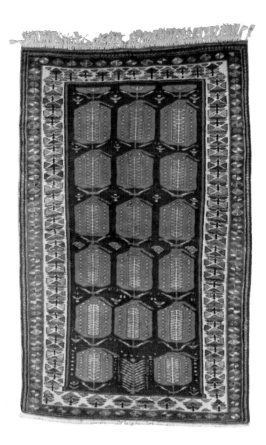

134 Ardebil
248 × 151 cm, 85,000 TK/m² (8′ 1″ × 5′ 0″, 55 TK/in.²).

135 Hamadan
Detail of a nineteenth-century runner, viewed from the back; 85,000 TK/m² (55 TK/in.²).
Victoria and Albert Museum, London.

flowers). Note that both the Senneh rugs illustrated are on cream grounds, which is unusual; Sennehs in other designs (e.g. fig. 497) are more on blue or red grounds. The weave here has the same characteristics as fig. 130. The *hashtguli* idea is also used in other areas which weave the boteh motif, such as the province of Khorassan. Indeed, old pieces from this area now in museums suggest that it may have originated there.

134 ARDEBIL
The next carpet, from Ardebil, is typical of the tribal kelleyis made in the south-eastern part of Persian Azerbaijan. Dealers in Tabriz might call it Ardebil, Meshkin or Khalkhal, but from its appearance the name Shah Savan would perhaps be better. The Shah Savan tribe does not seem to be Kurdish, as some carpet dealers suppose; it is a confederation formed at the end of the sixteenth century for political reasons, and many of the clans seem to be of Luri origin. However, it may be that their carpet weaving is influenced by that of the Kurds, just as the Beluchis of Khorassan are influenced by the neighbouring Turkomans. The Shah Savan inhabit large parts of southern and eastern Azerbaijan and spread as far south as the Saveh area west of Tehran. The Azerbaijan origin of the carpet illustrated is easily distinguished: the flat selvedge and the very tough, tight, though not necessarily very fine, double-wefted structure are unmistakable features. The weave, the kelleyi format and the bold uncompromising design might suggest Kakaberu, but the flat selvedge would preclude this origin; more important, however, is the colour combination – the red is too bright and the other colours are too light for a Kakaberu piece. True, the Kolyais, close Kurdish neighbours of the Kakaberu, often produce a similar red, but the Kolyais always use a single-wefted construction. Another typical clue is the Caucasian-looking border, for present-day Persian Azerbaijan and Russian Azerbaijan in the Caucasus have common traditions dating back many centuries. In this kind of Ardebil only kelleyi sizes are made; concerning the name Ardebil see also p. 100.

135 HAMADAN
There are many hundreds of villages around the town of Hamadan, all with distinctive designs and weaves. Generally the boteh is used only as a subsidiary motif (cf. fig. 729, from Mehriban), but occasionally one comes across a rug where the weaver has produced a boteh design of her own. In such cases the design is no guide to the origin – the key factor in such cases are the weave and the colours (which are dealt with in detail in the relevant sections on Hamadan designs). The piece illustrated here is from the Victoria and Albert Museum Textile Study Rooms collection and shows a fascinating interpretation from the Hamadan region dating from perhaps a century ago.

136–140 OLD CAUCASIAN
In the nineteenth and early twentieth centuries the boteh motif was used by weavers throughout the Caucasus, in a diversity of form and richness of imaginative invention unsurpassed by any other weaving area. Several examples are shown here, and another two appear in figs. 9 and 112. Old Caucasian rugs like these are available only from specialist dealers, but are worth illustrating here because of the different interpretations they reveal within a fairly small geographical area. The Marasali prayer rug from the Baku area (illustrated in fig. 112) includes a strictly geometric form of the motif whose jagged edging seems to suggest a flame; the figure at the base of the boteh could represent the cup of a torch. By contrast, the Genje botehs shown in figs. 138 and 136 are clearly interpreted as plant forms, the one sharply geometric and the other fully curvilinear, but the carpet shown in fig. 137 treats the motif in a highly abstract form in the ground, in a pattern known as *chibukli*, the Turkish for a (smoker's) pipe. This type is woven in both floral and geometric forms in many parts of the Orient, but especially in Khorassan, Qum and Genje. In this example the boteh appears in the border as well as the ground; in the border many of the botehs take the form of birds. This may be accidental, but there will certainly be theorists who will interpret the ground as a

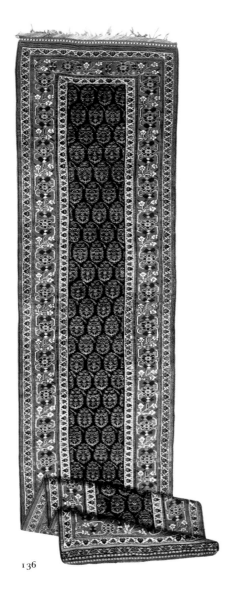

136

137

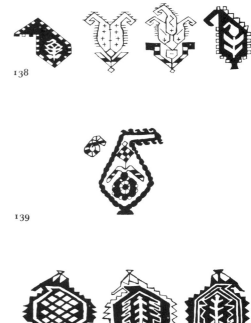

138

139

140

136 Genje
Runner, full size 445 × 100 cm, 120,000 TK/m^2
(14′ 7″ × 3′ 3″, 77 TK/in.^{2}).

137 Genje carpet with *chibukli* pattern
348 × 120 cm, 100,000 TK/m^2
(11′ 5″ × 3′ 11″, 65 TK/in.^{2}).

138 Boteh motifs from Genje carpets.

139 Boteh motifs from a so-called Kabistan carpet
(Kabistan is not a place – the name is probably a
carpet dealers' invention, but could possibly be
derived from Kobi, a village near Baku).

140 Boteh motifs from a Shirvan carpet.

representation of the Garden of Eden and the border as the birds and animals who
stand on guard around it.

141 KAZAK

Modern Caucasian rugs are made under controlled conditions similar to those that
prevail in India or China. Unlike Indian practice, however, the designers of the
Soviet State manufactories keep strictly to the traditional design elements of the
Caucasus (although not to the traditional designs of their own respective region).
Their re-interpretation is often rather mechanical and stereotyped – the standardization of qualities and the separation of weaver and designer tends to produce
rather soulless results, the dullness of the designs being surpassed only by the
insipidness of the colours. The boteh is used in several forms, but always as a subsidiary motif, as this illustration of a new carpet from the Kazak district shows. There
is none of the wealth of elaboration found in old Caucasian rugs, and the famous
flame of Baku, where oil and natural gas have sprung from the ground for centuries,
has apparently been snuffed out. More details of the typical features of modern
Caucasian rugs will be found in the chapter on Geometric Designs.

141 Kazak
Detail showing use of the boteh as a subsidiary
motif.

142 GEBBEH

As in north-west Persia and the Caucasus, the tribal weavers of Fars province produce a wide range of designs, again including several versions of the boteh, especially in the style of rug known as the Gebbeh (literally 'unclipped', a reference to the shagginess of the pile.) One version has been shown in fig. 113; a second is shown here. Genuine Gebbehs are rugs made by nomads for their own use. Rustic simplicity and indeed a certain wilfulness of design (and colouring) give the rugs an unaffected freshness which is much sought after, especially for use in a modern decor. Most Gebbehs measure about 220×110 cm $(7'\,3'' \times 3'\,9'')$; a width of 135 cm $(4'\,5'')$, as seen in this rug, is rare.

143–146 TURKOMAN

The Turkoman tribes, who are located mostly in Afghanistan and Russian central Asia, make little use of flower or plant motifs in the Persian style and do not usually include the boteh in their carpets at all. The two principal exceptions are illustrated here. The first shows a distinctive version found in the Beshir rugs of both Afghanistan and Russia. Notice here the suggestion of a tree design, although it is sometimes claimed that this is not a boteh design at all, but a representation of the two ancient Chinese motifs of the dragon and the phoenix (see also fig. 174). Early examples of this design support this interpretation, and it would certainly accord with Grote-Hasenbalg's assertion that the Beshirs are not a true Turkoman tribe, but that the name is corruption of 'Bokhara' (see p. 190). This theory is highly speculative, but it is certainly possible that Beshir weavers developed this design from motifs introduced into the area by Timur's Chinese artists towards the end of the fourteenth century.

The second Turkoman boteh design is one used in the borders of carpets from all over northern Afghanistan, although it is not normally found in Turkoman goods from Persia or Russia. The three botehs grouped together in the Kaldar example form an unprepossessing but subtle and effective motif, which, once one

142 Gebbeh
226×135 cm, 67,000 TK/m² $(7'\,5'' \times 4'\,5'', 43$ TK/in.²).

143 Beshir
205×105 cm, 160,000 PK/m² $(6'\,9'' \times 3'\,5'', 103$ PK/in.²).

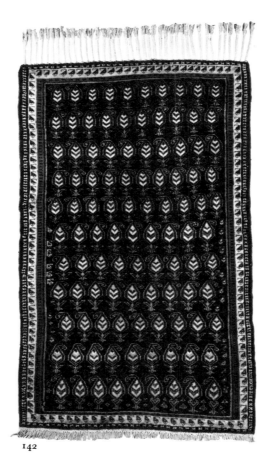

142

143

is made aware of it, seems to occur in almost every Afghan carpet one looks at; but here again it must be doubted whether the motifs are intended as botehs in the usual sense (the Turkomans call the motif 'judor', which means 'almond'). The Heriz and Shirvan examples illustrate a similar design much used in the Caucasus and Azerbaijan (where there are also many weavers of Turkoman origin): although the boteh shape is hinted at in these two rugs, it is more likely that the motifs represent opening flower buds linked together in the way that bud or palmette motifs are usually treated in carpet borders. It may thus be pure accident that the Afghan version looks like a boteh. It is cases like this which must make us very suspicious of attaching universal labels to motifs; quite often there are all sorts of influences at work to determine the particular shape which a motif acquires, and these influences can make nonsense of too dogmatic theories.

147, 148 BAKHTIARI

Bakhtiari carpets are made by Armenians, Kurds, Lurs and other settled tribes in the province of Chahar Mahal va Bakhtiari, south-west of Isfahan. They are not made by the nomadic Bakhtiari tribe, who live further west and have no significant carpet production. A very large range of qualities is made, from the coarse, single-wefted products in geometric designs from villages like Borujen, Farah Dumbeh and Boldaji, through medium-fine double-wefted carpets from Shalamzar and Shahr Kurd, to the fine double-wefted products, generally using floral designs, of Saman and Chahal Shotur. A wide diversity of designs are used, too, but one in particular predominates, the so-called 'garden design', consisting of rectangular panels containing a variety of different 'garden' motifs, from summer houses to grape vines and from individual stylized flowers to fully fledged cypress or weeping willow trees. More details will be found below, in the section on panel designs.

In the panels, the boteh often figures as one of the plant forms – in various shapes and styles, depending on the stitch and character of the particular village's production. Between them, the two Bakhtiari carpets illustrated show five different forms

144 The 'judor' pattern used in an Ersari rug from Kaldar, Afghanistan.

145, 146 The same idea as used in Heriz and Shirvan.

144

145

146

of the motif. A particular feature which distinguishes these botehs from those illustrated in the preceding pages is the three-dimensional effect created by the placing of one boteh outline behind another with the hooks at their tops bent in opposite directions. To the author this clearly suggests one of those plant forms which opens at the top – a leaf-bud, perhaps, or a hazelnut husk – or a pine cone. Not all Bakhtiari botehs have this characteristic, but it is more common there than in any other geometric version of the motif.

149 CHAHAL SHOTUR

The finest Bakhtiars are more or less curvilinear – often one can sense the influence of the neighbouring city of Isfahan – but they always retain a certain angularity as a reminder of their peasant origins. The character of the botehs in this carpet from Chahal Shotur (in the panel and in the border) lies halfway between the geometric style seen in the Caucasian rugs shown on the preceding pages and the truly floral version used in the Qum panel design in fig. 159.

150 QUCHAN

A rug from Quchan provides another example of botehs used as subsidiary motifs. Quchan is a small mountain town north-west of Meshed in eastern Persia. The town is the centre of a fascinating and unique carpet-producing area, since it is surrounded by an area occupied by Turkoman and Beluch tribes, with their own very significant carpet output. Quchan and the neighbouring villages, however, are Kurdish. The Kurds have lived here since the beginning of the seventeenth century (see p. 192), but the designs of their rugs are often strongly influenced by the neighbouring Beluchis and Turkomans. But the true Kurdish character manifests itself in many details – from the names of the villages, like Kolyai and Shirvan, to things like the

147, 148 Boteh motifs in Bakhtiari carpets.

149 Boteh motifs in a Chahal Shotur carpet.

148

149

150 Quchan (detail);
full size 234 × 147 cm, 79,000 TK/m²
(7′ 8″ × 4′ 10″, 51 TK/in.²).

151 Shahr Babak
153 × 113 cm, 202,000 TK/m²
(5′ 0″ × 3′ 8″, 130 TK/in.²).

150

151

152 Shahr Babak
203 × 150 cm, 269,000 TK/m²
(6′ 8″ × 4′ 11″, 174 TK/in.²).

flat selvedge (typical of Caucasian Kurdish rugs). The border of the rug illustrated also shows a clear link with the Caucasus. Most rug sizes exist, but small pieces are very rare. The most common types are kelleyis. More notes on Quchan will be found on p. 195.

151, 152 AFSHARI
The Afshari tribes, settled mainly around the three centres of Sirjand, Shahr Babak and Rafsinjan in the region of Kerman in south-east Persia, weave perhaps the widest range of different designs produced in any one area of the Orient. A visiting buyer could easily find a hundred different designs in current production, maybe many more, and certainly enough to produce a book devoted to Afshar designs alone. The author of a more general survey is obliged to select a few typical examples and simply disregard the rest. The boteh appears in many variants, two Shahr Babak examples being illustrated here. The geometric form of the motif seen in the second of these is the more typical of the Shahr Babak region – indeed the first

153 Beluch
189 × 101 cm, 168,000 PK/m²
(6′ 2″ × 3′ 4″, 108 PK/in.²).

154 Luri
267 × 159 cm, 55,000 TK/m²
(8′ 9″ × 5′ 2″, 35 TK/in.²).

might well have been woven not in Shahr Babak but in Pariz village, on the road to Rafsinjan. A fascinating feature of fig. 151 lies, however, in the links it suggests with north west Persia and the Caucasus. In this case the historical connection is well documented, for the Afshars are of Turkoman origin and for many years lived in the Lake Urmia region. Several Persian rulers from the seventeenth century onwards deported rebellious Afshar groups at various times. Most notably, when Nadir Shah, himself an Afshar, seized power in Persia in the early eighteenth century after the Afghan invasion, he smashed the opposition of the Afshars of the north-west by transporting thousands of tribesmen to the inhospitable desert area between Shiraz and Kerman where their descendants still live. Many Afshars still remain in northern Persia, however, and in Turkey as well, and their influence on carpet design in the north-west is strong. Some of the finest Bijars are made by Afshars, for example. Is it pure coincidence that the rather odd shape of the botehs in fig. 151 is the same as that of the main pair of botehs in fig. 131? In the case of our second example the botehs are of course used as a background pattern. This is a common feature in several Shahr Babak designs, more details of which will be found in chapter IV. Note here the 'barber's pole' binding of the selvedge, and in particular the general colouring of the rug. The rosy-brown shade is the key clue to the recognition of the Shahr Babak rugs, as this colour is not used anywhere else in the Orient. Another distinctive feature is the subdued grey-green used as a subsidiary colour.

153 BELUCH
The Beluchis constitute one of the great tribal groups of Persia; their territory lies on either side of the modern Afghan-Iranian frontier. Among their many designs are several versions of the boteh, one of which is illustrated. This version is perhaps not particularly distinguished – the Beluch designs shown in figs. 435–7 have more flair, and it may be for this reason that the boteh design is not encountered very often in Beluch rugs, but it does illustrate very well how the asymmetry of the motif gives life to the repeating pattern. For a general note on Beluch rugs see pp. 139 and 193.

154–156 LURI, QASHQAI
One of the most attractive of the tribal versions of the boteh is the old Qashqai design illustrated here, though it is more often found nowadays in the coarser form illustrated in the Luri piece from the Shiraz region. Note how in the Qashqai the boteh takes on yet another different form. One of the fascinations of this version, too, is the link it indicates with the Caucasus (cf. fig. 136), spotlighting the unity of the culture of the Turki-speaking races despite their wide dispersal and subjection to greatly varied historical forces. Note also that in both these rugs the top of the motif in most cases inclines in both directions, producing a version which is much more nearly symmetrical than usual.

The floral botehs

The majority of the variant forms illustrated in the preceding pages have been of tribal or peasant origin and represent a spontaneous geometric stylization, be it of a mango, a parrot, an acorn, a flame or whatever. The same vitality and universality have of course also been a source of inspiration to master designers throughout Persia. There is probably no source of manufactured carpets that has not at some time or other produced a version – or many versions – of the boteh design. In Meshed one may encounter a rather geometric form of the *hashtguli* boteh, but further south in Khorassan province, perhaps influenced by India, there is a tradition of refined and nicely balanced curvilinear designs. Qum tends to follow the fine weaves of Khorassan, while in Kerman the designers' imagination can run riot, as the loom-drawing shown in fig. 126 reveals. The possibilities are endless, but only a few of the refined versions have established themselves as distinctive designs in their own right: perhaps it is the earthy spontaneity that gives the peasant versions their strength, while the refined versions sometimes look either dull or weak or excessively elaborate and stilted.

155

156a

156b

155 Qashqai
175 × 100 cm, 160,000 TK/m²
(5′ 9″ × 3′ 3″, 103 TK/in.²).

156
The Qashqai boteh (a) as seen in fig. 155, compared
with the Genje version (b) shown in fig. 136.

157

158

159

157–160 QUM

Probably the best-known floral boteh design is the example illustrated in fig. 157: it is most often seen, on a cream ground, in dozars and in smallish carpet sizes (up to about 6 or 7 m²; 65–75 ft²), but – as with all manufactured rugs – every size and colour are possible. Note that all the botehs face in one direction (unlike the Serabend versions, where alternate rows always face in opposite directions). This rug clearly shows the influence of Khorassan on Qum designs (see fig. 161). For

160

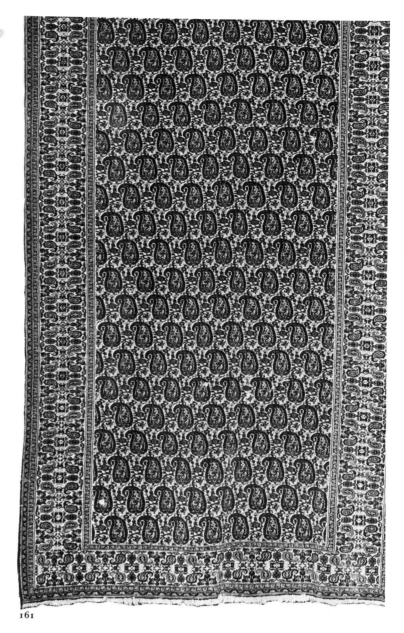

161

general notes on Qum cf. fig. 691. Figs. 158–60 all illustrate typical different treatments of the boteh as a subsidiary motif. It is these versions which perhaps come closest in modern Persia to the elaborate nineteenth-century Indian designs, well known in the West from copies made by manufacturers of fine textiles at Paisley in Scotland.

A full illustration of the Qum version of the Bakhtiar 'garden' design will be found in fig. 340; here, fig. 159 shows the boteh panel which is almost always found in it (in the Bakhtiar original the boteh occurs only from time to time). The design is very well drawn here – compare it with the Chahal Shotur version in fig. 332 – but most carpet lovers may well declare that the Bakhtiar version has more character. Similar motifs will be found in panel designs from Birjand, where they are made in an even finer weave than in Qum, sometimes with strikingly beautiful results.

161 KHORASSAN

Like Qum, Kashan and other towns in central Persia weave versions of an all-over floral boteh design. In many cases there are derived from nineteenth-century rugs produced in Khorassan. Today the centre of fine weaving in eastern Persia is Birjand, but in the nineteenth-century Qain and the surrounding area (known as the Qainat) were also important. It seems fitting to close the boteh section with a detail of one of the fine Qainat originals, which have inspired many of the Persian manufactured versions of today. This rug was presented to the Victoria and Albert Museum, London, in 1877 by the Shah of Persia.

157 Qum
204 × 134 cm, 334,000 PK/m²
(6′ 8″ × 4′ 5″, 215 PK/in.²).

158 Qum
213 × 132 cm, 665,000 PK/m²
(7′ 0″ × 4′ 4″, 430 PK/in.²).

159 Qum
Panel design (detail).

160 Qum
161 × 106 cm, 490,000 PK/m²
(5′ 3″ × 3′ 6″, 316 PK/in.²).

161 Khorassan
266 × 152 cm, 325,000 PK/m²
(8′ 9″ × 5′ 0″, 210 PK/in.²).
Victoria and Albert Museum, London.

2 THE HERATI PATTERN

162 The Herati pattern; this example, showing a 'Kaimuri' Indian carpet measuring 253 × 185 cm with 220,000 PK/m² (8′ 3″ × 6′ 1″, 142 PK/in.²) from Khamariah (see pp. 99 and 305), is one of the latest developments in the history of a design that has spanned several centuries.

Persia as the home of oriental carpets has not always been confined to the frontiers of present-day Iran. Over the past 2,500 years, during which, at least, we know that the carpet designs of today have evolved, the Persian Empire has expanded and contracted over many parts of central and western Asia, and significant changes have occurred in the racial make-up of the population – and of the rulers. As the historical maps on p. 343 show, the original Persian Empire (in the period in which the Pazyryk carpet was produced) stretched from the Mediterranean to the Hindu Kush, while centuries later Persia was for long under Turkoman and Mongol rule. In view of this, when we speak of 'Persian' designs, we should not think simply in terms of the boundaries of modern Iran. It is therefore quite natural for one of the most used and most widely spread of all Persian carpet designs to be named after Herat, today the second city of Afghanistan. Herat was founded, as Alexandria Areion, by Alexander the Great in 328 BC. It was already a major city on the Silk Route when Timur established his court at Samarkand in the fourteenth century. Shah Rukh (ruled 1405–47), one of the most enlightened rulers of the Mongol Timurid dynasty, chose Herat as his capital and turned it into the most important centre of learning and culture in central Asia. The city was held briefly by the Shaibani Uzbeks, but was recovered in 1510 by the Safavid Shah Ismail and remained an important city of the Persian Empire until 1857. During the critical period of the development of Persian carpet design Herat was the capital of Khorassan province and was thus the metropolis for the whole of eastern Persia, which region was the source of many important carpets of the sixteenth and seventeenth centuries. Among these, particular attention is focussed on three types: carpets in the fully fledged Herati design; carpets in a free-flowing all-over floral style, which seem to have been the predecessors of the first-mentioned group; and a related group in another, stiffer, all-over floral style, a group known as 'vase carpets'.

This said, it must immediately be admitted that, despite the existence of hundreds of sixteenth- and seventeenth-century carpets of all three types, we simply do not know precisely where or when any of them were made – not even for certain whether they are all really of east Persian origin at all. As the place of origin of the vase carpets Kerman is often suggested, for the floral 'Herats' Meshed is a possibility, and for the pieces in Herati pattern the villages of the Qainat in central Khorassan have a claim. As to chronology, it is suggested that the floral carpets and the vase design developed in the first half of the sixteenth century, and the Herati design somewhat later. But when it comes to specific pieces the experts offer widely different opinions, with discrepancies of more than a hundred years in dating and hundreds of kilometres in location. It would be beyond the scope of this book to present the various cases advanced by carpet experts. However, the reader should be aware of the historical background and of the stylistic associations of the Herati design, and it is hoped that the illustrations included here, taken together (and in conjunction with the vase designs on pp. 119 and 325–8) will contribute to an appreciation of the modern versions of Herati designs shown in this chapter.

163–168 TRIBAL HERATI DERIVATIVES

In the first place it is interesting to note the many connections with the Herati design to be found in the rugs of the present-day tribes of Khorassan (i.e. Turkomans, Beluchis and Kurds). These are illustrated in figs. 163–168, which, taken in order of appearance, reveal a backwards progression from the Turkoman göl – a medallion or flower-motif – to the Herati pattern. Any proposal that such a connection exists is anathema to the many passionate champions of the tribal rug, for there is an implied suggestion here that the Turkoman göl (cf. fig. 399), the 'holy cow' of the campaign for the recognition of the supremacy of nomad art, is no more than a debased derivative of a design from a Persian manufactory. To assert this might be going too far; but even if a connection exists we must also consider that when the Herati pattern first appeared it may have represented not an original idea by a skilled designer but a reflection of a design tradition already extant in the Herat region, and that the tribal rugs of the area may embody a much more ancient inheritance of the same tradition. The tribal rugs from Khorassan illustrated in figs. 163–6 show various treatments of the Herati design. Fig. 167 shows how the zigzag edges of the diamond shape seen in fig. 166 can be opened up to produce a leaf shape; the principal features of the Herati design are thus clearly revealed. Fig. 168 shows a floral manufactured style – from the village of Dorukhsh, in the heart of the Beluch area – similar to that of Birjand. If A. C. Edwards is right in believing the Herati pattern to have originated in the Qain-Dorukhsh-Birjand region, local tribesmen would have plenty of opportunity to transform the Beluch version (fig. 167) into that shown in fig. 166; the influence may also have been the other way round, but from time immemorial it has been the practice of nomads and peasants to introduce new designs by the simple expedient of copying what is selling best in the local manufactories. The conversion of the fifteenth-century geometric tribal pattern shown in fig. 398(g) into the floral version seen in fig. 398(h) shows how this kind of development can occur, and this example may indeed be one of the key pieces of surviving evidence concerning the evolution of the Herati pattern.

163 The standard Sarukh Turkoman design: a göl with zigzag edges alternating with a more rounded göl, 201 × 129 cm, 320,000 PK/m² (6′ 7″ × 4′ 3″, 206 PK/in.²).

164 The characteristic design of the Yamut Turkomans; there is usually only one type of göl, repeated in diagonal lines; 193 × 122 cm, 196,000 PK/m² (6′ 4″ × 4′ 0″, 126 PK/in.²).

163

164

165

166

165 A Beshir Turkoman rug from Afghanistan; 162 × 123 cm, 200,000 PK/m² (5′ 4″ × 4′ 0″, 129 PK/in.²). For a more fully developed Herati design woven by the Beshirs of Turkestan see fig. 236; the version shown here – clearly a derivative of the Herati design – is the more common of the two.

166 One of the many variants of the repeating-diamond idea woven by the Beluch tribes of Khorassan; 190 × 90 cm, 195,000 PK/m² (6′ 3″ × 2′ 11″, 126 PK/in.²).

167

168

167 A Beluch rug, of a type very commonly found in the area between Meshed and Herat; 218 × 128 cm, 115,000 PK/m² (7′ 5″ × 4′ 2″, 74 PK/in.²).

168 Dorukhsh: floral manufactured style; 307,000 PK/m² (198 PK/in.²).

77

169 Detail of a mid-sixteenth-century Cairo carpet, in which the distribution of the leaves and palmette motifs is organized according to a similar principle to that used in the Herati pattern. Victoria and Albert Museum, London.

169–173 SIXTEENTH-CENTURY PRECURSORS

There still exist many carpets of early times that reveal stylistic features which could well have influenced the development of the Herati pattern. The Turkoman connection strikes the observer who sees the geometric lozenge- or diamond-shaped frame as the outstanding feature of the design, but one may also ask how that frame originated. If one takes as the centre of the design not the flower which appears inside each diamond but the one which lies between the diamonds, then a quite different picture presents itself. At least as far back as the Ottoman carpets from Cairo, an example of which (formerly in Berlin) is in a style dated by Erdmann to 1540–50 (we show a similar piece in fig. 169), and the mosque tiles (fig. 171) from later in the century, Islamic designers were putting motifs together in a way which, to say the least, strongly foreshadows the Herati pattern. The Persian rug shown in fig. 171 is described by C. G. Ellis as mid-sixteenth-century Kerman; it shows delicately conceived palmette and lancet-leaf motifs rather clumsily put together, but the underlying structure of the design is very interesting because it reveals a basic idea, much developed in both the Herat floral and the vase carpets, which can

170 East or south-east Persian carpet, sixteenth century; 265 × 195 cm (8′ 8″ × 6′ 5″). Corcoran Gallery of Art, Washington, D.C. (W. A. Clark Collection).

also be seen as an obvious potential source for the Herati pattern. This piece clearly belongs to the group known as vase carpets (see also fig. 184 and index), but is less geometric in style than others of its kind and represents a link between the vase carpets and the Herat floral pieces (cf. figs. 738 and 776). The opening up of the layout to produce a structure dependent on flowing flower-stalks (called 'islimis') runs into difficulties in the upper portion of the rug, but provided later weavers with the key to interlinking all the elements of the design to a much greater degree than is possible with the layout of the Cairo carpet.

The rather unusual modern Bijar rug shown in fig. 200 has a Herati pattern which also clearly shows a layout based on the same principles. The underlying structure of fig. 170 can be elaborated in many different ways. The two versions shown here in figs. 172 and 173 may easily have been used to lead to the Herati pattern. There are no 'loose ends' in this kind of layout: the interdependence of all parts of the design will have been a valuable feature for designers producing carpets for use in mosques because it reflects an important aspect of the traditional Islamic view of the cosmos.

The most convincing exposé of the background material of this era is given by Werner Grote-Hasenbalg in his book *Der Orientteppich, seine Geschichte und seine Kultur*, one of the great classic carpet books; published nearly sixty years ago, it is still worth reading. Although some of that author's detailed observations have been superseded by the discoveries of later scholars, his principal line of thought is sound and is summarized below. Grote-Hasenbalg begins at the point where the flourishing edifice of Persian art was utterly destroyed by the Mongols in the thirteenth century.

In a series of campaigns beginning in 1219, Jinghis Khan, a Mongolian chieftain, subjugated northern China, East Turkestan and Persia through to the Caucasus and beyond. Baghdad, the capital of the Seljuq Turks, fell to the Mongol Empire in 1258. Fifty years later both Persia and Turkey achieved independence, but were overrun again in the 1380s and 1390s by Timur (Tamerlane), whose ferocious Mongol and Turkoman hordes conquered almost the whole of Asia, including northern India, Persia, the Caucasus and Turkey. In 1369 he established one of the most resplendent courts of all times in Samarkand – already a great city, being the pivotal point of the Silk Route, the principal artery of trade between East and West. Timur attached great importance to the arts and brought many Chinese artists to work in his new empire. Bokhara and Herat, both of them towns on the Silk Route, also benefited from the splendour of the Mongol court, Herat, in particular, becoming under Timur's successors an artistic centre of the first rank and the source of regeneration for Persian art. The effect of this Mongol influence was incalculable. Whereas in western Persia the stricter older style of carpet design survived, in the east a completely new, Chinese-influenced style began to emerge. Chinese motifs, which were later to assume such great importance, entered the field of carpet design.

174–179 THE STYLISTIC INFLUENCE OF CHINA

The cloud-band, the phoenix, the dragon and the palmette are all examples of motifs that first came to Persia with the Mongols and became absorbed into the carpet art of the fifteenth century; their significance and symbolism are set out in the captions to these illustrations. As has been pointed out in the Introduction, the palmette was a widely used decorative motif in Western Asia in ancient times. Whether the motif travelled to China via the Silk Route or through the art of the Scythians or other horsemen of the steppes, or whether it developed independently in China is not known. But it is certain that its use in the Islamic art of Asia was very limited until the Mongol invasions. It may thus be said to have been re-introduced into carpet art by the Mongol/Chinese influence. It is, however, impossible to trace this re-introduction in detail because of the non-existence of Persian carpets of the fifteenth century. By the early sixteenth the palmette was already fully established as a principal element of floral patterns.

According to Grote-Hasenbalg, there is an even more important feature of the Chinese influence than the introduction of individual motifs, and that is the impulse

171 Tiles from a Cairo mosque, mid-sixteenth century. Victoria and Albert Museum, London.

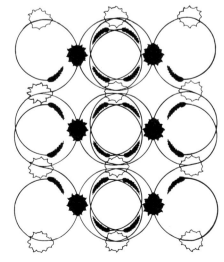

172, 173 Development of the Herati pattern.

174 The dragon and phoenix, as seen in an Anatolian rug of *c.* 1400; as symbols of the benign power of, respectively, the Chinese emperor and empress from early times, they later became the official 'coat-of-arms' of the rulers of the Ming dynasty (1368–1644).

175 The Chelsea carpet, perhaps the greatest of all sixteenth-century Persian carpets, includes the dragon and phoenix in its border (as well as a magnificent development of the Chinese cloud-band motif). The bird, *feng huang* in Chinese, is not strictly a phoenix: it is usually depicted with the body of a peacock, the wings of a goose or stork, and the tail of a golden pheasant. In Persia it became associated with the *simurgh*, the allegory of God in Sufi mystic symbolism. Since the dragon is seen as a symbol of evil, commentators often describe the dragon and phoenix as being depicted 'in combat' in carpet designs. There seems to be little evidence for this interpretation: the two creatures are simply depicted, as here, in the same way as heraldic beasts in European coats-of-arms.

176 Design incorporating lotus palmettes as used in a Chinese rug fragment of the sixteenth century. (Although other rugs with similar motifs are often held to portray paeony or chrysanthemum blooms, Lorentz is emphatic in stating that this pattern represents the lotus flower.)

177 Elaborate palmettes in a Kashan carpet of the mid-sixteenth century; 250 × 150 cm, 998,000 PK/m² (8′ 2″ × 4′ 11″, 644 PK/in.²).
This example also incorporates another Chinese motif, the so-called 'cloud-head' pattern (*yün tsai t'ou*). Yet another motif, the 'endless knot' or 'knot of destiny', may be observed in the border of the carpet depicted in the fifteenth-century miniature reproduced in fig. 616.

for greater freedom of expression and a more flowing, so to speak picturesque, style. Western Persia, he asserts, being furthest from the Chinese influence, preserved the strict Islamic style longest, while the new free style of design developed in Herat and eastern Persia. Figs. 178 and 179 illustrate the difference. The second of these, a north-west Persian medallion carpet, is one of several such pieces about which experts differ with regard to their dates. This carpet – illustrated by Grote-Hasenbalg (his fig. 44) – is described by him as 'around 1500', Dimand, who shows a similar carpet (his fig. 59), suggests an even earlier date. Erdmann's example (his fig. 99) is simply described as sixteenth century; he also illustrates a carpet (his fig. 79) with a less well developed design, which he attributes to the first half of the sixteenth century. Another piece in the McMullan Collection was attributed by Ettinghausen (*Textile Museum Journal*, June 1970) to Tabriz, second quarter of the sixteenth century. All these have a stiffness and angularity which Grote-Hasenbalg sees as a residue of the strict style of the fifteenth century. A point that he does not mention is that they all also use a geometric variant of the Herati pattern in the ground, suggesting links between it and the arabesques of Islamic art of an earlier period. Dimand (in his figs. 62–4) shows how the Tabriz designers gradually overcame this stiffness and introduced the flowing style seen in some Herat miniatures (figs. 617, 751). It is no longer possible to photograph Grote-Hasebalg's example of the flowing Herat style of the first half of the sixteenth century, since the carpet in question was in the Leipzig Museum collection and is now lost. The famous all-over carpet in the collection of the Österreichisches Museum für angewandte Kunst in Vienna is illustrated here in its stead, since it is stylistically very close to the lost Leipzig piece. Its origin may be eastern or central Persia; stylistically it shows the Herat floral style at its most elaborate and fully developed.

We have no firm datable evidence of the art of western Persia to confirm Grote-Hasenbalg's contention, and Erdmann has shown that it was not until about a hundred years after the Mongol conquests that the geometric style gave way to the floral in Herat. However, it does seem that Herat led the way in carpet design as an extension of the very important school of miniature painting and bookbinding and related arts which developed there in the fifteenth century. As the Mongol power waned (Timur's adoption of the Islamic religion of his conquered territories itself began the process of the 'Persianization' of the Mongol Empire) the cultural independence of the Ottoman Turkomans in Anatolia and of the Persians began to assert itself, until, at the end of the fifteenth century, the complete political breakdown of Timur's inheritance occurred with the establishment of: the Safavid Empire in Persia, between 1498 and 1510; the Ottoman Empire in Turkey and the rest of Asia west of Persia – a gradual process that lasted from Timur's death in 1405 until

176

177

179 Detail of a sixteenth-century north Persian carpet with a geometric precursor of the Herati pattern in the ground. Formerly collection Freiherr Tucher von Simmelsdorf, Vienna.

178 The flowing Herat style, in its most mature form, as seen in the 'Emperor's carpet' in the Österreichisches Museum für angewandte Kunst, Vienna; 760 × 325 cm, 495,000 PK/m² (24′ 11″ × 10′ 8″, 320 PK/in.²).

180

181

the accession of Suleiman the Magnificent in 1520; and the Moghul Empire – politically Mongol and culturally Persianized – in India and parts of Afghanistan, between 1525 and 1530.

Although no actual carpets from fifteenth-century Persia have been preserved, it is clear from the Herat miniatures that their designs were markedly geometric, which is sometimes claimed to be a reflection perhaps of a strict interpretation of the Islamic demand for the stylization of all living forms in art (see pp. 156–9, 270). The floral style which developed at the end of the century marked as abrupt a change as the difference between the Gothic and the Romanesque in Western art. The change was itself perhaps a reflection of, perhaps a contributing factor to, the resurgence of Persian political independence. In Grote-Hasenbalg's view, the Herat free style, as exemplified in fig. 178, was the foundation of the great flowering of the carpet art which spread throughout Persia in the sixteenth century, reaching its peak in the reigns of Shah Tahmasp (1524–76) and Shah Abbas I (1587–1629).

During this Golden Age, once the Safavid Emperors had established their power and transferred the capital, first to Ardebil, then to Tabriz, Qazvin and finally to Isfahan, it was the carpet manufactories of Tabriz, Isfahan and Kashan that were called upon to produce the monarch's sumptuous gifts to foreign rulers and the showpieces for mosques and palaces. South-eastern and eastern Persia faded from the limelight, but continued to produce large quantities of carpets, presumably mainly for local use. They came to be called Herat carpets because it was here, in the provincial capital, that they came to the attention of the outside world. But how many, if any at all, were made in Herat is open to question. Firm evidence is practically non-existent: interest centres on the general way the designs of the area developed.

A major problem in tracing the history of a design is that, when faced with a simple version and a more complex one, some experts will call the simple version a later debased form of the more refined one, while others will call it the original from which the more complex one was developed. The chronology of the floral Herat carpets and of the vase designs (which are often attributed to Kerman) is thus much in dispute. Once again, Grote-Hasenbalg's conclusions, with some modifications, may be cited (see notes below).

180–182 THE INDIAN DIMENSION

Quite early in the sixteenth century eastern Persia saw the beginning of a development in which the fine naturalistic balance and flowing proportions of the original Herat style gave way to over-massive and heavily stylized flower and leaf forms joined by long meandering stalks (islimis). Many influences were at work and the designs developed along several different lines. An important factor at this period, and one which is often neglected, was the cultural exchange between Persia and India. The last important successor of Timur was Babur, who inherited the province of Fergana, three times conquered and lost Samarkand, established himself securely as the ruler of Kabul and from there extended his power to found the Moghul Empire in India at the beginning of the sixteenth century.

At times there was conflict between the Moghul and Safavid empires, the worst-hit town being Kandahar in south-eastern Khorassan, which changed hands several times between 1595 and 1649. At other times the two powers were allied in common cause against other forces, but above all there was a cultural interchange derived from the common heritage of the Mongol rule, the Islamic religion and a common court language, Persian. There was thus as much intercourse in the period 1500–1700 between Herat, Kerman, Lahore and Delhi (via Kandahar and the Khyber Pass) as between Herat and Isfahan (which are separated by an impenetrable desert). Carpet historians draw attention to this when writing of the development of weaving in India but usually pay scant attention to the reverse influence in Persia. But the 'Indo-Isfahans', as the Herat-style carpets made south of the Khyber are called, represent an indivisible part of the development of the sixteenth-century east Persian carpet and as such had their own role to play in the crystallization of the separate designs that came to be established in the region. Figs. 180–90 illustrate a few of the important strains of the development, which,

180 Flower motifs in one of the most famous surviving sixteenth-century vase carpets (cf. fig. 270), the origin of which is believed to be Kerman. Victoria and Albert Museum, London.

181 Flower motifs in a seventeenth-century carpet from Lahore. Metropolitan Museum of Art, New York (formerly Kevorkian Collection).

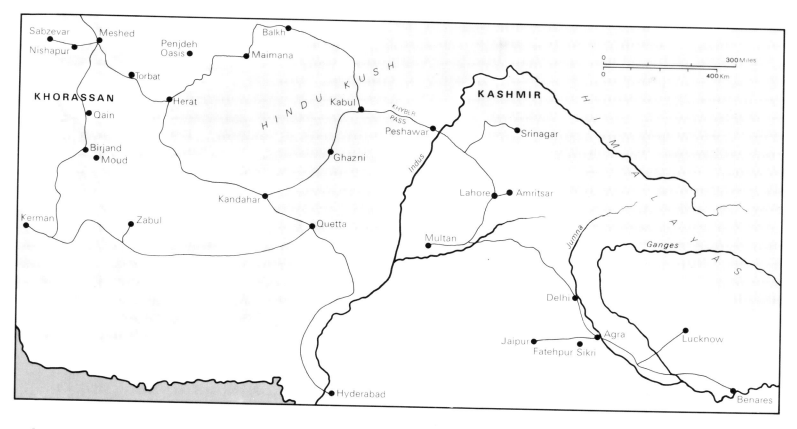

as Grote-Hasenbalg demonstrates, led not only to the Herati pattern, but, by 1700, to the Mina Khani and Joshaqan styles as well (see figs. 754–7, 599), and which, as is amply illustrated in many parts of this book, has remained a dominant influence on the whole of Persian carpet design ever since.

Map of northern India and eastern Persia in the late sixteenth century. For most of the century there was a steady interchange of trade and ideas between Delhi, Kandahar and Herat.

183–191 THE DEVELOPMENT OF THE HERATI DESIGN
Certain stylistic features not always noted by scholars seem worthy of comment. One is the relationship between the vase carpets and the floral Herat carpets. In his excellent notes on the vase design (*Textile Museum Journal*, December 1968) Charles Grant Ellis does not mention this point, although it was noted by Grote-Hasenbalg some fifty years earlier. A. C. Edwards points out that the floral Herat pieces could not have been woven without graph-paper loom-drawings and must therefore have been the products of a town manufactory, whereas Grote-Hasenbalg declares the vase carpets with their strict, symmetrical style to be the 'most perfect examples of Persian folk-art'. Were they perhaps a development one from the other – the semi-geometric vase designs being peasant derivatives from the floral style? Or did they develop separately from a common source? Could the geometric vase designs actually pre-date the floral ones?

An interesting feature linking the two groups is the way the Chinese cloud-band motif is handled. Is it accident that the vase in fig. 183 has a form so reminiscent of the cloud-bands of figs. 186 and 187? Either way up, the cloud-band can be converted into a vase at the flick of the designer's pen or by very elementary mis-reading of the loom-drawing by the weaver. Compare also the similarity between the cloud-bands in figs. 186 and the important lily motif at the very centre of fig. 739 which occurs also in the diagonal axes of this and most other vase carpets.

Another point rarely touched on by scholars is the importance of the introduction of leaf motifs some time in the course of the development of both the vase and the Herat floral types. This must have been a decisive innovation seized upon by designers as a means of pushing the development along lines which might have been difficult with the purely floral and animal motifs of the early classical carpets. How or when the elongated leaf motifs, usually called lancet leaves, arose is not known, owing to the uncertain chronology of all of these carpets. These motifs are absent in figs. 739, 186 and 270, but in one of the lines of development, clearly evident in figs. 188–90, they came to occupy a dominant position in the overall design and

182 Cartouches of inlaid *pietra dura* on the Tomb of Itimad-ud-Daulah, Agra (built 1622–8).

183 The most brilliant of the Kerman vase carpets: fragment of a sixteenth-century carpet now in the Österreichisches Museum für angewandte Kunst, Vienna (another fragment is in the Textile Museum, Washington, D.C.), showing – in the inner guard – the same cartouche shapes as those seen in the previous illustration.

184 Vase carpet, sixteenth century, in the Lamm Collection (Textile Museum, Washington, D.C.); this piece is considered by C. Grant Ellis to be the oldest of the group in the museum. The best-proportioned vase carpet, known as the Jeziorak or Figdor carpet, is shown in fig. 739.

184

183

they were the kéy to the conversion of the floral Herat carpets into the Herati pattern.

Whatever the origin of the Herati design, the form in which it is used in modern production is unproblematical: a flower is surrounded by a diamond-shaped framework of stalks with a large leaf set parallel to each of the four sides of the diamond. In many parts of Persia the leaf is regarded as a fish and the design is called *mahi* (meaning 'fish') or the 'fish-in-the-pond' design. However, this description seems to be a case of weavers – or dealers – reading their own fanciful interpretation into a new design adopted from a foreign tradition, in the same way as the

185

186

185 Detail of a Herat floral carpet, full size 265 × 180 cm (8′ 8″ × 5′ 10″), formerly in the Museum für Islamische Kunst, Berlin (now lost), dated by Grote-Hasenbalg to the first half of the sixteenth century, and by Erdmann to *c.* 1600.

186 Detail of a floral Herat carpet, 224 × 207 cm (7′ 4″ × 6′ 9″); this piece also has the characteristics of the sixteenth-century style. Victoria and Albert Museum, London.

187 A late sixteenth-century floral Herat carpet, 380 × 296 cm, 420,000 PK/m² (12′ 5″ × 9′ 8″, 271 PK/in.²). Carpet Museum of Iran, Tehran.

188 Detail of a seventeenth-century Indian carpet, full size 256 × 220 cm (8′ 5″ × 7′ 2″). Museum für Islamische Kunst, Berlin.

187

188

Indians refer to 'parrot' Serabends, discussed above in the context of the boteh motif.

The spread of the Herati design outside Khorassan (assuming it did originate there) is better known. There is a universally accepted but, here too, seemingly not very well documented tradition that in about 1730 or 1740 Nadir Shah transferred large numbers of weavers from Khorassan to central Persia – to the Ferahan region of present-day Arak, and the area across to Joshaqan, north of Isfahan. In the process he transferred the east Persian design concepts, paving the way for the development of the Mina Khani and Joshaqan designs (figs. 757, 599) as well as

189

190

191

189 An excellent example of the developing Herati pattern seen in a detail of the flowing, well-balanced design of a carpet formerly in the Kunstgewerbemuseum, Leipzig; although attributed by Grote-Hasenbalg to the first half of the seventeenth century, there is a conflict of chronology since the border seems much closer in style to those seen in figs. 66 and 178, while the layout of the ground is strongly reminiscent of that in fig. 179 (dated by Grote-Hasenbalg to 1500).

190 Detail of a Herati carpet, full size 990 × 358 cm (32′ 6″ × 11′ 9″), known to have been made not later than 1640 (from which date its presence in the palace of the Duke of Braganza is recorded). Thyssen-Bornemisza Collection, Lugano.

191 Detail of an antique Herati carpet in the Victoria and Albert Museum, London; the museum also owns a piece of almost identical design but woven with the Turkish knot and in the single-wefted construction typical of the Ferahan region.

stimulating the spread of the Herati design. There remains something of a mystery about the name Ferahan (often misspelt Feraghan). Today, Upper and Lower Ferahan are administrative districts north-east of Arak, adjacent to Tafrish. Although the famous antique Ferahan design may have originated in this area, the bulk of the production in the late nineteenth and early twentieth centuries seems to have come from a much wider area, with special emphasis on the region west of Arak towards Malayir. Whatever the explanation of this confusing situation, the Malayir-Ferahan carpets quickly became as famous as the Herati originals, and 'Ferahan design' is just as commonly used as a description as is 'Herati design'. This has become the typical traditional design in several parts of Persia, but it is in fact made almost everywhere and is found in both rectilinear and curvilinear forms, from simple peasant rugs to fine manufactured carpets. Once fully established, the Herati pattern was used as an independent design with the same degree of variation from one locality to another as is found with the boteh motif. The eighteenth-century carpet from Herat (in the Victoria and Albert Museum textile study collection) shown in fig. 191 captures well the essential flavour of the design. Here, the motifs are drawn rather larger than is normal for the design, but what is particularly fascinating about this version is the blending of floral and geometric styles which it incorporates. The weaver has introduced a number of curves into the execution of the pattern, but without obliterating its semi-geometric peasant flavour. This is a feature which will be noticed in many of the best versions of this design, and which no doubt contributes much to its universal appeal.

192, 193 SENJABI, BIJAR

The Herati design is woven throughout western Iran, from Tabriz right down to Khorramabad, each area having its own characteristic version. In Kurdish tribal rugs it appears in many guises, two of which – Senjabi and Bijar – are illustrated here. Although the simple rustic execution of the motifs is common to both, the two pieces are markedly different in almost every other respect, reflecting the wide variety of types found within the Kurdish weaving area. Senjabi is the name of one of the southernmost Kurdish tribes, but it is used rather loosely in the carpet trade to describe a range of tribal or village types of the Kermanshah area. The warmth of the colouring, the light brownish shade of the red and a single-wefted construction

192

193

194

on woollen warps are typical Senjabi features. The Bijar rug, on the other hand, has features which might remind one of the Kakaberu tribe – a coarse but tight and heavy double-wefted structure, the kelleyi format and a rather wild interpretation of traditional Bijar motifs (for a finer version of the border see fig. 103). However, the ground of this rug is light red and the whole appearance is bright and airy, which completely excludes Kakaberu as the origin. (Kakaberu rugs are always dark; many are predominantly dark blue with little use of red at all, but where any quantity of red is used it is a dark shade, even mahogany-coloured). Most carpet experts would therefore classify the piece as a Bijar, with the rider that it is not a true Bijar in the normal sense but a coarse peasant product, probably from some village in the Bijar area.

194 HASHTRUD

Another simple village form of the Herati design, from the mountainous Hashtrud region, on the northern edge of the Persian Kurdish area, reveals stylistic influence from the neighbouring Azerbaijan region: the leaf or 'fish' motifs have here become completely displaced and out of order. This is a not uncommon feature of Kurdish Herati pieces – one often encounters, for example, an all-over distribution of Herati leaves, but only a hint of the rest of the Herati pattern; and in the piece shown in fig. 532 the Herati pattern of the central medallion is quite dismembered. The Hashtrud (literally, 'eight rivers') region lies east of Lake Urmia. It has only a small output of rugs, which are sold in the Tabriz bazaar; they are also described as Shah Savan or Amroullah.

195–200 BIJAR

One of the great versions of the Herati design is that used in Bijar, the market for the finest and best Kurdish carpets. Whereas the previous illustrations have shown rugs made entirely of repeating Herati motifs, in the Bijar carpet the Herati design provides a background dominated by a large floral medallion. This combination of a basically floral centre on an essentially geometric ground is characteristic of many Bijar designs. Bijar is one of the fine weaves of Persia, so that technically there would be no problem at all in producing elaborate floral designs; however, the strongly geometric style of the traditional Kurdish tribal designs always makes

192 Senjabi
193×126 cm, 90,000 TK/m^2
($6'\ 4'' \times 4'\ 1''$, 58 TK/in.^{2}).

193 Bijar
248×141 cm, 85,000 TK/m^2
($8'\ 1'' \times 4'\ 7''$, 55 TK/in.^{2}).

194 Hashtrud
186×111 cm, 106,000 TK/m^2
($6'\ 1'' \times 3'\ 8''$, 68 TK/in.^{2}).

195

196

195 Bijar (Kurdi)
215 × 140 cm, 230,000 TK/m²
(7′ 1″ × 4′ 7″, 148 TK/in.²).

196 Afshar Bijar
348 × 249 cm, 270,000 TK/m²
(11′ 5″ × 8′ 2″, 174 TK/in.²).

itself felt in Bijar carpets. Note, by the way, the broad light-coloured outline to the medallion. This is a characteristic feature which is a useful clue to recognition of Bijar designs. Most of the production features a red ground, although blue and, occasionally, cream are also found. The sizes made are: pushti, zarcherek, zaronim, dozar, some kelleyis, and carpets of all sizes (though carpets under 8 m² – approx. 85 ft² – are rather rare). It is interesting that the centre part of the medallion in fig. 195 is used as an independent motif in the repeating-medallion Bijar piece shown in fig. 761.

The finest Bijars, as it happens, are woven not by Kurds but by a small clan of Afshars who live to the north of Bijar around Tekab and Tekkenteppe – presumably descendants of the tribesmen who escaped Nadir Shah's transportation in the eighteenth century (see p. 70). From the point of view of carpet design, there is little connection with the Afshars of the Kerman region: the Bijar Afshars produce carpets fully within the Kurdish Bijar tradition, although they are usually just a little more flowery, especially in their floral medallions, an example of which is shown (fig. 197). In the Afshar carpet (fig. 196), however, we see a third use to which the Herati design is put: this remains a Herati all-over, but by using three different ground shades separated by an outline of dark blue the weaver has produced a medallion-and-corner effect. This idea is used in many places – see fig. 230 (Birjand), fig. 223 (Saruq), fig. 227 (Ardebil) – but the Bijar version is unmistakable, mainly because of its more primitive execution. Note that the edges of the medallion are not parallel to the corners, nor are they symmetrical in themselves. The Herati pattern itself is also distorted, and another noteworthy feature is the extraordinary shapes which the medallion can adopt. The three examples illustrated (figs. 198–200) show some of these distortions which are the hallmarks of village weaving.

At this point it is worth quoting in full the paragraph Grote-Hasenbalg (1922) devotes (p. 62) to the collapse of the great Court Manufactories of the Safavid Empire, even before the Afghan invasion of 1722:

> The decline of Persian art is usually explained entirely by the argument that the artisans no longer understood the artistic concepts of earlier times. I would say this was the least important reason for the decay. I have already drawn attention to the dangers that attend an art which is founded only upon high technical skills and precious materials and is dependent on the most extravagant wealth. That Persian art followed this path at all no doubt has to do with the form of despotism in the Orient which drove all branches of art to extremes of showiness and to a refinement of technique down to the smallest detail, which were intended to proclaim the ruler's splendour and his power to the whole world . . . But there came a point where increased living standards coincided with a decline in the ruler's power and influence: there was no increased wealth to support the standards demanded and the pressure for simplification became overwhelming . . . Very often the person commissioning the work simply could not afford the desired degree of refinement. In countries like those of western Europe, where free art has always been more highly regarded than craftsmanship, the situation was different. The struggles to liberate the Netherlands (from Spain), which must surely have had a serious impact on the Dutch economy, were not yet at an end when the seventeenth-century school of Dutch painting led by Rembrandt reached its highest peak of achievement. But for these works the only materials needed were paint and canvas – and the genius of the artist. The collapse of the economic substructure destroyed the art of the great city manufactories. But the folk art of the mountain villages remained untouched by all this: it neither partook of the artistic opulence of the Golden Age, nor did it suffer by the latter's decline. It simply retained its identity and preserved its originality, the touchstone of its cultural significance.

What excites us about the best Bijar carpets is that this originality is coupled with the highest technical quality, for all their lack of elegance and manufactory perfection. They are seen again and again in prime positions in oriental carpet exhibitions because they combine all the qualities that we prize in this field of art: practically indestructible construction, magnificent colours, fine weave and unpredictable and deeply expressive independence of design.

197 Afshar Bijar: floral medallion.

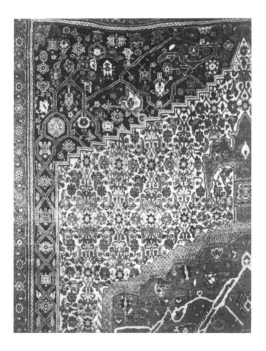

198–200 Herati motifs in Bijar carpets: three examples showing typical irregularities in execution; although of fine weave, Bijar's output is produced in villages, mainly without the controlled design work available in town manufactories.

201, 202 GOGARJIN, KOLYAI

We come now to two further Kurdish examples of the Herati pattern. Gogarjin is a village very close to Bijar, weaving a distinctive form of Bijar rug in the style illustrated; this, like all Bijars, is double-wefted. The Kolyai tribe, whose goods are marketed in Sonqur in the south of Kurdistan, weave their own version of the Bijar design, and, like all Kolyai tribal rugs, the example illustrated is single-wefted. The broad camel-coloured outer edge to the medallion is a typical Bijar trait, but the general coarseness of the rest of the rug betrays its more humble origin.

203 ZENJAN

Zenjan is a small, neat market town roughly halfway along the road from Tehran to Tabriz. Here three different carpet-weaving styles meet: the coarse double-wefted kelleyis and rugs of southern Azerbaijan (e.g. fig. 134), the fine double-wefted rugs of the Bijar area, and the coarse-to-medium single-wefted goods of the northern Hamadan region. The name Zenjan is used, confusingly, to describe some of the products of all three types. The single-wefted type is illustrated in fig. 580. The fine double-wefted category, made to the west and south-west of Zenjan, may be sub-divided again into three types, two of which have distinctive names: Qoltuq (see fig. 581) and Bidgeneh (see fig. 582). The third of the fine double-wefted types is

201 Gogarjin
162 × 105 cm, 202,000 TK/m²
(5′ 4″ × 3′ 5″, 130 TK/in.²).

202 Kolyai
224 × 130 cm, 141,000 TK/m²
(7′ 4″ × 4′ 3″, 91 TK/in.²).

201

202

illustrated here. Such carpets are made in the area between Zenjan and Bijar and many people at first glance think they are Bijars because they have the same general colours and designs as Bijar. There are, however, two noticeable features by which they can be distinguished. The first is a stiff gawkiness in the design: compare, for instance, the grace and elegance of the border of the Bijar in fig. 195 with the nondescript feebleness of the star-spangled lollipops in the piece shown here. Or again the sense of flowing movement in the Bijar medallion with the uninspiring dryness of the Zenjan one. The feature which always strikes one about the Zenjan 'Bijars' is that they look like Bijars that have not come out right, that have somehow failed to reach the required standard. The second distinctive feature is a corresponding stiffness in the weave: the structure – unlike that of Bijar – is not well balanced, but over-heavy in the warp and weft and underweight in the pile; the back of the carpet is thus excessively stiff, which, of course, in the long run impairs the wearing quality. The above comment may seem to read like an outright condemnation of the Zenjan Bijar, but that would be unfair. In the world of carpets all things are relative and a good Zenjan is always better than a bad Bijar. Also many Zenjans have the advantage of being much cheaper – only half or two-thirds the price of a Bijar of equal fineness – which can make them an attractive buy, although quite extravagant prices are sometimes quoted for Zenjans of unusual fineness.

203 Zenjan
200×129 cm, 197,000 TK/m²
($6'$ $6'' \times 4'$ $3''$, 127 TK/in.²).

204 SENNEH
Mention has already been made of the special distinctiveness of the rugs made in the Kurdish capital of Senneh. This also applies to their use of the Herati design, as illustrated here. This rug shows the standard interpretation of the Herati motif which is used for in-filling in many Senneh designs; this particular version, with its strange dismemberment of the pattern, is not generally used elsewhere in Persia. Note how the diamond has become a hexagon and the leaves merely rectangular shapes. All the motifs, moreover, are set out in simple vertical chains (with no

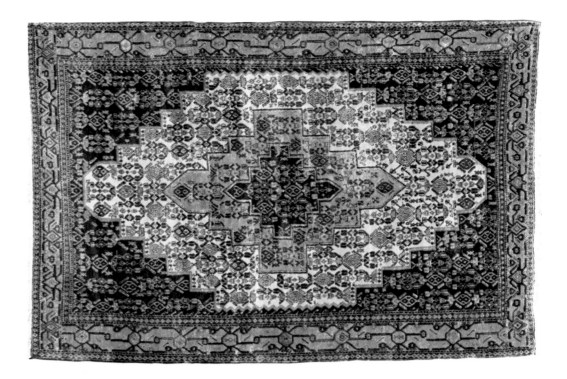

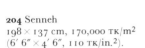
204 Senneh
198 × 137 cm, 170,000 TK/m²
(6′ 6″ × 4′ 6″, 110 TK/in.²).

feeling of the horizontal and diagonal interdependence which is so strong in most Herati patterns). For general comments on Senneh, cf. fig. 130. Note that the size of this rug, the standard Persian dozar size, is rare in Senneh; Senneh dozars are usually appreciably larger.

205, 206 FERAHAN

We now come to one of the best known of all nineteenth-century carpet designs, the Ferahan. It is no longer produced, but in its heyday it had a great reputation for quality combined with elegance and restraint. Carpets of this type were made in large numbers and many examples can be found in museums, stately homes and private collections, especially in England, where they acquired in the late nineteenth century the sort of popularity that is enjoyed, for example, by the Mir Serabend in German-speaking countries in our own times – and for the same reasons of tasteful restraint and economy of design and colour, durable construction with very good wool and suitability for use in a wide range of decorative situations. The old classical Ferahan was discovered by the European traders who began buying up Persian carpets for export from 1875 onwards. The type had two distinguishing features apart from its design: it always featured madder red (i.e. a shade on the browny-rose side of red), either as the ground colour or as the dominant subsidiary tone on the rarer cream or blue grounds; and it was usually in the kelleyi format, i.e. rather long in relation to its width. The supply of old kelleyis did not last for very long and towards the end of the nineteenth century, at the same time as importers based at Sultanabad (Arak) were beginning to develop the manufactured Saruq, they also began to organize the village production of Ferahans over a wide area of the Arak region. These goods were, of course, in more normal European or North American dimensions. For background notes on the Ferahan's origin see the first part of this section. Note that many other carpets were also called Ferahan; these were made in designs and in a fine double-wefted construction which, to avoid confusion, would be better described as Saruq. This situation has no doubt resulted from the extreme geographical vagueness of the word Ferahan, which is used very loosely to mean 'Arak area' in general. The Malayir-Ferahan of the kind depicted in fig. 205 was always single-wefted; the weave was rather like that of present-day Nenej or Jokar (see figs. 760, 211), but the pile was always clipped very close to give greater clarity and brilliance to the design. The style of the double-wefted Saruq/Ferahans is illustrated in figs. 603, 604 and 784.

Today, the Ferahan area proper, centred around the village of Farmahin, has a significant production of single-wefted rugs and runners in the Herati design. These come within the general category of Hamadan rugs, having similarities with both their neighbours in the Hamadan region, that is, with Borchalu to the west and with Tafrish and Rudbar, which are to the north and east. However, the new Ferahan Herati design, as seen in fig. 206, is very distinctive and quite unlike the red *mahi* version found in so many Hamadan villages (see figs. 210, 211). To begin with, it is mostly found on a dark-blue ground (sometimes also on a muddy dark red), often with rather sombre secondary colours which may tend to make the overall effect somewhat gloomy; secondly, the motifs are rather larger than those used in other Hamadan villages; and thirdly, the Ferahan Heratis are almost all without medallion. There are several variants, some more angular than others; most sizes are made, the commonest being: mossul (200 × 100 cm; 6′ 6″ × 3′ 3″), dozar (200 × 130 cm; 6′ 6″ × 4′ 3″) and runners in sizes such as 300–350 × 100 cm (10′ 0″–11′ 6″ × 3′ 3″) and longer.

207 BORCHALU

Borchalu is the name of a tribe centred on the villages of Khumajin and Kumbazan, a remote area east of Hamadan and to the west of Ferahan. This tribe is well known for a particularly successful version of the American Saruq design (see fig. 639), but a large part of their output is in the standard Hamadan village form derived from the nineteenth-century 'Ferahans' (compare fig. 205). Experienced dealers can

205 An old Ferahan carpet in the entrance hall of Hever Castle, Kent.

206 Ferahan
195 × 122 cm, 120,000 TK/m²
(6′ 5″ × 4′ 0″, 77 TK/in.²).

205

206

208

209

207

recognize Borchalu Herati rugs fairly easily from the neat, fine weave and from certain clues in the colourings; but for most people the principal distinguishing feature is the shape of the central medallion. Most sizes up to 4 m² (43 ft²) are made, but especially dozars and zaronims. Most Herati Borchalus are on red grounds, but blue and some creams are also found. A similar fine Herati rug is made in the village of Musa Khan Bolaghi, which lies to the west of Khumajin in the direction of Husseinabad.

208 RUDBAR
Next to Ferahan to the north is Rudbar whose production, in its weave and colouring, belongs to the Tafrish group (see fig. 555), but has its own distinctive version of the Herati design: quite like the Ferahan but more floral, and above all lighter in colour, with many cream grounds, some red and very few blue. A particular distinguishing feature of the Rudbar weave is the frequent use of pink wefts. Another, less easily recognized, feature is the soft, spongy feel to the wool frequently employed there. The lighter colours and the softer wool both link Rudbar with the Shah Savan tribe of Saveh (cf. p. 237 and map, p. 346). A wide range of rug sizes is made.

209 KHARAGHAN
A stylistic neighbour of the Ferahan Heratis is illustrated here. It has the same dark-blue background and the angularity of design commonly found in Ferahan, but there are subtle differences which a trained eye will notice. The overall colouring lacks the luscious warmth of the Ferahan area: the red, for example, is too hard. The wool is also a little harsher to the touch and the weave is not so fine. The origin of this example is Kharaghan, the name of a group of villages to the north-west of the Ferahan area.

210, 211 HUSSEINABAD, JOKAR
The Herati design is used in a large number of villages around Hamadan (and generally known locally as the *mahi* design), especially in a cluster of places to the south-east on the road to Malayir. These villages all have distinguishing features of weave and colouring which a trained eye can recognize. A Jokar piece is fine and neat but a Borchalu is finer and neater – one is reminded of Hugh Johnson's description of the individual wines of the Beaujolais region: 'Brouilly is grapy and rich, but Côte de Brouilly is grapier and richer'. Most of the *mahi* rugs are sold simply as Hamadan, but the layman can tell some of the different types from

differences in the design. Note that in the vast majority of the production a red ground is used; blue grounds are rare, and cream grounds even rarer, though both do exist. The biggest production comes from Husseinabad, and that name is often used to describe rugs in the *mahi* design made throughout the area. Husseinabad goods vary in quality from medium to very good. Fig. 210 illustrates one of the simpler weaves (better pieces will have 100,000–115,000 knots/m^2; 65–75 knots/ in.^{2}). Apart from Everu (see fig. 215), it is the only village with a significant output in the all-over Herati pattern, without a medallion (as illustrated here), but it also produces goods with its own rather small distinctive medallion (and corners). All sizes are made, from pushtis to large carpets, including narrow runners (60–80 cm wide; 2' 0"–2' 9") in all lengths.

Jokar also makes a range of sizes, especially large dozars (about $3\frac{1}{2}$ m^2 or 40 ft^2). The distinctive medallion is similar to the one used in Husseinabad, but larger. The weave, too, is similar to that of Husseinabad – perhaps even neater – but not as fine as in the better-grade Husseinabads. Jokar has, in effect, the same structure as Nenej (see fig. 760), with very good wool and a thicker pile than Husseinabad. To the north of the group is the main source of the cheap, small Herati rugs, Gombad. Gombads are mostly rather bright and crude, but above-average pieces are also to be found. Among the other sources of Husseinabad-type *mahis* are Ezanderian, which makes coarse cheap carpets (which are often wrongly sold as Husseinabads), and Ganjtepe, which makes fine, expensive carpets.

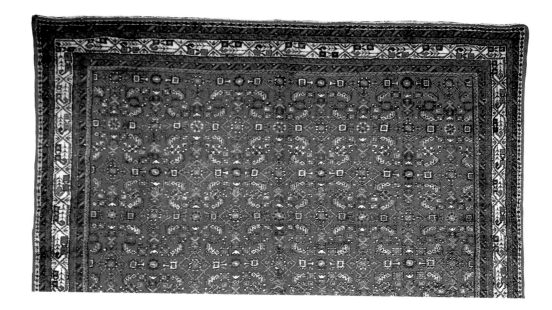

210 Husseinabad/Ezanderian area; detail of a carpet, full size 300 × 200 cm, 68,000 TK/m^2 (9' 10" × 6' 6", 44 TK/in.^{2}).

211 Jokar 222 × 137 cm, 96,000 TK/m^2 (7' 3" × 4' 6", 62 TK/in.^{2}).

212

213

212 Malayir/Borujird region
195 × 124 cm, 115,000 TK/m²
(6′ 5″ × 4′ 1″, 74 TK/in.²).

213 Lilihan
153 × 107 cm, 109,000 TK/m²
(5′ 1″ × 3′ 6″, 70 TK/in.²).

214 Enjilas
195 × 142 cm, 185,000 TK/m²
(6′ 5″ × 4′ 8″, 119 TK/in.²).

215 Everu
102 × 107 cm, 120,000 TK/m²
(3′ 4″ × 3′ 6″, 77 TK/in.²).

212 MALAYIR

South of Jokar and stretching as far as Borujird (see Hamadan area map, p. 346) there is a largish area producing single-wefted rugs of varying quality in a wide range of designs. The production may be as clumsy as the piece shown in fig. 655, or as neat and finely executed as the Herati rug shown here. This piece shows the stylistic influence of Jokar, but has the predominant dark blue which is characteristic of the Malayir and Borujird region (and also of the Nehavend and Tuisarkan group to the west, where Herati designs are normally not woven – see p. 259). The weave of this area is clearly distinguishable from that of the Jokar/Husseinabad group owing to the use of medium-blue wefts, against which the white warp-strings show up strongly as clear white specks all over the back of the rug. Apart from Alamdar, with its own characteristic design (see fig. 217) the names of the individual villages of the area are not used and the rugs are sold simply as Borujird or Malayir.

213 LILIHAN

Parallel with the unmistakable production in the American Saruq design (see fig. 638), the Armenian village of Lilihan also has a substantial output in the Herati pattern, as illustrated here. As is explained on p. 282, this is a single-wefted region, lying to the south of the Hamadan village area. The weave is medium-fine, with a normally very sound structure and good yarn. The colours are regrettably rather variable; not only are some of the subsidiary shades very crude (greens and orange, for example), but also the dark blue, which is the most common ground shade in Herati-pattern Lilihans, can have a very dead appearance, with grey, black or mauvy streaks. The red shades are usually sound, however, and the open layout of the Herati motifs creates a very appealing effect if the blue is properly dyed. All rug and carpet sizes are found, including some unusual dimensions like 200 × 170 cm (6′ 6″ × 5′ 6″).

214, 215 ENJILAS, EVERU

Enjilas products have always been among the very best of all Hamadan rugs. In the past their workmanship, design, colours and materials were all superlative, and to this day remain far above the local average. The price, of course, reflects this: even a good Husseinabad may be only a quarter of the price of a fine old Enjilas. Dark-blue grounds are common; red is also found. The illustration shows a piece which may be about forty years old; the natural madder red of the ground has mellowed to a superb warm shade with a tinge of rose. The Herati design – wherever it is made – is almost always successful; a true Enjilas shows us just how much better

214

215

216 Kemereh

perfection is than mere success. A considerable range of sizes exists, but dozars are the most common; they are almost always without medallion, but include the small corner motifs of the rug illustrated.

The next village to Enjilas is Everu, which is an important centre for mass-produced rugs in the Enjilas style. As often happens in the carpet trade, nomenclature is flexible – in this particular case Everu rugs are usually sold as Enjilas, but there is in fact no problem in distinguishing the genuine article from the cheaper copy. For one thing the fineness of stitch is easy to check: a good Enjilas will have at least 160,000 knots/m² (104 knots/in.²) while an Everu will rarely exceed 130,000–140,000 (84–90/in.²); in addition, almost every other characteristic sets the Enjilas in a class apart. The only feature Everu has in common with its illustrious neighbour is the fine yarn used; in everything else Everu is inferior. The quality varies from quite good to very poor. The design, as shown in the example illustrated, is pretty clumsy, but the worst feature is the colouring: crude red, heavy dark blue and, above all, a vicious synthetic turquoise-green. A wide range of rug and runner sizes is made, including such things as small squares, which are rarely found in Persian goods.

216 KEMEREH

To the south, outside the Hamadan region proper, there is a group of villages known as the Kemereh, some of which are still inhabited by descendants of the Armenians transported there by Shah Abbas I after the partition of Armenia between Persia and Turkey in the early seventeenth century. The two best known are Lilihan (cf. fig. 638) and Reihan (cf. fig. 467), which have their own designs. The others produce single-wefted rugs in the Hamadan *mahi* style which the layman can perhaps best distinguish by the lighter shade of red used in the area, for the Kemereh lies in a region that otherwise produces Saruq carpets, with their light madder rose, or Viss

216 Kemereh
209 × 137 cm, 130,000 TK/m²
(6′ 10″ × 4′ 6″, 84 TK/in.²).

217 Alamdar
217 × 137 cm, 86,000 TK/m²
(7′ 1″ × 4′ 6″, 55 TK/in.²).

218 Assadabad
207 × 137 cm, 98,000 TK/m²
(6′ 9″ × 4′ 6″, 63 TK/in.²).

219 Zagheh
208 × 142 cm, 102,000 TK/m²
(6′ 10″ × 4′ 10″, 66 TK/in.²).

220 Taimeh
167 × 106 cm, 209,000 TK/m²
(5′ 8″ × 3′ 6″, 135 TK/in.²).

carpets, which are equally light in colour (see figs. 645, 534). There is, however, also a distinctive design feature by which one can identify Kemereh rugs – the shape of the medallion, as illustrated here and again in fig. 585.

217–220 ALAMDAR, ASSADABAD, ZAGHEH, TAIMEH

In the Hamadan region proper there are several other villages that produce their own version of the Herati design. Typical of Alamdar are dozars and zaronims with a blue ground and the rather angular version of the design shown here. Alamdar lies to the south of Malayir in the direction of Borujird, and both the colourings and weave remind one of the latter – the warps, for example, appearing as very prominent white specks on the back of the rug.

Assadabad rugs, mainly dozars without a medallion, usually display a pleasant red, with a coarse but chunky weave. Here, too, the design is rather open (see illustration), with the peculiarity that the diamond motif is not the central feature of the design and hence does not occupy as important a position as it does in rugs made elsewhere. Assadabad lies at the top of the mountain pass on the road from Hamadan leading to the Kurdish area, and the design shows Kurdish influence, as a comparison with Kakaberu and Kolyai designs will confirm.

Just over the mountains from Assadabad, on the Hamadan side, lie Zagheh and Tajiabad and a group of villages weaving a full range of rug and runner sizes in the design illustrated in fig. 219. It is the shape of the medallion, together with the 'teeth' motif around it and the corners which help one remember the Zagheh design; the ground, however, is yet another version of the Herati motif. The quality is quite good, although the yarn is often suspect and the dyestuffs more than suspect. Another version of this design uses the same layout on a ground covered with biggish boteh motifs.

An example of a Taimeh rug is included here because of its superficial resemblance to Zagheh. In fact there is no possibility of confusing the two, Taimeh being a double-wefted rug of the Malayir/Jozan group, whereas all Hamadan rugs, including Zagheh, are single-wefted. Once again the ground is a special variant of the Herati design, although, as with Zagheh, the ground may also be filled with angular boteh motifs. For general details of the Malayir group, cf. fig. 653. Taimeh is unusual in that cream grounds, and lighter colours in general, are more common than in the other villages of the group.

217

218

219

220

221–229 SARUQ

Saruq is the name of a village on the edge of the Ferahan region which has given its name to the products of the whole area around Arak, the centre where the goods are marketed. The Herati is an old-established traditional design of the Saruq carpet, although today more carpets are perhaps made in other designs. Fig. 221, from the village of Viss, illustrates a type that would normally be called a Mahal, i.e. a grade II (but still quite good) Saruq. Note the neatness and regularity, which nevertheless do not degenerate into stiffness. Fig. 222 is a really fine all-over Herati Saruq rug from Ghiassabad (which, with Mahallat village, is probably the best known of the various villages in the region still capable today of producing very fine work): again there is exactness combined with warmth and charm. From the general appearance one may infer a relationship with the best Borchalu goods and other fine Herati rugs from the Hamadan area, but there is no possibility of confusing the two types since all Saruqs are double- and all Hamadans single-wefted.

Fig. 223 shows the best of all the new Saruqs, the Mesheriki. Here the all-over Herati is converted into a medallion-and-corner carpet by the same expedient as is used in the Bijar carpet in fig. 196. Mesheriki (Mashayekhi) is a manufacturer who, reviving a traditional Saruq idea, has exactly captured the half-geometric, half-floral nature of the Herati design. By retaining just the right amount of the rectilinear in a stitch which could easily produce perfect curvilinear designs, he has established a standard version of the design which is widely admired – and widely copied. Copies of Mesherikis are made in Bulgaria (fig. 226) and the author himself was responsible for starting one of the Mesheriki copies made in India (illustrated in fig. 162), but none of the copies have the flair of the Persian original. The prices of the originals, it must be admitted, are horrific, but the results produced rank with the best Bijar and Enjilas rugs as the modern pinnacle among goods using the Herati design. A fine village variant of the Mesheriki style is shown in fig. 225, another Ghiassabad rug; what this example lacks is the finesse of Mesheriki's colour-balance, but it is a very good rug nevertheless. The Bulgarian copy illustrated uses a good-quality yarn in a quite fine weave – although the production is fairly small the quality is considerably above that of the standard grade of other Balkan countries. But at the heart of the success of the Bulgarian 'Mesheriki' lie the same factors as inspire the original: the finely judged balance of colours and proportions of the design.

221 Viss
321 × 237 cm, 84,000 PK/m²
(10′ 6″ × 7′ 9″, 54 PK/in.²).

222 Ghiassabad
205 × 126 cm, 370,000 PK/m²
(6′ 9″ × 4′ 1″, 239 PK/in.²).

221

222

223

223 Mesheriki (Mashayekhi)
294 × 231 cm, 386,000 PK/m²
(9′ 8″ × 7′ 7″, 249 PK/in.²).

224 Mesheriki Saruq
Detail viewed from the back.

225 Ghiassabad
200 × 129 cm, 340,000 PK/m²
(6′ 6″ × 4′ 3″, 219 PK/in.²).

226 Bulgaria
322 × 221 cm, 250,000 PK/m²
(10′ 7″ × 7′ 3″, 161 PK/in.²).

224

225

226

227 ARDEBIL

It is confusing that there are five quite different types of carpet sold as Ardebil. The easiest to deal with is what is known as the Ardebil design, the Sheikh Safi carpet, which does not come from Ardebil at all – see fig. 702. Then there are the old-style kelleyis and runners from a fairly far-flung group of surrounding villages, woven in typical bold Azerbaijan designs and the heavy weave that characterizes the Persian southern Caucasus. These are illustrated in figs. 134, 508 and elsewhere (see index). The modern production of this same area apes the Russian Shirvan style: the goods are known in the trade as new-style Ardebils (see p. 225). Then there is an Ardebil town production which has the same structure as the old-style kelleyis but makes clumsily executed Tabriz designs. The clumsiness is accentuated by the fact that the designs are never unequivocally curvilinear or rectilinear. The

227

228

227 Ardebil
Detail of a carpet, full size approx.
350 × 250 cm, 188,000 TK/m²
(11′ 6″ × 8′ 3″, 121 TK/in.²).

228 Tabriz
Detail of a carpet (viewed from the back), full size
350 × 247 cm, 250,000 TK/m²
(11′ 6″ × 8′ 1″, 161 TK/in.²).

results are rarely attractive: the colours are usually crude and the sizes often too long in relation to the width, but the weave is firm and solid and the carpets are relatively cheap. In the 1970s these carpets were displaced by an entirely new kind of Ardebil carpet based on the same design concept as is used in the Mesheriki carpets and the Bijars shown in figs. 223 and 196. This type is woven, in all carpet sizes and most rug sizes, in a wide range of qualities (in densities of less than 100,000 to over 300,000 knots/m²; 65–195 knots/in.²), the finest pieces even having a part-silk pile. Some pieces are made on woollen warps, which is most unusual for Azerbaijan. The design layout is the same in all grades, although the medallion shape varies considerably. At present (1980) only blue-ground carpets are made, often using a poor dyestuff that tends to make the whole carpet look pinkish mauve. The weaving pattern on the back varies enormously from one piece to another, and in many cases does not look like Ardebil at all – some even look like Birjands. In all grades there are some very good pieces and others with a construction that is highly suspect. The worst pieces feel as thin as a rag, but the better ones are quite sound. The most attractive carpets are those where a proper deep blue is used for the ground and where the subsidiary colourings include a rich, medium leafy green and a fine madder-rose. These are the equals in appearance of good Saruqs and Bijars, and they demonstrate powerfully that the designers and colorists of Persia are still capable of producing new carpets of outstanding beauty. The fine goods of this type are called Sinehbaff, i.e. 'Senneh weave', a rather misleading description. The name derives from the supposed resemblance of the back of the finest pieces to that of Senneh goods; it does not imply the use of the Persian ('Senneh') knot, since all Ardebils are woven with the Turkish knot.

228 TABRIZ

Mesheriki has manufactories in Sarab and Tabriz as well as Arak, all making the same design – and to the same high standards. The layman has no hope of telling them apart. The professional will, however, detect the difference from the fact that the Tabriz version of any design always looks too stiff and rigid. This is a feature which can be seen in the Herati illustrated, which is typical of the standard production of many weavers in Tabriz; in these the accuracy of both the designing and the weaving, clearly seen in this piece (viewed from the back), seems to make the carpets too exact and perfect; they appear somehow too set and lack the natural flow of the Saruq versions. Nevertheless large quantities are made and sold in

229

230

231

229 Typical medallion shape used in the Birjand area.

230 Birjand
Detail of a carpet, full size
370 × 260 cm, 300,000 PK/m²
(12′ 2″ × 8′ 6″, 194 PK/in.²).

231 Qum
210 × 141 cm, 510,000 PK/m²
(6′ 10″ × 4′ 7″, 330 PK/in.²).

Tabriz in the Herati design, not only in the very fine type on a dark-blue ground as illustrated in fig. 228, but in every quality and colour conceivable, both with and without medallions. The colours can be problematical: as with other designs, Tabriz Heratis are often spoilt by poor dyestuffs and ugly colour combinations.

229, 230 BIRJAND
The area from which some authorities at least suspect that the Herati design came has its own considerable production in a distinctive style today. The finest carpets are from Birjand itself; a lower grade comes from the villages around Dorukhsh to the north-east and Moud to the south-east, although Moud also produces very fine pieces. The designs are all of the Herati all-over type converted into medallion-and-corner by the superimposed outline of the medallion and change of colour. In some cases the medallions are geometric, as with the Bijar carpet of fig. 196; others have curvilinear medallions. The circular medallion with the well-drawn pendants shown in fig. 229 is particularly common. All-over pieces in one ground colour are also made. Cream and blue grounds predominate; reds are also made but are rarer. Since early in the present century Birjand has had a very low reputation owing to several malpractices, including the universal use of the *jufti* knot (i.e. one knot on four warp strings instead of two, giving the carpet only half the weight in wool; see fig. 35). Today, however, much better carpets are produced. There are still plenty which are badly woven, thin and scruffy, but many manufacturers have managed to raise their standards and the best pieces are as fine as Mesheriki or finer, with the proper density and weight of pile and fine attention to details of colouring. A bad name, once acquired, is not easily shaken off, however, and even the best Birjands cost no more than half the price of Mesherikis. The design is more or less fully curvilinear. For a close-up of the weave see fig. 33. All carpet sizes are made (including squares), but rugs and runners in general are rare.

231 QUM
Another intriguing example of the similarity of design ideas between Birjand and Qum is illustrated here. Sometimes one must study the weave in order to tell them apart (see figs. 342, 343), but in this case there is no problem since the Qum rug shown is all silk and silks are rarely made in Birjand. Many rugs are produced in Qum in the layout illustrated – a medallion filled with Herati motifs set in a plain ground. The hexagonal geometric medallion shown is very common, but more

oval or rounded medallions with the same in-filling are also found. All the typical Qum colours may be found – that is almost every conceivable ground shade from bright reds and strong dark blues to pastel pink and light green – but always with an overall feeling of lightness and brightness, however strong or soft the main shades may be.

232 VERAMIN

As is explained on p. 330, the Mina Khani design, which is used in 90% of all Veramin carpets (cf. 757) seems to be a variant of the Herati pattern which developed in eastern Persia in conjunction with the Herati itself. Today, however, Veramin makes a particularly original version of the Herati design which is quite different from the Mina Khani, as a comparison of fig. 232 with fig. 757 shows, Although this variant of the Herati pattern is thought of as a Veramin design, it may also be found in other central and west Persian origins.

233–235 SOUTHERN PERSIA

The Herati design does not form part of the Kerman/Yezd design tradition, but various manufactured versions in a medium stitch have been made at various times in the past in Yezd. In the version illustrated the drawing is completely floral, with no attempt to preserve the geometric element found elsewhere. The output in this modern production is mainly on cream grounds in most rug and carpet sizes up to about 8 m² (85 ft²).

232 Veramin
Detail of a carpet, full size
320×210 cm, 325,000 PK/m²
($10' 6'' \times 6' 11''$, 210 PK/in.²).

233 Yezd
302×198 cm, 158,000 PK/m²
($9' 11'' \times 6' 6''$, 102 PK/in.²).

232

233

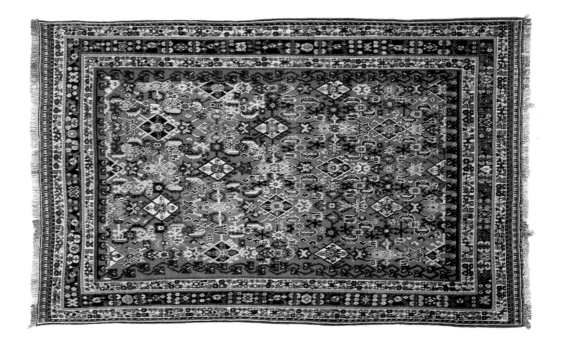

234 Qashqai
252 × 164 cm, 109,000 PK/m²
(8′ 3″ × 5′ 4″, 70 PK/in.²).

235 Abadeh *vagireh*
48 × 22 cm, 216,000 PK/m²
(1′ 7″ × 9″, 139 PK/in.²).

Another southern Persian area with no major tradition of using the Herati design is Fars province, with its Qashqai and Luri nomads. The Qashqai do, however, have a version which one occasionally encounters, (see fig. 234). Note the unusual feature of using a different colour for the centres of the diamonds. The town of Abadeh, at the foot of the Zagros mountains, on the edge of the desert, has a strong element of settled Qashqais in its population. The design which is used in the vast bulk of the local production is derived from a Qashqai original (see fig. 597). The same applies to the Abadeh version of the Herati design. Older Abadeh pieces look very like the example shown in fig. 234, but in recent times the more independent version shown in fig. 235 has developed; the piece shown is a weaver's sample, as used in several parts of Iran in place of graph-paper loom drawings. Here, too, the diamonds are in a different colour from that of the ground; note in the border a variant of the Zil-i-Sultan bird and vase (cf. fig. 271). For further notes on Abadeh see p. 264.

236 BESHIR
Yet another version which seems alien to the local tradition is illustrated here. It is made in Turkoman Russia and sold as Beshir. Attention has already been drawn (see p. 77) to the interpretations of the Herati design by the Beshir nomads of Afghanistan. Here we have another which is quite distinctive and unlike any other version of the Herati motif used elsewhere, yet it is clearly Turkoman in feeling. It is a good example of how designers working in a clearly defined tradition can take an established design from elsewhere and refashion it in their own mould.

The fact that such refashioning has always been done throughout the East has been illustrated in several examples in the preceding pages, but it tends to be forgotten nowadays. We are apt to say 'this design comes from that place and if anyone else uses it that amounts to mere imitation and is therefore inferior'. This was patently never the case in the past; and with the economic pressures affecting Asia at present it must not be thought to be the case now, or the art of carpet weaving will die out. It is fascinating in this connection to read what Grote-Hasenbalg has to say about the Ferahan Heratis of the eighteenth and nineteenth centuries: to him they represent an art in decline, a design torn from its folk-art roots and merely copied in another region. But ask any dealer or collector today and one will hear the highest praise for the old Ferahans. What Grote-Hasenbalg overlooks is the transformation and regeneration, the 'Ferahanization' of the Herati design. Of course in composed art what we value most are the great original achievements, but in folk art there are no originals, everything is copy. To be sure, each version at any stage of the tradition, including the beginning, was created by

236 Beshir
321 × 219 cm, 208,000 PK/m²
(10′ 6″ × 7′ 2″, 134 PK/in.²).

one individual, but not as an originator, not as a free creative spirit, rather as the tool of the tradition, the mouthpiece of the people, whose culture as a whole finds expression in the art he creates. Thus, tradition means copying, and this is something we must not forget when considering the manufactured copies which account for the majority of all carpets sold today – the complete output of China, Turkoman Russia and the Caucasus, which are copies of older styles from their own areas, and the huge output of India, Pakistan, Rumania, Bulgaria and Albania in copies of Persian designs. These modern pieces are no more copies than the old Ferahans were; what counts is not where the design originated, but what today's weavers have made of it.

3 TREE DESIGNS

We encounter trees, or large tree-like plants, with or without flowers, in two principal forms in carpets: as subsidiary elements in pictorial designs of many different kinds; and as the main motif around which a whole design is constructed.

The classification of tree designs into a separate section in this book poses some problems of cross-referencing, since trees occur in so many other forms. Apart from the designs shown in the following pages, the reader should also bear in mind the illustrations from several other sections:

(i) pictorial designs, because while some 'tree' designs represent no particular tree, others present quite realistic pictures;

(ii) animal and bird designs, because the trees often have animals and birds around them;

(iii) prayer designs, because trees are just the right shape to fit into the ground of a prayer rug;

(iv) vase designs, because the distinction between a single vase of flowers and a single tree is often lost and the two merge into one design;

(v) 'garden' designs.

237 THE 'TREE OF LIFE'

Frequent references will be found in books on carpets to the 'tree-of-life' design. We cannot today attach much importance to the ancient symbolism which is associated with many carpet designs, but there seems little doubt that at one time religious or mythological ideas had a great influence on carpet art. The reader who wishes to delve further into this subject should look at the series of lectures by S. V. R. Cammann printed in the *Textile Museum Journal* (Washington, D.C.) in December 1972. Some of the connections suggested seem rather far-fetched, but these essays contain a great wealth of background information on Islamic and pre-Islamic oriental mythology which certainly adds to our appreciation of the culture from which our present-day carpets are derived.

The 'tree of life' represents the connecting link between the three world levels of the ancient Orient: Paradise (in the sky), the world of men (on earth); and the world below (which, in terms of Christianity, may be likened to the notion of Purgatory). It was believed that these three were held together by a great vertical axis through the centre. The idea of depicting the world axis as a tree is very ancient and is found in many art forms besides carpets (and of course in European mythology as well as oriental), but we must always remember with oriental mythology that the language of symbolism is many-layered. One must be cautious of saying 'this represents that', for in the East all is suggestion and any symbol can have a host of different implications as well as hinting at other related symbols which themselves have a different host of secondary implications.

An awareness of possible mythological implications in tree designs needs however to be balanced by the knowledge that much of Persia is stony desert – this alone is sufficient reason why carpet designs should so often be filled with flowers and trees. Not only that: what of the *creators* of religious art? It is too easy to listen to Bach's

237 Wall sculpture from the palace of Ashurnasirpal II at Nineveh, ninth century BC. British Museum.

Mass in B Minor or Beethoven's *Missa Solemnis* – for many people among the absolute pinnacles of Western music – and conclude that the two composers must have been ardent Christians. They may or may not have been: the question is irrelevant to the greatness of their works, nor does one need to be a Christian to appreciate their greatness. Musicians are guided by musical impulses and obey musical rules, whether they are composing 'religious' music or operas. If Beethoven fought the angel for the key to the fugal Credo in the *Missa Solemnis* (as Wendell Kretzschmar tells us in Thomas Mann's *Dr Faustus*), it was a struggle for the technical means to carry his universal humanism to all who hear the work. The same principles apply in carpet design. The universal appeal of the 'tree-of-life' design – or of any other design – depends on the purely aesthetic consideration of the suitability of the motif in the given design situation and the degree of technical accomplishment in its execution. However, it must be remembered that in folk art there are no creators – the designs are representative of a cultural background and, as such, reflect the symbolism with which it is imbued. We shall therefore keep coming back to the cultural background in considering the extra layers of symbolic meaning underlying certain motifs.

The 'tree of life' as 'world axis' is by no means the only form of symbolic tree encountered in ancient art. From the apple tree of the Garden of Eden to the Druids' groves of Celtic Britain, we can find countless examples of trees with religious associations. Fig. 237 illustrates the sacred tree of Assyria flanked by two priests in symbolical bird form. This stone carving comes from the palace of Ashurnasirpal at Nineveh (ninth century BC). The 'tree' is constructed from the same palmette motifs as are seen in the stone 'carpet' illustrated in fig. 57, a further reminder of the particular importance of the palm-tree in western and central Asia (see also p. 54). These stone panels often include a symbolic representation of the national deity Assur, in a form similar to that frequently found in connection with

238 Samarkand
410 × 200 cm, 87,000 PK/m²
(13′ 5″ × 6′ 6″, 56 PK/in.²).

239 Sinkiang
216 × 146 cm, 120,000 PK/m²
(7′ 1″ × 4′ 9″, 77 PK/in.²).

Ahura Mazda, the sun-god of the Parsee religion, Zoroastrianism, which was the official faith of pre-Islamic Iran. Traces of the symbolism of these ancient religions may be found in carpet design to this day and some scholars, indeed, regard the bird symbols as a primary source of carpet motifs.

238 SAMARKAND
Now the second city of the Soviet central Asian republic of Uzbekistan, Samarkand was once the gateway to China. It was one of the principal cities, if not the very pivot, of the Silk Route, the main commercial artery of Asia until the Portuguese discovered the sea route around the Cape of Good Hope in the late fifteenth century. It thus became the western outlet for the carpets of the oases of the Tarim Basin (now the Chinese province of Sinkiang, but known to carpet men everywhere as East Turkestan). The principal production centres were Kashgar, Khotan and Yarkand; their carpets were known simply as Samarkands. Today they are collector's items, but they are not so rare as to be priceless, especially in the large long and narrow sizes (e.g. 500 × 200 cm; 16′ 6″ × 6′ 6″) which are typical. All their designs are strongly individual and quite unmistakable. The 'pomegranate tree' illustrated here was common in all three centres; it is most often found in red on a dark-blue ground. The weave is as distinctive as the design, a hard, dry-feeling structure, fairly coarse, with a markedly ridged back and a thin, close-cropped pile.

Hans Bidder's excellent book on the carpets of Eastern Turkestan draws attention to the antiquity of this design, which may well be linked to the symbolic tree of the ancient religion of Assyria (fig. 237). The earliest settlers of the Tarim Basin were Indo-Europeans; marauding Western Turks entered the region in the sixth century, but they were expelled by the T'ang Dynasty Chinese. After the latter's demise the area was incorporated into the great Tibetan empire of the eighth century; the Uighurs, or Eastern Turks, occupied it by the tenth; it fell to the Mongol empires of the thirteenth and fifteenth centuries and returned again to Chinese control in 1757/8. But the region was never entirely assimilated by any of these outside powers, so that the essential Indo-European cultural strain remained. Although East Turkestan is geographically isolated from the main areas of west Asiatic carpet production, its roots are firmly set in the traditions that inspire the designs of Persia and Turkey. Like the tree motif itself, the pomegranate also had important symbolic significance for the ancient world. Its use as a fertility symbol can be traced back to ancient Sumer; the Muslims carried both the fruit and its symbolism throughout the Old World, from Spain to China. It is possible that the many scaled motif looking like a pine-cone in the Pazyryk carpet (fig. 56) and the Nineveh panel (fig. 57) may be meant to represent a pomegranate. Note also the presence of the motif in the hand of the eagle-headed figure in fig. 237.

239 SINKIANG
Carpets are still made in the Tarim Basin – a low-quality controlled production sold by the Chinese government simply as Sinkiangs. Some of the designs, such as the 'pomegranate tree' illustrated here, are modelled quite closely on Samarkand originals. Others (see, for example, fig. 450) interpret the geometric East Turkestan style rather more loosely, but in neither case can they be compared with either the structure or colouring of the antique originals. The new production is made in different grades, some loose in weave and using very thin warps and wefts, giving a rather floppy construction, while other pieces have more body and a much heavier handle. The main features in their favour are the remarkably low price and the use of a very appealing soft yarn. A wide range of rug, runner and carpet sizes is made in a variety of ground shades, creams and buffs being most common.

240 CHODOR
A reminder from West Turkestan of the universal importance of tree forms in carpet motifs is contained in the detail reproduced here from the Chodor enssi shown in fig. 354. The panel design itself is discussed in detail on p. 153, but from a cursory glance at the panels one is apt to miss the fact that the 'garden' is full of trees, in this case trees with botehs. Another detail from the same rug is shown in

fig. 144, and from these details the reader will realize how much more there is to a good Turkoman rug than at first meets the eye and that the restraint described on p. 176 hides a wealth of imaginative and expressive detail in no way inferior to the more showy rugs of Persia.

241 GEBBEH

Tree designs crop up time and again in nomadic weaves. Their form is never standardized. They may include birds, fruit, leaves, flowers – all of these elements or none of them. And one can never say that a particular combination is the 'regular Gebbeh version' or the 'regular Niriz version' of the tree. Each one is different as each tree is different. The Gebbeh rug illustrated here is woven in natural undyed wools, in different shades of white, yellow and brown. This is rather unusual. The 'natural' Gebbehs are usually in the bold designs shown in figs. 478–80; tree designs are more often found in the 'coloured' Gebbehs (see p. 214), especially on red grounds. Of the latter, fig. 113 (with or without botehs), is a good example of the style one often finds.

242 LURI

The Lurs, one of the oldest tribes in Iran, are spread over the whole western side of the country, from Lar in the south, near the Persian Gulf, through the Zagros mountains and the province of Luristan right up into the Caucasus, to the river Pambak in the Kazak region just south of Tbilisi (Tiflis), and also into Turkey. The presence of the 'latch hook' in a design (see fig. 475) often indicates Luri influence in a particular area, but where the Lurs have merged with the local population their carpets are generally known by the local name: Lori Pambaks, for example, are thought of as Kazaks rather than Luri rugs. However, even if one limits the name Luri to the products of the Zagros mountains area, where the Lurs predominate, there is still a big range of types, all of which may include tree designs. The Gebbeh of fig. 113 is probably a Luri; the other main types are Ilam, Khorramabad, Behbehan, Owlad, Yalameh and Nasrabad. The principal features of these origins are detailed in the section devoted to bold geometric designs, beginning on p. 208. Here we have included only one tree design. This is a small carpet from the

240 Detail of a Chodor enssi.

241 Gebbeh
205 × 119 cm, 65,000 PK/m²
(6′ 8″ × 3′ 11″, 42 PK/in.²).

242 Luri
262 × 155 cm, 65,000 TK/m²
(8′ 7″ × 5′ 1″, 42 TK/in.²).

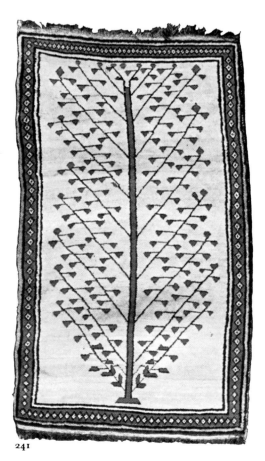

241

242

243 Niriz
190 × 141 cm, 70,000 PK/m²
(6′ 3″ × 4′ 7″, 45 PK/in.²).

area north and west of Shiraz which produces the fairly standardized· category of goods known simply as Shiraz Luris. They are fairly easy to recognize from several salient features: the size, which never varies much from 250 × 150 cm (8′ 3″ × 5′ 0″), the goat-hair or woollen warps, the firm but coarse ribbed structure, the shaggy pile and the overall light tenor of the colourings. From the wide range of designs made other examples are illustrated in figs. 453, 477 (see also index).

243 NIRIZ

Halfway between Shiraz and Sirjand lies the village of Niriz, which is the production centre for a rather low-grade type of Shiraz rug. Shiraz is really an incorrect description because the Niriz production is influenced by many different factors. The bulk of the production is in a medallion-plain version of the Qashqai *hebatlu* design (fig. 595), but unlike these rugs from the Shiraz area, the warps and wefts of Niriz goods are of cotton, which makes the weave very like that of the cheaper Afshar types, such as Sirjand. Some of the more unusual designs also show strong Afshar influence, and the colourings, too, are more characteristic of Sirjand than Shiraz – the red, in particular, is brighter than the Shiraz red. Yet another influence certainly comes from the Arab nomads living in the countryside to the north. Within all these influences, however, Niriz has a distinct style of its own. The tree design illustrated here is a good example: while certain elements are strongly reminiscent of Afshar work the general style is clearly recognizable as Niriz. Note, too, the wealth of realistic detail within the stylized overall conception.

244–246 AFSHARI

As with the boteh design (see figs. 151, 152), the Afshars have dozens of versions of the tree motif, some forming just a small element in a larger design (as in fig. 244), others dominating the whole rug (as in figs. 245 and 246). Figs. 244 and 246 both illustrate how close is the connection between tree motifs and the concept of the vase design, while fig. 245 – with several different trees, birds, animals, botehs, the two medallions, sundry stylized flowers and purely abstract rosettes – shows how difficult it is to classify the richly decorative products of the tribal imagination. This vision of Paradise, this dream of a richly watered garden, of superabundant nature, epitomizes the universality of the appeal of the nomad rug. In view of the wealth of the designs the Afshars use, the layman's design knowledge will not be enough on its own to enable him to recognize a particular place of origin. To take an obvious example, what is it that permits us to state categorically that the tree in fig. 241 is a Luri Gebbeh tree, the one in fig. 243 is a Niriz tree, while fig. 246 illustrates a Sirjand Afshar tree? The answer is that this is one of the cases where recourse must be had to the other more subtle clues mentioned in the Introduction. With Afshari rugs, the first clue is an additional design element: their makers love to include birds, animals and little human figures scattered all over the place, sometimes quite realistically drawn, but more often like curious little puppets. The Afshars are not the only weavers to do this but it is certainly a very characteristic element which helps in identifying their goods. The other points are: colour, warp and weft materials, sizes, wool, weave. It takes experience to recognize subtle variations in these features, but the principal differences are shown in the table opposite.

247 BELUCH

There are many Beluch tribes weaving rugs over a wide area of Persia and Afghanistan, from Serakhs in the north to Zahedan in the south and Ferdaus in the west to Gormach in the east. There are also many more tribes in this area which weave rugs in the Beluch style and whose output is always classed as Beluch in the carpet trade. Note that Beluch rugs do not come from Beluchistan. The tree motif is very important in filling the ground in the typical prayer designs made in many parts of the Beluch area, but most especially by the Afghan Beluchis, whose rugs are usually called Herat Beluch, for no better reason than that traders are totally ignorant about their true origin. However, the rug illustrated is from Persia: it is an old piece, woven on woollen warps (modern Persian Beluch rugs usually have cotton warps). The exceptionally fine weave brings out the delicate details of the

244

245

246

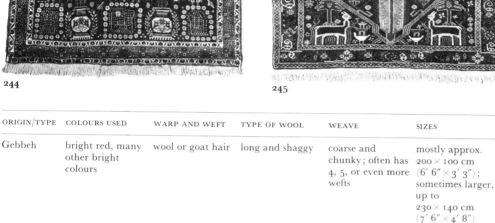

ORIGIN/TYPE	COLOURS USED	WARP AND WEFT	TYPE OF WOOL	WEAVE	SIZES
Gebbeh	bright red, many other bright colours	wool or goat hair	long and shaggy	coarse and chunky; often has 4, 5, or even more wefts	mostly approx. 200 × 100 cm (6′ 6″ × 3′ 3″); sometimes larger, up to 230 × 140 cm (7′ 6″ × 4′ 8″)
Niriz	bright red, very distinctive medium blue, very dark blue; overall colouring rarely as bright as Gebbeh	formerly wool, now cotton	average quality and height	coarse; pink wefts visible on back	smallish dozars and zaronims
Sirjand	light red, warm dark blue, and a limited range of other shades; more light blue than in Gebbeh or Shahr Babak goods	cotton; old pieces sometimes made with wool	average quality and height	finer than Niriz, but also showing pink wefts; ridged back and much firmer to the handle, with more body	pushtis, zaronims (both fairly rare) and dozars; the last two types usually very large (180 × 130 cm and 250 × 160 cm, i.e. 5′ 10″ × 4′ 3″ and 8′ 3″ × 5′ 3″, respectively)
Shahr Babak	dull brownish red, sometimes mauvish; much ivory and grey-green; dark blue (almost black) used sparingly; overall colouring generally restrained	cotton	fine and very soft, often clipped very thin	fine or very fine, but construction rarely sturdy	all rug sizes (i.e. up to 3½ m²; 40 ft²)

244 Shahr Babak
150 × 112 cm, 211,000 PK/m²
(4′ 11″ × 3′ 8″, 136 PK/in.²).

245 Shahr Babak
202 × 141 cm, 248,000 PK/m²
(6′ 7″ × 4′ 7″, 160 PK/in.²).

246 Sirjand
93 × 68 cm, 108,000 PK/m²
3′ 1″ × 2′ 3″, 70 PK/in.²).

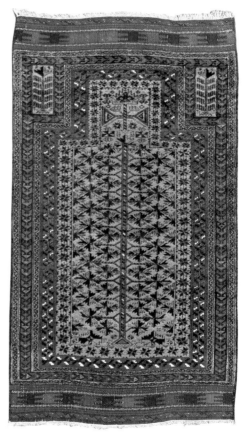

247 Beluch
134 × 73 cm, 256,000 PK/m²
(4′ 5″ × 2′ 5″, 165 PK/in.²).

design with unusual clarity. Note the two additional tree motifs in the spandrels beside the prayer *mihrab*. The spandrels in Beluch prayer rugs are often occupied by the so-called 'hand of Fatima'; several theories have been offered to explain this feature. The most likely one is that the five fingers serve as a reminder to the believer of the five cardinal principles of Islam: faith, prayer, pilgrimage, fasting and charity (*Shahada, Salat, Haj, Ramadan*, and *Zahat*). Another noteworthy feature is the broad kilim 'skirt' at both ends: in old Beluch goods such kilims were one of the glories of the overall composition, but they are very rare in modern rugs. Another Beluch tree motif can be seen in fig. 105.

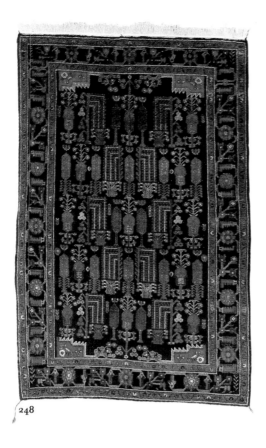

249

250

248 Zenjan
238 × 159 cm, 169,000 TK/m²
(7′ 10″ × 5′ 2″, 109 TK/in.²).

249 Kurdish
236 × 176 cm, 110,000 TK/m²
(7′ 9″ × 5′ 9″, 71 TK/in.²).

250 Kurdish
295 × 152 cm, 92,000 TK/m²
(9′ 8″ × 5′ 0″, 59 TK/in.²).

251 Cypress tree in a Shalamzar Bakhtiari carpet.

252 Willow tree in a Shahr Kurd Bakhtiari carpet.

253 Rose bush in a Boldaji Bakhtiari carpet.

254 Grape vine in a Bakhtiari carpet.

255 Flowering shrub in a Saman Bakhtiari carpet.

256 Tree branches in a Shalamzar Bakhtiari carpet. This motif is a direct derivative from the panels of the eighteenth-century garden carpets (cf. fig. 346).

248–250 KURDISH

Trees (and flowers) often feature in Kurdish rugs. The piece illustrated in fig. 250 is typical of a design made throughout Kurdistan, as well as Luristan. Its origin goes back hundreds of years, but such pieces are still made with all the individuality and freshness found in many examples of the design seen in museums and antique collections. Fig. 249 dates from the eighteenth century and is particularly valuable for the unmistakable connection it reveals with both the Joshaqan design (see figs. 7, 8) and with vase carpets (e.g. fig. 180). Here is a perfect example of the way nomad weavers have borrowed the ideas of the great manufactories, set their own imprint upon them and developed an independent tradition from them. The rug from the Zenjan area (fig. 248) shows a further development of the idea in a village manufactured style which is typical of much of rural Persia. This is an exceptionally good example of the Kurdish-influenced production described on p. 91. Note here, as there, a certain stiffness in the design which the weaver of the rug shown in fig. 250 has succeeded in avoiding completely.

251–257 BAKHTIARI

The evolution of the Bakhtiari panel design from eighteenth-century garden carpets is illustrated in figs. 327–339. Within these 'gardens' tree motifs are widely used. Sometimes the trees are quite naturalistic and easily recognized; in other carpets, such as figs. 255 and 256, the motif is reduced to an indeterminate stylization of tree or bush forms.

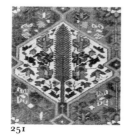
251

252

253

254

255

256

257 Typical tree border in a Boldaji Bakhtiari carpet. This is the most easily remembered feature of Boldaji goods.

258 SHALAMZAR

This rug comes from the village of Shalamzar in the southern Chahar Mahal, but the design is woven in many of the villages that make double-wefted Bakhtiari rugs, and in some of the areas of single-wefted production too. The design is one of those that fit into several possible categories, involving as it does elements of bird, tree, vase and prayer types. The prayer *mihrab* may be omitted in some cases, but the vase is always present, as are the strikingly drawn birds, the particular shape of the latter being one of the immediately recognizable features. In rugs of this type excellent natural dyestuffs are very often found, and the quality varies from medium to quite fine. Outstanding examples will fetch very high prices – as much as Saruqs or Bijars of considerably finer weave. The design is made in dozar sizes only.

259 KHARAGHAN

Another distinctive tree design, very weird and always just like the present example, is made in the Kharaghan district north of Hamadan, and also by the Shah Savan

258 Shalamzar
208 × 148 cm, 132,000 TK/m²
(6′ 10″ × 4′ 10″, 85 TK/in.²).

259 Kharaghan
161 × 104 cm, 109,000 TK/m²
(5′ 3″ × 3′ 5″, 70 TK/in.²).

258

259

tribe near Saveh. For the difference between Shah Savan and Kharaghan, see fig. 536. The design illustrated is most often found on a cream ground in zaronim size, but other sizes and colours do exist.

260–265 ISFAHAN, TABRIZ, KERMAN, KASHAN, NAIN, QUM

All the towns of Iran that use a fine weave produce designs with trees as the principal motif within a prayer-rug layout. They are not prayer rugs in the proper sense but are produced commercially in a range of sizes from pushti up to about 6 m² (70 ft²) in area, the most common size being the dozar. In cases of doubt the weave and colouring are the only sure guides to the origin, but all the pieces shown in figs. 260–265 are recognizable to experts on the basis of their design style alone. Indeed, all six origins are instantly identifiable purely on the basis of the pieces illustrated here; this is remarkable proof of the independent identity preserved by all Persian production areas, whatever designs they use.

The Kashan of fig. 263 is a silk carpet of a type made in considerable quantities (in both silk and wool) between the two World Wars, although this piece, with its rigid central axis, may be somewhat older. Perhaps the most important feature of the Kashan style is the perfect balance of its proportions: the Kerman of fig. 262 includes no more detail than the Kashan but looks crowded by comparison. Other Kashans of the same era are illustrated in several sections of this book. The strength of the Kerman carpet design is its exuberance. The tree designs are derived from ancient carpets such as figs. 327 or 696; but here the Kerman designer has gone much further than his illustrious predecessors in the abundance of the floral elaboration: every inch of both ground and border must be crammed with richly coloured blossoms. This is a characteristic feature which may be observed in other Kerman designs (see fig. 309 and index).

The most striking stylistic feature of the Tabriz tree rug (fig. 261) is its use of perspective. This is a rare element in Islamic art: the restriction of all representation to two-dimensional forms constitutes a widely accepted compromise between the artists' search for expression and the religious law's ban on the portrayal of living things. The use of perspective here is a facet of the Tabriz tradition of universal adaptability of design, linking fig. 261 with fig. 361 and many others like it.

Nain rugs (fig. 262), the finest of all modern Persians, are made in hundreds of villages in the area around Nain. Some of the best pieces come from places as far

260 Isfahan
158 × 111 cm, 837,000 PK/m²
(5′ 2″ × 3′ 8″, 540 PK/in.²).

261 Tabriz
220 × 144 cm, 220,000 TK/m²
(7′ 2″ × 4′ 9″, 142 TK/in.²).

262 Kerman
277 × 178 cm, 320,000 PK/m²
(9′ 1″ × 5′ 10″, 206 PK/in.²).

263 Kashan
302 × 209 cm, 360,000 PK/m²
(9′ 11″ × 6′ 10″, 232 PK/in.²).

264 Nain
121 × 80 cm, 713,000 PK/m²
(4′ 0″ × 2′ 7″, 460 PK/in.²).

260

261

262

263

264

afield as Biabanak, over 200 miles out into the desert. Isfahan used to have a small production equally fine (as well as a large output in medium grades), but typically Isfahan in style and clearly distinguishable from Nain. Now, however, the style of Isfahan has become so like that of Nain that even experts sometimes cannot tell them apart. Nain prayer designs are not very common but they are occasionally found: for a rug which is so fine and expensive that many people prefer to hang it on the wall, the prayer-with-tree motif is an obvious choice.

Similar ideas as the basis of a prayer design are used in the superfine Isfahan shown in fig. 260. One clue to the difference between Nain and Isfahan is the use of silk. Nain rugs usually have cotton warps and woollen pile with the outlines of the design edged in silk. Isfahans mostly have an all-wool pile but use silk for the warps. Note that figs. 261–3 all employ the same border design, but all three show evident stylistic differences which are as helpful clues to the origin as are the differences in the tree motifs themselves. A similar style (not illustrated) is also found in the northern half of Khorassan province, in rugs of various sizes (dozars are the most common). They are usually village products, inferior in weave to the Meshed and Kashmar carpets which they otherwise resemble. They are much coarser than the other rugs shown in this group and are also easily distinguished by the bluish red and the very heavy dark blue which are typical of the region.

As has already been noted, Qum makes a panel design based on the Bakhtiari 'garden' style. In this various tree motifs are used, but the same comments apply as in the case of the boteh motif (see fig. 159). Beyond this there is a huge range of designs made in Qum. Tree designs are common, with or without a prayer *mihrab*.

265 Qum
218 × 139 cm, 278,000 PK/m²
(7′ 2″ × 4′ 7″, 179 PK/in.²).

Fig. 265 shows a typical Qum version of a design also used in Kashan and Isfahan. There are several stylistic features which indicate that this piece is from Qum (the shape of the border motifs, for example, and the colours, especially the red), but there is a further clue in that parts of the motifs in the woollen ground are woven in silk. Although this practice is not unknown elsewhere, it is a particularly common feature of the modern Qum production. Qum also employs a design including groups of trees arranged in a layout similar to that seen in the present example. Many ground shades are used including several – such as light blue – which are rarely found elsewhere.

266

267

266 Wall panel from the mid-seventeenth century Fort, Lahore.

267 Kaimuri 'Shah Jahan' rug, 148 × 107 cm, 220,000 PK/m² (4' 10" × 3' 6", 142 PK/in.²).

266, 267 THE SHAH JAHAN STYLE

The great Moghul emperors of India, Jahangir and Shah Jahan (who built the Taj Mahal), established a very distinctive style in art. The carpets woven in the Punjab at that time – often called Lahore carpets – made use of the same motifs and the same decorative style as are found in the palaces and monuments of the period (fig. 266). Many examples of this art will be found in carpet collections in museums. In recent times, several attempts have been made to revive this style in India as a means of giving a more recognizably Indian flavour to the huge output which has blossomed in Kashmir, Gwalior, Agra itself and the Benares district. The rug shown in fig. 267 illustrates one such attempt; the original which inspired it is in the Metropolitan Museum of Art, New York. The rug shown, made in Khamariah, near Benares, is not a copy but has many features in common, notably the naturalistic treatment of the chrysanthemum plant (not strictly a tree design, of course!) and the very un-Persian feature of not having outlines to separate the individual colours in the leaves. The similar treatment of flowers in the wall panel in Lahore, shown in fig. 266, should also be compared with figs. 180 and 249; from this comparison one can see how strongly interdependent some designs are in widely separated parts of the Orient.

268 DÖŞEMEALTI

The student of carpet design often has cause to marvel at the ability of the peasant weavers of the Orient to create exciting and expressive forms out of the simplest of geometric motifs (see, for example, figs. 101 and 484). The Anatolian village of Döşemealti provides a further example of this: the key to its effectiveness is the openness and bold simplicity of the layout and the elusive significance of the motifs, which at one moment resemble some form of tree of life, at others shady trees in a flowery park, and at others a purely abstract elaboration of 'latch-hook' and related motifs. The border design and the all-wool structure are sure indicators of the Döşemealti origin, but the main design itself is also quite commonly encountered. For general notes on Döşemealti see fig. 495.

268 Döşemealti 188 × 120 cm, 82,000 TK/m² (6' 2" × 3' 11", 53 TK/in.²).

4 VASE DESIGNS

Some of the 'trees' in the designs in the preceding pages are really overgrown bunches of flowers emanating from a vase. This is a common feature. Designs based on one or more vases of flowers, with or without medallion, are found in many old carpets, but even in early examples the distinction between flowers and trees is blurred.

270 VASE CARPET
Several 'vase' carpets of the classical period are illustrated in this book – see index. The one shown here is perhaps the best known of all – a huge, finely woven piece displayed in a prime position in the Victoria and Albert Museum, London. It is packed with elaborate detail but retains a measure of balance in the layout and proportions of the motifs that is missing in other examples of the genre. The vases seem to have originated in the Chinese influence described in the context of fig. 279, but in Persian hands they soon lost any sense they may have had of depicting functional flower-containers and became no more than a starting point for the elaboration of motifs that might embody 'tree-of-life' ideas, or may simply be decorative flowery pattern-work. The vases themselves are in fact superfluous and are omitted entirely in many pieces of the group. However, the design does also reflect the retreat from pure abstraction in carpet design that occurred in Persia in the sixteenth century, and in many modern derivatives of the idea this feature is emphasized, the vase often being drawn in naturalistic detail and used as the focal point of an elaborate floral display.

The original vase carpets have been attributed to different places by various scholars, but the most widely held view is that they came from Kerman. Mention is rarely made, however, of a piece of circumstantial evidence which supports this view, viz. the large number of vase designs woven by the Afshars of Kerman province. The propensity of the nomad and peasant weavers to plagiarize the best-selling lines of their local manufactories has been noted elsewhere in this book; the striking stylistic similarities between figs. 244, 275 and 270, for example, may thus indicate the last of these examples as being the source for the first two. As fig. 309 demonstrates, there are other possible sources, but then the Kerman tile panels shown may well have been inspired by the vase carpets. Further comparisons may be made between figs. 183, 739 and 765 (vase carpets) and figs. 272, 273, 276 and 562 (Afshar vase designs).

271 ABADEH
Many village weavers in Persia use designs consisting of a repeating pattern of vases of flowers. Of these one of the best known is called Zil-i-Sultan after a nineteenth-century governor of Isfahan. It is illustrated here in a rug from Abadeh, a small town about halfway between Isfahan and Shiraz. Almost the whole production from Abadeh today is in the *hebatlu* design (see fig. 597), but occasional pieces are found in other designs, too; fig. 234 illustrates another, and in the past it was the Zil-i-Sultan design which dominated the production. It is now used in both carpet and rug sizes, usually on cream grounds. The general characteristics and colourings

269 Pao-Tu
An early twentieth-century rug incorporating one of the most ancient of Chinese motifs; 122 × 62 cm, 92,000 PK/m² (4′ 0″ × 2′ 0″, 59 PK/in.²). Cf. fig. 279.

270 Vase carpet
519 × 325 cm, 390,000 PK/m²
(17′ 0″ × 10′ 10″, 252 PK/in.²).
Victoria and Albert Museum, London.

270

271

272

273

271 Abadeh
160 × 117 cm, 149,000 PK/m²
(5′ 3″ × 3′ 10″, 96 PK/in.²).

272 Shahr Babak
173 × 122 cm, 190,000 PK/m²
(5′ 8″ × 4′ 0″, 123 PK/in.²).

273 Shahr Babak
126 × 109 cm, 170,000 PK/m²
(4′ 1″ × 3′ 7″, 110 PK/in.²).

274 Typical Kerman vase motif.

described on p. 264 apply to all Abadehs. The idea of flanking the flower-vases with a pair of birds, to produce a pattern known also as *gol-i-bolbol* (= 'rose and nightingale'), is used in other weaving centres, too. A related bird-and-flower design from Veramin is shown in fig. 758.

272–275 AFSHAR

Owing to the miraculous diversity of the Afshari designs, this name will inevitably crop up in almost every section of this book. The Afshars (as also in the case of the boteh) have several ways of interpreting the vase-design concept, as illustrated here in two Shahr Babak rugs. The geometric version of the first is perhaps the more classical and shows more of the features which are immediately thought of as typically Afshari, although the origin of the design may be regarded as a variant of the Zil-i-Sultan pattern (fig. 271). The second shows the influence of Kerman, as a comparison with figs. 262 and 773 will confirm. The Shahr Babak weaving area is actually a full 125 miles from the city of Kerman but the characteristic Kerman manner of treating sprays of flowers (fig. 274) often makes itself felt in the tribal rugs of the province (general notes on Kerman will be found on p. 321). A further splendid Afshar version of the vase design is shown in fig. 275, which is a variant of the tree pattern illustrated in fig. 244.

276 SIRJAND

A considerably cruder approach to the use of vases is seen in this Sirjand Afshar rug. The differences between the fine rugs of Shahr Babak and the coarser production of Sirjand are explained on p. 111. It is worth drawing attention here to the similarity, which sometimes strikes one, between Afshar rugs and those produced by the Kurds in the area of western Iran from which the Afshars were expelled in the seventeenth century. Large, angular vases and primitive, stiff flowers are common in Kurdish rugs, but it is above all the boldness of the design shown in this rug that reminds us of the Kurds. Happily, there are several simple clues to help us tell the origins apart. Kakaberu Kurdish rugs are double-wefted, as are Sirjands, but they are much chunkier and heavier; they are also much more sombre in colouring owing to the use of a blackish-blue and a very deep shade of red, whereas the Sirjand red is light and glowing. The Kolyai Kurds have a similar light red, but their rugs are always single-wefted. Another clue is to be found in the sizes made: Kolyai and Kakaberu rugs are almost always long and narrow, while the shape of Sirjands usually tends to be squarish.

In origin the Afshar tribes are Turkoman. They entered Persia probably with the Seljuqs and were settled in the Kurdish region of central and eastern Anatolia and north-west Persia during the period in the fourteenth and fifteenth centuries when one Turkoman clan after another came to dominate the Tabriz-based government of Persia. The Afshars' turn came when they formed part of the seven-clan Kizil Bash confederation which swept the Safavids to power in 1501. Kizil Bash lancers formed the Imperial Guard and their reputation lasted throughout the empire for centuries. To this day descendants of Nadir Shah's garrisons in Afghanistan live in several towns of that country. After the transportation of the Afshars to the Kerman region they became largely assimilated with the local population, and today no distinctively Turkoman Afshar design style is discernible.

277 QASHQAI

Next we come to one of the famous old Qashqai designs which used to be fairly common when the average Qashqai weave was similar in fineness to that of today's good-quality Afshars. The design shown is derived from an original believed to have been woven in Lahore in the seventeenth century, although a south Persian origin – even Shiraz itself – has been suggested. In view of the close connections between southern Persia and north-west India (see p. 82), it is possible that versions of the design may have been woven in both areas. However, in southern Iran today the design has become rather rare and will no doubt soon join the many other splendid Qashqai designs that are no longer woven; although quite fine rugs are still made by the Qashqais, one thinks of the present-day products of this still largely nomadic group of south Persian tribes as being coarse-to-medium (but well made) goods which are generally a cut above the average of other rugs from Fars province. This was not always the case. Unlike some other tribes, such as the Beluchis of

275 Shahr Babak
139 × 106 cm, 211,000 PK/m²
(4′ 7″ × 3′ 6″, 136 PK/in.²).

276 Sirjand
230 × 162 cm, 95,000 PK/m²
(7′ 6″ × 5′ 4″, 61 PK/in.²).

275

276

277 Qashqai
303 × 219 cm, 156,000 TK/m²
(9′ 11″ × 7′ 2″, 101 TK/in.²).

Khorassan or the 'Mauri' Turkomans of Afghanistan, who are today still capable of producing rugs as fine as anything made by their forefathers, the Qashqai have lowered their standards dramatically. A hundred years ago, they produced rugs so fine that it is difficult to believe they were made by human hand. This degree of fineness naturally enough meant that the Qashqai also had a very wide range of designs; why these should nearly all have disappeared is not clear, but perhaps the importance of Shiraz as a trading centre has made the Qashqai area more accessible than that of other tribes to the degrading influence of Western commercialization. Whatever the reason, it is now only in the simple Gebbeh rugs (see index) that the Qashqai's rich treasury of designs can be suspected. Nevertheless, the Qashqai carpet of today remains a sound product and, as in the case of the piece shown here, can on occasion rise to quite exceptional levels of imagination and execution.

278 CHAHAL SHOTUR
Although vases did not figure in the original garden carpets of the seventeenth century, they have for a long time constituted an important item in the array of

motifs used to fill the panels of Bakhtiari garden designs. Other vase motifs may be observed in figs. 332 (Chahal Shotur) and 333 (Saman). Note, too, the use of a vase in the Shalamzar rug shown in fig. 258.

269, 279 CHINESE

The two Chinese carpets illustrated in figs. 269 and here could easily figure in the section on pictorial designs, so true-to-life is their style. They have been included in this section because of the importance of vases in Chinese carpet design, both old and new. The rug in fig. 269 would have been made in the early twentieth century in northern China, and comes into the category usually traded as Pao-Tu or Suiyuan, the names respectively of the main town and the province from which most examples of this type originated. Regrettably, no more than this is known about the production because, before the Second World War, none of the experts discussed Chinese rugs in their books in any detail, and since the post-war Revolution the sources have been completely closed to Western researchers. Nevertheless, thousands upon thousands of old rugs have reached the European market in the past twenty years and the demand for them has stimulated the Chinese into producing new rugs in this old style alongside the standard new-style production described on pp. 32f. The modern piece illustrated here is typical of this 'old style' or 'antique finished' Peking production. The two types are easy to tell apart because old Pao-Tus are of better quality. Both kinds have fairly flimsy warps and wefts, but the 'antique finished' goods have a thinner yarn, less tightly packed and with less body. Even when worn and thin, Pao-Tu goods still feel firmly put together, whereas the new goods are more decorative than durable.

The use of vases in carpet designs derives, according to Hans Lorentz, from the simple fact that phonetically the Chinese word for vase, *p'ing*, has the same sound as the word meaning peace. This kind of aural/visual pun lies behind much of the ornamentation of Chinese rugs. For example, the word for a table (*an*) also sounds like that for tranquillity; in the same way, *ju-i*, the Buddhist symbol of a sceptre, can be thought of as *ju*, meaning 'according to', and *i*, meaning 'wish'. Thus, a vase on a table combined with a sceptre expresses the sentiment: 'May you find peace and tranquillity according to your wishes.' Consequently vase motifs have been used for a very long time in Chinese rugs, both as centrepieces of a design (Lorentz illustrates – in his pl. 22 – a seventeenth-century Ming Dynasty rug displaying a vase full of sprigs, the symbol of the Taoist Immortals) and as subsidiary motifs such as those found as in-fill patterns in the ground of medallion carpets.

278 Chahal Shotur (detail).

279 Peking 'antique finished' 131 × 195 cm, 96,000 PK/m² (4′ 3″ × 6′ 3″, 62 PK/in.²).

280, 281 KASHAN, TABRIZ

Before the Second World War, Kashan was one of the great manufacturing centres producing rugs and carpets of the highest quality. The vase-of-flowers design shown here is identifiable as Kashan both from its colourings (see p. 295), and from the weave and small details of the design which go to make up the Kashan style. However, this type of pretty little rug could just as well have been made in any of the other great manufacturing towns – Tabriz, Isfahan, Kerman, Arak and elsewhere. It is an example of the exquisite trifles which Persian weavers have always been capable of producing. A more developed version of this idea is shown in the prayer-design section, figs. 303, 304.

A more ambitious Tabriz vase design is illustrated in fig. 281. The piece belongs to the family of *Zirhaki* designs, the full version of which is illustrated in fig. 366. The designer has allowed himself considerable licence: note for example the swords in the upper border, the allegorical figures in the principal vase and the drinking horns and the intrusion of the crown of the *mihrab* into the border. The work of Tabriz designers is often marked by the kind of macabre wildness to be seen in this piece.

282, 283 KASHMIR, AGRA

Like the Afshar rug illustrated in fig. 275, these two Indian rugs could with equal justification be included in the section on prayer designs, the vase being framed in a *mihrab* like a prayer rug: the distinction here between 'vase' and 'prayer' design is a rather artificial one and serves to underline the point made on p. 126 that the

280 Kashan
85 × 66 cm, 378,000 PK/m²
(2′ 9″ × 2′ 2″, 244 PK/in.²).

281 Tabriz
157 × 105 cm, 318,000 TK/m²
(5′ 2″ × 3′ 5″, 205 TK/in.²).

280

281

282

283

prayer-rug layout provides the designer with a useful and stimulating framework within which to accommodate a 'one-way' design. The theory that the wealth of flowers and birds depicted within the arch represents a vision of the Garden of Eden glimpsed through the portals of Heaven is one that can be neither proved nor refuted. It is a nice idea to attach to a prayer design, but one must remark also that the arch-shaped layout provides a neat solution to the technical problem of how to round off a design based on a vase of flowers. The two rugs illustrated here represent two extremes in quality in the new Indian production. Fig. 282 shows an all-silk rug woven in a fine double-wefted construction in Srinagar: when properly executed this type constitutes one of the pinnacles of modern Indian weaving, although the bulk of the production is plagued by fraudulent 'langri' weaving (see fig. 35). Fig. 283 shows a single-wefted piece woven in the double-weave technique in Agra; the production here is very varied in design (several other examples are illustrated in this book), but the quality is mostly poor and the colouring dull. They are, however, surprisingly cheap and there are exceptional pieces to which these criticisms do not apply; in such cases they represent good value for money.

282 Kashmir
200 × 128 cm, 440,000 PK/m²
(6′ 6″ × 4′ 3″, 284 PK/in.²).

283 Agra
154 × 91 cm, 191,000 PK/m²
(5′ 1″ × 3′ 0″, 123 PK/in.²).

5 PRAYER-RUG DESIGNS

Prayer rugs have been used in Muslim countries (which embraces the whole of the carpet-weaving Orient, including parts of China) for hundreds of years. The orthodox Muslim prays five times a day and is enjoined to find a 'clean spot' to do so. Prayer rugs are used to provide this in mosques, in the home and outdoors. Three standard sizes are found: 120 × 80 cm (4′ 0″ × 2′ 9″), which is the most common size among nomads since it is small and easy to carry; 150 × 90 cm (5′ 0″ × 3′ 0″), the Persian zaronim size, which in Turkish is called *namazlik* – literally 'prayer rug'; and the Turkish *seççadeh*, which originally also meant prayer rug, being derived from the Arabic word for obeisance or 'prostration'. The word 'seççadeh' is used today purely as an indication of size – in Turkey about 180 × 120 cm (6′ 0″ × 4′ 0″), the equivalent (slightly larger) size in Persia being called 'dozar' (cf. p. 30). The Persians, of course, also use the word 'sedjadeh' in areas like Hamadan and Tabriz (where the population has a large Turki-speaking element), but here too it is the size, and not the function, that is meant.

284–286 THE USE OF 'MIHRABS' IN ISLAMIC ARCHITECTURE
In early mosques there was always a stone – the *qibla* – set in the wall and pointing towards the holy city of Mecca; later, this spot came to be decorated by the representation of an arch-shaped niche known as a *mihrab*, and this is the shape which is almost universally adopted in prayer-rug designs. Cammann draws attention to the wide-ranging significance that gates and arches have had in the East since earliest times: the name Babylon itself means 'Gate of the Gods' and in the world of Islam the *mihrab* may certainly be thought of as suggesting the gateway to Paradise in inmost Heaven, as well as, in the realm of Sufi mysticism, the threshold of infinite wisdom. Genuine prayer rugs are still made and used in many parts of the Orient, but they are rarely found in the carpet trade. Many weaving areas, however, have appreciated the purely decorative value of the prayer design and there is a large output of rugs of this type in all sizes made specifically for export to the West. The use of the *mihrab* as a decorative rather than as a strictly symbolic element is not new, nor is it restricted to the carpet trade, as the architectural examples shown in figs. 284–6 reveal. The basic architectural shape, moreover, may be as simple as in fig. 285, as elaborate as in fig. 286, or as severe as in certain prayer rugs (e.g. figs. 319 and 320).

It is perhaps appropriate at this point to remind the reader of a feature of the Islamic world which is often overlooked by Westerners, namely the indivisibility of the various aspects of Muhammadan life. There is no distinction in Islam between the spiritual and the secular, and thus no division of art into sacred and profane. From earliest times the mosque was both the place of worship and the political forum, and the leaders were at once priests (*mullahs*) and political leaders. Significantly, the 1979 Iranian revolution was led by the *ayatollahs*, demonstrating that in the true spirit of Islam the two functions are one. Any rug may therefore also serve as a prayer rug, and the designs illustrated in the following pages would be better entitled 'archway' designs: it is a decorative and historical convention that has

284 Colonnades in the Diwan-i-'Amm (Hall of Public Audience), in the Red Fort, Agra; under Shah Jahan (reigned 1627–58) *mihrabs* were extensively used in secular architecture.

285

emphasized this shape above all others as a 'prayer rug'. The prayer-rug layout was no doubt originally devised for a religious purpose, or if it already existed as an 'archway' design before the advent of Islam, it was certainly adopted for religious use. But it is a layout which for centuries has inspired designers to create elaborate versions of a purely decorative nature, just as architects throughout the world have seen in the arch and the vault an opportunity for artistic expression and decorative elaboration far transcending the test of their technical skills posed by purely functional demands. Qum and Kashan (figs. 302–304) in central Persia and Hereke (fig. 301) in western Anatolia are the towns one immediately thinks of today as sources of elaborate 'secular' prayer rugs. However, there are many others too, notably those in the Indian sub-continent such as Lahore, Srinagar and Agra; however, not all places that could weave this style do so – prayer rugs are rare in Arak, for example, and almost unknown in Bijar.

286

287 KAYSERI

Today, the largest range of prayer designs is woven in Turkey, and this is the one region where a buyer may still find appreciable numbers of rugs actually woven for religious use. The Kayseri piece illustrated here, however, most definitely does not belong to this category: this Anatolian type is in fact mass-produced by the ton in artificial silk (mercerized cotton or rayon). The design itself is ancient; examples of carpets which may be as much as 600 years old have been preserved, and these were undoubtedly used in mosques for several men praying at once (but not as 'family prayer rugs', as some dealers call them: strict segregation is normal, and no Muslim man would ever dream of praying in the company of the women of his household). The design shown is also made in wool in Kayseri, as well as in other places, most notably Sinkiang in China (see overleaf). There is no fixed rule about the colourings; in the artificial-silk goods of Kayseri much use is made of pastel

285 Prayer niche in the Sultan Hasan mosque, Cairo.

286 *Mihrab*-shaped vaulting in the bazaar in Kashan.

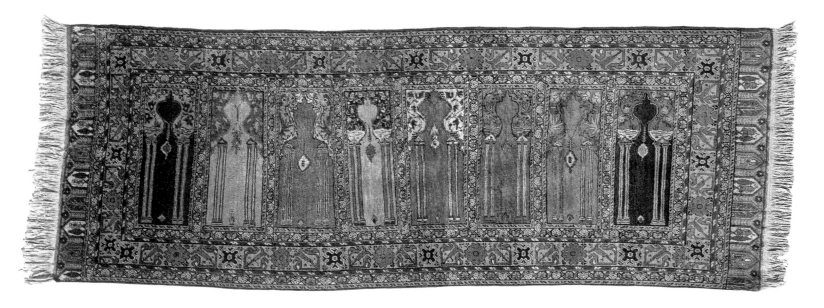

287 Kayseri saph
222 × 85 cm, 125,000 TK/m²
(7′ 3″ × 2′ 9″, 81 TK/in.²).

shades and strong yellow, but there is no shade at all that will not be encountered in these goods.

288 KHOTAN

At first sight it appears odd that the Kayseri *saph* design should be found both in central Turkey and in western China but (leaving aside modern manufactured copies from places like Pakistan) only rarely elsewhere. The carpet illustrated dates from the eighteenth century. A similar type is still made in the Tarim Basin area today and is sold by the Chinese under the name Sinkiang (see p. 108).

There is no obvious connection between the 'Samarkand' rugs of Khotan, Kashgar and Yarkand and the prayer rugs of fifteenth- or seventeenth-century Turkey, but the existence of the same design in two such widely separated areas is interesting for two reasons, cultural and commercial, either of which may explain the puzzle.

Firstly, it highlights the cultural connection between the two regions. Although the facts are well enough known, little attention – certainly too little – is paid to the influence on carpet design of the migrations of the Turkish races. The early history of the Mongols, Uzbeks, Turks and Turkomans, to be sure, is shrouded in mystery. They certainly populated central Asia two thousand years ago; but within the large expanse of central Asia it is not known who lived where and which racial groups were related to which or descended from whom. However, the Turks are mentioned in Chinese records of the sixth century AD and left inscriptions of their own in northern Mongolia in the eighth century. During the tenth century they were converted to Islam by Sunni missionaries from the Samanid state centred on Bokhara. From then until 1500 successive waves of Turkish invaders dominated the history of central and western Asia (see p. 343).

The first to establish a great empire was Tughril, the grandson of Seljuq, a tenth-century Turkish chieftain. From his central Asian power base he conquered Persia (fall of Isfahan 1043) and the Arabian Empire, capturing the capital of the Islamic world, Baghdad, in 1055. Within the Turkish forces the most warlike group were the Turkomans, and while Tughril consolidated the heart of his new empire, the Turkoman marauders were sent off to the frontiers. Tughril's nephew and successor, Arp Arslan, led them into the Caucasus and Anatolia, smashing the Byzantine army at Manzikert near Lake Van in 1071. Byzantium, the Christian East Roman Empire, was known in the Islamic world simply as Rome, or Rum. The Seljuq Turkomans carved themselves a large slice of Anatolia from it in the eleventh and twelfth centuries, hence the name Seljuqs of Rum. Thus by AD 1200 Turkoman links were established right across Asia from Mongolia to Anatolia.

These links were reinforced by the second shock wave from the East, when Jinghis Khan's Mongol and Turkoman hordes swept down from Mongolia and established an empire ruled from Peking that embraced the whole of western Asia

288 Khotan
320 × 110 cm, 106,000 PK/m²
(10′ 6″ × 3′ 7″, 68 PK/in.²).

and penetrated deep into Europe. The destruction of the official Seljuq control by the Mongols left the Turkomans on the Islamic-Christian frontier in Anatolia in a position to indulge their taste for freebooting raids in all directions. One chieftain, in particular, Osman, gained especial fame and set in motion the founding of a Turkoman state in the fourteenth century which was to become one of the world's great powers: the Ottoman Empire, which lasted for six centuries. Its development was diverted (but not seriously interrupted) by the third great wave from the east, that of Timur (see p. 99). The Ottoman state was incorporated into the Mongol Empire in 1402, but retained its identity and its Turkoman rulers, although they at first held power as Timur's vassals. By the middle of the fifteenth century the renewed expansion of the Ottoman Empire in western Asia and, from c. 1500 onwards, its permanent armed conflict with Persia and other eastern neighbours severed its direct connection with the Turkoman heartlands in Central Asia. It is clear, however, that at least from 1050 to 1450 there were countless opportunities for carpet designs to be exchanged between Khotan and Kayseri. Indeed, many examples of individual motifs of Turkoman origin will be found spread all over western Asia – see, for example, figs. 394, 398, 475, 500.

What is perhaps puzzling in view of the useful nature of the *saph* (the deployment of several large *saphs* on the ground in a mosque is a very practical way of achieving order among a crowd of praying Muslims) and of the wide dispersal of the Turkoman tribes is that the design is rarely found in other places: the Turkomans of West Turkestan and Afghanistan do not use the design, nor do the Turkomans of the Caucasus. This must make us wonder whether the design's transfer from Khotan to Kayseri (or *vice versa*) occurred for historical reasons at all. The second possible explanation could well have been a commercial one. Thus, for example, a traveller on the Silk Route may have happened to see and admire the Turkish original and copied it or had it copied in Khotan. But in our awe of the past, it is easy to think that everything was pure and noble and that artisans were simply inspired by high artistic ideals without a profit motive; as a result we may tend to overlook the fact that when Shakespeare or Molière speak of rich merchants they mean men who on their travels found new and unusual lines of merchandise which they could sell at home at a fat profit. Perhaps that is how the Turkish *saph* design found its way to Khotan. We must always bear in mind that in the world of oriental carpets, manufacturing – the production of rugs on strictly commercial lines – has always existed and has often been responsible for goods of outstanding cultural value.

289 GHIORDES

Also from Kayseri in central Anatolia (cf. fig. 287) there are very fine rugs in natural silk, based in the same way on ancient designs. The workmanship is of the highest order, in many cases equalling that of Hereke (see fig. 301), although the average Kayseri is less fine. Less well known, but exactly comparable, are the fine silk rugs

289 Ghiordes
134 × 92 cm, 640,000 TK/m²
(4′ 5″ × 3′ 0″, 412 TK/in.²).

290 Döşemealti
185 × 118 cm, 65,000 TK/m²
(6′ 1″ × 3′ 11″, 42 TK/in.²).

289

290

of the other great manufacturing centres of Turkey. One such, an early twentieth-century piece from Ghiordes, in the Izmir region of western Anatolia, is illustrated.

290 DÖŞEMEALTI

The rugs shown in figs. 289 and 301, on the one hand, and figs. 293–296 on the other, illustrate two typical features of modern Anatolian production: the accurate copies of classical designs, and the simple village products following a purely local tradition. Figs. 290 and 300 represent a third category, in which ancient designs are adapted to fit an established modern manufacturing style. The border, the whole colour-scheme and many details of the subsidiary motifs seen here are typical of Döşemealti (the style is unmistakable – see also figs. 268 and 495), but the design is another variant of the tulip Ladiks of the eighteenth century (cf. fig. 292). It remains something of a puzzle that, in order to see the triangular *mihrab* at the top of the rug, the tulips must be viewed upside down. This feature of the layout is already present in the earliest examples. In fig. 297 the position of the ewers seems to imply that the design can be thought of as usable either way up.

291 KASHMIR

The antique Turkish prayer-design style, with bold open designs and elaborate borders, has been woven in Kashmir for at least fifty years, perhaps more. The Ghiordes design seen in fig. 289 is found there on gold, blue, green, red and rust grounds. There are certain features which enable one to distinguish a Kashmir rug in a Turkish design (such as this one) from a modern Turkish piece, even when both are copies of an antique original. The Turkish village rug is recognizable by its woollen warps (Kashmir invariably uses cotton), but this is not a universally reliable guide since manufactured Turkish goods often use cotton warps. Above all it is the luscious yarn and the colours that one notices – the Kashmir is finely woven, brightly coloured, with a thin pile of fine imported wool. The Turkish rug is more sombre, coarser, more peasant-like in every respect, less set and regular in its style; or else, in the finest Turkish production, it has a verve and panache that the Kashmir rug never achieves. However, it is only when one sees the two together that one realizes how striking the differences really are.

291 Kashmir
181 × 122 cm, 260,000 PK/m²
(5′ 11″ × 4′ 0″, 168 PK/in.²).

292

293

292 Ladik, late eighteenth century,
228 × 109 cm, 155,000 TK/m²
(6′ 8″ × 3′ 7″, 100 TK/in.²).
Metropolitan Museum of Art, New York
(Gift of James F. Ballard).

293 Konya
132 × 87 cm, 88,000 TK/m²
(4′ 4″ × 2′ 10″, 57 TK/in.²).

292, 293 LADIK, KONYA

The power of the Ottoman Empire grew during the latter part of the fifteenth and the sixteenth centuries, and with it the demand from the Court for fine carpets. In prayer designs several standard styles of a generally ornate floral nature were established by the Court manufactories in Bursa, which Osman had made his capital in 1326, and in Cairo, which fell to the Ottomans in 1517. Many of the prayer rugs produced in manufactories today are based on these classical Ottoman originals. However, surviving seventeenth- and eighteenth-century rugs from many other centres (such as Ghiordes, Kula, Ladik and Konya) reveal a more geometric, abstract flavour, of which modern copies also abound, e.g. figs. 289, 290 and 297.

The 'tulip' Ladik of fig. 292 reflects the proximity of Ladik to Konya, which was the Seljuq capital from 1097 to 1307. Some of the oldest known carpets of the Islamic world are from Konya: their strict geometric style is an unmistakable documentation of the Turkoman connection. This much later piece, dated by Dimand to the end of the eighteenth century, is still reminiscent of the racial background, especially when compared with nineteenth-century Turkoman *enssis* (see fig. 325). Fig. 293 shows a modern rug from the same general area, for which Konya remains the marketing centre (one of several important collecting points in Central Anatolia). Note the distinctive border, which has a red pattern on a dark-blue ground and which is a typical feature of the current Konya production.

294 KEÇIMUSLU

Within the basic framework of the prayer-rug layout Anatolia produces an endless variety of designs, some of which are illustrated in figs. 293–296. They are completely unstandardized and there is little one can say about them except that their designs reflect the broad spectrum of inspiration which is enshrined in the ancient weaving art of the peasants of Anatolia. The rug illustrated here comes from a village in the region of Konya. The border shade is green, the plain ground red, the latter being streaked by 'abrashes', those variations in colour which are common in village and tribal products and which constitute one of the 'imperfections' that make oriental carpets so vibrant with life. Note also the use of another variant of the 'judor' motif in the innermost guard (see figs. 145, 146).

294 Konya Keçimuslu
184 × 114 cm, 92,000 TK/m²
(6′ 1″ × 3′ 9″, 59 TK/in.²).

295 Kavak
190 × 120 cm, 95,000 TK/m²
(6′ 3″ × 3′ 11″, 61 TK/in.²).

296 Yuntdag
163 × 110 cm, 63,000 TK/m²
(5′ 4″ × 3′ 7″, 40 TK/in.²).

295 KAVAK

In this piece we encounter a green ground – not a common colour in rugs in general, since green is the special colour of the Prophet; but in Turkey, where the peasant rugs mostly employ a wider range of colours than is found in the village products of Persia, green is less rare. The use of a 'tree-of-life' motif is quite common in prayer rugs – see p. 106 and also the Beluch rug shown in fig. 247. The large number of borders, or rather guards, used in the piece shown here is one of the characteristic features of Turkish prayer rugs. Note also the up-turned ewers in the corners, looking unfortunately like policemen on point duty. Cammann asserts that these are symbols of life-giving water, although they may also be regarded as simply ritual vessels reminding the believer of the cleanliness of both body and mind associated with prayer. The reason why the ewers, and other motifs in prayer rugs, are upside-down may be that the rug itself was woven upside-down so that when the worshipper – kneeling in the centre of the rug – slides his hands forward towards the top at one stage in his prayers they will glide freely with the lie of the pile. Rugs like this may well be woven from the weaver's head, without the guidance of design paper, and if he happens to slip in a few motifs of his own which appear the right way up while he is weaving, they will appear upside down when the rug is taken down from the loom and viewed in the normal way.

296 YUNTDAG

With all the 'meanings' which we attach to symbols in oriental carpets we must of course remember that we are talking about what may have been the *original* significance of a motif or idea. There must be no suggestion that this meaning is necessarily still valid today. In some cases it may be, but in others the weaver is in cultural terms so distanced from the design's origins that it can mean no more to him than pretty patterns to occupy his nimble fingers. In consequence, there are many designs whose original implications are completely lost. In the rug here the hooks at the top of the *mihrab* might just represent 'sun-birds', the ancient mythical creatures that guard the gate of Paradise, and the ragged-winged 'eagles' that fill the ground might just have something to do with a 'tree-of-life' idea. They may also be related to the Turkoman pattern found in the side borders of fig. 325, but they are so far removed from anything definitely recognizable that we can only assume that the modern weaver, like the beholder, can have little conception of any religious or mythological intent in the design. Does that make it a bad rug? If we answer no, then we must ask whether the more certain meaning we can attach to the symbolism of other rugs contributes to making them good rugs; logically the answer in that case would need to be no as well. We can point to the play of colours here, to the striking Caucasian-style border, to the mystery of the motifs in the ground, and we can declare this piece fascinating for aesthetic reasons. However, there is no doubt that the interplay of forms and colours in not the only factor that influences our assessment of why an oriental rug is fascinating, and so we are driven to conclude that a rug is good if you like it, just as the money value of a rug is simply 'what someone is willing to pay for it' (see p. 28).

297 RUMANIA

The Turkish prayer designs of old are copied not only in modern manufactories in Turkey but in many other areas, too, including Rumania. Unlike the Kashmiris who have an ancient weaving tradition of their own, but use the designs from many origins, re-interpreting them in a typically Kashmiri style, the Rumanian 'antique Turkish prayer rugs' are painstaking imitations of ancient pieces. The designs and colours of museum pieces are copied accurately and the rugs are then washed time after time and burnt and sandpapered until they become threadbare and tatty and the fringes begin to fall to pieces, just as if they had been in use for three hundred years. But it is still fairly easy to tell the new 'antiques' from the originals: one immediately senses that the result is too good to be true; and one can confirm one's suspicions by putting one's nose to the rug, for all Rumanian carpets have a strange and unmistakable oily smell. Of course this sort of brilliant counter-feit makes one wonder what it is about the museum-piece original that makes it

297

298

297 Rumania
175 × 119 cm, 120,000 PK/m²
(5′ 9″ × 3′ 11″, 77 PK/in.²).

298 Ezineh
150 × 84 cm, 62,000 TK/m²
(4′ 11″ × 2′ 9″, 40 TK/in.²).

worth thousands of pounds, while the almost indistinguishable copy will fetch only a few hundred. Is the original better? Many examples in the carpet world show that the words 'good' and 'better' often have no real meaning at all. Not only does the aesthetic value often conflict with the functional value but the aesthetic value itself is hotly contested. The rug illustrated here clearly demonstrates the truth of the argument that a carpet is worth what someone is willing to pay for it: no other value judgement is possible. If a Turkish antique will fetch a higher price than a Rumanian forgery then the antique is not better, but it is worth more; the relationship between price paid and intrinsic merit is unfathomable. Several different Anatolian designs and many more of Caucasian origin are produced in this class of Rumanian goods, often sold under the name 'Transylvanian'. This rug, like fig. 290, is based on a Ladik original of the type shown in fig. 292. Note in this version the striking connection with the Takht-e-Jamshid design of the Kolyais (fig. 553).

298 EZINEH
The village of Ezineh, near Çannakkale in north-west Anatolia, is the source of a large number of rugs in simple geometric-designs, described in detail on pp. 233 and 240. Within this output examples will be found in which some use is made of traditional designs from other areas. The design illustrated here is based on the style of the Yagçibedir rugs (see fig. 577). These also appear occasionally with a prayer-*mihrab* layout, but Yagçibedir goods are always much finer and more elegant than the Ezineh copies. Whereas in other designs the simplicity of Ezineh is the key to success (see fig. 527, for example), here the recipe fails because the weave and materials are not adequate to capture the charm of the Yagçibedir original. The subtle effect of the latter's simple red motifs on an intense blue background derives from the use of fine yarn and a fine weave, sharp contours and gradations in colour; in the Ezineh copy the blue looks dead, the red hard, the outlines coarse and indistinct, and the design clumsy and inconsequential. The rug shown is thus more interesting as an illustration of the difficulties encountered in creating new designs outside the scope of an established tradition. For a successful new Ezineh see fig. 543; and for a successful adaptation of Yagçibedir motifs see fig. 457.

299 Pakistan
161 × 96 cm, 380,000 PK/m²
(5′ 3″ × 3′ 2″, 245 TK/in.²).

300 Melas
167 × 99 cm, 126,000 TK/m²
(5′ 6″ × 3′ 3″, 81 TK/in.²).

299 PAKISTAN

Pakistan produces two distinct types of prayer design: the Persian-style double-wefted floral goods, of which the rug illustrated in fig. 310 is an example, and single-wefted double-weave merchandise which reveals stylistic similarities with the Turkoman designs illustrated in figs. 323 and 404, although the prayer-niche layout in this second type looks more Turkish than Turkoman. They are woven in many different grades. The cheapest are primitive in design, colouring and execution, but in the finer grades a considerable wealth of detail may be introduced. The rug shown here is an example of one of the best categories woven.

300 MELAS

The history of many of the carpet-producing towns of Anatolia reaches back to antiquity. Bergama, for example, lies close to the site of the ancient Hellenic city of Pergamum; and the modern name Kayseri is derived from the epithet Caesarea applied by the Romans to the city of Mazaca in the first century B C, at which time the city already had a history spanning more than five hundred years. The precise origin of Melas is not recorded, but the district of south-west Anatolia where the town lies (ancient Lydia), including the valley of the River Maeander, was settled by the Hellenes in the second millennium B C.

The textile tradition of the region goes back more than 3,000, perhaps 4,000 years (see p. 33), which makes it probably the oldest of today's carpet-producing areas where the existence of textile weaving in antiquity can be proved. The principal town of the area was Miletus, one of the greatest cities of the Ionian Confederacy, a port with a flourishing trade over much of the Mediterranean. The rise of Phoenician naval power and later the dominant military position, first of the Persians and then of Athens, reduced Miletus to a purely provincial centre.

It passed into Roman hands in the second century B C and was seized from the Byzantine Empire by the Turkomans in the late thirteenth century A D. The catastrophe of the Graeco-Turkish war (1922–23), which followed the dissolution of the Ottoman Empire after the First World War, robbed the area of many of its weavers who, being of Greek origin, fled to the safety of Greece. Nevertheless, the region today remains famous for its slit-kilim tapestries, the modern representatives of the tradition of Arachne (see p. 33). In terms of pile rugs, Melas is known largely for one style only, prayer rugs of the type illustrated in figs. 109 and 300. It is quite common for the borders to be so dominant as to swallow up the ground of the rug almost entirely. The bold geometric border and open layout of geometric motifs in the ground are other distinguishing features, but the easiest way to recognize the new rugs of Melas is by their colouring, as illustrated in fig. 109. No other place produces quite this combination of grey-green, grey, rust, dull yellow and brown. Like all Turkish village rugs, the Melas goods have woollen warps and wefts; the woollen pile is usually clipped very thin. The range of sizes woven is very limited – almost all the production is in the seççadeh size.

301 HEREKE

The most elaborate Turkish designs are made in Hereke, which, while it produces several types of wool and silk merchandise, concentrates on the finest and most expensive grade of all-silk rugs. There has always been a great manufacturing tradition in Turkey, and some sixty years ago towns like Sivas, Smyrna (Izmir) and Sparta had as large an output and as great a range of designs as Tabriz or Kashan. The whole Turkish production collapsed in the 1920s after the Graeco-Turkish war, and it was not until the mid-1960s that renewed demand, especially from Germany, led to the revival which is now in full swing. All parts of Turkey have benefited from this new interest, and we now see once again the same structure in the art of weaving which was apparent before the collapse: a wide range of tribal and peasant goods in geometric designs, with manufacturing units in places like Kula and Hereke which are capable of producing any design. Of all these, Hereke is the acknowledged leader. If finest means best in the carpet trade, then Hereke makes the best rugs in the Orient. The materials (all silk) and colourings are excellent and the designs imaginative and wide-ranging.

301

302

301 Hereke
150 × 100 cm, 830,000 TK/m²
(4′ 11″ × 3′ 3″, 536 TK/in.²).

302 Qum
214 × 138 cm, 570,000 PK/m²
(7′ 0″ × 4′ 6″, 368 PK/in.²).

The Hereke carpet production began with the establishment by Sultan Abdul Hamid in 1890 of a Court Manufactory as an extension of the existing textile works. Pieces produced there before the First World War now fetch very high prices. From the beginning the designs were based on the ornate style of Bursa and Cairo (see pp. 131, 270, 329 and fig. 169) and meticulous copies of these sixteenth-century originals still form the backbone of the output. Other pieces have as their inspiration stylistically related Persian rugs of the same era, and in the course of time twentieth-century designers have added their own derivatives, still within one basic floral style. Several pieces are illustrated in this book (see index); the rug shown here is representative of the Bursa type, examples of which may be seen in museums throughout the world.

302 QUM

The biggest Persian centre for silk rugs is Qum, and here too a wide range of prayer designs is woven, no doubt for the simple reason that people often prefer to hang silk rugs on the wall rather than lay them on the floor, and for this purpose one-way designs of the prayer arch type are very suitable. Commercial production did not begin in Qum until 1945, so that in this case we cannot speak of traditional designs, but the one illustrated here is widely made and is one of the most successful. The colourings, in particular, are often less jazzy than in other typical Qum designs, much of the effect deriving from a nice balance between rose and soft green.

303–306 KASHAN

In its pre-war heyday Kashan also produced many exquisite pieces with prayer designs, often with pillars supporting the *mihrab*, as in fig. 303, or else with elaborate vase designs such as those shown in figs. 304 and 306. It is interesting to compare figs. 304 and 305. The thirteenth-century wall panel has clearly inspired the twentieth-century designer. In essence the latter has simply taken over the design structure and basic style of the tiles and adapted them to incorporate a realistically drawn vase and, of course, all the floral detail of the later era. The puzzle is: in view of the undoubted interchange of ideas in all Islamic decorative art, why did the style of the wall panel not appear in thirteenth-century carpets? Since no carpets from thirteenth-century Kashan survive we cannot, of course, be sure that it did not, but

303

304

305

303 Kashan
209 × 131 cm, 330,000 PK/m²
(6′ 10″ × 4′ 3″, 213 PK/in.²).

304 Kashan
208 × 131 cm, 320,000 PK/m²
(6′ 10″ × 4′ 3″, 206 PK/in.²).

305 Tiled wall panel from the Maydan Mosque, Kashan, dated AD 1226 (623 AH).

306 Kashan
220 × 143 cm, 345,000 PK/m²
(7′ 3″ × 4′ 8″, 223 PK/in.²).

307 Agra
155 × 100 cm, 190,000 PK/m²
(5′ 1″ × 3′ 3″, 123 PK/in.²).

306

307

the suggestion that such a style existed in carpet design before 1500 flies in the face of all the currently accepted theories. However, it is certain that an earlier floral style gave way at some time to the strict geometric stylization of the fourteenth-century Anatolian carpets, since the Pazyryk carpet (fig. 56) displays a fully curvilinear technique. Attention is always drawn in this connection to the *hadith*, the sayings traditionally attributed to the Prophet, which, if strictly interpreted, proscribe the representation of living forms in art. It is asserted that it is because of this that flowers and other plant forms appear in carpets in a stylized geometric form. It is an assertion little questioned by carpet scholars, one of the *idées reçues* passed on from generation to generation. The whole concept is, however, badly

308

309a

309b

in need of investigation by a scholarly comparison of the known evidence of early Islamic art. More notes on this subject will be found on p. 156; the important point here is that the patterns of fig. 305 fully obey the injunctions of the *hadith* and yet remain entirely curvilinear in style. Perhaps it was not Islamic religious precepts at all that caused the switch from floral to geometric carpet designs, but some other force occurring at a later date than the imposition of Islamic law in central Asia – the thirteenth- or fourteenth-century Mongol invasions, for example.

Note in all three rugs illustrated (figs. 303, 304, 306) the unmistakable unity of style; see, for example, the way the vases are employed, and compare them also with fig. 280.

307 AGRA

The Kashan piece illustrated above (fig. 306) is, like figs. 280–3, as much a vase design as a prayer rug, and the comments made on p. 124 apply equally here. This particular vase design appears in a variety of forms in Kashan, often showing an affinity with Joshaqan motifs. This latter connection is apparent in the new Agra copy illustrated here, as a comparison with figs. 599 and 600 will confirm. This rug is one of the single-wefted pieces described on p. 288, and is further evidence of the rapid development in the use of classical Persian designs that has taken place in India in the course of the 1970s.

308, 309 KASHMIR

The word Kashmir is used rather loosely in the carpet trade to describe a wide range of fine carpets and rugs from various parts of the north of the Indian sub-continent, including both the Indian and Pakistani Punjab and sometimes even places as far afield as Agra. The finest goods are, however, made in Srinagar, the capital of Indian Kashmir, itself. Many of them are all silk. Others, like the rug illustrated here, are part-silk, part-wool, but with a much higher proportion of silk than in Qum part-silks – in the latter only individual motifs are woven in silk to highlight the appearance of the rug, whereas in the example illustrated almost the whole of the ground is silk. The Kashmir designs are all taken from classical Persian originals. The rug shown is typical of the style woven in Kerman around the turn of the century – the so-called Laver-Kermans. One is reminded of the tile designs of Kerman (fig. 309) which are much more light and flowery, much less classically restrained than those of the great mosques of the early Safavid period.

308 Kashmir (Srinagar)
183 × 123 cm, 650,000 PK/m²
(6′ 0″ × 4′ 0″, 420 PK/in.²).

309a, b Tile panels at the entrance to the Madrasseh (Theological College) and Bath House of Ibrahim Khan, Kerman, 1816–17.

310

311

310 Lahore
208 × 130 cm, 508,000 PK/m²
(6′ 10″ × 4′ 3″, 328 PK/in.²).

311 Kashmir
213 × 153 cm, 550,000 PK/m²
(7′ 0″ × 5′ 0″, 355 PK/in.²).

310–312 LAHORE, AMRITSAR, AGRA

Among fine goods from other sources in the Indian sub-continent, one of the best – from the Pakastani Punjab – is represented in fig. 310. Indeed, from the picture alone many experts might well guess a central Persian origin for the piece. Only the weave and handle (especially the wool) reveal the Pakistani origin. In Amritsar, a few miles away in the Indian Punjab, and in Indian Kashmir to the north, one of the prayer designs most commonly found is the one illustrated in fig. 311. This is usually made in dozar sizes and usually on cream grounds, though other colours are also woven. The quality can vary enormously: in northern India it is not only a question of the fineness of the weave but of the basic structure, which is often not at all sound. The fine weaving for which Kashmir has traditionally been famous often conceals a very shoddy approach to the basic principles of good craftsmanship, so that many pieces will be found to be lacking in body. A properly made rug should feel both firm and flexible to the handle; but in Kashmir too many pieces are flexible and flabby. Good pieces, however, like the one illustrated, can be rated among the best-woven rugs of the Orient today. The same design is made in yet another version in Agra in the single-wefted double-weave construction described on p. 288. In the illustration (fig. 312) the difference looks small, but in fact the price of the Agra rug is only about a quarter of that of the Kashmir, and the reason for this will be apparent to anyone seeing the two rugs side by side. The Agra is inferior in every detail of design and colouring, and even the most tightly packed rugs made there cannot be described as having a 'firm, flexible handle'. They sell because they are cheap and exceptionally finely woven for the price, the fine weave permitting a degree of floral detail not normally to be found in this price-range.

313–325

Apart from the large numbers of prayer rugs woven by the Turks, the leading producers of tribal goods today are the Turkomans and the Beluchis. These two ethnic groups are not related, the Beluch language being a Persian dialect, similar to that of the Lurs, while the Turkomans speak a form of Turkish. However, they live in the same area – broadly the three-nation frontier region that lies to the east of the Caspian Sea, with Mazar, Meshed, Ashkabad and Herat as the main towns. Whereas the Turkomans live mainly in the north of this region and the Beluchis mainly in the south, there are many points of contact, and this is often revealed in their carpet designs.

The Beluchis, some nomadic and some permanently settled, inhabit large areas of both Persia and Afghanistan. They are split into a large number of tribes or clans, most of whom weave rugs, all clearly of one stylistic family, but with an infinite variety of individual local interpretations, about which, alas, very little is known. The carpet trade distinguishes two essential categories – Meshed Beluch and Herat Beluch. The Meshed goods, woven on the Persian side of the frontier, have cotton warps and wefts, (they used to be of wool and just occasionally still are) and are finely woven, with dark blues and reds predominating. There are various styles of design and size. Herat Beluch goods, made in Afghanistan, are woven on woollen warps and are generally coarse and floppy, with a wide range of colours both bright and dull, but not often sombre like the Meshed goods. The production is dominated by prayer designs. Within these two main categories some further degree of differentiation is possible: sometimes the actual tribal name is known, and at least the principal bazaars where each type is bought and sold can be ascertained. Both categories also include many items traded as Beluch but woven by other tribes working within the Beluch stylistic tradition. One may cite, for example, the Arabs of Ferdaus, the Taimani, Aimaq and Timuri, who are to be found in various parts of central and western Afghanistan and eastern Persia, the Jamshidi north of Herat, and many more. Indeed, modern research suggests that very few of the rugs we know as 'Beluch' are actually woven by tribes of Beluch origin. The name has been retained in this book, but it should be regarded more as an indication of type than of origin. The prayer rugs shown in figs. 313–9 are all from Afghanistan. A Meshed Beluch prayer rug is shown in fig. 247.

313 KOUDANI

This rug is an outstanding example of Beluch weaving art. The imaginative intricacy of the mosque design is matched by the deep glowing colours and the magnificent wool. In their best pieces, the Beluchis use a very fine silky yarn which, when tightly packed (as in a rug as fine as this), feels like deep plush or velvet. The colourings are typical of those associated with the southern part of the Afghan Beluch area. In particular, the sombre mauvish brown is highly characteristic and quite unmistakable – nothing quite like it is used anywhere else.

314–316 BELUCH

Considering the very wide area over which the Beluch tribes are spread it is not surprising that there is such a huge variety of interpretations within the basic prayer-arch type. The Mushwami, a group of Pashtun or Persian origin who live mainly in the Herat region, near Karokh (to the north) and Ghurian (to the west), are famous for magnificently and richly adorned, intensely sombre tapestries, which are usually executed in a variety of flat-weave techniques. Their pile rugs, too, are of the first grade; they are characterized by excellent wool and a fine weave which shows off to great effect the intricate detail of the geometric patterns. The same may be said of the rug, from the small Haft Bolah tribe of the Ghurian district, illustrated in fig. 315. Note here also the remarkable restraint in the use of colour – the weaver has really used only red, white and blue with a tiny amount of yellow.

312 Agra
186 × 122 cm, 288,000 PK/m²
(6′ 1″ × 4′ 0″, 186 PK/in.²).

313 Koudani Beluch
134 × 81 cm, 210,000 PK/m²
(4′ 5″ × 2′ 8″, 135 PK/in.²).

314

315

316

314 Mushwami Beluch
132 × 87 cm, 223,000 TK/m²
(4′ 4″ × 2′ 10″, 144 TK/in.²).

315 Haft Bolah Beluch
140 × 88 cm, 128,000 PK/m²
(4′ 7″ × 2′ 10″, 83 PK/in.²).

316 Shindand Beluch
139 × 87 cm, 128,000 PK/m²
(4′ 7″ × 2′ 10″, 83 PK/in.²).

Again and again we must note that the tribal weaver's combination of outstanding workmanship and artistic restraint can achieve just as much visual impact as the showy elaboration of the town manufactories. Figs. 314 and 315 represent exceptional pieces; the more pedestrian grade of Herat Beluch goods is represented by the rug from the Shindand region (fig. 316). Here, the stylistic essentials are the same, but the much inferior craftsmanship produces a less impressive result. Even at this level, however, Beluch rugs are original and decorative – as well as being cheap, especially in relation to the fineness of their weave.

317 DOKHTAR-E-GHAZI
This rug is characteristic of the Dokhtar-e-Ghazi, one of the best-known Beluch tribes, who are located not far from Herat. The design used is a difficult one to bring off because the slender red lines of the motif set against a usually very dark-blue background often tend to leave the pattern very indistinct. However, the Dokhtar-e-Ghazi work is often very fine and in well executed pieces the red glows against the dark blue and the design breathes that inexplicable combination of repose and vibrancy which imbues many of the small repeating patterns of the Orient.

318 CHICHAKSU
The village of Chichaksu produces the finest of all Herat Beluch rugs. Modern production is on an organized basis employing weavers who for the most part are not Beluchis at all. There are eight or nine grades, from medium-fine to very fine – and prices from high to extremely high. The goods are made with quite good yarn, although the rugs are often thin and flimsy, and lacking in body. They are given a primitive kind of antique finishing treatment in the region of origin, which sometimes spoils the colours but often produces very agreeable shades of rust and dark blue. Every piece is different, but all look very much alike owing to the weavers' rather strict adherence to the principal elements of the design, as in the rug illustrated. In recent times the Chichaksu production has been extended to embrace a range of additional designs, some of which have no connection whatever with the traditional Beluch style. Chichaksus are often traded as 'haft [seven] mihrab'.

317 Dokhtar-e-Ghazi Beluch
123 × 110 cm, 95,000 PK/m²
(4′ 0″ × 3′ 7″, 61 PK/in.²).

319 TAIMANI

A coarse type of rug is woven in the wilds of the mountains east of Herat, in the province of Ghor. The weavers there may be Beluchis but are more often from the Taimani or Timuri tribes, both of uncertain origin but who have learned the art of weaving from their Beluchi neighbours. The rugs often contain appalling shades of mauve and orange (most appalling when used in combination with one another), but they are produced with dyes so fugitive that the colours often quickly fade to agreeable brown shades. Although this region, too, has seen the introduction of organized production in recent years, one may still find rugs – made for local use rather than for export – which are often full of unspoilt individual character, despite their rough weave and improbable colours. The rugs are often adorned with a double fringe, as in fig. 45. Note, in the rug illustrated, the use of the motif seen in fig. 395b. The same general style of design as that shown here is also used in *sumakh* prayer rugs (decorated flat weaves) from the same area, usually sold as Kuchi (i.e. gypsy) – an indication of the carpet trade's extreme vagueness about the Beluch and related areas.

320–325 TURKOMAN

There is a huge range of prayer designs to be found among the wealth of the old Turkoman patterns of Afghanistan. What is puzzling is that so few of them seem to be woven today. Eight or ten years ago the author saw dozens of pieces every month passing through the stocks of a London importer; today we see them only as occasional pieces in parcels of old goods. When will someone in Afghanistan remember them?

The only one in large-scale production today is the Daulatabad (fig. 320), made by both Turkoman and Uzbeki tribesmen in and around the town of that name south of Andkhoy. This is an interesting item because many years ago excellent fine carpets were produced in a style similar to the Alti Bolagh example shown in fig. 412. The reputation of Daulatabad was such that many exporters chose the name as a trade name for any better than average Afghan rug. Hence Afghan rugs from all sorts of origins are often labelled Daulatabad. Today, however, although the output in Daulatabad, apart from goods in the prayer design shown, is very small, some of the prayer rugs from there are outstandingly well made.

318 Chichaksu
143 × 95 cm, 160,000 PK/m2
(4′ 8″ × 3′ 1″, 103 PK/in.2).

319 Taimani
100 × 89 cm, 65,000 PK/m2
(3′ 4″ × 2′ 11″, 42 PK/in.2).

320 Daulatabad
119 × 79 cm, 196,000 PK/m2
(3′ 10″ × 2′ 7″, 126 PK/in.2).

319

320

321

322

323

321 Kizil Ayak
120 × 81 cm, 94,000 PK/m²
(3′ 11″ × 2′ 8″, 61 PK/in.²).

322 Kunduz
111 × 65 cm, 119,000 PK/m²
(3′ 8″ × 2′ 1″, 77 PK/in.²).

323 Jangalarik
120 × 74 cm, 115,000 PK/m²
(3′ 11″ × 2′ 5″, 74 PK/in.²).

324 Sarukh(?)
125 × 84 cm, 244,000 PK/m²
(4′ 1″ × 2′ 9″, 157 PK/in.²).

325 Yamut enssi
132 × 110 cm, 355,000 PK/m²
(4′ 4″ × 3′ 7″, 229 PK/in.²).

326 Shirvan
129 × 95 cm, 180,000 TK/m²
(4′ 3″ × 3′ 1″, 116 TK/in.²).

The other designs illustrated in this group – and countless others like them – are often of average or less than average quality; it is the charm of the design used that makes these rugs collectors' items. The Kizil Ayak rug (fig. 321) is unusual in that some of the motifs are in green (a colour very rarely used in Afghan goods), while others are woven with camel hair. Camel hair is much softer than wool – in this rug the wool looks positively bristly beside it – and it is thus not often used in carpets. The Kizil Ayaks, a Turkoman tribe of uncertain origin, are found throughout northern Afghanistan; they are noted for rather more flamboyant designs than most of their Turkoman neighbours. Kunduz (fig. 322) is the most easterly of the major market towns for Afghan Turkoman goods. Several tribes are represented among the weavers of the region, of whom the Suleimans, the Dalis and the Beshirs are perhaps the most important. The design used in the prayer rug illustrated is also found as an all-over pattern in carpet sizes. It is not a göl, of course, but a representation of the *minbar*, the focal 'pulpit' of the mosque set up next to the *qibla* (see fig. 285), from which the *mullah* addresses the faithful, the magistrate proclaims the laws and the invader formerly received the submission of conquered peoples. Note that in fig. 323, the Jangalarik rug (the name is that of an Ersari subtribe from the Andkhoy region), a lamp is seen hanging in the niche of the *mihrab*. This is not a universal practice in mosques, but the lamp is often depicted in prayer rugs. Cammann suggests that this feature is connected with a verse in the Koran: 'Allah is the light of the heavens and the earth. The symbol of His light is a niche in which is a lamp.'

The rug shown in fig. 324 goes further than the other examples illustrated in the portrayal of the mosque, reflecting a western Afghan tradition seen in Beluch rugs as well as in Turkomans. Indeed, it is not quite certain that this is a Turkoman rug at all; it could have been made by the Jamshidi tribe, one of the many small non-Turkoman clans who inhabit the area between Herat and the Penjdeh oasis and have a small output of fine rugs that look like a cross between Beluch and Turkoman styles. The design of this rug, however, has much of the Kizil Ayak style (fig. 321) about it; while the very fine, firm, ribbed weave suggests a Sarukh origin (see fig. 409). Even if a proper documentation of the area were to be produced, the inter-

324

325

326

mingling of the clans and copying of designs from one area to another has been so extensive that it is doubtful if a clear picture will ever emerge.

The last rug illustrated in this Turkoman group, fig. 325, is an 'enssi', held by some to be the traditional Turkoman prayer rug *par excellence*. The thorny problem of this design is discussed on p. 153, in the section devoted to panel designs. The rug shown here is a Yamut piece attributable to the early nineteenth century, incorporating the traditional *mihrab*-shaped form at the top of the ground.

326 SHIRVAN

Finally, this Shirvan rug is an example of the Caucasian production described in detail on p. 230. The design is derived from the huge manufactured output of north-eastern Azerbaijan and Daghestan in the nineteenth century and harks back beyond that to the concept of alternating flowers within a lattice-work pattern, the use of which seems to go back at least as far as the sixteenth-century vase carpets of east or south-east Persia (cf. also figs. 386, 767). Although the modern Shirvan production is fairly wide-ranging, this particular design is normally found only in the colours of the piece illustrated and in rug sizes. As in the case of all the modern Russian copies of old designs, the price is low in relation to the fineness of weave and the quality of the materials used, but this factory production suffers from a stiff, mechanical look, underlined by the use of cotton warps and wefts.

6 GARDEN AND PANEL DESIGNS

When Timur overran central Asia in the fourteenth century he had thousands of artists and craftsmen brought from the four corners of his empire to embellish his capital, Samarkand. However, the modern traveller who marvels at the mosques and mausoleums, public buildings and monuments, will search in vain for Timur's palace: he never built one. He remained a tent-dweller, a nomad of the steppes, to his dying day. What he did build were nine magnificent gardens in which the imperial tent could be set up: for the garden, with avenues of cool and shady trees, beds of colourful flowers and brooks where water flows eternal, is the nomad's idea of Paradise. This does not apply only to the steppes of central Asia; the reader who has not visited Iran can hardly conceive how unutterably desolate the landscape is in most of the country. It is not just the great Kavir-e-Lut – covering a huge part of the east of the country – which is desert: almost the whole of Iran lies on a great plateau averaging 1,200 m (4,000 ft) or more above sea-level. Rivers are very few, so that in effect most of the towns and villages must be thought of as oases. For the rest, one encounters endless wastes of grey-brown desert – not sand, but dry dust, rock and stone. Amid this mournful landscape the traveller will not be surprised to find the resplendent 'gardens' woven into the carpets which cover the floors of houses, and we need look no further than the weavers' environment to find their motivation for this design.

327–330 THE CLASSICAL GARDEN CARPETS

One may call all Persian carpets 'woven gardens', the artistic precipitate of the nomad's dream. But there is also an ancient tradition of weaving designs which directly imitate the special formal layout of the Persian garden (fig. 328). What is probably the most famous carpet in history had such a design. It was produced (in what technique is not known – probably kilim or felt, rather than knotted) for the palace at Ctesiphon of Chosroes (Khosroes) I, one of the last Persian emperors before the Arab conquests of the seventh century AD. It is reported to have been some 27 m (90 ft) wide and five times as long, and its fabric was embellished with silk and thousands of pearls and jewels. Chosroes used it on the floor in winter to 'remind him of the spring'. The Muslim conquerors tore the carpet to pieces as booty when Ctesiphon fell in 641; but the sacred aura of the garden was enshrined in the Koran, where the faithful are promised a Paradise containing 'four gardens, beneath which waters flow'. Although the 'spring of Chosroes' clearly proves that the idea contained in the garden carpet is older than Islam, the description of the celestial gardens in the Koran will certainly have been drawn upon by later artists working on the design.

Many attempts have been made to re-create the pattern of the legendary 'spring of Chosroes'. A modern Kerman version appears in fig. 347, but the oldest known piece, now in the Jaipur Museum in India (fig. 329), seems to have originated as a development of the vase design in southern Persia in the early seventeenth century; a variant of perhaps somewhat later date appears in fig. 327. The conversion of the garden into a formalized panel design (fig. 330) seems to have occurred during the

327 North Persian garden carpet, seventeenth or eighteenth century, 527 × 425 cm (17' 3" × 13' 11"). The Burrell Collection, Glasgow Art Gallery.

327

328

329

330

328 Persian garden in Mahun, near Kerman; the carpet shown in fig. 347 was woven in this village.

329 Detail of a south-east Persian garden carpet, full size 840 × 370 cm (27′ 7″ × 12′ 2″), certainly woven before 1632. Jaipur Museum.

330 North-west Persian garden carpet, eighteenth century, 925 × 327 cm (30′ 4″ × 10′ 9″).

eighteenth century. By this date the idea was being used in north-west Persia, but opinions among the world's carpet scholars as to exactly where vary. Iten-Maritz, disagreeing with Erdmann, sees the whole tradition as originating in Isfahan in the sixteenth century as a development of the ideas of Bihzad, the most famous of the classical Persian miniature painters. Bihzad was a product of the Herat school at the end of the fifteenth century, but moved to north-west Persia with the Safavid Court after the collapse of the Mongol Empire in 1510. He did not live to see the establishment of Isfahan as the Persian capital, but his work strongly influenced his successors. He was famous for the technical innovation of presenting scenes from a bird's-eye view and it is to this feature in the garden carpets that Iten-Maritz draws attention.

331–339 THE BAKHTIARI PANEL DESIGNS

Today, the garden design is associated with one area, the Chahar Mahal. This is a fertile hilly region south-west of Isfahan on the slopes of the Zagros mountains. Beyond the mountains is the territory of the Bakhtiari tribe, a Luri group who produce no carpets of consequence but who are famed for their spectacular annual migration with their herds from the plains of Khuzistan near the Persian Gulf to summer pastures in the mountains. In the early nineteenth century some of the leaders of this tribe settled as gentry in the Chahar Mahal; their name was appended to that of the province and has been used for the carpets of the area ever since. The weavers are of very mixed origin: Lurs, Kurds, Armenians and others, with a considerable stiffening of Turkomans from the time of the Seljuq invasions.

The oldest known Bakhtiari carpets date back to perhaps 1800. Between the examples shown in figs. 329 and 331 there is the intermediate stage shown in fig. 346, a design which already has a strong Bakhtiari flavour. The further stages in the breakdown of this design into straightforward repeating panels is not documented in existing carpet literature, which is perhaps surprising in view of the immense popularity which these goods enjoy and of the outstanding artistic merit of the best pieces.

Within the province of Chahar Mahal va Bakhtiari there are scores of villages making different versions of the panel design, which is known locally as 'kishti' – meaning compartment. A Bakhtiari expert can tell at a glance what are the distinguishing features in weave and colour – the warm pinks and leafy greens of Feridan, the firm handle and rich gold of Shalamzar, the stiff robustness of Shahr Kurd, the fine wool but heavy brownish-red shade of Farah Dumbeh, and so on, but no proper survey of the distinguishing features of each village has ever been published. The principal design elements are more or less interchangeable, and in this book the differentiation must be restricted to the following few notes:

Boldaji (fig. 337): a small town on the southern edge of the Chahar Mahal. Makes average-grade single-wefted rugs and carpets in large numbers; they are typical of the production of large parts of the province, with little subtlety of colour or elegance of design, but sound and honest, hard-wearing everyday village goods.

Feridan (fig. 336): at the other end of the scale in the single-wefted types – still robust, but quite fine, with thick pile, a very distinctive, even wayward design (in

331 Shahr Kurd
350 × 245 cm, 119,000 TK/m² (11′ 6″ × 8′ 0″, 77 TK/in.²).
A good-quality carpet from the capital town of Chahar Mahal province; when properly constructed, Shahr Kurd goods can be very robust, but other pieces may appear stronger than they really are.

332 Chahal Shotur
318 × 205 cm, 168,000 TK/m² (10′ 5″ × 6′ 9″, 108 TK/in.²).
Compared with other Bakhtiar goods, Chahal Shotur carpets have that little bit extra to offer – in design, colouring, yarn and weave.

331

332

333 Saman (detail); full size 350 × 250 cm, 141,000 TK/m² (11′ 6″ × 8′ 3″, 91 TK/in.²).
The best Saman goods also hold their own against those of Shahr Kurd and Chahal Shotur; although the Saman weave is slightly less fine, the carpets are distinguished by a magnificent shade of madder-red and a wealth of other vegetable-based colours. Cf. fig. 255 for another detail from this carpet.

334 Shalamzar (detail); full size 310 × 215 cm, 84,000 TK/m² (10′ 2″ × 7′ 1″, 54 TK/in.²).
The carpets of Shalamzar, though double-wefted, are fairly coarse; they often have a densely packed pile and will give excellent wear. The typical border seen here is a useful aid to identification; the panels are less elegant than in the more finely woven goods.

333

334

335 Shalamzar
212 × 155 cm, 125,000 TK/m²
(6′ 11″ × 5′ 1″, 81 TK/in.²). A vase-and-bird design from Shalamzar is shown in fig. 258; the diagonal-panel layout shown here also always includes birds. Note that the dark panels are actually black, which – though not often used in Persia – is very effective in the right setting.

336 Feridan
323 × 178 cm, 132,000 TK/m²
(10′ 7″ × 5′ 10″, 85 TK/in.²).
Another bird design; the whole design is based on only three different panels, but the use of nineteen different shades in a completely random distribution produces a dazzling effect. For a single-wefted Bakhtiar, the weave of this carpet is quite fine.

335

336

which parrots figure prominently), with a huge palette of shades, mostly based on bright natural dyestuffs. Feridan is a small administrative district on the Armenian northern edge of the province. The carpet shown is from Chadegan.

Shalamzar (fig. 335): one of the most attractive of the cheaper double-wefted types, fairly coarse, with a firm but flexible handle and nicely judged colourings, including gold and warm madder red. There is also a distinctive border (as seen in fig. 334), which, however, is not exclusive to Shalamzar. In view of their more reasonable price, these goods often represent the best value for money among Bakhtiari carpets. See also fig. 258.

Shahr Kurd (fig. 331): used to be called 'Deh Kurd' ('Kurdish village') but has now been upgraded – *shahr* means town. It is the capital of the province and centre of the double-wefted production. The use of two wefts makes the carpet feel more solid – although this is deceptive – the carpet is no more hard-wearing just because more cotton has been packed into the back. It is what is on the front that counts, so that a good thick-pile Feridan will easily outlast many a Shahr Kurd. Usually rather bright in colour and stiff in design, it is the double-wefted counterpart to Boldaji, but can also rise to much better grades on occasion.

Saman (fig. 333): one of the finer double-wefted types, better known for rather stiff medallion designs in which a particular brown rose shade is prominent; also produces attractive panel designs.

Chahal Shotur (fig. 332): a village near Shahr Kurd which is universally acknowledged to be the home of the finest Bakhtiars. See fig. 633. Panel designs are made, but they are somewhat rare.

Bibibaff: not a place at all, but literally 'woman's' weave, or – more specifically – 'grandmother's' weave, i.e. particularly fine work.

There is a very odd and limited range of sizes made in the Bakhtiar region: no small rugs, no runners, very few 350 × 250 cm (11′ 6″ × 8′ 3″) carpets. The production thus consists of: dozars; 250 × 150 cm (8′ 3″ × 5′ 0″); kelleyis 320 × 150 cm (10′ 6″ × 5′ 0″); carpets 300 × 200 cm (10′ 0″ × 6′ 6″) and all large sizes from 370 × 270 cm (12′ 0″ × 9′ 0″) upwards. Some places make only dozars, but the majority of villages make most of the sizes. There is still a considerable production using vegetable dyes; these dyes may be found in particular in the many carpets between twenty and thirty years old at present readily available on the market. The vast majority of the region's output is in the panel design, although many other types are also found (see index).

The panels may be arranged diagonally, as in fig. 335, but outside Shalamzar, Chahal Shotur and Bain (figs. 339, 748) this is rare, the rectangular arrangement being much more common. The panels may be arranged to form a pattern (either of colour or of design) in themselves, or they may be put together on a completely random basis. Apart from the motifs illustrated in figs. 147–9, 251–7 and 278, countless other items more or less associated with gardens are encountered, from simple stylized rosettes to fountains and summer-houses.

337 Boldaji
315 × 162 cm, 112,000 TK/m²
(10′ 4″ × 5′ 6″, 72 TK/in.²).
The distinctive tree border and the prominent use of green are easily recognizable features.

338

339

338 Boldaji
238 × 155 cm, 80,000 TK/m²
(7′ 10″ × 5′ 1″, 52 TK/in.²).
A carpet with a strictly rectilinear design typical of the best products among the coarse Bakhtiari peasant weaves. Note the outstanding delicate vegetable colours.

339 Bain
214 × 162 cm, 124,000 TK/m²
(7′ 0″ × 5′ 4″, 80 TK/in.²).
Another rug with outstanding colours; in this example, the curvilinear design reveals that it is a manufactured piece. Note the use of French-style floral bouquets (cf. fig. 711).

340

341

342

343

344

340 Qum (detail);
full size 222 × 139 cm, 277,000 PK/m²
(7′ 3″ × 4′ 7″, 179 PK/in.²).

341 Birjand (detail);
full size 290 × 198 cm, 370,000 PK/m²
(9′ 6″ × 6′ 6″, 240 PK/in.²).

342 Qum weave.

343 Birjand weave.

344 Rumania
350 × 250 cm, 110,000 PK/m²
(11′ 6″ × 8′ 3″, 71 PK/in.²).

340–343 QUM, BIRJAND
The finely woven manufactured panel designs have already been mentioned on p. 73. To distinguish their origins one needs to see the weave, as illustrated in figs. 342, 343. As far as design goes, there is normally a much more limited range of motifs and styles than are to be found in the Bakhtiari area. The colours can also be quite crude, Qums in particular having a sharp bright red. However, careful washing of raw new carpets can soften and harmonize the tones and some of the results can be quite brilliant. Qums are made with a pile either of wool, of wool with some motifs in silk, or entirely of silk. Birjands usually have an all-wool pile, but some pieces with part-silk are also found. The panel design is fairly rare in Birjand, though quite common in Qum, where it is woven in dozars, zaronims and all standard carpet sizes (but not runners).

344 RUMANIA
The panel design lends itself readily to copying under manufacturing conditions, but great skill is needed to compensate for the loss of that spontaneity which so charms us in the peasant Bakhtiari carpets. The version illustrated, in the standard Rumanian Bucureşti quality, avoids the strident colours often used in this type of merchandise and manages to pack in a great deal of detail, with almost all the panels being treated as *mihrabs*, rather as though the overall design were a cross between a garden design and a multi-panel *saph* (see figs. 287, 288). However, the composition inevitably has a rather mechanical appearance and one is left wondering whether a fine machine-made carpet would not be equally acceptable.

345–347 KERMAN
Two very much better manufactured carpets are shown here. If Erdmann is right, the garden design originated in Kerman. The top designers of that city have always delighted in the design and to this day produce remarkable versions which owe nothing to Bakhtiari originals. The style illustrated in fig. 345 is mostly woven in the so-called 100/50 quality (about 500,000 knots/m²; 320 knots/in.²), the finest grade made in Kerman today, and is generally available only in quite large carpet sizes. The particular piece shown here is, however, in the 80/40 grade, the established standard quality of the best manufacturers in Kerman.

Fig. 347 shows a further example of current Kerman design and colouring skill, which may be compared with fig. 346 – an eighteenth-century piece using the same design. The museum piece represents a simplification of the original Chosroes garden designs; instead of trying to illustrate a complete formal garden the layout is reduced to produce a simple medallion design. The brooks, though, are retained and we are reminded of the concept of Paradise as four gardens beneath which waters flow. The modern Kerman is available in a range of carpet sizes from about 7 m² to 12 m² (80–130 ft²) and, like fig. 346, is woven in the 80/40 quality. If only the quality of the weaving in Kerman were as good as the work of the designers and colourists, the city could still lay claim today to the pre-eminence allotted to it by A. C. Edwards, who wrote in 1948: 'Forty years ago, when she turned from shawls to carpets, Kerman took the lead and she has held it ever since.' And again: '... the best carpets in the world are conceived and woven by its people.' Regrettably, this is no longer so, the fabric being deficient from beginning to end. Kerman's designers are, however, unrivalled anywhere. More detailed notes on Kerman will be found in the last section of this book (see p. 292).

348, 349 OWLAD, YALAMEH

When 'Owlad' carpets first appeared on the market in Isfahan, foreign buyers did not know what their origin was, and the seller – sensing that he had an exclusive and potentially lucrative line – did not wish to reveal his source and described the origin as 'Pashkuhi', a name which has stuck. Meanwhile, the buyers went away, proud to be able to impress their friends and competitors with their new-found knowledge of a tribe which had not previously been known to weave carpets.

345 Kerman (detail),
full size 266 × 186 cm, 325,000 loops/m²
(8′ 9″ × 6′ 1″, 210 loops/in.²).

346 North-west Persian garden carpet, eighteenth century; originally larger – present size
376 × 264 cm, 87,000 TK/m²
(12′ 4″ × 8′ 8″, 56 TK/in.²).
Victoria and Albert Museum, London.

347 Kerman
327 × 232 cm, 330,000 loops/m²
(10′ 9″ × 7′ 7″, 213 loops/in.²).

345

346

347

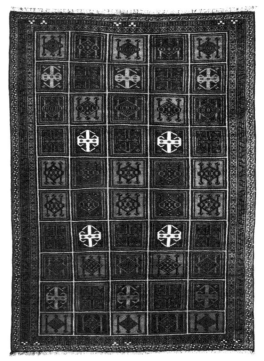

348 Owlad/Pashkuhi (detail);
full size 308 × 215 cm, 55,000 TK/m²
(10′ 1″ × 7′ 1″, 35 TK/in.²).

However, Pashkuhi could be translated roughly as 'over the hills and far away'. The name by which these rugs are more properly known – Owlad – is itself open to doubt, for the word simply means 'clan' or 'tribe'. There are many *owlads* in the Bakhtiar region, but the one with which we are concerned is a group of Lurs (or perhaps Bakhtiars) living near Naghun in the Zagros mountains on the south-western edge of the Chahar Mahal.

The name Pashkuhi had an official existence in earlier times. In pre-Safavid Persia the peoples of the Zagros mountains were divided into the Great Lurs in the south and Little Lurs in the north. The main tribes of the Great Lurs were the Bakhtiari, Mamassani and Kuhgalu; the northern group was divided into Pish-Kuhi and Pusht-i-Kuhi (or Pash-Kuhi), meaning cis- and ultramontane. It is unlikely that these ancient administrative divisions have anything to do with the Owlad carpets of Naghun. The design shown here is quite different from the main body of Owlad designs and obviously shows Bakhtiari influence, but it is easily distinguished from the Bakhtiar carpets of the Chahar Mahal by the stiff simplistic design and the gloomy blue and red colour combination from which all the lighter rose, gold, cream, and green shades of the Bakhtiar carpets are absent.

Another tribal group living in the province of Chahar Mahal va Bakhtiari are the Yalamehs, who are settled mainly in villages around Talkhuncheh. Full details of their production are given on p. 217. The designs, colours, construction, range of sizes made and materials used are quite unlike those of the Bakhtiaris, but the panel or garden idea is frequently used in various forms. Fig. 349 illustrates a typical example.

Outside the Bakhtiari region there are various tribal and peasant designs in which the field is divided into panels. For the most part these have no discernible connection with the eighteenth-century garden design. There are, for example, Turkoman carpets in which the göls are set in panels; the Genje-type pieces (see figs. 439–442) are another group. A few individual items are illustrated in the following pages; the rest will be found in the sections devoted to all-over designs and repeating medallion designs.

350 BELUCH
Large parts of western Afghanistan and eastern Iran are populated by nomadic and semi-nomadic Beluch tribes who make prayer rugs of the type illustrated in figs. 313–9 and the long narrow pieces shown in figs. 434–6. The respective Afghan or Persian origin of these rugs is fairly easy to distinguish. However, when it comes to the carpet sizes woven in the area the distinctions are less clear. The type shown in fig. 476 is generally found in Herat, the one in fig. 350 more often in Meshed, but there are many pieces which could be from either side of the border. The carpet illustrated here has woollen warps, which is fairly unusual for modern Persian Beluch goods (although universal in Afghan Beluchis). The design shows Turkoman influence, both in the panels (cf. fig. 400) and the border (cf. figs. 419, 427, 430), and indeed the very idea of a panel design among Beluch goods seems somehow foreign to their normal design concepts. The colours of this type are also rather untypical of the Meshed Beluch style, being lighter in overall tone and using an attractive rusty shade of red. One disadvantage for many buyers is that the sizes made tend to be long and narrow, not only in the rug format illustrated but also in carpet sizes, where dimensions like 400 × 250 cm (13′ 0″ × 8′ 0″) are not uncommon. For a detail of the border of a similar rug see fig. 101.

351 QUCHAN
The designs used in the Kurdish enclave around Quchan, north of Meshed in eastern Persia, have been subjected to a multiplicity of influences over many centuries. It was the rising power of the Ottomans that first drove this group of Kurds out of the Caucasus and Anatolia; but they lived in various parts of Persia before being moved for political reasons to the Turkoman frontier region. They thus brought with them designs which had already been influenced by the upheavals of

349 Yalameh
300 × 213 cm, 140,000 PK/m²
(9′ 10″ × 7′ 0″, 90 PK/in.²).

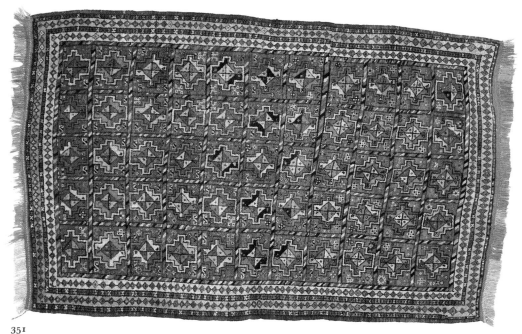

350

351

fifteenth- and sixteenth-century Asia. The area where they settled is also the meeting point of at least three types of design: the small repeating patterns of the Beluchis, the bolder patterns of the Turkomans and the endlessly varied town manufactory designs of Khorassan and Meshed. The latter mostly have little influence on Quchan rugs. Most apparent in the designs are the traditions of their Caucasian origin, but Turkoman and Beluch influence is also very strong. The carpet shown in fig. 351 reveals the typical synthesis that results: one can see the connections with other styles but the carpet nonetheless has a markedly independent style of its own. Notes on the Quchan construction will be found on p. 195.

352 GEBBEH

The simplest form of panel design, whose appeal lies largely in the colour combinations (as in the work of Paul Klee or other twentieth-century painters), crops up fairly often in the tribal rugs of Fars province. Sometimes the panels are completely plain, as seen here, but in other pieces tiny motifs appear at random, giving a similar effect to that seen in the well-known kilims of the region. The loose structure of these very decorative rugs often suggests a Luri origin, but they may be made anywhere between the Owlad area and the Persian Gulf coast. Further notes on Gebbeh rugs are given elsewhere (see index).

353–355 THE 'ENSSI'

The *enssi* (or *engsi*) has always excited the interest of collectors both for the unusual layout of the design and for the exceptional workmanship that is usually put into it. Considerable confusion has been caused in respect of this design by the contention that the *enssis* are prayer rugs, but now it seems fairly certain that they are not. Their use is described by Károly Gombos in an excellent essay (*Heimtex*, April 1979) on the treasures of the Budapest Museum of Applied Art. He writes:

Almost all Turkoman women wove carpets . . . especially among the nomadic tribes with their own flocks, where the raw materials were readily available . . . The Turkomans used hand-knotted products for many purposes. It is generally true of the Orient that furniture was little used, even in town houses. This was especially the case, however, with the animal-breeding peoples, for whom it was vital that all household items should be easily transportable and should fit into the yurt, which itself had to be easy to construct and dismantle and carry from place to place. The yurt, in which the nomadic Turkomans lived, was no more than a circular felt tent on a wooden lattice frame. Its average diameter was about twenty feet, the inside height about ten feet. The total weight, including the wooden frame and all accessories, was about three hundredweight, which is the

350 Beluch
238 × 138 cm, 169,000 PK/m²
(7′ 10″ × 4′ 6″, 109 PK/in.²).

351 Quchan
249 × 161 cm, 59,000 TK/m²
(8′ 2″ × 5′ 3″, 38 TK/in.²).

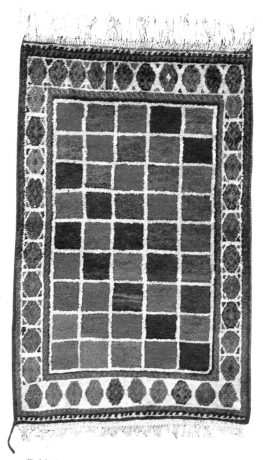

352 Gebbeh
174 × 102 cm, 68,000 TK/m²
(5′ 8″ × 3′ 4″, 44 TK/in.²).

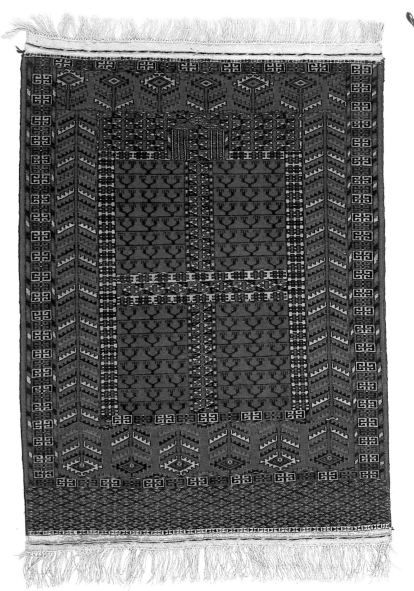

353

354

353 Bokhara enssi
134 × 100 cm, 310,000 PK/m²
(4′ 5″ × 3′ 3″, 200 PK/in.²).

354 Kaldar enssi
249 × 171 cm, 205,000 PK/m²
(8′ 2″ × 5′ 7″, 132 PK/in.²).

average load for a camel . . . Inside the yurt everyone had his assigned place, determined by strict customs. Opposite the entrance, behind the hearth, was the place for the guest, to the right were the womenfolk, the provisions and the household implements, while on the left, on the men's side, were the clothes, the saddles and the harnesses. In the centre, under the dome-shaped roof, lay the hearth. The servants' place was beside the entrance. The chieftains owned yurts of the richest equipment and adornment, but even the simplest yurt would be decorated with a woven tent-band, a *kapunuk* (knotted arch shape hanging over the entrance) and an *engsi* (tent entrance curtain). The floor of the yurt was covered with felt carpeting, on top of which lay pile carpets . . . The wooden frame opposite the entrance was hung on the inside with pile bags, usually two *chovals* and two *torbas* . . . The *kapunuk*, *engsi* and tent-band (*yolami*) were on the outside . . . The carpet accompanied the Turkoman from the cradle to the grave . . . The pile-carpet was used for the trousseau bag, the swathing cushion, the cradle, the corn storage bag, the salt container, the comb and mirror bag. It was used for the saddle-cover, the belt, the fodder-bag and the knapsack of the proud Turkoman riders, and to this day it is employed for the magnificent covers and hangings of the camel that carries the Turkoman bride as well as the many bags and containers for the bridal yurt . . . We must look more closely at the Turkoman prayer rugs and the *engsi* carpets which were used as tent doors, since these two types are often confused by scholars and collectors alike . . . Yet it is very easy to distinguish the two. The prayer rug is always smaller than the *engsi*; even more important is the appearance of a horn-shaped motif above the mihrab [see fig. 321] . . . In

the Turkoman language *engsi* is unambiguous: it means tent entrance-curtain....
Its form and proportions were determined by the size of the yurt; it is usually
100–140 cm wide and 150–170 cm high.

Gombos goes on to explain that the *mihrab* shape which appears at the top of some
enssis (fig. 325, for example) does not indicate that they were intended as prayer
rugs (it is hardly likely that the nomad would take down his tent door five times a
day to pray). This arch-shape is a relic of pre-Islamic Turkoman symbolism,
representing the shape of the yurt itself, meaning home and security. The cross-
shaped layout of the centre of the *enssi* led to the use of the word *hatchlu* (derived
from the Turkish word for cross) to describe these rugs. Gombos disputes the theory
that the cross shape derives from that of the mighty door panels of the buildings of
Khiva or Bokhara, but does not suggest an alternative explanation. Cammann puts
forward the interesting idea that the *enssi* represents not only a physical but also a
metaphysical door: the four panels depict, he claims, the four gardens promised to
the Muslim in innermost Paradise. This cannot be proved, of course, but would
accord well with Gombos's insistence on the supreme importance of the yurt as the
home and the symbolical centre of Turkoman life. Whether there is thus a connection with the Persian garden carpets of figs. 327–49 it is impossible to say: as
with all Turkoman designs, the origin of the *enssi* patterns must remain a mystery
since we possess no really old examples. Perhaps further research will reveal evidence
in other art forms which will throw light on the matter.

A nineteenth-century *enssi* is illustrated in fig. 325; figs. 353–355 show examples
of modern production in this design. The finest examples of all are made in factories
in Kabul, capital of Afghanistan, but outstanding pieces may be found in all the
traditional Turkoman areas as well. There are also countless imitation *enssis* from
Pakistan, in every lurid colour for which that country is notorious. The Suleiman
(fig. 355) comes from the Andkhoy region and is woven in the typical standard grade
of that area. Within this category one may find pieces in every rug size which are
clearly not intended for practical use: they are produced commercially for export
and merely draw on the *enssi* design for decorative purposes. They may also be
found with only two panels, sometimes indeed with only one. The Chodor piece
from Kaldar on the Amu Darya (fig. 354), the frontier between Afghanistan and
the U.S.S.R., is of exceptional quality, with a splendidly balanced firm and flexible
handle. The göls of the border and of the cross-beam are those of the Chodor tribe,
known to us from nineteenth-century carpets but nowadays submerged among the
other tribes of Afghanistan. The 'Bokhara' *enssi* (fig. 353) is of a type woven in
Ashkabad, the capital of the Turkoman S.S.R. Here, too, one finds pieces in quite
small sizes, produced solely for export.

Among interesting design features in all *enssis* one may draw attention to: the
trees and other motifs of plant (or perhaps bird) origin which feature within the
panels and also in the borders; the extremely diverse patterns used in the beams of
the 'cross', which may include many different göls (see fig. 399), but sometimes
suggest the brooks between the gardens of the eighteenth-century garden carpets;
and the unusual asymmetrical panel at the bottom of the rug whose function in the
layout of the design has never been explained. Note also that in *enssis* actually used
as yurt doors there is no fringe at the top of the rug: the kilim is left unfinished and is
simply turned over and sewn to the back of the rug. An additional plait of material
is woven into the top kilim and used to produce loops at both top corners by which to
suspend the rug; this is clearly visible in fig. 354. Almost without exception *enssis*
have red grounds.

355 Suleiman enssi
204 × 150 cm, 167,000 PK/m²
(6′ 8″ × 4′ 11″, 108 PK/in.²).

7 PICTURE DESIGNS; ANIMAL AND BIRD DESIGNS

356 Chinese pile rug in 'tapestry' style; 184 × 143 cm, 110,000 PK/m² (6′ 1″ × 4′ 8″, 71 PK/in.²). Cf. note to fig. 381.

357 Kerman 335 × 200 cm, 504,000 PK/m² (11′ 0″ × 6′ 7″, 325 PK/in.²).

Strong pictorial elements may be noted in several categories of design illustrated in the preceding pages, from willow trees and nightingales to vases and mosques. But although the borderline between a real picture and one which simply contains representational elements is ill-defined, very few of them could be called fully fledged pictures.

Of course, the finer the weave the easier it is to produce a pictorial effect. In fact, however, picture rugs tend not to be dependent on fineness of stitch but more on local tradition. The representation of human or other figures in art is forbidden to Muslims – not in the Koran, as is sometimes asserted, but in the *hadith*, the sayings attributed to the Prophet (cf. p. 136). Some areas observe the injunction rigidly but others disregard it entirely. It is often said that the interpretation of this rule depends on which of the two main Muslim sects the weaver belongs to – i.e. that the Sunni Muslims of Turkey and Afghanistan interpret the dogma most strictly, while the Shi'a doctrine, which gained complete ascendancy in Persia from about 1500 onwards, is much more liberal in its attitude. However, this is one of those facile explanations prevalent in the carpet trade which are passed on from writer to writer with no attempt to check the evidence. It may be convenient to explain the differences in this way, but it is a theory which has no basis in fact.

Sunna is an ancient Arabic word, which, before the advent of Islam, meant the acceptance of convention, respect for the ancestral customs of the tribe. It was thus as much a political and social term as a religious one. In the Islamic world it retained this force. At the root of its application is the belief that Muhammad was the last of the Prophets and received the final revelation of God's word. Anything beyond or after what was revealed to the Prophet is beyond the pale and must be expunged. The *sunna* came to be equated with the practice and precept of the Prophet as set down in the Koran and related in the *hadith*. One of the sayings expresses the extreme Sunni view: 'The worst things are those that are novelties. Every novelty is an innovation, every innovation is an error and every error leads to hell-fire.' The worst offences in Islamic law were *bida* and *ghuluww*, innovation and excess, two forms of going beyond traditions, showing disrespect for the belief in the finality of the revelations of the Prophet. Elsewhere, however, the *hadith* states: 'Difference of opinion in my community is evidence of Divine mercy.' The differences between Muslim sects often hinge upon the question of where to draw the line between difference of opinion and genuine *bida* or *ghuluww*. In the end it is the political aspect of the *sunna* which decides the issue: the Muslim creed tolerates almost any variant interpretation as long as it is not subversive and represents no danger to the fabric of society or the power of its rulers. Shi'ism also arose for political reasons. After the death of Muhammad in 632 AD, the leader of the movement, the Caliph, was elected by his disciples. However, the rivalries among the various factions in Mecca exploded into civil war. In AD 656 the third Caliph, Uthman, was murdered by supporters of Ali, Muhammad's cousin and son-in-law, who was proclaimed his successor. Uthman however, had been the leader of one of the most powerful pre-Islamic clans of Mecca, the Umayya, and for twenty-five years there was bitter

357

conflict between the Umayyads and the Shi'at Ali – Ali's party, who came to be known simply as the Shi'a. Ali himself was murdered, and the climax came when his son Husayn, the Prophet's grandson, and his Shi'ite followers were massacred on the tenth day of Moharram, 61 AH (AD 680).

The Sunni Umayyads preserved their power; but the Shi'a sect had their martyr and for centuries remained an opposition group, questioning the very validity of the power of the Caliph. This 'questioning' stance was paralleled in theological argument, too. Muslim theologians had a duty to use their reason and judgment in interpreting the Koran and the *hadith*. According to the Sunni view, this process was completed by *c.* AD 900, by which time, by general consensus, all the important questions had been answered. The Shi'ites rejected this view and claimed the right to continue innovative interpretation of the *sharia*, the Holy Law. In fact, however, both the political and theological differences between the Sunnis and Shi'ites were purely theoretical. In practice the Shi'ites were just as conservative as the Sunnis, and the Sunnis just as independent in their judgements as the Shi'ites.

By the thirteenth century the Shi'a survived only among isolated groups. The simultaneous attacks of the Crusaders in the west and the Mongols in the east led to a closing of the ranks behind Sunni orthodoxy. Dissenters then began to turn to the Sufi mystic movement. This had its roots in the teachings of several ascetics at the very beginning of the spread of Islam. By the tenth century it was a recognized movement within Islam which concentrated less on the law and dogma of the Koran and the *hadith*, more on their implications for man's soul and the search for his inner self. The Sufis were organized into brotherhoods, like little monasteries, each headed by a sheikh (the Arabic word for spiritual master). In the course of time the followers of certain sheikhs were seen as clearly defined religious orders, like those of Christianity. Different orders came to be identified with different objectives: some were missionaries, others looked after the poor, and some had a decidedly political bent, the sheikhdom passing from father to son in hereditary succession. Sufism placed much greater emphasis on respect for individual teachers than did orthodox Muhammadanism, and this gave new impetus to Shi'ism. The Shi'a had always venerated Ali, and one group – the Twelver Shi'a – had set up eleven of his descendants as saintly leaders above all others, calling them the Imams (it is said that the return of the twelfth, who disappeared in the ninth century, will coincide with the Day of Judgement). Now the Sufi convents threw up new leaders to be individually revered, among them Sheikh Safi ad-Din al-Ardabili, who founded an order in Ardebil (north-west Persia) early in the fourteenth century. After his death in 1334 his successors began expanding the order, setting up cells in most parts of Persia and eastern Anatolia. By 1450 the Safawiyya, as they were called, were claiming the temporal title of Sultan for their leaders; and in 1501 Sheikh Ismail took advantage of a rebellion of Shi'a Turkomans against their Ak Koyunlu masters in eastern Anatolia to seize power in Azerbaijan. The Turkomans (known as the Kizil Bash, and so called on account of their red headgear) had been adherents of the Ardebil convent for decades and now provided Sheikh Ismail with the élite troops he needed to sweep away the crumbling Mongol power and declare himself Shah of Iran. Within ten years he established a powerful empire dominating western central Asia, with Shiism as the state religion. His military strength, his expansionist policies and his control of the silk trade routes aroused the emnity of the Ottomans, who declared a holy war and called upon all orthodox Sunnis to quell the heretic.

Thus, at the beginning of the sixteenth century, when the fundamental changes in carpet design referred to on p. 274 took place, there were opposed two mighty powers, Turkey and Iran, the one Sunni, the other Shi'ite; it is quite clear that in this context the religions must be thought of as a political force. The old Shi'a 'questioning' attitude, the willingness to accept innovations, were harnessed to fire the nationalist cause and renew the ancient independence of the Persian state, while the Sunni traditionalism and respect for the established order were used by the Ottomans to secure the political *status quo* and as propaganda to sustain the troops against a dangerous military threat in the east at a time when their main concern was with the thrust into the Balkans in the west. The effect of the two doctrines on carpet design was minimal. The powerful anti-dogmatic influence of Sufism, which

358

359

existed in both sects, may have had a role to play. But if the great changes in Persian carpets were linked with the resurgence of Shi'ism then the latter is an expression of the changes, not their cause.

There is no want of evidence in the art of the Islamic world that Muslim sovereigns, like rulers everywhere, were not at all scrupulous in observing the rules – in this case those concerning representational art. As Cammann has pointed out, we have – from the Sunni courts of Moghul India and Ottoman Turkey – thousands of paintings of supposedly forbidden subjects, and in the realm of carpet design itself the Ottoman Court manufactories of Bursa and Cairo and the Indian manufactories of Lahore produced rugs just as floral as any of the Safavid Persian goods. In works destined for the imperial or royal courts the artists could quite freely represent flowers, animals, and even people, depending on the relative liberality of their patrons' views. It was the much more conservative common people, perhaps following very literal-minded spiritual leaders, who interpreted the religious rules more strictly; and one may add that from a practical standpoint – without the benefit of graph-paper loom-drawings – they were obliged to adopt geometric stylization anyway. Above all, as Grote-Hasenbalg convincingly argues, the courtly art neither impressed nor influenced the style of the traditionalist weavers in their mountain villages, and when the economic foundation for the Safavid extravagance collapsed and the elaborate designs disappeared, the village weavers continued making traditional geometric designs as before.

Today's picture designs thus fall into three main categories:

(1) the guardedly geometric figures and animals of certain tribal and village areas;

(2) those used by the successors of the ancient court tradition, the town manufactories in Tabriz, Kerman, Qum and elsewhere, producing goods largely for export;

(3) those of non-Muslim areas like China, Kashmir and the Christian parts of Iran and the Caucasus (e.g. Armenian districts).

360 KERMAN

Kerman was well known before the First World War for its exceptionally fine carpets made for export in a wide range of designs. Of these, the most spectacular were the curiosities depicting kings of England, Emperors, figures from the Bible etc., examples of which still turn up on the international auction market from time to time; one such is illustrated here. These carpets were woven in various villages of the Kerman region from about 1890 onwards, just as fine Kermans still are

358 Majnun throws himself on Layla's tomb, Indian miniature painting illustrating a mid-fifteenth-century romance; this is a typical example of the secular representational art that flourished at the court of the Sunni Moghul emperors.

359 The Muhammadan creed on a seventeenth-century pulpit title dating from the time of the Sunni Ottoman empire; the naturalistic floral pattern would, strictly, be forbidden if the *hadith* were to be interpreted literally. Victoria and Albert Museum, London.

360

361

360 Laver Kerman
249 × 178 cm, 1,640,000 PK/m²
(8′ 2″ × 5′ 10″, 1,056 PK/in.²). Victoria and Albert
Museum, London.

361 Tabriz
290 × 201 cm, 320,000 TK/m²
(9′ 6″ × 6′ 7″, 206 TK/in.²).

362 Tabriz
158 × 117 cm, 120,000 TK/m²
(5′ 2″ × 3′ 10″, 77 TK/in.²).

362

today. One village, north of the city, is called Ravar, and this is the name which is used for whole production, though normally in the corrupt spelling Laver.

361 TABRIZ
The modern equivalents of rugs of the above types are pieces like this Tabriz example. Most fine-weave manufacturing centres – Kashan, Qum, Birjand, Nain etc. – are capable of producing this sort of item but the vast majority come from Isfahan or Tabriz. Other designs have included the heads of famous figures, e.g. John F. Kennedy or the late Shah of Iran. Rugs of this kind are especially popular with Persian retailers, who feature them on the walls of their shops in both Persia and Europe. A similar type of merchandise is produced for the tourist trade in Afghanistan.

362 TABRIZ
A certain curiosity value attaches to the banknotes, flags, maps and similar designs woven in parts of Turkey, as well as Tabriz in north-west Persia, about 60–70 years ago. A typical example is illustrated.

Another interesting type, found in Isfahan, is a pile-rug chessboard. It is not as easy as it might seem to weave a chessboard – few weavers anywhere can get the tension on the loom exactly right to produce a perfectly square shape (which more-over must not curl at the edges) of anything less than about a square metre (or yard). One trick is to weave half a dozen all together on one loom and cut them up afterwards – this minimizes the risk of distortion. Chessboard designs are not only woven in Isfahan: Tibetan weavers, for example, produce much coarser but still quite attractive examples. Items of this sort are all harmless fun, and there will no doubt always be collectors interested in curiosities of this kind, but we must turn elsewhere for rugs in which the pictorial style is not an end in itself but is made subservient to the weaver's artistic goal.

357, 363, 364 HUNTING DESIGNS
There has always been a great classical tradition of carpets depicting hunting scenes. The earliest known carpet includes pictures of elks (fig. 56), and one of the most famous of all the Shah Abbas carpets, a sixteenth-century silk hunting carpet now in Vienna (cf. fig. 365) is filled with motifs of horsemen spearing or shooting deer and other animals.

Today the home of the hunting rug is Qum (fig. 363), although examples of very similar designs are found elsewhere: Isfahan, Veramin, and Kerman, for example, all produce rugs which the layman might confuse with fig. 363, and a similar design is woven in silk in China – one of the latest developments in the realm of carpet design. The Qum rugs may be wool with silk or all silk, and vary from tiny pushtis (say, 60 × 40 cm; 2′ 0″ × 1′ 3″) to carpets about 4 m² (43 ft²) in area. Hunting rugs are often noticeably better in quality and colouring than other Qums – they represent, as it were, a manufacturer's *pièce de résistance*. The Kerman shown in fig. 357 is of a similar class.

Tabriz, too, can 'make any design' and traditionally has several versions of the hunting scene woven in all sizes; fig. 364 illustrates a typical example. The Tabriz hunting design is often woven in a much coarser stitch than this, and although the Tabriz design style often has a rather stiff appearance the degree of realism achieved can be quite remarkable despite the low knot-count.

365 KASHMIR
The hunting designs shown in the preceding illustrations are all-over 'one way' patterns. But it need not be so. Many of the great classical Persian carpets which are the inspiration of modern hunting designs have medallions, with the animals and figures distributed around them. The most famous of these – and, along with the Ardebil carpet (fig. 702), undoubtedly the most famous among all oriental carpets – is the silk hunting carpet in the collection of the Museum für angewandte Kunst in Vienna. This piece is believed to have been woven in Kashan or some other central Persian manufactory about the middle of the sixteenth century. With over $1\frac{1}{2}$

363 Qum
202 × 133 cm, 390,000 PK/m²
(6′ 7″ × 4′ 4″, 252 PK/in.²).

364 Tabriz
171 × 125 cm, 191,000 TK/m²
(5′ 7″ × 4′ 1″, 123 TK/in.²).

365 Kashmir (detail);
full size 441 × 301 cm, 570,000 PK/m²
(14′ 5″ × 9′ 10″, 368 PK/in.²).

million knots/m² (970 knots/in.²), it is the finest of the Safavid carpets. The design is not symmetrical, the figures illustrating a large-scale Court hunt in which more than fifty hunters chase a total of 157 animals. We know from contemporary reports that the Safavid monarchs treated their courtiers and guests to elaborately prepared hunts in netted-off areas of woodland in which hundreds or even thousands of animals were trapped. The word 'paradise' is derived from the Persian term for an enclosed hunting park.

It has already been noted that Kashmir can reproduce more or less any design. The piece depicted in fig. 365 represents one of the pinnacles of modern Indian weaving. When properly executed (one must always make this reservation when speaking of Kashmir), these carpets are in no sense inferior to those of the fine Persian manufactories. There was a time when one bought Indian rugs because they were cheaper than Persians; today there are many occasions when one should consider buying the Indians because they are better.

366

367

366 Kashmar
290 × 194 cm, 187,000 PK/m²
(9′ 6″ × 6′ 4″, 121 PK/in.²).

367 Kerman armori
202 × 137 cm, 500,000 loops/m²
(6′ 7″ × 4′ 6″, 323 loops/in.²).

Naturally, for a design as complex as this a very fine weave and large format are necessary. Modern copies such as this example are therefore fairly rare. It is also extremely difficult to copy the colours of the original: its ground colour is a subtle shade of peach which is almost impossible to reproduce accurately; and the whole carpet is a nightmare for the photographer, the silk pile having such a brilliant sheen that the colours change when viewed from different angles.

366 KASHMAR

The town of Kashmar in Khorassan province, between Meshed and Birjand, weaves carpets in a variety of styles and in a stitch which may also be described as intermediate between Meshed and Birjand. The design shown here, which has become established as 'typical' of Kashmar, in fact originated in Tabriz, where it is still occasionally produced. It is called *Zirhaki*, i.e. 'under the earth', and represents items found in some of the thousands of ancient archaeological sites of Iran – pots, vases, statuettes, mythical figures, etc. The centre of the medallion often incorporates a further picture of a mosque or some other building (also a feature of some Kashan rugs). Kashmar carpets are not cheap and the design can often look wild, but, once the crude new colours have been toned down by age or washing, the carpets have enormous appeal and their unique design makes them rather special. They are made mainly in standard metric sizes: 300 × 200 cm (10′ 0″ × 6′ 6″), 350 × 250 cm (11′ 6″ × 8′ 3″) and 400 × 300 cm (13′ 0″ × 10′ 0″); rug sizes are rare, especially in the design illustrated. Naturally, with so much detail to be accommodated, the design is most effective in the larger sizes. Apart from the design illustrated, Kashmar is also noted for new carpets in the traditional Kashan style (see p. 298).

367, 368 KERMAN ARMORI

The coat-of-arms of the Shah of Iran is a design motif which figured frequently in Persian carpets made before the 1979 revolution. The traditional symbols – rising sun, lion and sword – may appear in rugs from any Persian source, from the simplest geometric rug designs of the nomads and villagers to the finest products of town manufactories. The piece illustrated comes from Kerman; it was made in very small quantities in the finest stitch now employed there, the so-called 100/50 quality, which means 100 warp strings (i.e. 50 knots) to the *gireh* (about 7 cm; 2¾ in.) in the width of the carpet and 50 knots in the length. 'Armori' rugs of this kind are usually found on red or blue grounds and in sizes of about 3 or 4 m² (30 to 40 ft²).

368 Lion and Sun depicted on a thirteenth-century tile from Kashan.

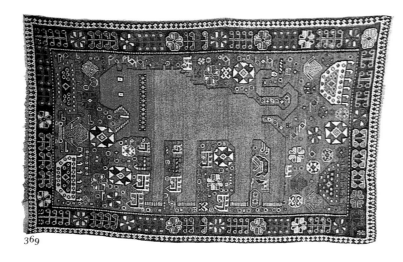

369

370

369 Lion (and other animals) depicted in a Qashqai gebbeh rug.

370 Lion depicted in an old Caucasian rug.

371 Shahr Babak
180 × 137 cm, 220,000 PK/m²
(5′ 11″ × 4′ 6″, 142 PK/in.²).

372 Qashqai 'horse'
(a representation of a head from a pillar at the palace of Darius at Persepolis).

373 Camel and bird motifs in a Qashqai gebbeh.

374 Peacocks filling the ground of a Beluch rug.

375 Deer slipped into the corner of a Kolyai rug.

371

372

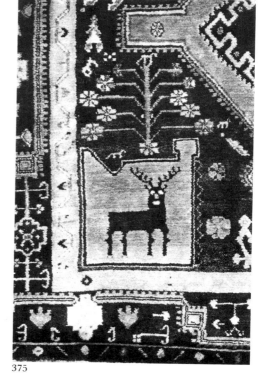

373

374

375

376

377

378

369–375 ANIMAL MOTIFS IN TRIBAL RUGS
The Shahr Babak group of Afshar villages often incorporate bird and animal motifs into their rugs, sometimes in great profusion, as shown here. The Afshars are probably the most prolific of all the Persian tribes in this respect, but other places of origin and their typical pictorial elements are illustrated. (Notes on these origins will be found in other sections of this book – see index.) The Qashqai lion rug (fig. 369) belongs to a special category woven by various tribes of Fars province; the lion seems to be related to the stone figures which since pre-Islamic times been placed over the graves of fallen heroes in this region.

376 YÜRÜK
The nomads of Anatolia, as may be judged from the history of the area outlined in several places in this book (see index), are racially so mixed that it is often not possible today to apply a specific name to them. They are thus simply known under the generic name of Yürük, which means 'mountain people'. The charming naive rug shown here is something of a rarity. Its origin may perhaps be sought in the trade-mark (which features three camels being led by a man) of one of the great carpet-manufacturing companies established in Anatolia before the First World War. Perhaps a peasant weaver thought the pattern would be a good basis for a design into which he could also introduce his own imaginative embellishments.

377 GHURIAN
Pictorial elements are found in several different types of Beluch or Beluch-style rug. The mosque-pattern of the prayer rug in fig. 313 is one example; the birds illustrated in fig. 374 are another. An important group of Persian Beluch rugs, produced in a fine weave on woollen warps, features a chicken ('morgh'), which is often used as a talisman in the Orient to ward off the 'evil eye'. The bird is usually set in a plain light-brown square panel in the centre of the rug, with end-panels and border in the typical dark-blue and red shades of Persian Beluch goods. The rug illustrated here, however, comes from Afghanistan, from the region of Ghurian, between Herat and the Persian frontier. Scenes or subjects from Persian history and legend are the inspiration: one is reminded here of the terrifying raids of the wild Mongolian riders of Jinghis Khan who were so sure in their saddles that the whole army seemed to be composed of creatures with the bodies of warriors and the legs of horses.

378 MESHED
The rug illustrated is another quaint pictorial piece of the kind found in areas with a manufacturing tradition, in this case Meshed. The rug shown reveals more of the character of the surrounding villages than of the Meshed town production. The origin of the design is not known. Perhaps it was intended as a *vagireh* (see p. 62); or possibly a weaver who had executed an order for a large figural carpet for a town contractor had some yarn left over and decided to make a small picture rug while the loom drawing was still at his disposal.

376 Yürük
140 × 85 cm, 103,000 TK/m²
(4′ 7″ × 2′ 9″, 66 TK/in.²).

377 Meshed
97 × 154 cm, 210,000 PK/m²
(3′ 2″ × 5′ 0″, 135 PK/in.²).

378 Ghurian
142 × 88 cm, 154,000 PK/m²
(4′ 8″ × 2′ 11″, 99 PK/in.²).

379 Ning-Hsia
190 × 110 cm, 37,000 PK/m²
(6′ 3″ × 3′ 8″, 24 PK/in.²).
Victoria and Albert Museum, London.

380 Pao-Tu
231 × 162 cm, 55,000 PK/m²
(7′ 7″ × 5′ 4″, 35 PK/in.²).

379–385 CHINA AND TIBET

We now turn to the large and important group of pictorial designs from China and Tibet. The subjects represented fall into two main categories: on the one hand, flowers, landscapes and items of everyday life; and on the other, animals, scenes and symbolical objects from Chinese mythology and philosophy.

379

The latter group is the more important, especially in older rugs, several examples of which are included here since, although rugs of this type are no longer made, there are still many thousands of pieces for sale in shops and warehouses all over the world. The most famous and rarest are the dragon-design temple rugs from Ning-Hsia, the province of Inner Mongolia just beyond the Great Wall of China at the heart of the ancient Silk Route. These rugs, made for Buddhist temples and monasteries, have the dragon laid out in sections so as to link up and form a continuous body when the rug was hung, wrapped around a pillar. Note at the base the representation of mountains, clouds and sea, which have appeared on rugs in this stylized form for at least two or three hundred years.

380

Dragons figure prominently in the Chinese rugs of the pre-Revolution period, i.e. before 1950. Such rugs are often named after Pao-Tu, the principal city of Suiyuan Province, but a more accurate attribution of their origin is not possible since almost nothing is recorded about them in the West. A magnificent start was made by Hans Lorentz, whose book *A View of Chinese Rugs* was the first to provide some of the missing details on the fascinating subject of the Chinese carpet, but much more needs to be published before we can speak of a proper documentation of this area. However, from the point of view of identification at least the style is unmistakable. The vast majority of what we know as Pao-Tu rugs have a dark-blue ground, very open in design layout and with a large number of pictorial motifs. The weave is strikingly coarse (on surprisingly thin cotton warps), but the pile is thick and lustrous. Above all, the intense dark blue has a compelling glowing warmth (fig. 382), which is further enhanced by the simplicity of the design. The present example shows a rug with a beige ground, a much rarer type.

In China the dragon is seen as a benign creature, quite unlike the fierce monsters we encounter in Western myths. Traditionally, it is one of the Four Supernatural Creatures, powerful but merciful, and by extension symbolic of the Emperor; it has been called the 'genius of strength and goodness'. It is often depicted, as here, in association with a flaming (or sacred) pearl, the meaning being that the dragon, symbol of the Emperor, is always striving to reach the pearl, the sign of perfection. The fact that the dragons in this carpet have five claws suggests that the piece was made after 1912, since before then only items made for the Emperor or his family were allowed to have five-toed dragons; all other dragons had to be content with four or three toes, according to the rank of the owner. In 1912 the Empire was abolished and thereafter anyone could have five-toed dragons, and of course nearly everyone did. Note that the design has no outlines: instead the colours are separated by an incision in the pile (known as carving).

381

In the late 1920s a new style of manufactured Chinese carpet began to emerge, with a heavy warp and weft, a firm ridged back and a thick pile. All the designs were carved. After the Revolution it was this style which was exclusively adopted by the Communist régime and the older Pao-Tus were banned. Four categories of design were established (entitled 'Esthetic', 'Peking', 'Floral' and 'Self-tone embossed') and a large number of different grades were introduced. A list of these different types will be found in the Introduction. They are made in Tientsin, Peking, Shanghai and many other centres. Dragons are used mainly in the 'Peking' designs, but they are also found in 'Florals'. There was a period during the Cultural Revolution (in the mid-1960s) when dragons, flying horses, mythical dogs and similar motifs strongly associated with China's ancient culture were not considered

381

382

381 Peking
244 × 154 cm, 88,000 PK/m²
(8′ 0″ × 5′ 0″, 57 PK/in.²).

382 Pao-Tu
160 × 100 cm, 93,000 PK/m²
(5′ 3″ × 3′ 3″, 60 PK/in.²).

suitable for use in carpets and other handicraft products, and for some years dragon designs disappeared from the market. However, subsequent political changes led to a reprieve for these old designs and they are now freely available again in the West. From the point of view of draughtsmanship and execution they are extraordinary pieces of work; no other production area of the world achieves a fully pictorial effect with a mere 90,000 knots/m² (58 knots/in.²). Even more stunning are the 'tapestry' style pieces in a slightly finer weave (fig. 356). Every single knot is different: the rug is built up like an incredibly complex jig-saw puzzle with thousands of tiny pieces to produce an effect akin to Impressionist paintings.

382–384

Old Pao-Tu rugs contain countless pictorial motifs, including complete scenes, often made in landscape format (i.e. wider than they are long). In other rugs the scenes appear in 'peep-hole' panels on the intense blue ground, as in fig. 382. For a detailed account of the meanings of the many and various symbols and motifs used the reader should refer to Hans Lorentz's *A View of Chinese Rugs*. The phoenix, as depicted in fig. 383, was the emblem of the Empress, analogous to the dragon symbolizing the Emperor. At its appearance the world was supposed to enjoy peace and happiness. The *feng huang*, to give it its proper name, is not strictly a phoenix in fact, but a mixture of stork, peacock and pheasant. In Chinese art both the dragon and the phoenix were symbols of felicity and complement each other. The story illustrated in fig. 384 is derived from Chinese symbolical legend. Every four thousand years the fungus of immortality grows at the top of a high mountain and lasts for twenty-four hours. The crane, symbolizing divine power, transports the deer, representing mankind, to this hallowed place to eat the fungus. The tree is often depicted with twenty-four leaves.

385

Weaving has been carried on in Tibet for centuries, but until recently the rugs produced there were almost unknown in the West. The change came with the Communist Chinese invasion of 1959, as a result of which many thousands of Tibetans fled to Nepal and northern India, where a considerable weaving industry was established. In Nepal the Swiss Red Cross provided development aid which

383 Pao-Tu
185 × 133 cm, 57,000 PK/m²
(5′ 1″ × 4′ 4″, 37 PK/in.²).

took the very practical form of organization of the production and an outlet for the rugs woven. More recently the Chinese have started their own production in the Tibetan capital, Lhasa, which is the origin of the piece illustrated in fig. 110. The bulk of the production in Tibet proper is in a 200 × 100 cm size (6′ 6″ × 3′ 3″; equivalent to a single bed) the rugs having originally been used to sleep on. They are produced with a soft woollen pile on cotton warps, using the so-called Tibetan knot, a complicated construction with the basic configuration of the Persian knot (although the first knot in the row is Turkish, as it often is in other central and east Asian types which employ the Persian knot). The complications arise from the

385

384 Pao-Tu
122 × 64 cm, 73,000 PK/m²
(4′ 0″ × 2′ 1″, 47 PK/in.²).

385 Tibetan
173 × 94 cm, 57,000 Tibetan knots/m²
(5′ 8″ × 3′ 1″, 37 Tibetan knots/in.²).

fact that the knots are not tied singly but in a whole chain of knots looped over a rod as the row progresses. A full technical explanation of this method is given in Lorentz's book, and an even more detailed portrayal in Philip Denwood's excellent monograph *The Tibetan Carpet*. However, it is also possible to see the technique in operation in Europe, for the same procedure is employed in the carpets made in the State-run Gobelins Manufactory in Paris. (It is not, to the writer's knowledge, used anywhere else in the world.)

In fig. 385 we see the coat-of-arms of the Dalai Lama, the spiritual leader of the Tibetan Buddhists who now lives in exile in India. This is a motif frequently found in the Tibetan refugee carpets made in Nepal. The best of these are of better quality than the Chinese Tibetan rugs, with a thicker pile and chunkier weave. The designs used draw heavily on the treasure-house of traditional symbolism in Chinese culture; this rug features two 'snow-lions' – mythical creatures associated with the Buddha, and perhaps connected with the Chinese lions (or dogs) of Fo (Fo means Buddha). Further notes on this splendid article will be found on pp. 237 and 248.

IV Geometric designs

1 GEOMETRIC ALL-OVER DESIGNS

386 Kolyai shirshekeri
193 × 135 cm, 67,000 TK/m²
(6′ 4″ × 4′ 5″, 43 TK/in.²).
The lattice-work of the field is probably a distant
derivative of sixteenth-century vase designs. See
also fig. 461 and p. 330.

387 Saryk (Sarukh)
311 × 240 cm, 274,000 TK/m²
(10′ 2″ × 7′ 1″, 177 TK/in.²).
This is a nineteenth-century piece; note that the
Turkish knot is very rarely used in Turkoman
carpets today.

There are basically two different types of carpets with repeating geometric patterns. The first, of which fig. 386 is an example, is the more recent in origin since its many different forms represent geometric abstractions of the all-over floral carpets of sixteenth-century east and south-east Persia. The second type is perhaps more interesting since it is much older. It is based on the simple repetition or alternation of one or more geometric motifs. The earliest known antecedents of this layout are the Pazyryk carpet (fig. 56) and the Nineveh floor panels (fig. 57). But in respect of the carpets we use today the oldest known prototypes are the Turkoman pieces of the Seljuq and early Ottoman empires; in 1909 a group of carpet fragments dating from the thirteenth century were discovered in the Ala-ad-Din Mosque (formerly the principal mosque of the Seljuqs) at Konya. Others, perhaps woven in the fourteenth or early fifteenth century, were found at the Eşrefoglu Mosque at Beyşehir, some 45 miles (70 km) from Konya. From about this period onwards there are paintings by Italian, German, Dutch and Flemish masters which depict Anatolian carpets the designs of which are based on repeating geometric polygons, some enclosing figures of animals, others strictly abstract, in a style similar to that of the Persian rug seen in fig. 616, and others again with the more ornate, though still geometric flavour of fig. 390. The stylistic development of these early Anatolian carpets is splendidly set out by Erdmann (see bibliography) and by Charles Grant Ellis in the *Textile Museum Journal* (December 1963).

Erdmann's contention, however, that the Turkomans were the inventors of the technique of knotting is less convincing. His neglect of Bidder's valuable notes (see fig. 238 and p. 248) and his virtual dismissal of the evidence of the Pazyryk carpet from his assessment have very much the air of an adaptation of the facts to suit his theory, which is that the knotting technique originated among the nomads of Central Asia and was not brought to Iran and Western Asia until the Seljuq invasions. The plain fact is that we do not know who first invented the technique. At the time the Pazyryk carpet was woven the Persians were already a major power; but the existence or otherwise of carpet weaving in the time of the Achaemenian kings Kourosh (Cyrus), Darius and Xerxes is not documented. The Achaemenian stylistic features of the Pazyryk carpet do not prove anything: it may have been made *by* them but could just as well have been woven *for* them; and the Nineveh floor panels suggest the style could have had a wide currency over a large area and a long period. Recent scholarship has suggested the Armenian area of the south-western Caucasus as the Pazyryk carpet's origin, but this remains purely speculative. It is moreover by no means impossible that the technique may have been discovered by different peoples at different times.

The root of the attraction of geometric designs for Erdmann and other experts of the German school is their relative genuineness and purity. They *are* more genuine in the sense that they are woven in a traditional style, which once perhaps had a religious basis, handed down over generations from mother to daughter. Each weaver re-interprets the design in her own way, but always within the parameters of her own tribe's cultural heritage. These rugs may thus truly be

387

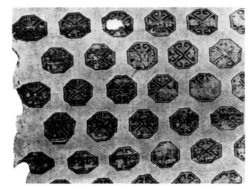

388

389

388 Turkoman carpet (fragment), Konya, thirteenth century.

389 Turkoman carpet (fragment), central or western Anatolia, *c.* 1400.

390 Western Anatolian carpet, sixteenth century. This carpet has stylistic affinities with the geometric Mamluk carpets woven in Cairo in the fifteenth and sixteenth centuries. Similar octagonal motifs are also found in the carpets produced in Spain during the Muslim occupation.

called the expression of a whole people, in the same way as folk-songs are, and unlike the famous carpets of the Persians, which are more often the artistic expression of one individual designer or school of design.

Erdmann adds the theory that the making of the early Turkoman carpets developed as an independent textile art within the limits set by textile techniques, whereas the elaborate designs of Safavid Persia derived from other fields of Islamic art, especially the art of the book. This, he says, is the reason why the Turkish carpet retained its character throughout the period of the seventeenth to nineteenth centuries, when the Safavid traditions in Persia collapsed. This argument, however, contains an element of special pleading: the Safavid designs were produced just as much within the confines of textile techniques – except that the techniques were different from those used by the Turkomans; while the Turkoman designs themselves were unquestionably influenced by other art forms, just as the Persian ones were (cf. fig. 616). The rise and fall of Safavid Persian art is much better explained by Grote-Hasenbalg in the passage quoted on p. 89.

With all the rug-producing tribes of the Orient a wealth of anthropological information is embodied in their carpet designs. One may be struck, for example, by the design affinities between certain nomad or peasant rugs from the Isfahan region of Persia and some of the Kazaks from the Tiflis area of the Caucasus. The reason: both types are made by Luri tribesmen.

Nowhere is this cultural heritage more thoroughly developed than in the carpets of the Turkoman tribes of central Asia, which are illustrated in the following pages. In Asia Minor the Turkoman designs of the Seljuq and early Ottoman era were resolved in later centuries into styles we know as Turkish or Anatolian, rather than specifically Turkoman. Far away from the cosmopolitan influences of Anatolia, however, in the Turkoman heartlands of central Asia – Turkestan – something much closer to the original style was preserved. No central Asian Turkoman carpets have come down to us from the Seljuq or early Ottoman period: the oldest-known pieces are not more than two centuries old, which makes their history less well documented than that of any other carpets of the Orient. But if some Turkoman designs of today seem to show the influence of Persian manufactories (see figs. 163–5) there seems little reason to doubt that others are direct descendants of a style already clearly expressed in the carpets of Anatolia in the thirteenth to sixteenth centuries. Apart from the internal visual evidence, apparent, for example, in a comparison of figs. 388–90 with figs. 391–3, or of figs. 394 and 423 with fig. 422, there is a striking factor: in the two hundred years from the

390

391

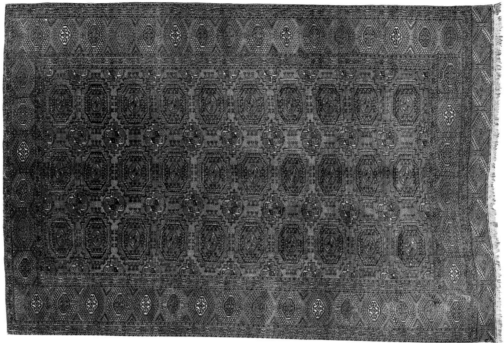

392

393

391 Dali carpet from Kala-i-Zal, Afghanistan.
265 × 195 cm, 140,000 PK/m²
(8′ 8″ × 6′ 5″, 90 PK/in.²).

392 Salor, nineteenth century,
287 × 206 cm, 244,000 PK/m²
(9′ 5″ × 6′ 9″, 157 PK/in.²). See p. 175.

393 New Kizil Ayak, northern Afghanistan,
142 × 73 cm, 92,000 PK/m²
(4′ 8″ × 2′ 5″, 59 PK/in.²). See p. 184.

oldest-known examples to the present day the designs of Turkestan have scarcely changed in essence at all. There is almost nowhere in Persia of which this can be asserted, which lends further support to the idea that the Turkoman designs of today are still quite close to those of 500 years ago and more.

Turkoman influence remains strong in all the areas which the tribes, with their Mongol allies, occupied between six hundred and a thousand years ago. It is evident in the carpets of East Turkestan (figs. 528, 569, 570) and in many parts of Persia (compare, for example, fig. 442 with fig. 441). In some cases in Persia only the names remain, Saruq, for example, or Borchalu (see figs. 645, 639), but in Azerbaijan countless motifs are still in use which reveal the Turkoman legacy. In the Caucasus this is even more marked: fig. 500 shows several examples of Caucasian motifs of Turkoman origin. And, of course, in Anatolia itself there are many designs which still show the imprint of many centuries of Turkoman occupation (compare, for example, fig. 390 with fig. 541). However, when we speak of Turkoman rugs today we mean the products of the area that used to be called West Turkestan. They come from several clearly defined districts (these are shown on the maps on pp. 175, 347): the Bujnurd and Gombad region of north-east Persia, Ashkabad and neighbouring towns, the oases of Merv and Penjdeh, a string of towns along the Amu Darya in Soviet Turkmenistan, a broad strip of northern Afghanistan stretching from Maimana to Kunduz, and isolated parts of western Afghanistan, north of Herat. Like many parts of Asia, this region has been overrun time and

394 A carpet of Anatolian Turkoman origin, of a type often referred to as 'Holbein carpets'; detail from an anonymous painting – *The Somerset House Conference* – dated 1604. The principal göl is still used today in Turkoman carpets (cf. fig. 422). National Portrait Gallery, London.

395 The principal göl (a) seen in fig. 394 embodies simplified 'knot of destiny' motifs. If these are eliminated (b), a simple geometric motif results; variants of it are used throughout the Beluch and Turkoman areas (cf. fig. 319).

395

again, but the Turkomans became established here in a dominant position after successive waves of their tribes poured in between the tenth and fourteenth centuries, first under Seljuq, then accompanying Jinghis Khan and later amid the 'armies' of Timur. After the collapse of Timur's empire various rulers established themselves for greater or longer periods, but for the most part the whole of Turkestan was split into small principalities, originally called Khanates but later known as Emirates. The most important of these was the Khanate of Bokhara, whose capital became the trading centre for most of the carpets of West Turkestan. Relations with Persia were always strained and the Sunni Turkomans often joined in alliance with the Ottomans of the West and raided the Persian frontier areas. However, from *c.* 1700 onwards the Khanates were under constant threat from the north as the power of Muscovite Russia began to expand. At the same time there was constant warfare among the Turkoman tribes themselves and by 1868 most of the northern half of West Turkestan was no more than a Russian protectorate. The final Russian conquest of the whole area took place shortly after the Revolution, and in 1924 the present states were proclaimed – Turkmenistan for the western half, Uzbekistan for the east, with Tajikistan and Khirgizistan forming the link with East Turkestan, which is now in China.

The southern part of old Turkestan became part of Afghanistan when that country's borders were finally established at the end of the nineteenth century. Prior to that it had shared in the amazingly chequered history of Afghanistan. In the time of Darius the Great the whole area was part of the Persian Empire. After Alexander's campaigns Afghanistan, then known as Bactria, was under Greek rule for two hundred years, interrupted by the Parthians from the west (Persia) and the Mauryans from the south (India). During the period of the rise of Rome in the Mediterranean, Bactria saw the beginning of a 1,500-year long series of invasions by nomadic peoples from central or eastern Asia displaced by events in China or Mongolia. The first great Afghan empire of the eastern peoples was that of the Kushans or Yueh-chih, but in the first half of the third century AD the region again became part of Persia under the Sassanids. They in turn relinquished power to invaders from the east, the Hephthalite Huns, but regained control of the territory south of the Amu Darya by about 565, at which time the first Turkic peoples gained control north of the river. The Arab conquest and conversion to Islam took place in the eighth century, but the Arab rule faded before the power of the Samanid state centred on Bokhara in the ninth and tenth centuries. The Seljuqs having passed to the west at the end of this period, another Turkic Empire arose in Afghanistan, that of the Ghaznavids (997–1186). Jinghis Khan, and then Timur, reinforced the Turkoman and Mongol control of the region, but the founding of the Safavid and Moghul Empires of Persia and India led to the division of Afghanistan between the two, accompanied by four hundred years of internal fratricidal strife. By now the ethnic patterns of the country were basically settled, with Pashtuns occupying the southern half, and the north divided between Tajiks, Uzbeks (see p. 180), Hazaras, Aimaqs (the latter two being of Mongoloid race but speaking Indo-European dialects) and sundry small groups like the Turkomans and Beluchis. Note that the word Afghan does not denote a race or language – its original meaning is uncertain; but basically when we speak of Afghans we mean the Pashtuns. There were brief periods between 1500 and 1900 when a single power ruled Afghanistan, notably after the crushing of the Safavids in 1722 and the establishment of Ahmad Shah's Durrani Pashtun empire. For the most part, however, the Afghan tribes (as L. Duprée notes), 'having resisted all comers for centuries, fought among themselves when no comers were available'. The final crystallization of modern Afghanistan occurred when the Russians had pressed south through Turkestan as far as they could and Britain had pushed north from India as far as she could: the territory that was left in between became Afghanistan.

There is only one set layout for the traditional designs of the whole Turkoman area: several rows of repeating octagonal or other polygonal motifs, known as göls, on a red or (occasionally) blue ground, usually interspersed with another set of repeating motifs (secondary göls), the whole encased in a rich array of narrow geometric borders. Sometimes one of the borders predominates, but often they are all of equal importance. The five carpets illustrated in figs. 387, 392, 396, 397 and 400 are old or antique pieces from the Russian part of Turkestan. Such goods are still to be found in the trade, but they are rare collector's items available only from specialist dealers at very high prices. What they illustrate is the magnificent variety that can be achieved within the confines of the one rigid formal layout. They all keep strictly to the schema outlined above, but all look quite different from one another. The essence of Turkoman design is restraint: the ability to make so much out of so little, to achieve a remarkable depth of expression by combining and re-combining the simplest little twists and odds and ends of design elements.

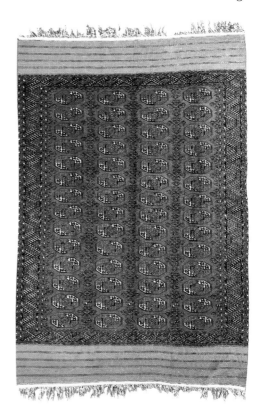

396 Kizil Ayak, nineteenth century. 268 × 240 cm, 142,000 PK/m² (8′ 9″ × 7′ 10″, 92 PK/in.²).

Map of northern Afghanistan.

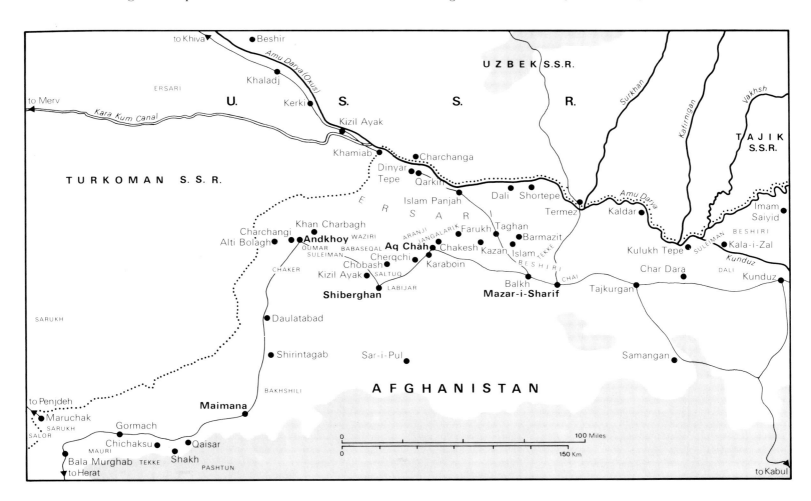

397 Chodor tent-bag face, early twentieth century.
87 × 128 cm, 186,000 PK/m²
(2′ 10″ × 4′ 2″, 120 PK/in.²).

398 Early Turkoman göls:
(a) basic outline of the medallion of a Mamluk
carpet of *c.* 1500;
(b) pattern from a sixteenth century Anatolian rug;
(c, d) pattern from a sixteenth-century Anatolian
rug, and the same pattern as used in Spanish rugs of
the Islamic period;
(e) a sixteenth-century north-west Persian
adaptation;
(f) the simplest derivatives of the original idea,
widely used in Caucasian carpets;
(g) The rug pattern most commonly depicted in
fifteenth-century Persian miniatures;
(h) a curvilinear derivative of the same pattern, as
used in a Persian miniature (British Library, Or.
6810) of 1494.

398

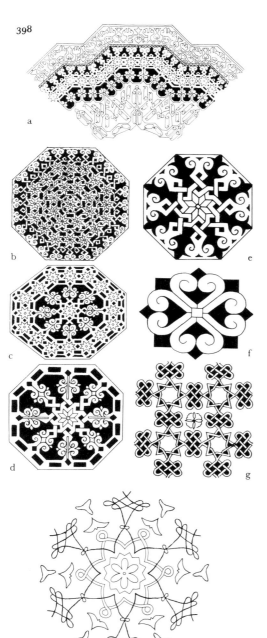

A striking example of this has been referred to in the context of fig. 144, where the most rudimentary form of the boteh is turned into a fascinating border design of quite distinctive character.

The göls themselves have great individual significance and some authorities attach much greater symbolic meaning to them than to any other oriental carpet motifs. W. Loges, the author of the best available book on Turkoman carpets, distinguishes between göls, meaning the heraldic primary motifs of each tribe, and güls, motifs similar in construction but of secondary importance. In the past most people have assumed that the word göl is an etymological variant of the Persian or Sanskrit word 'gul' or 'gol', meaning flower, and that the Turkoman motifs represent stylized flower forms. Thomas Knorr, however, states that göl is an ancient Turkish word meaning clan or family; and several other authorities have drawn attention to features of the göls whose origins owe nothing to floral forms. If Loges' assessment is right perhaps the göls are clan 'coats-of-arms' and the güls are derived from flower patterns. Certainly it is now accepted that each tribe had its own göl and that when one tribe conquered another in battle the defeated were obliged to use the victor's göl in their carpets and abandon their own. The origins of the göls were often associated with the heraldic birds which each Turkoman tribe adopted as its device. One class of early Anatolian Turkoman rugs, widely portrayed in fifteenth-century Italian paintings, is based on repeating panels incorporating birds or other animal forms (fig. 174 illustrates one example). And even today bird forms may be distinguished in several göls commonly used in Afghanistan and Turkoman Russia. Such motifs undoubtedly had religious or totemistic origins in pre-Islamic Asia, being used to propitiate the gods or ward off evil spirits.

Unfortunately it is not possible to rely on the evidence of the göls as a means of identifying the origins of Turkoman carpets: even in quite early times some tribes at least made rugs strictly for sale, and if one design sold better than another they would weave it, whatever its totemistic significance. Today there is even more borrowing and interchange of motifs between clans. Still, a knowledge of the origins of the göls can help in identifying rugs, and it can be quite fascinating to observe and note the combinations and re-associations of various motifs that one encounters.

398, 399 TURKOMAN GÖLS

In an article in the *Textile Museum Journal* (December 1963) Charles Grant Ellis sheds interesting light on the early göls and their possible association with the Mamluk carpets. His drawings form the basis of the group shown in fig. 398 along

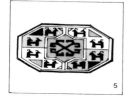

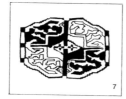

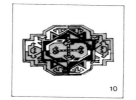

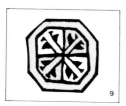

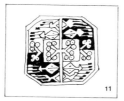

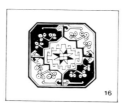

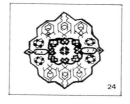

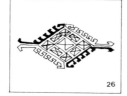

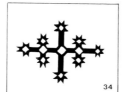

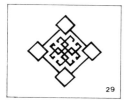

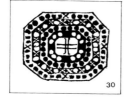

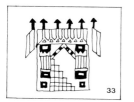

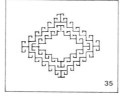

399 The principal motifs (göls) used in Turkoman carpets of today:

(1) Penjdeh – modern derivative of nineteenth century Saryk or Salor göl (cf. fig. 392).

(2) Kizil Ayak – simplified version of Saryk göl, often called 'Afghan Pendi'.

(3) Sarukh – woven by Saryk tribes in Afghanistan (cf. fig. 407); note the connection with sixteenth-century Anatolian Turkomans.

(4) Aranji – Ersari variant woven in Afghanistan; a similar pattern is used by the Labijar Ersaris.

(5) Chobash – Ersari weavers in Afghanistan use this pattern, derived from the 'tauk nushka' göl of the Chodors; note the double-headed creature in all four quarters – perhaps a derivative of the Scythian gryphon (cf. fig. 59), and a reminder that once all Turkoman tribes had bird figures as their emblems.

(6) Chodor – a nineteenth-century göl no longer woven in this form, but found in simplified versions in many areas (cf. fig. 319).

(7) Tekke – the principal göl of the most important Turkoman tribe; now the main motif of Russian and other Bokhara carpets (cf. figs. 400–5). Note here, too, relics of bird forms in the inner ornamentation.

(8) Alti Bolagh – simple Ersari form of the Tekke göl, used in the Andkhoy region.

(9) Jangalarik – another Ersari version, from the Shiberghan region.

(10) Mauri: less rounded, this göl was used in the nineteenth century by most of the Turkoman tribes except the Ersari, although it was originally perhaps the property of only one of them; it occurs today in Mauri goods from Afghanistan and in copies woven in Pakistan and northern India.

(11–16) Typical variants of the best-known Ersari göls of the Andkhoy/Shiberghan/Aq Chah regions: (11, 12) Taghan; (13, 15) Suleiman; (14) Farukh, with unusual asymmetrical quartering; (16) Saltuq.

(17) Bastardized göl from a Chobash rug; the outer edge is from Kazan and the trefoil ornament from Taghan (mixtures of this kind are common).

(18) An old Suleiman göl showing Persian influence, used by several tribes of the Andkhoy/Aq Chah area.

(19) Chakesh – an Ersari göl of the Aq Chah area.

(20, 21) Kazan, Dali – two Ersari göls with an outer edge reminiscent of those in fig. 390.

(22) Babaseqal – the most florid of the Ersari göls (cf. fig. 472).

(23) Charchangi – another Ersari göl showing links with sixteenth-century carpets (cf. fig. 394); note here, too, the bird figure relics in the internal details.

(24) Kizil Ayak – the version of the Charchangi motif woven in Russian Turkestan (cf. fig. 422).

(25–27) Yamut – the 'kepse' göl (25) found in carpets of both Afghanistan and Russian Turkestan; the commonest göl (26), found in Persian, Russian and Afghan carpets; also used by some Ersari weavers; a third type (27), found mostly in Russian Turkoman goods.

(28) Waziri – a non-traditional göl, used only in Afghanistan (cf. fig. 427).

(29) Dali – the principal motif of Persian Yamut *soumakhs* (flat weaves), also used as a secondary göl in north-west Afghanistan, is employed as a primary göl by Dali and other Ersari weavers of north-east Afghanistan.

(30) Beshir – a göl often used as a central medallion in carpets in Herati and other designs woven by Beshirs in Russian Turkestan; here, too, we may detect links with fifteenth-century Anatolian göls.

(31) Beshir – a simple floral göl, probably derived from the Persian Mina Khani design.

(32) Kizil Ayak – one of the very many designs used by the Kizil Ayaks of Afghanistan which lie rather outside the mainstream of the Turkoman tradition.

(33) Kunduz – motif based on the *minbar* (mosque pulpit), used by Ersari weavers in north-east Afghanistan.

(34–36) Three secondary göls used by Turkoman tribes – the Taghan, Suleiman, and Tekke, respectively; although attention is focused mainly on the primary göls of the Turkoman tribes, each tribe also has one or more secondary göl, often as distinctive as their principal motifs.

with the outline of one of the most commonly used göls of fourteenth- and fifteenth-century Turkoman Persia. The göls (or güls) in use in the Turkoman regions today are illustrated in fig. 399. None of these is hypothetical or historical: all but one are drawn from carpets woven between 1970 and 1980.

400 TEKKE

The most important of the Turkoman tribes in the nineteenth century was the Tekke. They occupied most of the habitable part of what is now the Turkoman S.S.R. (Turkmenistan) between the Caspian Sea and the River Amu Darya. In the course of the first half of the century their territory expanded to engulf that of other tribes, in particular the Salor and later the Saryk in the valley of the Murghab between the Merv (Mary) oasis and the Afghan frontier. The Tekke illustrated has several features which suggest an early nineteenth-century dating. It has less than 300,000 knots/m² (194 knots/in.²), counting 40 knots to the decimetre (about 10 per inch) across the width and 72 per dcm (about 18 per inch) along the length in the typical flat-backed double-weave structure described on p. 182. Later carpets have a much finer weave than this, often well in excess of 400,000 knots/m² (260 knots/in.²). The narrow border is also typical of the earliest-known Tekke pieces. The only main feature of the oldest rugs which this one lacks is the alternation of dark and medium blue in the quarters of the centres of the göls; here they are all dark blue. In other respects the two göls used are entirely typical of the two traditional principal Tekke ornaments. Note the broad striped 'skirt' at both ends of the carpet; in most Turkomans (e.g. fig. 396) this is executed in kilim weave, but here it forms part of the pile.

400 Tekke
162 × 126 cm, 288,000 PK/m²
(5′ 4″ × 4′ 1″, 186 PK/in.²).

401 Persian Turkoman
200 × 140 cm, 319,000 PK/m²
(6′ 7″ × 4′ 7″, 206 PK/in.²).

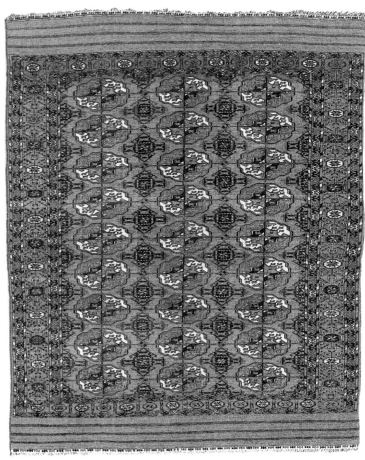

400

401

401 PERSIAN TURKOMAN

There are several groups of Turkomans in north-east Persia, mainly Yamuts and various Tekke sub-tribes. Today it is not always possible to distinguish the products of the various groups. In the rug illustrated the main elements of the design are Tekke, but the structure is firmer, with a more ridged back, than one would expect in a Tekke product. The Persian Turkoman goods come from a tiny area between Bujnurd and Gombad Qabus, just east of the southern end of the Caspian Sea. The output is small and the products not particularly popular in the West since they often have a great deal of white in the design, which makes it 'busy', and they are excessively prone to puckering. Some of the most interesting pieces are 100% silk. Otherwise they have all the typical traditional Turkoman characteristics: very fine yarn, woollen warps and wefts, a slightly bluish red and very dark (but not gloomy) blackish-blue. The Iranian Turkomans also sometimes use large amounts of green, not always to good effect, a mistake usually avoided by their Russian and Afghan brothers. Only rug sizes are made.

402 RUSSIAN BOKHARA

Bokhara, nowadays the third city of the Uzbek S.S.R. (Tashkent being the capital and Samarkand the second city), was for hundreds of years a key centre of one of the branches of the ancient Silk Route, the principal artery of trade in antiquity. In the course of its nearly two thousand years of history, Bokhara has enjoyed several periods of fame. The name comes from the Sanskrit word for a monastery. By the time of the Arab conquest in AD 709 the city was already a flourishing cultural centre. It reached its peak in the tenth century as the capital of the Samanid

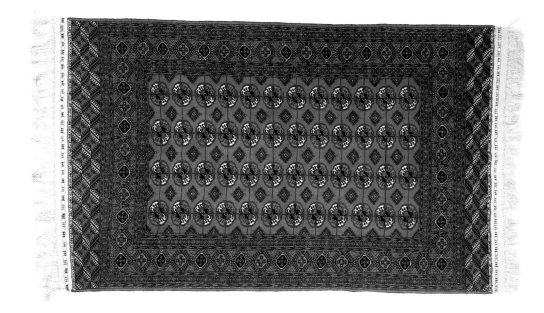

402 Russian Bokhara
214 × 133 cm, 295,000 PK/m²
(7′ 0″ × 4′ 4″, 190 PK/in.²).

Empire. The regions to the north and east of the River Amu Darya (Oxus) was called Transoxiana ('beyond the Oxus') in antiquity, and Ma Wara an-Nahr, which means the same thing, by the Muslims. The early inhabitants were all of Iranian stock and spoke Iranian dialects, but by the sixth century the region had come under Turkish control. The Samanids, however, were of Iranian origin, natives of Balkh, then in Khorassan, now in Afghanistan. Their empire reached deep into what is now Iran and also embraced most of Turkestan. Their 125-year rule saw a Persian cultural renaissance, including the re-introduction of the Persian language (albeit in Arabic rather than the ancient Pahlavi script) which had been suppressed when Arabic became the *lingua franca* of the Muslim world. In 999 the Turks regained control of the area and for hundreds of years Bokhara formed part of the states whose centre of gravity lay rather to the east. The rulers remained Turkoman or Mongol, but by the fourteenth century the governors of Ma Wara an-Nahr were Muslims, while the area east of the Syr Darya, Mughalistan, kept to the ancient shamanistic religions. Timur re-established unity but after his death his empire was split between countless sons, grandsons, and great-grandsons. This led to the final separation of east and west Turkestan. It was centuries later that East Turkestan, despite its largely Iranian, Turkish and Mongol population, became acknowledged as belonging to the Chinese sphere of influence, but the decisive step came with the concentration of power *c.* 1400. Timur's most powerful successor, Shah Rukh, moved his capital west from Samarkand to Herat (see p. 74) and sent his son Ulugh Beg to Bokhara as his deputy. Both cities flourished for 100 years, Bokhara again reaching a cultural peak overshadowed only by that of Herat itself.

In the meantime significant developments had occurred to the north. The area known as the Golden Horde, the Khanate of Kipchak between the Urals and the River Irtysh, had been allocated by Jinghis Khan to his grandson Shaiban. During the reign of Ad Allah Uzbek Khan (1313–40) the region was converted to Islam. A hundred years later the Uzbeks, as they now called themselves, began to move south but, just as they were poised to cross the Syr Darya into Shah Rukh's empire, internal squabbles halted their advance. With the accession of Muhammad Shaibani, the Uzbeks were again united and quickly swept away the fading power of Timur's successors. Shaibani himself was killed in 1510 while fighting Shah Ismail of Persia at Merv. The Uzbeks thus lost Herat but the realm he established throughout the northern half of West Turkestan endured. It was split into three Khanates: Bokhara, Khiva (previously called Khwarezm) and Kokand. Although the next four hundred years represented a period of gradual decline the Khanates remained until the Communist revolution led to the formation of the modern state of Uzbekistan. As carpet producers, the Uzbeks are of minor importance: the tribe is better known for its kilims, although one sometimes encounters pile products, especially bags, cradles and the like. One Uzbek motif, though, the göl illustrated in fig. 440, is found over a very wide area, documenting the tribe's ancient links with the Uralic/Altaic Turkomans.

Bokhara's interest to the carpet lover lies in its importance as the principal market place for the output of the whole of the Turkoman tribal areas. The name Bokhara has long been used to indicate any rug in the Tekke design illustrated in figs. 400 and 402, although the production area was always hundreds of miles away. Today the description is further extended to include such items as Pakistan Bokharas (see figs. 404, 405). Modern Russian Bokharas are made mainly in Ashkabad and a string of small towns reaching across to the Caspian Sea, and in the Merv (Mary) oasis on the river Murghab. They are standardized in design and style, although there are countless minor variations. It is not easy for the layman to distinguish between the various fine Bokhara types. Some of the noteworthy features of the modern Russian production are the use of attractive rich dark green and medium dark blue in small quantities in the göls and elsewhere – indeed richness and warmth of colour in general; the pattern shown in fig. 49 which is embroidered on the kilim; the Cyrillic letters 'TCCP' (Turkoman S.S.R.) which are sometimes woven into the border; and – unfortunately – a characteristic defect consisting of fine grooves in the pile running lengthways down some of the warps. All sizes are made, although the output of pieces over 4 m^2 (43 ft^2) is small; carpets are often long and narrow. All carpet sizes are more expensive per square metre than rug sizes.

405 MAURI

The Turkomans have fled Russian oppression at various times in the past 120 years, the latest flood of émigrés occurring during Stalin's purges in the 1930s. Most of these refugees have settled in Afghanistan and small groups of them in various parts of the country, mainly Tekkes and Yamuts to the north and north-east of Herat, produce what are today the finest Bokharas of all, with usually well over 300,000 knots/m^2 (194 knots/in.^{2}). The rug illustrated here has an unusually low knot-count. The Afghan rugs are called Mauris after the Merv (Mary) oasis, where the weavers originated. Their carpets are much better made than the current Russian production but often have too strongly contrasting colours. These pieces are also

403 Mauri Afghan
174 × 133 cm, 220,000 PK/m^2
(5′ 8″ × 4′ 4″, 142 PK/in.^{2}).

often clipped far too thin; some, however, are made with natural dyestuffs and the best of these may be numbered amongst the best carpets being made in the world today. Only a limited range of rug sizes is made. The price of good pieces is very high.

404, 405 PAKISTAN BOKHARA

Fine carpets have been produced in Kashmir and the Punjab for centuries. About 1950 the Pakistanis seized on the Bokhara design (rather as the Indians adopted the Mir Serabend twenty years later), and Lahore and the surrounding area now have a huge output of medium-quality 'Bokhara' rugs (fig. 404). They are usually utterly lacking in character, often crudely coloured or drab and washed to give a very artificial-looking sheen. They are sometimes sold as Turkoman and, if in any doubt, the buyer should demand to know the country of origin. The easiest way to recognize them is that they are woven on cotton warps, unlike the genuine Turkomans which, without exception, have woollen warps. The Pakistan Bokharas are also much cheaper than the genuine article. In fairness one must add that the finest rugs (with 250,000 knots/m^2 – 160 knots/in.^{2} – and more) are often technically very well made (fig. 405); but it seems a pity that so much energy should be expended on aping a nomadic style in modern manufactories when the nomads themselves do the job so much better.

406 PENDI BOKHARA

The southernmost point of Russian Turkestan is the Penjdeh Oasis, inhabited mainly by the Salor and Sarukh (Saryk) tribes. The former are now very few in number, but their göls are woven by the Sarukhs, which is the reason for the confusion which may be felt by readers comparing the göls shown in this book with the Salor and Saryk göls found in antique carpets. The modern Russian production in the design illustrated in fig. 406 is sold under the name 'Pendi'; it represents the best of the new Turkoman goods from the U.S.S.R. (apart from the Enssis). Apart from the design the most striking feature is the dark-brown or aubergine ground.

404 Pakistan Bokhara
175 × 94 cm, 197,000 PK/m^2
(5' 9" × 3' 1", 127 PK/in.^{2}).

405 Pakistan Bokhara
240 × 170 cm, 270,000 PK/m^2
(7' 10" × 5' 7", 174 PK/in.^{2}).

406 Pendi Bokhara
182 × 128 cm, 212,000 PK/m^2
(6' 0" × 4' 2", 137 PK/in.^{2}).

404

405

406

407 Sarukh
196 × 126 cm, 340,000 PK/m²
(6′ 5″ × 4′ 1″, 220 PK/in.²).

The weave is also different from that of the other fine Turkomans, having the more ridged back of the Afghan Sarukhs (see fig. 409). Almost all the output is in dozar size.

407 SARUKH
Sometimes called Sarukh (or Saryk) Mauri because they are the same grade and price as the Tekke and Yamut rugs illustrated in fig. 403, the goods – of which this rug is a typical example – come from Maruchak and the surrounding area, just over the Afghan border from the Penjdeh Oasis. They are mostly on dark-blue or aubergine grounds, with the typical Turkoman red predominating as the main border colour. They are very tightly woven, with a firmer, more robust handle than Mauri or Russian Turkoman rugs, with the ridged back shown in fig. 409. Again only a limited range of rug sizes is made.

408 Mauri weave (double weave).

408, 409 MAURI AND SARUKH WEAVES
In most fine Turkoman rugs the 'double-weave' technique, shown in fig. 408 (and referred to in the Introduction – see p. 22), is used. The back of the rug is completely flat and both loops of the knot are visible; this may make the rug look twice as fine as it really is. In a classical manufactured Persian weave the knot is 'square', i.e. if there are 10 knots to the inch (2.5 cm) across the width of the rug, there will be 10 knots to the inch down the warp; with double-weave, however, it is quite common to find 10 knots per inch across, but 20 knots per inch in the length. This is achieved by using very thin wefts between each row of knots and very fine yarn for the knots themselves, while the two warps around which each knot is tied are kept side-by-side. The knot is thus only half as long as it is wide, hence the very large number of knots in the length of the rug, while because the warps are side by side both loops of the knot can be seen in the width. The construction is shown diagrammatically in fig. 37; the effect is demonstrated in fig. 408: the eye registers each loop on the back of the rug as a separate knot, whereas in fact each knot (in the width) has two loops. Thus, a double-weave rug with 10 knots per inch in the width × 20 per inch in the length looks as fine as a 20 × 20, which in a Persian carpet would be very fine indeed. The disadvantage of the double-weave technique is that, since all the warps are side by side, the back of the carpet is very thin, and this makes for a rather unstable floor-covering. It also causes the grooves in the pile referred to in the note on Russian Bokharas (p. 180). It is also extremely difficult to achieve a perfectly even tension in all the weft threads in this weaving method; uneven tension causes the puckering referred to on p. 179 and if the warps are loose the 'handle' feels empty – i.e. the rug lacks body. It requires above-average weaving skill to make a sound structure using the double-weave technique.

409 Sarukh weave (ridged back).

Technically much more reliable is the ridged back (fig. 409) used by the Sarukhs (and in Pendi Bokharas). Here the alternate warp strings are on two different levels. This is shown diagrammatically in both fig. 36 and fig. 419, which reveal clearly how alternate warp strings are half-buried in the structure of the carpet and the eye registers a series of ridges across the back. The back itself is thicker and, because alternate warps are raised, there is an overlap of knots in the width of the rug. The weaver must therefore put in more knots to the inch in the width and compensate for this by using a thicker weft and thus weaving fewer knots to the inch in the length of the rug. Consequently a double-weave rug of 200 knots/in.^{2} will have 10 knots in the width and 20 in the length; but a ridged-back piece with 200 knots/in.^{2} will have 14 in the width and 14 in the length. Owing to the *trompe l'œil* effect of double-weave, the former will look finer, but the ridged back has overlapping warps and a thicker weft and feels much firmer to handle.

Considerable confusion has arisen in recent years over the terminology applied to these two different structures used in Pakistan and Kashmir. The ridged-back structure used for Persian designs is called 'singles' to distinguish it from double-weave. 'Singles' therefore implies good quality and sound construction without *jufti* knots. 'Doubles' does not, however, mean the opposite; it is used to describe goods with two-ply yarn, i.e. a double pile-thickness, in the single-wefted weaves. Both terms are thus used to indicate superior quality, but superiority of different kinds in different goods.

410 MAURI

Among the Afghan Mauri rugs of the Herat region one sometimes encounters the design illustrated here. This is not based on traditional Turkoman göls but is the creation of Mauri weavers of the time of Zaher Shah, the last king of Afghanistan (1933–73), and is named after him. Since it is contained within the limits of the Mauri style (although avoiding the division into quarters which characterizes the most ancient Turkoman göls) it has proved popular with weavers and buyers alike and may now be found not only in Mauri rugs but also in Beluch and similar products of western Afghanistan, as well as in a range of copies from Pakistan (see fig. 520). All kinds of ground colours are now available, but the original Zaher Shahi Mauris had white or cream grounds.

411 MAURI SHAKH

In Afghanistan there are two groups of Tekkes whose weave today is quite different from that used in old Turkestan. One is in Barmazit, near Balkh in the north, the

410 Mauri (Zaher Shahi design) 157 × 110 cm, 413,000 PK/m^2 (5′ 2″ × 3′ 7″, 266 PK/in.^{2}).

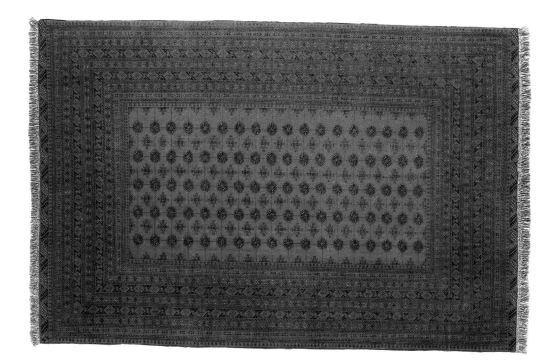

411 Mauri Shakh 350 × 245 cm, 180,000 PK/m^2 (11′ 6″ × 8′ 0″, 116 PK/in.^{2}).

other is further west in Shakh, near Maimana. The first group's products are sold as Barmazits, the second as Mauri Shakhs. Both are very similar and, as far as the retail trade is concerned, often interchangeable. In construction they are like a super grade of Daulatabad or Alti Bolagh goods (see figs. 320 and 412) – indeed it is better to think of them as the finest grade of Afghan rugs rather than as the coarsest type of Mauri. For, despite the name Mauri Shakh, they are not much like other Mauri goods, having heavy warps and a very tight ridged back. They sometimes suffer from the same faults as Daulatabad goods: the over-tight wefts produce fearful distortions of shape and cause the very close-clipped pile to open up into lengthwise grooves. The better pieces are, however, extremely robust and offer the buyer the richness and warmth of the Bokhara style at a surprisingly modest price. A wide range of sizes is made.

The Ersari carpet

As a result of the Soviet system of levelling and standardization, modern Russian Turkomans have been deprived of much of their individuality and it is to Afghanistan that we must look for today's repository of the vast treasure-house of ancient Turkoman designs. The actual fabric of the standard grade of Afghan carpets is different, being heavier and coarser in every respect; but the designs are unmistakably Turkoman. It seems to have been about the middle of the nineteenth century that Turkomans on the left bank of the Amu Darya (in what is now northern Afghanistan) began to develop what we now know as the Afghan carpet. No entirely satisfactory explanation has been offered as to how or why this coarser, more rugged style of rug developed but, apart from the Mauris and Sarukhs described above, all Afghan rugs of today are coarser in weave and thicker in pile than the Russian Turkoman rugs. It may simply be that most Afghan rugs are woven by Ersaris, who have always used a coarser structure than the Tekkes and Sarukhs who make the Russian goods, but there are probably other historical and cultural reasons, too. A comparison may perhaps be drawn with Azerbaijan where the Russian north and Persian south have developed similar designs along different lines (see p. 225). Within Afghanistan there is a huge output with a remarkable range of qualities, some quite fine and thick and solid as boards, some coarse and rough, almost with the daylight showing through. Ridged or semi-ridged backs are more common than double-weave, and the vast majority of the output is woven with red grounds, combined with the traditional dark blue and other shades of red, plus white where appropriate to the design tradition.

Sometimes the red is too sharp and many different washing techniques have been developed in England and in Switzerland to tone down the colours. The most famous of these transforms the reds to rich golden shades, but all tones between rose, copper and brown are found. These washes have the additional advantage of softening the white into cream – in an unwashed carpet the white is often too stark and makes the design look 'busy'. Most of the distinguishable types in Afghanistan are woven by sub-tribes of the Ersari. The tribes are spread over a large area of northern Afghanistan, however, and a proper classification needs to indicate both the tribe and its locality. This is a very complex matter since most of the villages take their name from the local tribe. Thus, Kizil Ayak rugs (fig. 393) are made in the village of Kizil Ayak, north-west of Shiberghan; but Kizil Ayaks are also made in countless other villages throughout northern Afghanistan. Again, fig. 415 illustrates a rug with the typical Suleiman göl; from the star-rosette in the main border we know that this piece comes from the Andkhoy region, but the Suleiman of Kala-i-Zal also use the same göl, but with a different border; the rosette border is used by all tribes of the Andkhoy region (e.g. the Alti Bolagh, fig. 412).

The reader will appreciate that it is therefore possible to give only a brief insight into the rich world of Afghan Turkoman designs within the confines of this book. It is to be hoped that some scholar will soon produce the full documentation of the subject which it so richly deserves; time is running out, however, for commercial pressures are fast leading to a disintegration of that cultural unity of the clans that gives the designs their individuality.

412

413

One other general point that needs to be made about Afghan carpets is that they are almost without exception at present undervalued on world markets. One can buy a really well made, solid and reliable Andkhoy Suleiman for less than half the price of a comparable Hamadan rug, or, at the other end of the scale, one can still find a magnificent 40-year old Chodor enssi or Beshir carpet for not more than two-thirds of the price of a Chinese carpet of similar age and quality.

Generally speaking, Afghans are found in all carpet, rug and runner sizes, but not all districts make all sizes; and in all districts all sizes over 6 m² (65 ft²) are rarer than smaller sizes, because most Afghan carpets are woven on horizontal looms laid on the floor of the traditional tents, called yurts. The yurts are not big enough to accommodate looms over 3 m long, and hence larger sizes are woven out of doors – this being practicable only in summer. Note that Afghan carpets frequently (though not invariably) have the flat selvedge seen in fig. 40.

412, 413 ALTI BOLAGH

One of the finest ridged-back structures among the medium-fine grades is woven at Alti Bolagh, near Andkhoy (see map, p. 175). Alti Bolaghs in the style of fig. 412 are often sold under the names of Daulatabad or Barmazit, an incorrect description since the goods from both these sources are finer than Alti Bolagh; indeed the writer has on more than one occasion seen Alti Bolaghs described as 'Mauri' and wondered whether ignorance is worse than dishonesty in the carpet trade or vice versa.

412 Alti Bolagh
197 × 128 cm, 171,000 PK/m²
(6′ 5″ × 4′ 2″, 110 PK/in.²).

413 Alti Bolagh
295 × 219 cm, 164,000 PK/m²
(9′ 8″ × 7′ 2″, 106 PK/in.²).

414 Jangalarik (detail);
full size 187 × 131 cm, 95,000 PK/m²
(6′ 1″ × 4′ 3″, 61 PK/in.²).

415 Suleiman (detail);
full size 280 × 183 cm, 110,000 PK/m²
(9′ 2″ × 6′ 0″, 71 PK/in.²).

416 Taghan (detail);
full size 210 × 151 cm, 85,000 PK/m²
(6′ 11″ × 4′ 11″, 55 PK/in.²).

417 Farukh (detail);
full size 182 × 146 cm, 82,000 PK/m²
(6′ 0″ × 4′ 9″, 53 PK/in.²).

'Afghan Bokhara', being vaguer, is less objectionable. This type always has white in the göls and the border, as well as the traditional reds and blues. Some pieces are found with blue grounds. From the same region comes the carpet shown in fig. 413; here the göls used are those of the Suleiman tribe of Andkhoy. The best carpets of this type are magnificent pieces of work. They are less firm than the Mauri Shakh goods but are more sound in construction: there is no need to weave finer than the design demands and it is certainly wrong to sacrifice the other important elements in a carpet's construction merely in pursuit of a finer weave. This is not to say that Alti Bolaghs do not also suffer from faults such as bad shapes and open grooves in the pile noted on p. 180, but that this fault is almost inherent in the construction of certain Turkoman types whereas in Alti Bolagh it is not. Production of Alti Bolaghs today is tolerably well organized so that most sizes are available.

414 JANGALARIK

The only Ersari tribe to use the small göl containing two white quarters are the Jangalarik who are mainly settled east of Aq Chah. The bulk of their output is coarser than that of Alti Bolagh and, although the construction is often remarkably dense, the carpets are generally classified with the wide range of average-grade Ersari goods from the Aq Chah region. Many other designs are produced by the Jangalariks in small quantities, most notable of which is a prayer type with a dark-blue arch over a plain red ground in which hangs a *mihrab* lamp.

415–419 THE STANDARD AFGHAN ERSARI

The traditional type of Afghan rug is best exemplified in the group of examples, woven between Andkhoy and Mazar-i-Sharif, shown in figs. 415–18. All four are woven with a nicely balanced semi-ridged back: that is, one shed of warps is on a higher plane than the other but the difference is not so great that the second half of each knot is buried in the back of the rug (see fig. 419b). This construction, if properly used, is perhaps the best of all, giving a firm yet flexible handle. The designs of this group are all coloured without the use of white, which emphasizes and intensifies their restraint. Again, a wide range of sizes is available. The Suleiman carpet is from Andkhoy, the Farukh from the Shiberghan area, the Taghan and Chakesh are both from villages between Aq Chah and Mazar-i-Sharif. Andkhoy Suleimans may often be finer than other goods of this region, but the best-made pieces are frequently those from Chakesh.

415

416

417

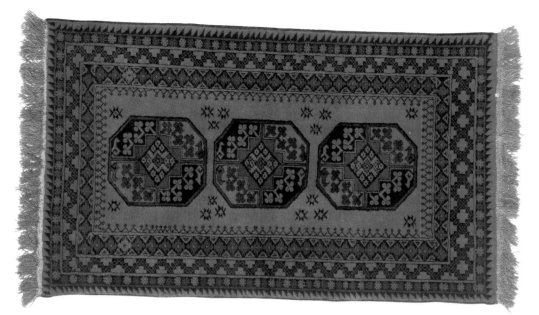

418 Chakesh
200 × 122 cm, 95,000 PK/m²
(6′ 7″ × 4′ 0″, 62 PK/in.²).

419
(a) Fully ridged construction as used in Alti Bolagh rugs: alternate warps are raised to such an angle above the bottom row that the left-hand half of each knot is buried in the construction and from the back only the firm ridge created by the right half of the knots is visible.
(b) Semi-ridged construction typical of most Ersari weaves: the shed between the two layers of warps is less pronounced. On the back of the rug the eye registers the ridges created by the right-hand half of each knot, but the left half is still visible in the 'valleys' between the ridges.

420, 421 KAZAN, DALI

The Kazan tribe of the Aq Chah/Mazar-i-Sharif area (fig. 420) and the Dali tribe of the Kunduz region (fig. 421) both use göls edged with a broad band of geometric patterning which reminds one strongly of the motifs shown in figs. 390, 398. But the inner details of the göls and the structure of the rugs are different between the two areas. The features which the Kazan göl shares with those of the Farukh and Chakesh tribes (figs. 417 and 418) are reflected in the weave and colourings also. The Kunduz group is visibly different in character. A striking aspect of the Dali rugs is their often sombre overall colouring. This is discernible in fig. 391, a 40-year-old carpet with a very muted overall colour scheme. Originally the carpet was probably rather gloomy, but age has softened and lightened the colours and the effect is now very compelling. Note the special kilim decoration (see also fig. 48).

The colours of the Dali rug, from the important Kunduz-region centre, Imam Saiyid, were probably produced with natural dyestuffs, called *rang-i-chub* in Afghanistan (i.e. 'wood colour', a reference to the shrubs and roots which are the source of many natural dyes). Note the use of light blue, which adds richness to

419

420 Kazan (detail);
full size 197 × 135 cm, 81,000 PK/m²
(6′ 5″ × 4′ 5″, 52 PK/in.²).

421 Dali Imam Saiyid
172 × 114 cm, 95,000 PK/m²
(5′ 8″ × 3′ 9″, 61 PK/in.²).

420

421

422 Russian Kizil Ayak
292 × 176 cm, 190,000 PK/m²
(9′ 7″ × 5′ 9″, 123 PK/in.²).

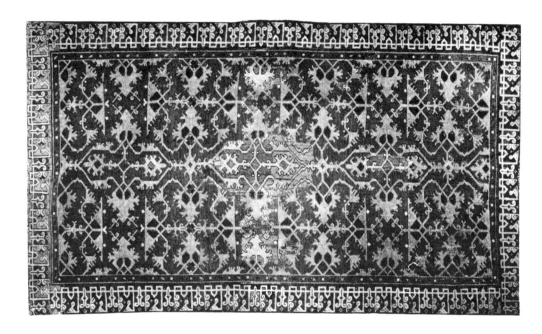

423 Uşak
170 × 107 cm, 155,000 TK/m²
(5′ 7″ × 3′ 6″, 100 TK/in.²).
This so-called 'Lotto' rug from Anatolia, made in
the sixteenth century, belongs culturally with the
other early Turkoman pieces shown in figs. 390, 394.
Victoria and Albert Museum, London.

the colouring without disrupting the balance. The Persian guard in the border
(cf. fig. 82) and the use of the same motif within the göl is unfortunate, not because
it is wrong for modern weavers to try new design elements but because it does not
work. The Persian motif is so out of place that it introduces a jarring note. Göls
similar to those shown in figs. 391, 420 and 421 are used also in the modern production of Russian Turkestan (see below), in and around the Ersari town of Kerki
on the Amu Darya.

422, 423 RUSSIAN KIZIL AYAK
The Turkoman output in the Soviet Union is limited to a handful of standardized
designs woven under manufacturing conditions. Kizil Ayak is a small town in the
Soviet Ersari area of Turkestan, but it has never been clarified whether the Kizil
Ayaks are an Ersari sub-tribe or an independent group. In Afghanistan the design
of fig. 422 is woven by the Charchangi, who are certainly Ersaris; it is only the
Russians who call the design Kizil Ayak. The Kizil Ayaks of Afghanistan weave a
very wide range of designs (see figs. 323 and 393, also fig. 399), all quite different
from fig. 422. The two göls used in the Charchangi layout are both demonstrably
ancient. The more rounded main göl, incorporating a variant of the Chinese 'knot
of destiny', is found in Turkoman carpets of sixteenth-century Anatolia (fig. 394)
and of fifteenth-century Persia (fig. 616 illustrates a related motif), while the cross-

425

424

shaped secondary göl is a principal feature of the so-called 'Lotto' carpets of Turkoman sixteenth-century Uşak (fig. 423). Most Russian 'Kizil Ayaks' are made in sizes of 4–6 m² – 43–65 ft² – but a limited range of other sizes is also available. Red is the only ground-shade used. A rather unfortunate mauve tone often spoils the subsidiary colours. As with all Turkoman goods, the warps and wefts are of wool.

424 Russian Yamut
200 × 140 cm, 319,000 PK/m²
(6′ 7″ × 4′ 7″, 206 PK/in.²).

425 Afghan Yamut
110 × 82 cm, 129,000 PK/m²
(3′ 7″ × 2′ 8″, 83 PK/in.²).

424–426 YAMUT

Another class of new Russian Turkoman goods is sold under the name Yamut. This is the name of the third largest Turkoman tribe (the Tekkes and the Ersaris being the largest); like the Ersaris, the Yamuts are split into many sub-tribes, but their names are rarely used in the carpet trade. The tribe is dispersed over a very wide area, the three main concentrations being around Khiva in the northern part of the Turkoman S.S.R., along the eastern shores of the Caspian Sea in both the Turkoman S.S.R. and in Persia, and in various parts of north-west Afghanistan. In the modern Russian production many features are shared with the Kizil Ayak carpets described above, but the output is larger and a greater range of sizes is available. Much more white is used in the designs, which sometimes creates a 'busy' effect, but the use of a number of different shades of red for the ground colours increases the variety available. The three principal designs used in the Russian production are illustrated in this group, but of the three rugs shown only fig. 424

426 Afghan Chakesh in Yamut design (detail);
full size 201 × 157 cm, 73,000 PK/m²
(6′ 7″ × 5′ 2″, 47 PK/in.²).

is of Russian origin, the other two being Afghan. Fig. 424 shows a rug that is considerably finer than most Russian Yamuts, which are normally woven with a density of some 200,000–230,000 knots/m² (130–150 knots/in.²).

The rug shown in fig. 426 is not a Yamut but a Chakesh, from the same village as fig. 418. The Russian Yamut shown in fig. 164 also incorporates this design. It is still fairly common to find old carpets from Russian Turkestan in this design. They often have a very dense pile, attractive brown or aubergine grounds and surprisingly low prices, considering their age and quality. They have the disadvantage of a long, narrow format and frequently suffer from physical defects like creases or cockling and serious distortions of shape. The Afghan Yamut shown in fig. 425 includes one of the most appealing of Turkoman göls, called *kepse* by the Russian expert Moshkova. This göl is widely used in the new Russian Yamut production. The Afghan version lacks the fineness of weave of the Russian goods, but compensates for this with its magnificent colouring.

427 WAZIRI

The design shown here is not an ancient Turkoman pattern, but belongs – like the Zaher Shahi (fig. 410) – to the small group of successful creations by individual designers within the Turkoman tradition. The Waziri are a confederation of weaving groups in the Mazar-i-Sharif area; the design is named after a nineteenth- or early twentieth-century Wazir (government official) who originated it. It is often woven, as in the example shown, on a dark-blue ground. The weave is usually quite fine, with a firm, ridged-back, structure.

428 KUNDUZ

Close-covered grounds in small repeating patterns are rare in Turkoman pile carpets. The design illustrated here is the standard pattern used in the superb fine Yamut *soumakhs* (flat-weaves), which are still woven in Iran and which also occur, generally in a coarser weave of Uzbek or Turkoman origin, in Afghanistan. In pile carpets the design is unusual, but may be encountered in goods from various origins in Afghanistan. The example illustrated comes from the Kunduz region of eastern Afghanistan.

429, 430 BESHIR

There is some doubt as to the meaning of the word Beshir as applied to carpet designs. Certainly the Beshirs of present-day Afghanistan consider themselves to be Turkomans and a tribe in their own right. Some modern authors describe them as a sub-tribe of the Ersari; others doubt this conclusion. Grote-Hasenbalg, moreover, describes the name Beshir as a corruption of Bokhara and uses it to describe nomadic goods of Mongol, Uzbek and other sundry and indeterminate origins produced over a wide area, from Herat to Samarkand. The two possibilities are

427 Waziri
264 × 205 cm, 138,000 PK/m²
(8′ 8″ × 6′ 9″, 89 PK/in.²).

428 Kunduz
134 × 109 cm, 122,000 PK/m²
(4′ 5″ × 3′ 7″, 79 PK/in.²).

427

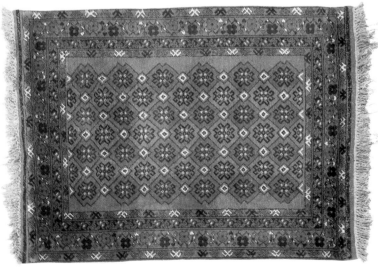

428

429

430

not necessarily mutually exclusive. The evidence of the designs supports Grote-Hasenbalg, for they are distinctly un-Turkoman in flavour in most instances. Very often they look like nomadic copies or re-interpretations of designs used in Persian or other places of origin, which suggests the work of people with very much less cultural unity than one usually finds in Turkoman tribes. Within the group of designs we call Beshir, however, it is perfectly possible that some are of genuinely Turkoman origin and it may be simply the ignorance of traders and scholars alike which causes many disparate types to be lumped together under one name. The reader may form his own judgement of the matter by comparing figs. 143, 165, 236 and 429–32, and by comparing these with the standard Turkoman types illustrated in the present section of this book. It will be seen that the Beshir rugs have a wide range of design types; they also have a wider palette of shades (often including gold). A particular feature is that the göls are not hexagonal, nor are they quartered in the way that W. Loges claims all Turkoman principal göls should be.

The design illustrated in fig. 429 is plainly a variant of the Mina Khani pattern which originated in Khorassan in the seventeenth century and has been copied by Beluch and other tribes ever since (cf. figs. 434 and 757). But, as with the copies of other east Persian designs illustrated in figs. 236 and 432, a clearly discernible Beshir style is evident. This kind of Mina Khani Beshir is found in many different qualities in both old and new goods from a wide area of northern Afghanistan. A typical simple Aq Chah derivative of the same idea is illustrated in fig. 430.

431, 432 BESHIR

It seems likely that we must look back as far as the Mongol conquests of Central Asia for the origins of the Beshir designs, and in particular to the fifteenth century, during which the three great cities of Samarkand, Bokhara and Herat became the flowers of Timur's empire, paving the way, under the guidance of Chinese artists, for the great renaissance of Persian art that accompanied the rise of the Safavid dynasty. Just as during this period Chinese ideas and motifs (such as the cloud-band, palmette, dragon and phoenix) entered Persian carpet art, so also were they adopted by some of the nomadic tribesmen who wandered from oasis to oasis in this arid region on both sides of the river Amu Darya. The so-called 'dragon and

429 Beshir (detail);
full size 252 × 159 cm, 136,000 PK/m²
(8′ 3″ × 5′ 2″, 88 PK/in.²).

430 Beshir (detail);
full size 132 × 72 cm, 91,000 PK/m²
(4′ 4″ × 2′ 4″, 59 PK/in.²).

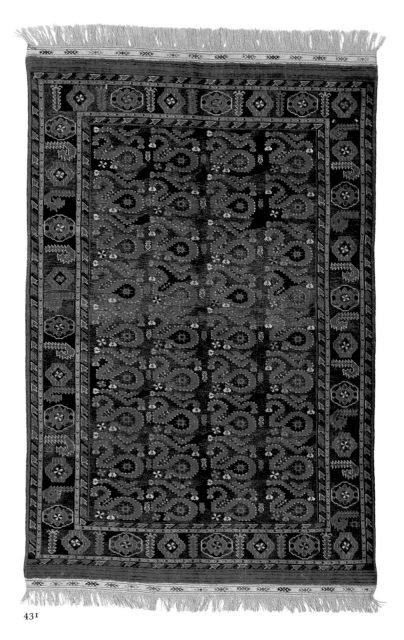

431

432

431 Beshir
264 × 162 cm, 176,000 PK/m²
(8′ 8″ × 5′ 4″, 114 PK/in.²).

432 Beshir
124 × 83 cm, 184,000 PK/m²
(4′ 1″ × 2′ 9″, 119 PK/in.²).

phoenix' design of fig. 143 is an example; fig. 431 shows another example. This particular Beshir design is not found in Afghanistan, only in the Russian Turkoman group. The easiest feature for the layman to recognize is the snake-like motifs in the ground: whether these are derived from the cloud-band motif or represent a derivative of dragon patterns is hard to say. A comparison with old Caucasian rugs using dragon motifs suggests the latter. Some authorities consider the motifs to be stylized tulips. The colouring, too, is noteworthy because of the large blocks of pale shades in the ground, which may vary in tone from grey-green to light blue. The weave and structure are the same as for all new Russian Turkomans (see above).

Yet another Russian Beshir is illustrated in fig. 432. Here, too, the origin of the design is East Persia, the leaf-like principal motif being developed from a small element of the Herati pattern (see figs. 165, 224; cf. also fig. 528).

433 QUCHAN

The rug shown is clearly influenced by the designs of the Salor Turkomans, as illustrated in fig. 392, but the colourings are quite uncharacteristic of Turkoman goods, and the border is plainly Caucasian. The key to the mystery is the small town of Quchan, just north-west of Meshed near the mountain frontier of Iran with Turkestan. Jenny Housego notes that the Kurds who weave in this area have had a very troubled history, being partly of Anatolian, partly of Caucasian origin, having fled to northern Iran to escape persecution from the Ottoman Turks in the sixteenth century, only to be moved on by Shah Abbas in 1602 to help secure his

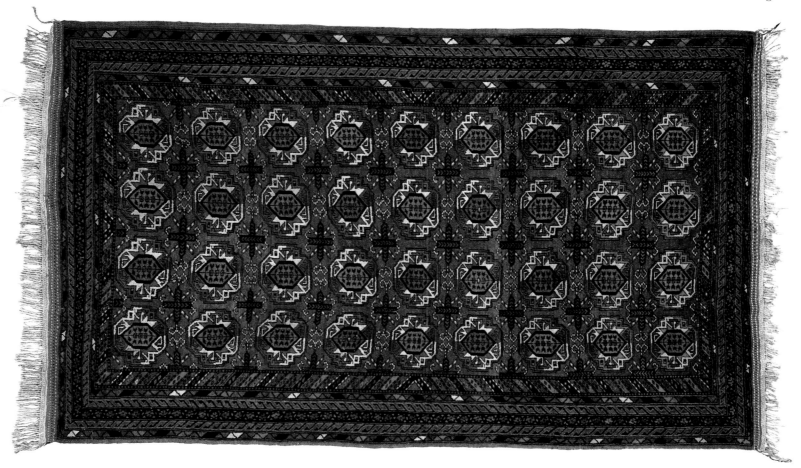

433 Quchan
252 × 155 cm, 106,000 TK/m²
(8′ 3″ × 5′ 1″, 68 TK/in.²).

north-east frontier against the Uzbeks. In the course of time they have softened their strict Azerbaijan-related style by the incorporation of motifs from their Turkoman and Beluch neighbours. Their rugs are not to everyone's taste, being often uncompromisingly wild and shaggy in both structure and design. However, if one is seeking a rug of unspoilt character which really reveals the true meaning of tribal art, then Quchan is one of the few sources today of genuine collector's items.

434–436 BELUCHI

The Kurds of Quchan are not the only tribal weavers to reflect the influence of the Turkomans in their designs. The Beluch villagers and nomads of eastern Khorassan and western Afghanistan use many design elements which are clearly of Turkoman origin. But the eclecticism of the Beluch tribes is revealed even more strongly in their adaptations of the designs of the Persian town manufactories. Figure 434 shows a Mina Khani design derived directly from the all-over patterns of east Persia used in the sixteenth to eighteenth centuries as illustrated in figs. 755 and 757 (a modern version). The border is based on a typical Turkoman motif. Figures 435 and 436 are further removed from the manufactured originals. The alien influences, such as the basic Herati-pattern layout, and the traces of the Uzbek göl (cf. fig. 440) are digested and incorporated into a design style which is independently and un-mistakably Beluch. All three rugs fall into the large category of Persian rugs known simply as Meshed Beluch. Regrettably, the products of the Beluch tribes in both Persia and Afghanistan are ill-documented. The principal point noted by carpet experts is the difference between the Iranian and Afghan types rather than the differences between one Persian Beluch and another. Predominant among the Persian production are all-over geometric patterns of the types shown, although others are also found (see figs. 153, 167, 247). Various shades of red and dark blue are the principal colours used but cream grounds are also found, and orange, gold, white and green are used in small quantities as secondary colours. Persian Beluch rugs were traditionally made only in 200 × 100 cm (6′ 6″ × 3′ 3″) and 100 × 60 cm (3′ 3″ × 2′ 0″) sizes, but in recent years the weavers have responded to international

434

435

434 Beluch
204 × 100 cm, 83,000 PK/m²
(6′ 8″ × 3′ 3″, 54 PK/in.²).

435 Beluch
201 × 97 cm, 111,000 PK/m²
(6′ 7″ × 3′ 2″, 72 PK/in.²).

Note that the weave of these two rugs is much
coarser than in most Persian Beluch goods.

demand and now more or less all rug and runner sizes are available. Persian Beluch
rugs are very fine – the finest of all the tribal weaves in large-scale production today
– and pieces with over 200,000 knots/m² (130 knots/in.²) are quite common; but
the dark colours depress the price and even outstanding pieces cost no more than,
say, an average Shahr Babak Afshari with a weave only two-thirds as fine. Almost
all Beluch rugs have the flat selvedge seen in fig. 40, often of goat hair.

437 DAGHESTAN
Although most rugs from Daghestan have bold repeating patterns, some fully
developed all-over designs are found, just as they always were in the northern

436

Shirvan region, which provides much of the inspiration for the Daghestan output. Note in this example a slightly floral touch, such as is mentioned also with regard to fig. 545. Here, it may perhaps suggest a connection with the Mina Khani design; another interesting comparison is with fig. 767 (Yezd). The present design brings a certain fluidity to a type which may otherwise suffer from being too set and regular. The structure, colours and other details are as noted on p. 210. The juxtaposition of this Derbend rug and the Beluch of fig. 436 is both surprising and illuminating. The problem of identification is easily disposed of, for Derbends are single and Beluchis double-wefted; and one needs to have seen only one piece from each origin to realize that one could never confuse the two different colour-styles. But what of the design? Some would say that the similarity is pure chance: there are only a limited number of possible permutations of repeating geometric patterns, so some of them are bound to look alike. To the author, however, the affinity suggests ancient cultural links – perhaps a common ancestor in the Mina Khani group, or maybe the heritage – one may even say the cultural debris – of one of the many marauding tribes that swept across the whole of Asia in the Middle Ages. It is by no means impossible that both rugs are based on a Turkoman göl deposited, as it were, in both north-east Iran and the northern Caucasus by a tribe which in the course of time made its way from central China to the Bosphorus. Perhaps even more interesting, however, is the difference between the designs rather than the similarities. Throughout the Orient every area puts its own imprint on the designs it employs. Often this has to do with the people's concept of colour in any given area; but it is also influenced by the way the motifs are handled and the subsidiary motifs with which they are associated. Every inch of fig. 436 proclaims a Beluch origin, while fig. 437 declares in an equally positive manner that it was woven in Daghestan.

438 QUCHAN

As is noted above, Quchan is the market place for a small group of Kurdish villages above Meshed in the mountains which form Iran's north-east frontier. Neither the coarse, floppy structure of the Quchan rugs (woollen or goat-hair warps, two woollen wefts) nor their designs or colours remind us of the products of the main Kurdish weaving areas of western Iran, but one frequently encounters striking similarities with Caucasian and Anatolian Kurdish styles. Both figs. 438 and 439 illustrate this and at the same time document the powerful individuality of Quchan.

436 Beluch
141 × 73 cm, 137,000 PK/m²
(4′ 7″ × 2′ 5″, 88 PK/in.²).

437 Derbend
198 × 128 cm, 144,000 TK/m²
(6′ 6″ × 4′ 2″, 93 TK/in.²).

437

438

The double-headed heraldic motif of fig. 438 reminds us of the bird and animal forms which predominate in Central Asian motifs and emblems of the earliest times, but what gives the rug its strength is the skilful – one should perhaps rather say instinctive – use of the random colour scheme.

439–442 THE LAKHARBI GÖL

The Quchan rug shown in fig. 439 demonstrates most strikingly how powerful an influence has been exercized on carpet design by the migrations of the Turkic tribes over the past millennium, for the design of this piece can be shown to be based on one of their most ancient motifs. Today, we associate it particularly with the tent bags and flat weave products of the Lakharbi Uzbek tribe, but its ancestry certainly predates the separation of the Uzbeks into an independent clan in the fourteenth century. It made its way to Western Asia at an early date and is found in some fifteenth-century European paintings in which Anatolian rugs are depicted. It is quite possible therefore that the Kurds of Quchan did not acquire the design from their Uzbek neighbours – contact with whom was limited for long periods to manning the barricades to repulse lightning plundering raids – but rather brought it with them from their Anatolian homelands. The Quchan villages constitute a small production area, so that the supply of goods is limited. The bulk of the production is in kelleyi sizes – up to 4 m (13′ 0″) or so long but never more than about 170 cm (5′ 6″) wide. Goods in the 3–4 m² (32–43 ft²) range are also found, but small rugs are rare; no carpet sizes are made.

439

440

441

438 Quchan
228 × 144 cm, 72,000 TK/m²
(7′ 6″ × 4′ 9″, 46 TK/in.²).

439 Quchan
250 × 160 cm, 62,000 TK/m²
(8′ 2″ × 5′ 3″, 40 TK/in.²).

440 Lakharbi göl.

441 Detail from the central panel of a triptych by Hans Memling, *Madonna and Child with Saints*, *c.* 1485, showing a carpet design based on the Lakharbi göl. Kunsthistorisches Museum, Vienna.

The 'Lakharbi' göl is used in rugs and runners in various villages of Azerbaijan and eastern Turkey; fig. 442 illustrates a piece from the Lamberan area (see also fig. 507). One village with a substantial output in this design, mainly in kelleyi format (i.e. over-wide runners), and with a distinctive wide border, is Dodan in Persia, close to the (Turkish) Kurdish area between Lake Van and Lake Urmia. The most spectacular version used to be made in the Russian Kazak town of Genje (now called Kirovakan, on the western border of the Azerbaijan S.S.R.). Old Genjes are amongst the most sought-after collector's items, but the design is no longer made in the modern Russian production. Other rugs employing this motif are occasionally found throughout Persia.

442 Azerbaijan
316 × 104 cm, 91,000 TK/m²
(10′ 4″ × 3′ 5″, 59 TK/in.²).

442 KARAJA

This carpet illustrates a point that the reader must bear in mind with respect to many of the designs illustrated in the next section of this book (repeating medallion designs), namely, that a chain of repeating medallions in a narrow rug can assume an entirely different aspect when treated as an all-over pattern in a large carpet. The most obvious examples of this are to be found in Afghan carpets (see fig. 472), but the Karaja carpet illustrated is another case in point. The surprising feature is the fact that actually very few carpet-weaving origins take advantage of this possibility. In Persian Azerbaijan, for example, with all its wealth of repeating

443 Karaja
350 × 251 cm, 69,000 TK/m²
(11′ 6″ × 8′ 3″, 45 TK/in.²).

444

445

446

444 Behbehan
279 × 139 cm, 46,000 тк/m²
(9′ 2″ × 4′ 7″, 30 тк/in.²).

445 Gebbeh
198 × 125 cm, 84,000 рк/m²
(6′ 6″ × 4′ 1″, 54 рк/in.²).

446 Owlad
305 × 214 cm, 68,000 тк/m²
(10′ 0″ × 7′ 0″, 44 тк/in.²).

geometric patterns, only Karaja produces carpets with all-over repeating medallions. The reader should refer to fig. 506 to see the difference in overall effect created by this procedure. Karaja carpets are made mostly on red grounds, but blue and cream are also found. All standard carpet sizes are available. For notes on the structure and design see p. 227. In the example shown the reader will observe further evidence of the lasting effect of the Turkoman conquests on the designs of north-west Persia.

444–446 GEBBEH, BEHBEHAN, OWLAD
Attention is drawn in the section beginning on p. 212 to the special predilection among the Luri tribes of south-west Persia for the hooked-diamond motif. How varied and how endlessly fascinating the motif may be when used in a repeating pattern is shown by these rugs from three important Luri groups. Note, for example, how the weaver has achieved a reciprocating effect in the interlocking hooks in most of the medallions of fig. 445; or how the two chains of polygons in fig. 444 are laid out so as to produce the effect of a third chain down the centre. All the pieces shown here are typical of their individual origins, notes on which will be found on pp. 214–6.

447, 448 KULA, QASHQAI

These two carpets offer an opportunity to compare a modern Turkish re-inter-pretation with a Persian original. The Qashqai piece is of a kind no longer readily found in the Orient. Its 'floribunda' style, the amazing wealth of ideas, leave the beholder stunned, unable to take in so much detail at the first encounter. This is because the design, for all its symmetry and planned layout, is in fact not regular: almost every motif is differently coloured and a great deal was clearly left to the weaver's discretion. There cannot have been a fully drawn and coloured design from which the weaver worked. Although the basic layout may have been pre-scribed, the things that attract us – the wealth of detail and the richness of the colouring – were provided by the weaver's imagination. If this was a piece made to order (which is perfectly conceivable), it can only have been executed by a weaver fully steeped in the Qashqai or Shiraz cultural tradition. In a latter-day manu-factured copy this is impossible, for economic considerations demand that in repeat-ing designs the basic design unit is isolated, drawn by a designer, painted by a colourist and then given to a weaver, who is told to 'weave this pattern in one corner and then repeat it in the length and breadth of the carpet until the required size is reached'. To paint a loom-drawing in the full size of the carpet and colour each motif differently would be quite unrealistically expensive for this kind of design, and more than that: the weaver could never follow it. It would take an eternity to weave because at every knot she would have to look at the drawing to see what colour to use. Thus by its very nature the Kula copy – and any other version woven outside the Shiraz area – can have only a fraction of the appeal of the original.

447 Qashqai
213 × 157 cm, 130,000 PK/m²
(7′ 0″ × 5′ 2″, 84 PK/in.²).

448 Kula
308 × 222 cm, 137,000 TK/m²
(10′ 1″ × 7′ 3″, 88 TK/in.²).

447

448

For the layman there can be some difficulty in recognizing Kula copies of other origins. Where the original has cotton warps the distinction is easy, for Kula uses woollen warps, but many of the designs woven in Kula come from places where woollen warps are still standard – the Yalameh of fig. 485 is an example. One helpful clue is the fact that the wool used in Kula is impregnated with a particular oil during the spinning process which gives the yarn an unmistakable smell. This is the same smell that helps identify Rumanian carpets; and it is also sometimes found in new Caucasian goods. The tribal rugs of Persia and Turkey are mostly made from hand-spun yarn, which smells like any other fresh wool. The biggest clue, however, is the colouring. Kula suffers the typical disadvantage of manufactured carpets aping the nomadic style: the makers can copy the design but do not have the courage to copy the bold colours. For a nomadic weaver, unburdened by the enfeebling awareness of good taste and restraint which marks our Western industrial civilization, will put together great masses of uncompromisingly contrasted colours. Sometimes the result is not so much spontaneous as excruciating, but where, as often happens, a weaver has an innate sense of what colours will work, the result has a richness and fresh brilliance which makes up for all the products of lesser artists which do not come off. There is a risk in juxtaposing all those bright colours. The nomad, weaving for herself, will take the risk and live with the result, but the manufacturer, with his eye on the export market, cannot afford to take that risk. For him it is better to make ten mediocre rugs which are sure to sell than eight disasters and two masterpieces. Thus, Kula Yalamehs and Kula Qashqais are weaker in colouring, harmonious through dullness, with a tired-looking rusty shade of red, a greyish tone of green and much use of brown and ochre. The example shown in fig. 448 is neat, accurate and clever, but it can never hope even to hint at the expressive power of fig. 447. Note in both carpets the ever-present influence of the Turkomans – for example in the border (cf. fig. 415), around the edge of the ground of fig. 447 (cf. fig. 395), and in the motif derived from fig. 398.

449 Rajasthan
189 × 121 cm, 232,000 PK/m²
(6′ 2″ × 3′ 11″, 150 PK/in.²).

449 RAJASTHAN

In fig. 86 is shown part of an old Shirvan rug from the village of Pirabadil. The design, with the geometric 'ram's-horn' motifs, is one of the dozen or so most easily recognized patterns of traditional Caucasian carpets and is used as much in new Russian Kazaks and Shirvans as in old goods. The present example shows another modern version of the design, woven in Jaipur (the capital) and in many surrounding villages of the province of Rajasthan in northern India. A considerable range of the more finely-detailed Caucasian designs is produced in Rajasthan today, mostly in a very fine weave and with a thick and dense pile. They are produced on cotton warps and wefts in a single-wefted double-weave construction. In relation to their fineness these rugs are cheap, though they suffer the disadvantage of a rather dry yarn. All sizes, from mats to large carpets and runners, are found and they are available in a variety of colour-styles, from beige and gold tones to strong reds and blues.

450 SINKIANG

The Sinkiang goods described on p. 108 are also made with various repeating all-over patterns, some having a distinctively Turkoman flavour reflecting the ancient culture of East Turkestan, others, like this rug, reminding us rather of Caucasian styles. The characteristics of structure and colouring noted earlier are the same for all designs.

451, 452 GEBBEH

The general note on Gebbeh rugs on p. 214 remarks that, from the point of view of design, anything is possible. The two rugs illustrated perhaps demonstrate the point. Like the Turkoman rug of fig. 428, the first of the Gebbeh examples brings flat-weave goods to mind, in this case the kilims of the Lurs and Qashqais north of Shiraz; but no specific connection can be cited – only the 'laughing colours' and the unpredictability of the design, which are, of course, the features by which the rug will be judged.

450 Sinkiang
185 × 94 cm, 88,000 PK/m²
(6′ 1″ × 3′ 1″, 57 PK/in.²).

451

452

453

Figure 452 shows a rug of the type woven with undyed yarns – the streaks in the ground are the result of this and give the rug a vibrancy which would be completely lacking in one containing colours dyed to perfect consistency by the use of modern techniques. It is astonishing to discover that the design used in this rug also appears on a carpet portrayed in a Persian miniature of *c.* AD 1360; while the connection may be purely accidental, it serves to remind us that we should take nothing for granted in the realm of carpet design.

453 LURI

Jenny Housego, in her excellent study *Tribal Rugs*, makes the point that the Lurs of southern Persia tend to go for bold, uncluttered designs, while the pieces with a great amount of detail are more often of Qashqai origin. Figs. 478 and 548 bear out this idea. However, there are exceptions, and the design shown here is an example. In structure and style this piece clearly belongs to the Shiraz Luri group which includes figs. 154 and 242. Note that the goat-hair warps are finished in an unfringed kilim at one end. This is somewhat unusual in Luri goods, being more characteristic of the Kurdish rugs woven further north.

454, 455 SHAH SAVAN

The origins and distribution of the Shah Savan tribe are described in interesting detail by Jenny Housego. They seem not to have any ethnic connection with the Kurds, but their rugs often reveal Kurdish influence reflected both in designs and in structure. The 'boteh' border of fig. 454 taken alone, would unquestionably be called Kolyai or Kakaberu by most carpet experts, but it is much more difficult to suggest a stylistic background for the wild and uncompromising design of the rug's ground. Indeed it is not possible to say what the motifs in fact represent, their original form being lost in the mists of antiquity. The rug's appeal lies in the splendid natural dyestuffs and the mystery of the composition, features it shares with many tribal products of the Elburz mountains (Taleghan) and the Persian foothills of the southern Caucasus.

451 Gebbeh
215 × 140 cm, 68,000 TK/m²
(7′ 1″ × 4′ 7″, 44 TK/in.²).

452 Gebbeh
190 × 109 cm, 81,000 PK/m²
(6′ 3″ × 3′ 7″, 52 PK/in.²).

453 Luri
247 × 158 cm, 51,000 TK/m²
(8′ 1″ × 5′ 2″, 33 TK/in.²).

454

455

Figure 455 illustrates a design woven by the Shah Savan tribe of the Saveh area and by Persian villagers in the Kharaghan region. What it represents is a mystery. A crown is suggested; or a bowl of fruit and flowers. Another theory links the pattern with the so-called cemetery design: certain old Turkish prayer rugs contain a repeating pattern of vignettes containing a small building and a cypress tree. Modern scholars have poured scorn on the idea that a weaver should wish to represent a cemetery in his prayer rug: a more likely explanation is that the vignettes show miniature gardens derived from the ideas explained above in the section on garden designs. Whatever the source for this design, the stylization is so complete that a definite conclusion is no longer possible. The similarity of the border with certain Bakhtiar designs (e.g. fig. 257) suggests a further possible explanation: a tribal adaptation of the French flower-cluster used in Bakhtiar carpets and many other origins over the past century (see below and figs. 707–11).

456 GEBBEH
This Gebbeh illustrates an indisputable example of a tribal weaver's copy of a manufactured design, for the repeating motifs in the ground, which the author has heard described unkindly as cauliflowers, are in fact roses, derived from the nine-

454 Shah Savan
195 × 110 cm, 110,000 TK/m²
(6′ 5″ × 3′ 7″, 71 TK/in.²).

455 Shah Savan
203 × 132 cm, 166,000 TK/m²
(6′ 8″ × 4′ 4″, 107 TK/in.²).

teenth-century *gol farang* design. French-inspired rose motifs were the principal element of a carpet style that had a certain vogue in many parts of Persia and elsewhere; some examples are illustrated in the section beginning on p. 313. Where the Shiraz weavers may have picked up the design it is impossible to say. The Gebbeh rugs in which it is used mostly have a very firm ridged-back structure, which looks like Qashqai work, but it is hard to be sure with this wayward article. Wherever they got the design from, they have developed it into a version of their own: fig. 456 may represent a bastardized form when set against a nineteenth-century *gol farang* original, but it is nothing if not a Gebbeh. What matters, as is stated elsewhere, is not where the design came from but what the weaver has made of it.

457 YAGÇIBEDIR
Narrow runners are not among the traditional types made in Anatolia, but they have been made in and around Sindirgi (Yagçibedir) and Döşemealti since about 1970 in response to West European demand. There is nothing particularly clever about making up the design illustrated in fig. 457 – it consists merely of the repetition of the geometric flower which is a subsidiary motif in most Yagçibedir rugs. The more surprising then that the runner has such a striking effect. It emphasizes the very important role played by colour – colour combinations and colour balance – in the appeal of oriental rugs: it also reminds us of the great value of tradition in the artistic achievements of the Orient. The design illustrated works because the weavers of Yagçibedir rugs know that this colour combination and this kind of motif – this traditional stylistic conception – have always worked. The construction is the same as in the rug illustrated in fig. 577.

456 Gebbeh
148 × 87 cm, 93,000 PK/m²
(4′ 10″ × 2′ 10″, 60 PK/in.²).

457 Yagçibedir (detail);
full size 300 × 57 cm, 84,000 TK/m²
(9′ 10″ × 1′ 10″, 54 TK/in.²).

458–460 SMALL REPEATING PATTERNS FROM CHINA AND PERSIA
It is surprising how differently we react to the Chinese and the Persian way of doing the same thing. A naïve observer from another planet would surely say that the ground patterns of figs. 459 and 460 are in essence the same, but to a carpet-lover whose response is coloured by all he knows of the cultural background, the expression of the two rugs appears quite different. The old rug shown in fig. 458 illustrates one of the many typical methods the Chinese adopted to produce a harmonious and restful overall effect. The picture designs of figs. 381–5, and the bold layout of carpets like those shown in figs. 713–19 no doubt served other objectives, but in the case of fig. 458 the impression is given that the weaver sought to make his carpet unobtrusive, its effect achieved only by the gentle interplay of colours. The symbolism of Chinese carpet design, as Lorentz fully explains, is social rather than metaphysical. The artistic goal is not expression but decoration. With this in view the weaver chooses a simple repeating lattice pattern as the most obvious and efficient way of turning a striking plain ground into a quiet decorative one. Figure 459 takes the idea a stage further: the lattice-work is opened up and each segment is filled with a stylized flower-motif. Unlike the boteh designs, however, where it was noted how the asymmetry of the principal motif fills the repeating pattern

458 Old Chinese
263 × 129 cm, 77,000 PK/m²
(8′ 7″ × 4′ 3″, 50 PK/in.²).

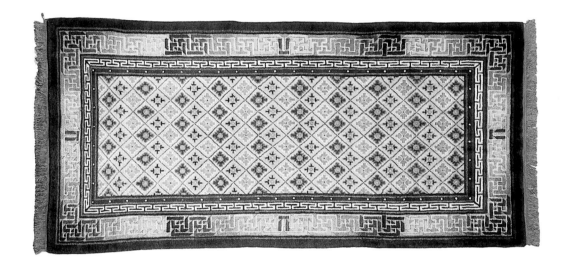

459 Peking 'Antique Finished',
186 × 93 cm, 101,000 PK/m²
(6′ 1″ × 3′ 0″, 65 PK/in.²).

460 Senjabi
67 × 57 cm, 138,000 TK/m²
(2′ 3″ × 1′ 10″, 89 TK/in.²).

with life (cf. p. 52), the pattern of alternating flowers in the Chinese piece is kept free of expressive feeling.

The Senjabi rug is quite another matter. Here we encounter all the ideas about Persian folk-art which keep presenting themselves in the course of this book; the hooked diamond (see fig. 475) with its varying associations for varying tribes, Cammann's 'sunbird' theory (p. 208), the possibility of repeating diamond panels being derived from the south-east Persian vase carpets or having a common ancestry with the Herati pattern (cf. figs. 166, 465). Then there is the question of the colouring: the wilful randomness of the colour distribution is clearly intended to produce anything but a quiet, unobtrusive effect. This does not mean it is not decorative, but that it is also an expressive vessel for the individual weaver's imagination. Of course, the Chinese rugs, too, reflect a cultural background in the folk-art sense, for they reflect the Chinese striving after an ideal beauty, an absolute to be achieved in all art by imitation and convention. This makes their beauty universal, but also anonymous; it appeals to us through its very foreignness. To the Western eye, however, it is the Iranian art, reflecting the struggles of the individual, that is closer to our own cultural traditions.

The rugs shown in figs. 458 and 459 are typical examples of their respective categories, which are more fully described elsewhere (see index). Figure 460 shows one side of a nomad donkey-bag. One often comes across these in the area of the Senjabi tribe, the southernmost weaving clan of the Kurdish group. Once they have served their purpose as transport or tent storage-bags the back is cut off and they are used as mats. Apart from this kind of piece the Senjabis also weave rugs which resemble those of the Kolyais, but are unmistakably distinguished by the use of a rusty shade of red, a tone which is never found in Kolyai rugs.

386, 461 KOLYAI

Most of the designs from the Kurdish areas of western Iran are bold and angular (see figs. 530–3 and 549–51), but one of them, known either as Bandi-Kurdi (i.e. stripe or ribbon design), or better as Shirshekeri (milk and sugar or honey), consists of an elegant all-over lattice-work. The design is unmistakable, and so are the colours: the lattice-work is dark blue (or dark green) and the panels are honey and cream-coloured. There are usually also little red flowers, suggestive of strawberries and cream, rather than milk and honey. The design is often referred to simply as Mina Khani. As with the Daghestan rug shown in fig. 437, it is certainly likely that the present form of the design is a Kurdish re-interpretation of the Mina Khani design as it developed in the eighteenth century in west-central Persia (see p. 329), but the author has never seen this theory documented. Three different types are made:

1 Traditional Kurdish kelleyis (i.e. about 240 × 130 cm; 8′ 0″ × 4′ 3″) woven single-wefted by Kolyai tribes near Sonqur, in the normal (very good) Kolyai quality and at the normal price; but only in this size or something near it – fig. 386 shows a typical example although smaller than average in size.

2 New manufactured carpets and rugs woven in the same region, but on an organized basis, and offering sizes not otherwise made by the Kurds, e.g. zaronims and 300 × 200 cm (10′ 0″ × 6′ 6″) carpets; the weave here is very fine and the quality excellent, but the price quite high (up to as much as twice the price of the traditional kelleyis).

3 A similar manufactured type including larger carpet sizes in a fine double-wefted structure rather like Bijar; fig. 461 illustrates one such piece, photographed from the back to show the weave. The price of these can be very high indeed.

All three types sometimes have medallion designs with a Shirshekeri ground. In the manufactured goods, pieces with a red ground are sometimes found, but otherwise the whole output is in the camel colour illustrated. Shirshekeri is used in Farsi as an adjective simply meaning 'buff-coloured'.

462, 463 BORUJIRD

The Borujird design shown in fig. 129 is one of the rarer types from the area around this small market town. A much more common one is shown in fig. 462. A comparison with figs. 753 and 754 will reveal that this is once again a western Persian derivative of the floral style of sixteenth-century Herat. As with the version from neighbouring Nenej (see fig. 760), blue grounds predominate, adding to the

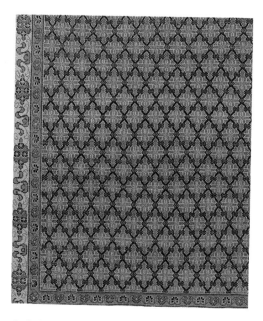

461 Shirshekeri pattern in a fine Kurdish carpet (detail).

462 Borujird
209 × 138 cm, 96,000 TK/m²
(6′ 10″ × 4′ 6″, 62 TK/in.²).

463 'Shah Abbas' palmette used as a repeating pattern in Oshturinan;
202 × 129 cm, 88,000 TK/m²
(6′ 7″ × 4′ 3″, 57 TK/in.²).

462

463

464 Mehrivan
311 × 229 cm, 65,000 TK/m² (10′ 2″ × 7′ 6″, 42 TK/in.²).

gloominess – previously referred to, – which makes Borujird goods unpopular, despite their fine lustrous yarn. The pattern of repeating 'Shah Abbas' palmettes in fig. 463 similarly reflects the design tradition based on geometric derivatives of classical motifs prevalent in the Borujird region. Oshturinan is one of the important production centres of the area. Both these types, like all Borujird rugs, are single-wefted; the technical notes given with regard to fig. 129 also apply here.

464 MEHRIVAN
Mehrivan (Mehriban) is the name of two quite unrelated important carpet origins in Persia. It is a district north of Hamadan, famous for fine runners and carpets as illustrated in fig. 642. There is also a village of the same name in the Heriz area of Azerbaijan. As applied to older goods, the latter Mehrivan represents the second grade of Heriz carpets (Heriz itself being the first, and Georovan the third), but today the name is more specifically applied to two distinct categories of newer goods: sound, medium-coarse carpets with a typical squarish medallion and distinguished by a brighter shade of red and a crisper appearance than is found in other Heriz goods; and, secondly, the all-over pattern illustrated in fig. 464. The red here is also typical, but cream grounds are also found. All-over designs are not common in the Heriz area today and this one certainly reflects the manufacturing tradition of the region from the early part of this century. The design has perhaps some affinity with the Herat-design derivatives of such places as Nenej, but the elaboration of the motifs is entirely in the Heriz-area style, and is always recognizable as such in the many variant forms which are found. Most rug sizes are found in small quantities, as in other Heriz villages, but the vast majority of the production is in medium carpet sizes.

465

466

465, 466 AFSHARI

The diamond-panel design of fig. 465 strikes one rather as somewhat foreign to the Afshar tradition. It is only made in the Sirjand area, not in the finer grades of the Shahr Babak group. Perhaps it represents a peasant re-interpretation of one of the all-over floral designs of eastern Persia illustrated on pp. 324–31; however, it is no longer possible to ascertain whether its origin might be the Herati pattern, the vase carpets or some garden design – or perhaps none of these. The use of the design in Sirjand is fairly common; it almost always appears in the extra-wide dozar size illustrated. There is no difficulty in recognizing the origin in view of the structural features detailed on p. 111. Figure 466, on the other hand, is immediately identifiable as Shahr Babak by its appearance alone. There is a trace of stiffness in the layout which is rather uncharacteristic, but the motifs themselves are very typical. Note here, too, the rather square format. General notes on the main Afshar types will be found on pp. 69, 120, 222.

467 REIHAN

The Armenian rugs of Lilihan and the Kemereh are described in several sections of this book (see index); a third type from the same region comes from the Muslim village of Reihan; the standard design is shown here. It is woven in the Lilihan single-wefted structure in a range of rug and carpet sizes. A more refined variant of the design is found in Saruq carpets, but the version shown here is always instantly recognizable as Reihan. Its origin must, of course, be – like the Borujird of fig. 462 – yet another geometric re-interpretation of the east Persian vase or Herati carpets, as a glance at fig. 755 will confirm. The Reihan output is small and the goods are woven almost exclusively with red grounds.

465 Sirjand 467
206 × 160 cm, 120,000 PK/m²
(6′ 9″ × 5′ 3″, 77 PK/in.²).

466 Shahr Babak
135 × 101 cm, 191,000 PK/m²
(4′ 5″ × 3′ 4″, 123 PK/in.²).

467 Reihan
145 × 120 cm, 128,000 TK/m²
(4′ 9″ × 3′ 11″, 83 TK/in.²).

2 GEOMETRIC REPEATING MEDALLION DESIGNS

468 Barjid
216 × 149 cm, 72,000 TK/m²
(7′ 1″ × 4′ 11″, 46 TK/in.²).

469 Chelabi
276 × 140 cm, 76,000 TK/m²
(9′ 1″ × 4′ 7″, 49 TK/in.²).

The separation of the following designs into a section of their own is perhaps not strictly justifiable on grounds of logic, for all of them could be fitted somehow into one of the three other categories of geometric designs in this chapter. However, a glance at the repeating medallion designs illustrated below will reveal that recognition is aided by having them so grouped. The category embraces all designs consisting of a single row or several rows of repeating (or alternating) medallions, such as form the basis of most of the runners made in the Orient, and those medallion designs on plain or covered grounds where the medallion's pendants are so enlarged or multiplied that they become, visually at least, further medallions in their own right.

468, 469 BARJID, CHELABI

The small Karabagh village of Chelabi, near the south-eastern edge of the Kazak area in Russian Azerbaijan, is the home of one of the most sought-after collector's items of the Caucasus, the 'Eagle' Kazak, or Chelaberd (the latter name being, according to Prof. Kerimov, a corruption of the village's real name). The number of medallions included depends on the length of the rug; small pieces may have only one medallion, or one whole and two halves. A much-repeated theory has it that the medallion represents the double-headed eagle with outstretched wings and claws which was the emblem of Imperial Russia. This association seems rather simplistic: at the very least the double-headed eagle has a heraldic significance reaching back far earlier than the time of Imperial Russian involvement with Azerbaijan; and Cammann reminds us that such a double-headed bird occurs frequently in oriental mythology as the beast guarding the entrance to Paradise. Other authorities have, however, cast doubt on the 'eagle' concept altogether, regarding the medallion as the stylization of a many-petalled flower and the idea of an eagle simply as the product of fanciful sales-talk. In fact, older versions of the design reveal features which can be traced back to the early Caucasian dragon carpets, a group (of highly controversial origin) discussed on p. 328. Whether, as a carpet-owner, one sees oneself as the keeper of mythical wardens of the Garden of Eden or as the unromantic observer of the abstract stylization of natural forms in decorative art, one will not escape the mysterious fascination of this powerful design and the appeal of its rich, soft colours.

The same design in an almost identical form is woven in Persian Azerbaijan over a hundred miles away, in Barjid, a village of the Karadagh region north of Heriz. The author has never seen any explanation of how such a distinctive design comes to be woven only in these two widely separated villages and nowhere else. The structure and appearance of the Persian version is quite different: whereas the Chelabi, like all old Kazaks, has a double-wefted structure with woollen warps and wefts, the Barjid has cotton warps and wefts and is single-wefted, with a weave closely related to the Karaja group to the south. The colours are best described as typical of Persian Azerbaijan – rose or ivory grounds with typical hard muddy reds and blues – giving a rather dead overall effect with none of the warmth and sparkle

469

470 Daghestan
197 × 139 cm, 150,000 TK/m²
(6′ 5″ × 4′ 7″, 97 TK/in.²).

471 Daghestan
210 × 134 cm, 155,000 TK/m²
(6′ 11″ × 4′ 5″, 100 TK/in.²).

of the Chelabis. Chelabi Kazaks come in various rug and kelleyi sizes; Barjids are found almost always in large dozar sizes, although the occasional wide runner may be found. A third origin copying this design (not illustrated) is Kars, one of the great cities of ancient Armenia (cf. p. 343); although today Kars is in Anatolia, the carpets produced there are all in old Caucasian designs, especially the bolder Kazak types. They are also no less copies than are the new Russian Kazaks, but they are executed with more imagination and individuality than the latter.

470, 471 DAGHESTAN
The Chelabi design is one that has been dropped by the Russians from the range now made in Armenia and Azerbaijan as 'new Kazaks'; but a variant of it is found in the new Daghestan carpets (fig. 470). Daghestan is the most northerly carpet-producing region of the Caucasus, although politically it is the southernmost province of the R.S.F.S.R., i.e. Russia proper. Before the Revolution a type of rug was made in Daghestan that is similar to what we now call Shirvan, but today the output is quite different. The rugs are immediately distinguishable because they are single-wefted (the only Caucasian type to be so). They are made throughout the province in two categories which are sold as Derbend (the cheaper grade) and Akhti-Mikrakh (the finer type). The difference between the two is not great; Akhti-Mikrakhs have a somewhat finer weave and a considerably finer, more lustrous worsted-type yarn. In view of the price difference the Derbends represent better value. The designs of both grades are identical, being based mainly on old geometric patterns employed in the northern Shirvan region; the range includes many patterns in a similar vein. The design of fig. 471 comes from Zeikhur (Shirvan) and represents, like the 'Eagle' Kazak, one of the most distinctive and easily identifiable of the old Caucasian patterns.

The big problem with the new Daghestans is their colours: one encounters brutally jarring contrasts of hard reds and fierce medium blues and big blocks of unharmonious colours including maroon, yellow, strange shades of green and a rose colour which is just too pink to be acceptable. However, if one can find a piece which has been skilfully washed to tone down these colour-clashes it is possible to acquire a well-made rug at an unrealistically low price. For further illustrations of Daghestan designs see index. The range of sizes made is surprisingly limited for a manufactured article: only large, squarish pushtis (e.g. 110 × 90 cm; 3′ 6″ × 3′ 0″), zaronims, dozars, short narrow runners and a small number of carpets up to about 6 m² (65 ft²) in area.

472 BABASEQAL
Babaseqal (sometimes written Kabaseqar, and in many other variant spellings, too) is the name of a clan of the Turkoman Ersari tribe living in the area between Andkhoy and Aq Chah; this clan has a small output of carpets. It is of course well known that Azerbaijan, in the Caucasus, was occupied by the Turkomans in the eleventh century and that many elements of Caucasian design are of Turkoman origin (see p. 224). One is therefore struck by the similarity between figs. 472 and 469. Whether this has any anthropological significance or is simply fortuitous cannot be said. In Babaseqal the medallions seem to represent flower forms which are less highly stylized than in other Turkoman göls. Their appearance as a chain of repeating medallions is of course purely accidental; as with all Afghan designs, a long and narrow shape automatically produces this layout from medallions which in carpet sizes form an all-over pattern (see figs. 387–432). The construction of Babaseqal rugs often reminds one of Alti Bolagh: the coarse to medium-fine weave has a ridged-back with heavy warps and wefts. The colours nowadays keep within the range generally found in Afghanistan, but more use is made of gold and ivory shades, and dark-blue or ivory grounds are more common than in other Ersari goods. The normal Afghan range of sizes is made (see p. 185).

473, 474 KHONJORESK
The two rugs shown are an old and a new example of the so-called 'cloud-band' Kazak. The curling motifs within the medallions are derived from the Chinese

472

473

474

cloud-band pattern which entered Persian carpet art after the whole empire (including Azerbaijan) was overrun by Timur at the end of the fourteenth century. The old Khonjoresk is a typical collector's piece, inspired by an expressive freedom and wealth of colour which are the sure signs of individual artistic imagination in the weaver. The new Kazak, a type produced in both Armenia and Azerbaijan, is quite a good copy: clean and sound in conception, with well managed corner-turns in the borders and subsidiary motifs strewn with calculated haphazardness across the ground. The calculated effect, of course, takes away much of the rug's character. There is no way that a modern manufactory can capture the elusive flair of the old Caucasian rugs. Old Kazaks are works of art (and are becoming priceless); new Kazaks are floor-coverings – well-made, often quite well coloured, and cheap: but they will never be the equal of 'old Kazaks', whatever their age.

The Kurds and Lurs

The Kurdish and Luri tribes, who occupy most of western Persia, belong to the oldest known of the Iranian peoples and their languages represent important early forms of the Aryan tongues. The Indo-Germanic languages form a whole family of dialects spoken in ancient times from east Turkestan, central Asia and northern India right through to western Europe. Within this vast area various major sub-groups are known to us – the Celtic, the Mediterranean, the Slavonic, the Sanskrit, the Germanic groups, etc. One of these is the Iranian group, within which again there is a wide range of dialects which are as much different languages as French and Spanish or German and Swedish. Apart from Farsi (modern Persian) and Urdu (Pakistani) one may mention Dari and Pashtu, the main languages of Afghanistan, both of which are Iranian dialects, Tajiki, spoken in the Tajik S.S.R.,

472 Babaseqal
121 × 65 cm, 143,000 PK/m²
(4′ 0″ × 2′ 1″, 92 PK/in.²).

473 Khonjoresk
254 × 114 cm, 95,000 TK/m²
(8′ 4″ × 3′ 9″, 61 TK/in.²).

474 Kazak
202 × 131 cm, 140,000 TK/m²
(6′ 7″ × 4′ 3″, 90 TK/in.²).

Map of the Kurdish and Luri weaving area.

Baluchi and many more, some spoken only by quite small clans. Often one may distinguish the languages according to their closeness to Old Persian; another important factor is how much Arabic the various languages absorbed during the period of Arab rule (seventh to ninth centuries).

From comparisons of archaeological records and the statements of ancient writers it seems possible that both the Kurds and the Lurs were aboriginal inhabitants of their respective regions. The Luri language is close to Old Persian; Kurdi is different but nevertheless related. The discernible evidence of the Kurds is the older. Although the name first occurs (as Kurtie and later as Kardu) in Assyrian documents, it seems that as much as 4,000 years ago they were established as the Gutu or Kuti tribe in the mid-Tigris area, from the Zagros mountains in the east to the Kuh-i-Shengar in the west. Their kinsmen, the Kassites (Kassu), ruled Babylon from *c.* 1800 to 1200 BC. By the sixth century BC several tribes in their present form can be identified, which makes their leaders the oldest aristocracy in the world. From the dawn of history they have fought tooth and nail against foreign domination, and although they are now split among several nation states they have to this day preserved a measure of independence which frequently disconcerts their rulers. From early times they have been pro-Persian. Their support of Kourosh and Darius earned them considerable autonomy within the Achaemenian Empire. After the Seljuq invasions the present regions of Persian Kurdistan and Kermanshahan enjoyed over 400 years of independence as the Khanate of Shahrazur. During the Turkish-Persian wars of the sixteenth century the region was occupied in 1514 by Sultan Selim I. Many Kurds were transported to the Caucasus by the Turks in an attempt to play them off against the Armenians, but the Kurds and Armenians joined forces with the Persians, and the Turks were driven out in 1536. Today the Kurds are concentrated in north-east Iraq, in eastern Turkey (with splinter groups in various parts of Anatolia), in the southern Caucasus and above all in Iran, where they occupy the province of Kurdistan and large parts of Kermanshahan and Azerbaijan, with small groups in many other places, such as Quchan.

The history of the Lurs is less flamboyant. They seem to be the aboriginal inhabitants of south-west Persia; their predominance in the Zagros mountains is perhaps the result of their having been driven there by early invaders of the Iranian plateau, rather as the Celts were driven into the mountains of western Europe by the invading Germanic tribes. The finest flowering of their culture occurred in the eighth century BC, when the Elamite Kingdom (see map, p. 343) developed into a great power in the region between Babylon and the Zagros mountains. Until the fifteenth century the tribe was split into the Great Lurs – the southern group – and the Little Lurs to the north (cf. p. 152). The Bakhtiars, members of the southern group, acquired great wealth and power over the centuries and have played a decisive political role in Persia on several occasions over the past two hundred years. The Lurs are often called Kuhi, which – like the Anatolian equivalent, Yürük – simply means 'mountain people'.

475 THE HOOKED-DIAMOND MOTIF
The Lurs, like all other Iranian tribes, have a wide range of traditional designs which are constantly being re-interpreted by individual weavers in countless variant forms. However, one particular design idea – the use of repeating diamond (lozenge) shapes – and one particular subsidiary motif – the 'latch hook' – occur again and again wherever there has been Luri influence in the design. It would probably be going too far to suggest that the hooked-diamond motif is the aboriginal property of the Luri tribes. To begin with, we know far too little about the Lurs to be able to make any such assumption, and, as Jenny Housego suggests, there are many rugs which we assume to be Luri which may in fact be the products of other tribes. The wide use of the motif in the kilims of Anatolia may mean that it is, culturally, the property of the Turkomans or other Turkic races and has merely been adopted by the Lurs in Iran. Whatever its origins, the pattern today always makes the carpet expert think of the Lurs, and it may thus be a useful clue in identification of carpets. What, if anything, the hooked diamond represents is a

a   b   c   d

475 Hooked medallion motifs in tribal kilims:
(a) Fethiyeh, western Anatolia; (b) Van, eastern
Anatolia; (c) Shah Savan, north-west Iran;
(d) Pashtun, Maimana region, Afghanistan.

subject of wide debate. As is true of all abstract carpet designs, one cannot prove
any theory, and the possible interpretations are endless, as noted above with regard
to the 'Eagle' Kazak (fig. 469). More to the point, perhaps, for the carpet buyer is
the uncanny expressive force the motif contains. Rather like a musical fugue, its
strict structural restraint is reassuring and convincing but allows for a huge
wealth of decorative elaboration and offers the weaver a great opportunity for
inventive use of colour. Its wide use in kilim work is not the immediate concern
of this book, but the illustrations here of flat-weave articles serve to reveal the
diversity of treatment which the basic idea is capable of inspiring. In figs. 477–86
several Luri-type diamond and hooked lozenge designs are grouped together, but
the motif will be found in many other designs in this section and in other sections,
too.

476 BELUCH

There is no reason why, when a carpet design appears in two geographically
separate areas, we should necessarily assume that there is a hidden connection.
The traditional insistence on doing so has led many authors, including no doubt
the present writer, to all sorts of questionable assumptions and assertions which
range from harmless speculation to seriously confusing factual inaccuracies. The
serious student of carpet design cannot escape the conclusion that the traditional
nomad and peasant carpets of Persia and the neighbouring areas reflect the essential culture of their producers and are thus anthropological documents as well as
objects of decorative art. Many carpet experts thus have that probing, inquiring
attitude of mind which is the inspiration of the successful archaeologist. What we
lack is the sound scientific training of the latter – hence the plethora of unsound
assertions; but that there is something worth probing and inquiring into – that
there *is* a reason why – we accept without reservation.

What then are we to conclude about the design of the Beluch carpet of fig. 476?
It is not an oddity, but typical of a small but regular output of the Beluch tribes
south of Herat in Afghanistan – one of the very few designs woven by the Beluchis
in carpet sizes. We cannot establish how it is that this design of the Fethiyeh kilims
of Turkey (see fig. 475a) is also used by the Beluchis of Afghanistan. Is it pure
chance? Is it perhaps related to the Herati design, or via the Herati design to the
Turkomans? See p. 77 for fascinating comparisons with similar motifs. If there is
a Herati connection, does the Beluch hooked-diamond motif represent a debased
peasant copy, or does it reflect a 'folk' tradition from which the Herati pattern was
developed? But fig. 476 also bears comparison with the Luri pieces seen in figs.
477ff. The Lurs and the Beluch both speak related Persian dialects, but the extent
of the connection has not been documented. Are the carpet designs evidence of a
closer relationship than is sometimes supposed? One of the great puzzles of the
Beluch carpet style is its extreme gloominess in colouring. Although good rugs have
a remarkably silky yarn, whose vibrant lustre fills the design with a powerful
expressive vitality, the basic idea is of a very dark colour combination indeed: the
dark blue is almost black, the subsidiary shades of dark green, dark red and brown
serve only to emphasize the effect to the extent that the pattern is sometimes almost
indistinguishable. Why? We do not know; but when we see the prominent use of
the latch-hook motif in the Luri carpets of Naghun (see fig. 484) and Khorramabad
(fig. 483), and in the rugs and kilims of Yağçibedir and Döşemealti in Anatolia –
many of which are gloomy to the point of excess – we are forced to conclude that it
is not merely because these weavers' local dyestuffs happen by pure chance to be
unusually dark: there must be some deeper cultural connection – the darkness of

476 Beluch
224 × 152 cm, 105,000 PK/m²
(7′ 4″ × 5′ 0″, 68 PK/in.²).

213

477 Shiraz Luri
258 × 160 cm, 94,000 TK/m²
(8' 5" × 5' 3", 61 TK/in.²).

the coloration and the expressive force of the hooked-diamond design must reflect some feature of their ethnographic heritage which is common to the peoples of all the above-named origins. And let there be no mistake about the expressive power – one can pore for hours over this dark, angular design and neither tire of nor fathom its mysterious fascination.

477 SHIRAZ LURI

The southernmost group of Luri weavers inhabit Fars province, in the region between the Persian Gulf and the southern end of the Zagros mountains. Their carpets are marketed in Shiraz. A typical design is illustrated here, but what a black-and-white photograph cannot reveal is the wide range of bright colours used – greens, light and medium blues, orange, gold, red and white – in a profusion which can sometimes prove a decided disadvantage. Rugs of this kind need a certain amount of patina to be acceptable in Western markets. The light-red shade and the light colours in general are unusual in Luri goods of most other areas. In the Shiraz type shown here only one size is made – approximately 250 × 160 cm (8' 3" × 5' 3"). Note that the warps are usually of shiny black goat hair. For other Shiraz Luri rugs see index.

478–481 GEBBEH

Gebbeh rugs are made by all the tribes of Fars province and no doubt by many settled villages as well. The Luri style predominates but the diversity is so great that the present writer has never met anyone who could offer a regular and consistent definition of the precise origin of any particular rug. Some traders describe the heavier or finer types as Qashqai, which though certainly right in general, is just as likely to be wrong in any given case. The name Qashqai is well known, and known for good quality, and that fact – for anyone trying to sell a rug – is sufficient reason in itself to describe the rug as a Qashqai. Gebbehs are made in two distinct types, the coloured and the naturals. In the former almost anything is possible in terms of both design and colour. Several types are illustrated in various parts of this book (see index); one of the typical Luri diamond-and-hook versions is shown in fig. 481. Here, too, the warps are often of goat hair, although wool is also used. Cotton warps in real Gebbehs are practically unknown (although common in cheap copies from elsewhere). Another geometric coloured type is shown in fig. 445. The 'natural' Gebbehs (figs. 478 and 479) are often made with undyed yarn in various shades of cream, white, grey, brown and black, with (in the best pieces) a warm mottled effect on the cream ground. The Luri influence may be less obvious here, but the designs are usually bolder than in coloured pieces, although the ground may also be covered with secondary motifs. The important thing about true Gebbeh designs is that they are not 'designed' – they are primitive, spontaneous and utterly unpredictable. Regrettably, their popularity has led to widespread copying of the genuine tribal pieces in manufactured articles throughout the Shiraz region. Manufactured Gebbehs, often known as Shulis after the tribe that makes them (fig. 480), are in many instances better in quality than the tribal ones, but they mostly lack the unspoiled character which is the very *raison d'être* of the latter. The quality is not intended to be hard-wearing, but Gebbehs should have a long pile – the word means 'unclipped' or 'long-haired'. The coloured Gebbehs sometimes have a remarkable number of wefts – even as many as eight or ten – between each row of knots, so that they sometimes look more like kilims with strips of pile across them. Only one basic size is made, approximately 200–230 cm (6' 6"–7' 6") in length and 100–120 cm (3' 3"–4' 0") in width. Just occasionally one comes across smaller sizes in the coloured types.

482 BEHBEHAN

From Shiraz the Luri tribes are spread out to the north-west throughout the Zagros mountains and right up into the Kurdish area south-west of Hamadan. The next market centre after Shiraz is Behbehan. The Luri rugs from this region are just as varied in design and colour as the goods from the Shiraz area, but in different ways. They tend to be gloomier than the Shiraz Luris, often with a

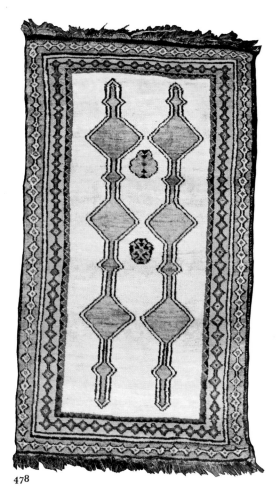

478

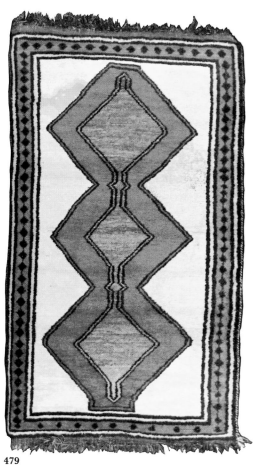

479

478 Gebbeh (natural)
205 × 108 cm, 54,000 PK/m²
(6′ 9″ × 3′ 6″, 35 PK/in.²).

479 Gebbeh (natural)
195 × 110 cm, 68,000 TK/m²
(6′ 5″ × 3′ 7″, 44 TK/in.²).

480

481

480 Gebbeh (Shuli)
210 × 106 cm, 100,000 PK/m²
(6′ 11″ × 3′ 6″, 65 PK/in.²).

481 Gebbeh (coloured)
220 × 138 cm, 82,000 PK/m²
(7′ 3″ × 4′ 6″, 53 PK/in.²).

482 Behbehan
253 × 135 cm, 53,000 TK/m²
(8' 3" × 4' 5", 34 TK/in.²).

mauvish red and some badly dyed shades of blue which have a grey-black appearance. Add to this the favourite Luri shade of bright orange (usually dyed with one of the fastest dyes known to man, which neither age nor chemical washing will tone down) and we have an example of the 'spontaneous' type gone wrong: clumsy designing and bad colours remain clumsy and bad whether or not they are the 'essential expression of a whole people'. The rugs are fairly coarse and are very often long and narrow; but they have a thick pile and heavy construction, and where natural dyestuffs are used (which is still fairly often) a piece with a strong individual character results. As with the Shiraz Luris, very many permutations of bold medallions and 'latch-hooks' are possible. The linking of the medallions in the manner illustrated is quite common. Behbehan Luris often have cotton warps, as well as the traditional goat hair or sheep's wool.

483 KHORRAMABAD
Moving further to the north-west through the Zagros mountains, the next principal market centre we encounter is Khorramabad. The products of this area are easily recognized. To begin with, they are generally in only one size – rather wide dozars (say 190–200 × 140–150 cm; 6' 3"–6' 6" × 4' 6"–5' 0"). Secondly, they all have cotton warps. Then there are the dark, gloomy colours of the rugs, which aspect extends even to the wefts, which are black, brown or dark grey, thus giving a very dark look to the back of the rug. If Behbehan reds are often tinged with mauve, here they are full-blooded mauve, again combined with very dark blackish blue and liberal doses of orange, the latter especially in rugs from Ilam, near the Iraqi frontier, which also belong to this group. The designs are still unmistakably Luri, but bolder and clumsier than other Luri types. Here, too, we often find another typical Luri design, the dominant medallion illustrated in fig. 578. The whole output is coarse – thick and shaggy – and only a small proportion can really be called pleasing in appearance. Khorramabads are at least hard-wearing and cheap, however, and they usually have those special features such as embroidered kilims and plaited fringes which suggest that the rugs were made for the weavers' own use.

484 OWLAD
To the east of the areas described above there are three Luri or Luri-type groups who produce a superior grade of goods. The first is Owlad, a clan located around

483 Khorramabad
235 × 143 cm, 71,000 TK/m²
(7' 8" × 4' 8", 46 TK/in.²).

484 Owlad
266 × 190 cm, 67,000 TK/m²
(8' 9" × 6' 3", 43 TK/in.²).

483

484

the mountain village of Naghun on the south-western edge of the Bakhtiari province (cf. note to fig. 348). Here again the colours are often rather gloomy, with dark red and dark blue predominating, relieved only by a little white, light blue or gold, but they improve with age; careful washing can also make a world of difference. Moreover, the finely detailed geometric designs are very attractive in themselves. Like the Turkomans, the Owlad Lurs can with finesse and subtlety produce an infinite variety of permutations of the same simple geometric elements. The most common type is illustrated here; and others are shown in figs. 348 and 446. The wefts are usually of red cotton, the warps of white cotton or black or brown goat hair. The wool is fine and silky and the best pieces are just what a traditional nomadic rug should be. The bulk of the production is in carpet sizes of between 4 and 7 m² (43 to 75 ft²). Note that the word 'Pashkuhi' as applied to these goods does not refer to the ancient tribal group of this name (see p. 152).

485 YALAMEH

To the east of the Owlad we find the Yalameh tribe, who seem also to belong to the Luri group, although some say they have Qashqai connections. The 'busy' appearance of their designs and the myriad of small details certainly seems more Qashqai-inspired – the Lurs usually tend to prefer bolder, uncluttered carpet layouts. If the Yalamehs are of Luri origin they make the most flamboyant goods of the whole group, using a wide range of mostly bright colours, with light reds, medium blues, buffs and leafy greens being particularly noticeable. The main weaving area is on the south-eastern edge of the Bakhtiari area near Shah Reza; the market town is Talkhuncheh, but the goods are usually bought in Isfahan. All sizes are made, from pushti to carpets up to 8 m² (85 ft²), but by far the most common are zaronims. Note that carpets always cost relatively more per square metre than rugs, sometimes much more. The Luri diamond medallion adorned with latch-hooks is usually present, often in the two- or three-medallion arrangement illustrated in fig. 485, but also in many other geometric layouts. Bakhtiari-type panel designs are also found (fig. 349). Yalamehs are medium-to-fine in weave and quite expensive, and are of all-wool construction, the best pieces having a considerably higher knot-count than the rug shown here and a superb silky yarn for the pile. Note the 'barber's pole' whipping of the selvedge.

486 NASRABAD

The most easterly Luri origin is called Nasrabad, the production area being just south-east of Isfahan, on the edge of the desert – which suggests that these 'Lurs' might also be Qashqais, or one of several rug-weaving Arab tribes. Nasrabads are the most exclusive rugs of the group, with a very small output which seems so far to have defied attempts at commercial bastardization. The prices asked, which are out of all proportion to the fineness of the weave, in fact reflect the demand for rugs with an unspoiled individual character. Only rugs and runners are made, usually in the Luri 'medallion-with-pendants' design illustrated. The colours are light and harmonious, with light red and camel or buff shades predominating. The construction, though coarse, is much more tightly packed and robust than that of the Yalamehs, which can be very floppy. The warps are usually of goat hair, but cotton-warped pieces are also found.

487–493 SHIRAZ

There are no carpets woven in Shiraz, the capital city of Fars province, except in the north-western suburb of Bulverdi, which used to be a separate village. However, the city is the regional market, and hence the name Shiraz is given to the products of many hundreds of villages and wandering tribes from all over the province. All the villages, of course, have their own names and styles of design, but very few are widely known, even to specialists in the trade. Much of the production is in the medallion/all-over style illustrated in fig. 594, but many variants of the repeating medallion idea are also found. All the designs are of tribal origin. Some of the tribes are permanently settled in villages, others are still nomadic or semi-nomadic. There is considerable racial variety in the region – Turki-speaking

485 Yalameh
150×95 cm, 141,000 PK/m²
(4′ 11″×3′ 1″, 91 PK/in.²).

486 Nasrabad
191×109 cm, 86,000 TK/m²
(6′ 3″×3′ 7″, 55 TK/in.²).

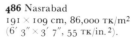

487

488

487 Qashqai
180 × 115 cm, 154,000 PK/m²
(5′ 11″ × 3′ 9″, 99 PK/in.²).

488 Qashqai
206 × 130 cm, 94,000 TK/m²
(6′ 9″ × 4′ 3″, 61 TK/in.²).

489 Qashqai end-frieze.
In Qashqai goods this kind of decoration is always
knotted, but in rugs made elsewhere it usually
occurs as part of the kilim (cf. fig. 48, Kala-i-Zal).

Qashqais (the largest carpet-producing group, with many sub-tribes), Farsi-
speaking Arabs, Lurs with their own special Persian dialect, Farsi-speaking
Persians of the Khamseh Confederation (not to be confused with the Khamseh
sub-district of Hamadan, see fig. 583) and other small groups of various Persian
and Turkic origins. This racial complexity is one important reason why differentiation between individual types is difficult and distinctions become blurred. Another
reason is the sheer inaccessibility of the countryside inhabited by nomadic people.
The largest weaving group in Fars is that of the Qashqai tribes. There are many
legends about how the Qashqais came to Fars and what the name means, but there
is no firm evidence. That most of them are of Turkic origin is certain, so it must be
assumed that they came to Persia with the Seljuqs, or at the very latest in the wake
of Jinghis Khan or Timur. Some clans of Luri, Kurdish or Arab origin joined the
confederation later. The group is divided into many individual clans, most of
which remain nomadic to this day. They spend the winters in the lowlands south
of Shiraz and migrate northwards in the spring to spend the summer in the Zagros
mountains. The area they inhabit extends a full 300 miles, from the southern edge
of the Chahar Mahal to Lar, near the Persian Gulf. Not all the clans weave, but
the goods produced by those that do represent the finest work of Fars province.
Today there is an output of exceptionally fine weave in lurid colours destined for
the Arab market of the Gulf States. The medium-fine carpets found in Western
carpet shops and illustrated in various parts of this book (see index under 'Qashqai'
and 'Gebbeh') are mostly old or semi-old pieces. The Turkic origin of the tribes
is clearly reflected in the carpet designs, which often contain motifs commonly
found in Caucasian carpets. In some cases old Qashqais are so like old Shirvans

490

491

that only experts can tell them apart. The oldest and best piece in the group illustrated here is fig. 487. Both this and fig. 488 contain many features which are typical of the Qashqai style. In both pieces the medallions contain reminiscences of the dragon and other animal motifs of early Turkoman and Caucasian carpets in forms which are probably related to the *hebatlu* medallions illustrated in fig. 595. The profusion of plant forms and animal figures are a characteristic feature of designs woven throughout Fars province. Figure 488 calls to mind the flowers seen in the vase carpets (see fig. 180) and the yearning of the nomad herdsman for the colour and the shady trees of the Persian garden. The ground in fig. 487 treats the plant forms in a more abstract and random fashion, scattering them through a thoroughly debased version of the Herati pattern. The weave of both carpets is firmer and has a more ridged back than most other Shiraz rugs. A further useful little clue to the Qashqai origin is the small square pattern which appears as a strip across both ends of the rug (fig. 489).

Figure 490 represents the best grade of Shiraz rugs. Many features are shared with the products of the Qashqais, including the border, which is commonly used in Abadeh (see fig. 597), where many of the weavers are settled Qashqais. The rug does not have quite the clarity and flair of the best Qashqai goods, however. The village rugs of Fars have a looser construction and a somewhat thicker, shaggier pile than those made by the neighbouring nomads. These features are evident also in figs. 491 and 492, which represent the standard grade of Shiraz rugs. Note the connection between the borders of figs. 491 and 349; the Qashqai border of fig. 490 is frequently found in seventeenth- and eighteenth-century Herat carpets. Figure 491 is a product of Arab nomads (see also fig. 494); fig. 492 of settled Persian

490 Shiraz
206×162 cm, 132,000 TK/m^2
(6′ 9″ × 5′ 4″, 85 TK/in.^{2}).

491 Shiraz
220×154 cm, 72,000 PK/m^2
(7′ 3″ × 5′ 0″, 46 PK/in.^{2}).

492 Shiraz
156 × 118 cm, 50,000 PK/m²
(5′ 1″ × 3′ 10″, 32 PK/in.²).

493 Shiraz
148 × 92 cm, 39,000 PK/m²
(4′ 10″ × 3′ 0″, 25 PK/in.²).

villagers. The definition and expressive urgency of the Qashqai style is missing; but these two simple peasant rugs contain attractive and original interpretations of the traditional style. Not so fig. 493, which illustrates a category of low-grade Shiraz goods which became common in the late 1960s. Shiraz rugs (like Hamadan rugs and Heriz carpets) had always been regarded as bread-and-butter merchandise by European importers: as fig. 490 shows, they had warm, appealing colours and richly inventive designs, and they were cheap. As Iran's oil wealth increased, however, the prices rose steeply and sales began to stagnate: faced with high prices for what were considered low-grade goods, buyers turned to other types (such as Afshars), which, although more expensive, seemed much more attractive and thus better value for money. The weavers of Shiraz, instead of improving their product to make the higher price more acceptable, took the opposite course: they cut both the price and the quality, using a coarser weave, fewer colours, inferior materials, less imaginative designs. The rug illustrated is typical of this development, and is typical of what may be found in Shiraz today. Meanwhile, the importers had discovered that the Indians could produce much better rugs at much less cost. Many buyers will still choose a low-grade Shiraz in preference to a high-grade Indian rug because the Shiraz is 'genuine Persian', with all the overtones of the ancient cultural traditions that the description implies, but the new cheap rugs of Shiraz have as much to do with the folk art of Persia as a tin of grape juice concentrate has with a bottle of Château Lafite.

494 BOWANAT
People are sometimes surprised to hear of Persian rugs being woven by Arab tribes; in fact this simply means that in various parts of Iran there are tribes of Arab origin, just as there are countless other ethnic groups. Their presence dates from the era of Persia's conversion to Islam. The Prophet Muhammad was from the very first a warrior-priest. The concept of the *jihad*, or holy war, was fundamental to his teachings. At first he secured the power-base of Islam in Arabia, and the subsequent spread of Islam was synonymous with the expansion of Arab power. Two centuries elapsed before the full extent of the Arab Empire was achieved – from the Atlantic coast of Spain through North Africa to the whole of Western Asia (except Byzantium) and thence through to the borders of India and China (see maps, p. 343). But the bulk of this territory was conquered in the first eighty years after the Prophet's death. The 400-year old Sassanian Empire of Persia collapsed under the Arab onslaught in the earliest years of this explosion of Muhammadanism. After eight years of siege and harassment a single battle near Nehavend in 641 was enough to open up the whole of Persia to the Arabs. The spearhead of their troops were small bands of fast-moving cavalry (mounted on horses or camels) who fanned out across vast territories, often leaving the reduction of fortified towns until later. Such a vast empire could, of course, not be occupied, only garrisoned: unlike the Turkomans, where the whole nation was migrating, the Arabs were out to subjugate and plunder, not to colonize. Thus, of all the races who have invaded Persia, the Arabs have had perhaps the least impact on the make-up of the population.

Among the most important of the Arab groups in modern Iran are those of the Ferdaus area of Khorassan, who weave Beluch-style goods, imitation cheap Gebbehs and a few other items in their own designs; and those of the area north and east of Shiraz, whose products bear a family resemblance to those of all the tribes of Fars province. The tribes are fairly widely dispersed over a large area from Shiraz to Abadeh and beyond. One of their main market centres is Bowanat (or Bohnad), which produces rugs in a rather distinctive design, as illustrated in fig. 494. The saw-tooth edging to the medallions is a typical feature, and so is the way the subsidiary motifs are coloured with quite large blocks of single shades – there is less of the minute detail one finds in other Shiraz rugs. The structure, too, is different to that used elsewhere in the province, having a fairly widely spaced but quite distinct ribbing on the back, which moreover looks very dark, owing to the almost black or dark-brown woollen wefts. The pile is long and dense and, the construction, although not as firm as that of Qashqai rugs, promises more wear than that of the run-of-the-mill Shiraz village goods.

494 Bowanat
173 × 129 cm, 122,000 TK/m²
(5′ 8″ × 4′ 3″, 79 TK/in.²).

495 Döşemealti
199 × 116 cm, 58,000 TK/m²
(6′ 6″ × 3′ 10″, 37 TK/in.²).

495 DÖŞEMEALTI
Leaving aside the tribal Veramin rugs, which have now completely disappeared
from the general market (see p. 330), there are no other clearly defined major Luri
groups beyond those already described; but there are countless small pockets of
Lurs in Turkey, Persia (especially Azerbaijan) and the Caucasus, and in many
places Luri-type designs predominate even though the Luri element in the population may be very small or even completely submerged. In Turkey the design that
is closest in appearance to Luri styles is the Döşemealti. This name refers to an
Anatolian village in which several variants of the two designs illustrated here and in
fig. 268 are woven – the one made up of latch hooks forming a tree-like shape, the
other having several (usually three) bold medallions on a plain field. Goods from
this village have several characteristic features: the ground is almost always red –
rather bright and hard when the rug comes off the loom, but with age or careful
washing this becomes a warm brown-red or rose shade; the red may also be quite
dark, and rugs in the design shown in fig. 268 are also found on dark-blue grounds;
in such cases one can detect a similarity with Beluch rugs. The corners of the ground
may be dark- or medium-blue, or they may be a rich, warm bottle-green, a colour
which is also found in other parts of the design. The border design (as illustrated

221

496 Shahr Babak
155 × 105 cm, 185,000 PK/m²
(5′ 1″ × 3′ 5″, 119 PK/in.²).

497 Senneh
147 × 110 cm, 220,000 TK/m²
(4′ 10″ × 3′ 7″, 142 TK/in.²).

here) is unmistakable, as also is the structure: the warps and wefts are of wool, the weave medium, quite firm but flexible to the handle. See also fig. 544.

496 SHAHR BABAK
The Afshars of Kerman province are another of the tribes of Persia who make use of the hooked diamond as a subsidiary motif, perhaps reflecting these tribes' Turkoman ancestry. In the piece illustrated, from the area of Shahr Babak (the market centre for the finest Afshar weaves), the chain of three diamond medallions is preserved, but they are set within three square-sided polygons, which themselves form the centrepiece of a large six-sided outer medallion. The idea of medallions within medallions is quite common, but the Afshars have a fascinating knack of balancing them so finely that one is never sure which part is the centrepiece and which the frame. This feature is also present in the Sirjand Afshar rug shown in fig. 559. For general notes on Shahr Babak rugs, see pp. 69, 111. Another Afshar type with repeating medallion designs comes from the Jiruft region, south-east of the Shahr Babak/Sirjand area. The goods are traded as Kuhi, which suggests a Luri connection (cf. p. 212). Indeed, they have many features that remind one of the Zagros Luris sold as Behbehans (cf. p. 216), but the designs and colours belong clearly to the Afshari tradition.

497 SENNEH
The use of a repeating diamond on a plain ground occurs widely among the Kurds of western Iran. The rug illustrated is from the Kurdish capital, Senneh; in this example, too, the eye is drawn to the polygonal framework within which the diamonds are set. Since the Kurds now occupy the same region as was once inhabited by the Afshars, before Nadir Shah had the tribe moved to the Kerman area in the 1730s, perhaps there is some cultural-historical link between figs. 497 and 496. As far as carpet identification is concerned, the Senneh is quite unmistakable, both from its weave, as described on p. 61, and from the special dismembered variant of the Herati pattern which is used to fill both the medallions and the corners of the rug illustrated. Note also the *hashtguli* design (cf. fig. 133) in the central medallion. This three-medallion design is one of the most common in Senneh: it owes much of its success to the brilliant lustrous yarn of Kurdistan, which enlivens the plain ground.

498, 499 KOLYAI, CHENAR
The typical Kolyai tribe version of this three-medallion design is shown in fig. 498. Many differences of detail are employed in the various individual villages of the region, but the basic framework remains the same. It is, however, confusing to find an almost identical version (fig. 499) made in Chenar, a Hamadan village belonging to the Zagheh group, quite close to the edge of the Kurdish area, and, to complicate matters further, a fairly accurate copy of the Chenar runners is made in Pakistan. The Pakistan copies are usually fairly easy to recognize from their double-weave construction, but in order to distinguish rugs from the two Persian sources, one must refer, as always, to the weave and to a series of other clues. Firstly, the sizes: Kolyais are always about 250 × 130 cm (8′ 3″ × 4′ 3″), although some fine manufactured goods in this design have recently appeared in other sizes, whereas Chenar goods are mostly zarchereks and narrow runners (although other rug sizes are also found). Next, colours: the Zagheh group is distinguished by appalling dyestuffs and some excruciating colour combinations, which the Kurds mostly avoid; the Zagheh shades of shocking pink and various 'electric' greens for example, are among the worst of the whole Hamadan region. Finally, the yarn is different, being more spongy and liable to felting in Chenar, and more resilient and lustrous in the Kurdish area. This is the most important difference, which will also always prove decisive in distinguishing the Persian rugs from Pakistan copies. A further variant of this basic design is made in another part of the Hamadan region, in the village of Faizabad in the Ferahan district. The speciality of its quite small production is rather wide runners. The colourings are attractively rich and warm in the typical Ferahan style.

498 Kolyai
230 × 133 cm, 88,000 TK/m²
(7′ 6″ × 4′ 4″, 57 TK/in.²).

499 Chenar
199 × 76 cm, 90,000 TK/m²
(6′ 6″ × 2′ 6″, 58 TK/in.²).

500–518 AZERBAIJAN

The present-day territorial limits of Azerbaijan – the Soviet Republic and the two Persian provinces – are shown on the map (see p. 345), but the region of the southern Caucasus, embracing also Soviet Armenia, Georgia and Daghestan and the north-east corner of Anatolia, has had a complex history. There are more languages spoken in the Caucasus than in any other area of comparable size in the world. They include Indo-European tongues like Armenian, Kurdish, Talish and Ossetic, Uralic/Altaic (Turkic) dialects such as Azerbaijanian, as well as others that do not belong to either of these two major groups which otherwise dominate the carpet-producing areas of western and central Asia. The region was one of the oldest known sites of bronze working. From *c.* 1200 BC onwards, but especially in the ninth and eighth centuries, the Kingdom of Urartu (Ararat), centred on the triangle of lakes Van, Sevan and Urmia, rivalled the power of the Assyrians. The Hayk entered the area from *c.* 600 BC onwards, founding the Kingdom of Armenia, which at the height of its power stretched from Kayseri to the Caspian. The influence of the ancient Scythians from the north and of the Medes and Persians, and later the Arabs, from the south, has left its mark, but for over 900 years the dominant feature has been that of the Turks, and more especially the Turkomans. The Seljuqs conquered the region in the early eleventh century (only Christian Armenia remained independent), and their language and culture have been influential ever since. In the thirteenth century the Turkomans became the nominal vassals of the Mongols, but their effective independence re-asserted itself at an early stage.

The capital of Azerbaijan, Tabriz, was a centre of learning and of the arts long before the rise of the Herat design school in the fifteenth century (see p. 274). The vizier of the first Islamic Mongol Il-Khans Ghazan and Oljeitü, Rashid-ad-Din, founded a library of 60,000 manuscript volumes and a school of painting there that were the envy of the Muslim world for the first two decades of the fourteenth

500 Turkoman motifs in Caucasian rugs.
Cf. (a) fig. 392 (main border); (b) fig. 325 (outer border); (c) fig. 401 (narrowest guards); (d) fig. 397 (bottom panel).

century. But by 1335 the Il-Khan dynasty (Jinghis Khan's successors in Persia; see p. 273) faded away and Azerbaijan was annexed by the Golden Horde, the Mongol state to the north. It was regained, however, in 1356 by the Jalayirids. After the collapse of the Il-Khani power Iran was split for a century or more into a large number of minor emirates. Among these, that founded in 1340 by Hasan-i-Bozurg was the most important. This so-called Jalayir dynasty controlled Iraq (Mesopotamia), Kurdistan and Azerbaijan. Their capital was Baghdad, but it was this west Persian petty emirate that was to become the nucleus for the later Safavid Empire. At the end of the fourteenth century the Kara Koyunlu Turkomans of Azerbaijan threw off the Jalayirid control. They were beaten by Timur, but regained Tabriz, their capital, in 1406. They resisted the efforts of Shah Rukh, Timur's successor (see p. 273), to include Azerbaijan in the east Persian Mongol Empire and after his death Jahan Shah (ruled 1438–68) extended the Kara Koyunlu domains at Timurid expense. A rival Turkoman clan, the Ak Koyunlu of Diyarbakir, overthrew Jahan Shah in 1468. Their great leader Uzun Hasan (ruled 1453–78) carried Tabriz to a high peak of imperial splendour and extended the Turkoman rule even as far as Herat (which was held only briefly, however). There are suggestions that some of the classic carpets usually attributed to the Safavids might perhaps have come from the workshops of late fifteenth-century Turkoman Tabriz (see fig. 179). Uzun Hasan's successor Yaqub incurred the unpopularity of his tribesmen by his strict Sunni orthodoxy and by his fiscal reforms, which greatly assisted the spread of Shi'ite propaganda from the increasingly influential Sufi convent of Ardebil that had been founded by Sheikh Safi at the beginning of the fourteenth century. The Safavid bid for temporal power began with campaigns in the Caucasus by Sheikh Heidar, a protégé of the Ak Koyunlu and kinsman by marriage of Uzun Hasan. After Heidar's death his son, Ismail, assumed leadership of the Safavids and occupied Baku and Shemakha in 1499. Taking advantage of the discontent with Ak Koyunlu rule he secured the support of a confederation of seven Turkoman tribes (including the Afshars) known as the Kizil Bash ('red turbans'), whose lancers swept away the Ak Koyunlu and established Ismail as Shah. The whole of Azerbaijan and the Caucasus were now included in the Persian state, but faced an ever-growing threat from the Ottoman Turks in the west. The Ottomans had defeated Uzun Hasan in 1473 and from then until the seventeenth century (and again in the eighteenth) war between Persia and Turkey flared at irregular but frequent intervals. Azerbaijan, Mesopotamia and Kurdistan were occupied many times by the Ottomans. Tabriz, for example, was in Turkish hands in 1514, again in 1534, 1538 and 1547; peace was concluded in 1555, but in 1585 the Turks again captured Tabriz, this time holding the city for eighteen years. The war continued until 1639, when the disputed lands were divided, Turkey holding Mesopotamia while Persia kept Azerbaijan. Armenia was split into two, a disaster for the inhabitants. Shah Abbas II, fearing a revolt in consequence, transported thousands of the Hayk to central Persia (which is the explanation for the Armenian presence in Lilihan, Feridan etc.). On the Turkish side a similar distrust led to endless persecution, culminating in the notorious massacres of many of the Armenian population in 1915, after which the remainder were driven into the desert by the Turks and Kurds and left to starve to death.

As Safavid power waned in Persia, Azerbaijan fell into open revolt, but Persian control was again established in 1735 by Nadir Shah, yet another ruler of Turkoman (Afshar) descent. By now, however, an even more ominous threat loomed before the Persian power in the form of the southward expansion of Muscovite Russia. The Russians had supported the revolt which Nadir Shah had crushed, but after his departure from the scene Persia was militarily a spent force, and in a series of short wars between 1795 and 1828 Russia was able to annex the whole of Azerbaijan and Armenia north of the River Araxes.

The centuries of Turkoman influence permeate the carpet style of both the northern and southern halves of the region, but it is the Persian manufacturing tradition, resulting from centuries of Persian rule, which dominates the production, even in the north of the region. In the nineteenth century the workshops of Kuba and many other towns and villages of the Shirvan district produced rugs of geometric design whose brilliant detail and magnificent colours cause many collectors to regard them as the highest pinnacle of the weaver's art. After the 1917 revolution the most northerly part, Daghestan, became part of the R.S.F.S.R., while Georgia, Armenia and Azerbaijan all became autonomous Soviet republics. Carpets are still made today in Daghestan, Georgia and Armenia, but the real home of Russian Caucasian carpets remains Azerbaijan and the skills and ideas of Azerbaijanian weavers are felt throughout the Caucasus. The language spoken in the region is Azerbaijanian (a Turkish dialect), which, even in books printed in Russia, has its own version of the Cyrillic script. It is not clear to what extent the people's independent spirit is a reflection of historical traditions or how much of it is merely an outlet for anti-Russian feeling; but it does seem that this complex racial mixture, from Scythians to Turks and Turkomans, from Persians to Kurds to Lurs, has developed an intensely nationalistic feeling and an idea of united independence which transcends the individual origins.

After 1828 the southern half of Azerbaijan remained part of Persia, with Tabriz the provincial capital, although no longer the capital of Persia itself. The weaving style of Persian Azerbaijan has developed quite differently from that of the Russian Caucasus, being altogether coarser, wilder in design, more rustic in character. Leaving aside the towns of Tabriz and Ardebil and the large carpet-making area of Heriz, the great speciality of Persian Azerbaijan is the production of rugs and, more especially, runners. Countless tiny and inaccessible mountain villages weave runners in a huge range of geometric styles. They all have a family resemblance but very few carpet experts can give an accurate name to many of them. We can distinguish the Meshkin/Ardebil group, the Sarabs, also Karaja and Lamberan, but the rest we simply call Azerbaijan. They can be any length from 200 cm (6' 6") upwards, and from 70 to 140 cm (2' 3" to 4' 6") wide. The vast majority are 100–110 cm (3' 3"–3' 6") wide, and this has tended to reduce their popularity in the West (most people want runners for halls and stairways around 70–90 cm – 2' 3"–3' 0" – wide). They are also rather stiff and uncompromising in design and colour – not crude or garish, but with hard reds and blues in combinations that lack a certain grace and that appealing warmth which characterizes the peasant goods of central and southern Persia (and the old goods of Russian Azerbaijan). The construction – cotton warp and weft, coarse weave with a heavy woollen pile – is extremely robust. The designs include almost all variants of geometric forms: some with close-covered grounds, some with bold repeating medallions; some have little human and animal figures, but most are made up of combinations of stars, hexagons, octagons, rhombuses, lozenges of all shapes and sizes. Two typical examples of the style are illustrated in figs. 442 and 502, and the reader may adduce more of the flavour of the region from the following more specific sections. One particular clue to recognition which is common to the whole region is the flat selvedge, as illustrated in fig. 40.

501–504 ARDEBIL AND MESHKIN

When, during the Second World War, the supply of Shirvans and other Russian Caucasian types dwindled to practically nothing, the weavers of Ardebil, near the Caspian Sea in Persian Azerbaijan, stepped in to meet the demand, changing their whole production from the thick, bold, heavy type shown in figs. 508 and 509 to the fine, thin goods of which fig. 501 is an example. A coarser and thicker – and generally cruder – grade of this style was adopted in the neighbouring town of Meshkin (on the road north-west to Ahar), narrow runners being the speciality, although some rugs and carpets are also made. Ardebils of this so-called 'new style' are not easy to distinguish from Shirvans. There is a stylistic difference in design, and to the trained eye the weave also appears different, but it is difficult to express this difference in words, or even by photographs. A few small clues sometimes help. Ardebils, for example, often include little human and animal figures, and this feature is not usually found in new Shirvans. The Ardebil colourings are more varied, with subtle pastel shades often prominent, although a crude, hard red sometimes also makes itself felt. Another clue is to be found in the binding of the

501 Ardebil
292 × 136 cm, 120,000 TK/m²
(9' 7" × 4' 5", 77 TK/in.²).

502 Meshkin
303 × 102 cm, 76,000 TK/m²
(10′ 0″ × 3′ 4″, 49 TK/in.²).

503 Ardebil weave.

504 Shirvan weave.

selvedge of the new Ardebils: the goods are made under manufacturing conditions in which several pieces are often woven together as one piece of work on a single loom. The rugs are cut apart afterwards, which means that the edges have to be specially bound, the result being a rather thin cylindrical selvedge of white cotton, instead of the traditional Azerbaijan flat selvedge which, of course, is woven with the rug.

The Meshkins are not difficult to distinguish from their Russian counterparts, the Erivans and the Kazaks. The Russian goods are obviously the products of factory-controlled conditions, while the Meshkins are just as obviously not. The whole structure of the Meshkins is more uneven; the flat selvedge is bigger and rougher; and above all the uneven colourings have the obvious imprint of peasant dyeing techniques – mauvish blue, constant streaks and changes of colour, garish light blues and green and large blocks of sandy yellow. Within the one basic style a wide variety of designs is made. Apart from the pieces shown here, another typical example will be found under the medallion section (see fig. 546).

505 HERIZ
The Heriz area, at the heart of Persian Azerbaijan, is important mainly as a producer of carpet sizes. Some rugs are made, however, as well as a small quantity of runners. The coarse, chunky construction of Heriz, is of course, ideally suited to the requirements of the runner format and, with the wonderful madder-based colourings used in the area, Heriz pieces may be the most attractive of all Azerbaijan runners. The characteristic Heriz medallion has to be considerably simplified for the narrow size, but the essential flavour is always preserved. Note here the pendants of the central medallion, which suggest a link with the Chelabi shown in fig. 469.

506, 507 KARAJA AND LAMBERAN
On the western edge of the Heriz carpet-weaving area is a large group of villages, with Karaja as its centre, with a very distinctive style of their own. The correct Persian name would be Gharadjeh, but the local Azerbaijanian-speaking population – unable to manage Persian pronunciation – have corrupted it to Karaja. (There are so many different races and languages intermingled in the weaving areas of the East that almost every name may be pronounced in several different ways – which may in turn result in quite astonishing differences of spelling when transliterated into the roman alphabet.)

The Karaja design, as illustrated – two different bold medallion shapes with hooks that are not quite 'Luri' hooks, on a ground covered with a myriad of geometric motifs – is unmistakable. There are also other features which make Karaja easy to recognize: it is one of the few sources of single-wefted goods, with white cotton warps and blue-grey cotton wefts. The selvedge is the usual flat Azerbaijan type. The colours are easily remembered, once seen – a warm medium red with small amounts of many other shades (untypical of Persian Azerbaijan, this), including medium and light blue and a lovely medium green. All sizes are made, including carpets and especially those narrow runners that are so much in demand in Europe.

To the west and north of Karaja is another region, known as Lamberan, where the same design is used, but in a stiffer style and in a coarse double-wefted structure (like a cheap Tabriz) and distinguishable from Karaja also by its much less harmonious use of colour. An unpleasant hard red is the main problem but another sometimes arises from a structural fault typical of the Tabriz village region (and of certain other areas, too). The fabric feels very firm to the handle – as stiff as a board, on occasion – but on examining the construction one discovers that the strength is 'all in the back', that is, the warps and wefts are disproportionately heavy in relation to the pile, which is thin and whiskery. In this case the solid handle is deceptive, for the carpet will not give satisfactory wear. However, if Lamberans avoid this fault, and if the colours are well balanced, they can be a good buy. Various rug sizes are common here; the runners are in the traditional width of one metre or so. Carpet sizes and narrow runners are not made.

505

505 Heriz or Ahar area
319 × 104 cm, 70,000 TK/m²
(10′ 5″ × 3′ 5″, 45 TK/in.²).

506 Karaja
195 × 138 cm, 75,000 TK/m²
(6′ 5″ × 4′ 6″, 48 TK/in.²).

507 Lamberan
195 × 142 cm, 139,000 TK/m²
(6′ 5″ × 4′ 8″, 90 TK/in.²).

506

507

508, 509 ARDEBIL

The runners and rugs known in the trade as 'old-style' Ardebils may come from anywhere in the south-eastern end of the Caucasus, from the Russian frontier near Akstafa down into the Elburz Mountains which skirt the Caspian. They often have a distinctly Kurdish look about them, especially in the kelleyis, of which fig. 134 is a typical example. These often represent the best value to be had in Azerbaijan since it is always claimed that rugs in this size are difficult to sell. Whereas the much-sought-after narrow runners are often grossly overpriced, the out-of-favour kelleyis are always relatively underpriced – and the chances of finding a really outstanding piece in this size are much greater because the selection available is better. Carpet dealers (and their customers), who have been brought up on stocks of machine-made carpets in formats – 10 × 8 ft and 12 × 9 ft, or 250 × 350 cm and 300 × 400 cm – designed to fit the proportions of rooms in Western houses, cannot easily be weaned from the idea that oriental carpets may

508 Ardebil
309 × 109 cm, 65,000 TK/m²
(10′ 2″ × 3′ 7″, 42 TK/in.²).

509 Ardebil
316 × 105 cm, 92,000 TK/m²
(10′ 4″ × 3′ 5″, 59 TK/in.²).

510 Sarab (detail);
full size 343 × 85 cm, 130,000 TK/m²
(11′ 3″ × 2′ 9″, 84 TK/in.²).

be treated differently. And yet it is often a nonsense to fill a whole room with a Heriz carpet and clutter it with furniture so as to destroy the artistic composition. (Does one listen to a Beethoven symphony while watching a film on television?) A kelleyi, however, precisely because of its long and narrow format, could well suit the layout of a modern house, which may have spaces free of furniture where these old Azerbaijan rugs can be displayed to full effect.

In both kelleyis and runners the range of designs in eastern Azerbaijan is unlimited, but the style always has the flavour of the two pieces illustrated, with bold medallions interspersed with a variety of motifs derived from the full range of the peasant traditions in Persia. Figure 508, for example, includes hooked diamonds and two different boteh forms as well as the conventional geometric stylizations of flower and leaf forms common in Azerbaijan. The weave is dense and solid, varying from about 60,000 to 120,000 knots/m² (39 to 78 knots/in.²). The colours are variable, but mostly harmonious and subdued.

510, 511 SARAB

West of Ardebil, on the road to Tabriz, lies the village of Sarab, which is the collecting centre for some of the hardest-wearing runners in the world. Of course, as with all unqualified statements about oriental carpets, there are exceptions. There are plenty of new Sarabs which have a heavily packed back combined with a thin pile; they feel very solid but are not hard-wearing because the weight is all in the back. However, the good average Sarabs made during the last fifty years, many of which are still available on the international market, are tightly packed with heavy woollen yarn, and these will last for generations. Some older pieces have woollen warps and wefts, but cotton is more common. The sizes begin at just under 200 cm (6′ 6″) long and go up to 5–6 metres (16′ 0″–20′ 0″) or more; most Sarabs are 100–110 cm (3′ 3″–3′ 6″) wide, but narrower pieces are also be to found. Two principal design layouts are used: the repeating diamond medallions shown in fig. 510 and the 'sergeant's stripes' design of fig. 511. The border design of fig. 510 is also noteworthy. The outer guard contains a well thought-out version of the reciprocating border, which may be found anywhere but is particularly popular with Caucasian weavers: the dark-blue central outline produces two shapes which interlock, each being the mirror image of the other. The main border guard contains a pattern used in this form only in Sarab, although older pieces in museums suggest that in origin it is a variant of sixteenth-century east Persian borders. The camel colour used in the ground is one of the principal characteristics of Sarab. The 'sergeant's stripes' design always uses this same shade for the stripes. The red is typical of the shade which the Azerbaijanians obtain from madder root (see also p. 267 *re* Heriz carpets). Many new Sarabs are characterized by the use of an ugly synthetic red which produces a crude contrast with the dark blue and white of the design, but a discerning buyer can still find plenty of runners with the genuine old madder shade.

512 MESHKIN

We show here a *nabati* Meshkin, i.e. a runner coloured with natural dyestuffs. Like many other goods sold under the name of Meshkin, such pieces are not woven in the town itself but in one of the surrounding villages. The weave is fairly coarse, but the pile is thick and heavy, giving quite a sound structure. The colours, as often happens with natural dyes, are warmer and richer than those of other Azerbaijan goods. Only narrow runners are made, and at present the range of lengths available is limited, 400 × 70 cm (13′ 0″ × 2′ 3″) being the most common. This production is, however, a fairly recent development and the range available may increase as demand grows. Though coarse, these runners have considerably more appeal than the garish pieces which were the standard Meshkins produced in large quantities in the 1960s and 1970s.

513 ERIVAN

North of the Russian frontier from Karaja lies Armenia, whose inhabitants have long been associated with hand-made carpets, both as weavers (in many areas, such as the Bakhtiari province) and as traders world-wide. In Armenia today there is a large production in 'new Kazak' designs, and also in a type named after the capital, Erivan. As with all new Russian Caucasian goods, many designs are available, of which two are illustrated in this book (the second is based on figs. 749, 750). The design shown here, diamond medallions with 'latch hooks', is quite common, especially in rug and runner sizes. It has the stiff appearance, the standard cotton warps and wefts and the unclassical colours that characterize most of the new Caucasian output. The Erivan colours are often very sweet – 'bedroom colours', one might say – with the inclusion of pink, light turquoise green, pale blue, yellow ochre and the like.

511 Sarab (detail);
full size 440 × 90 cm, 100,000 TK/m² (14′ 5″ × 2′ 11″, 65 TK/in.²).

512

512 Meshkin nabati (detail);
full size 438 × 80 cm, 76,000 TK/m² (14′ 4″ × 2′ 7″, 49 TK/m²).

513 Erivan
315 × 78 cm, 165,000 TK/m² (10′ 4″ × 2′ 7″, 106 TK/in.²).

513

514–517 NEW CAUCASIANS

The huge wealth of ancient geometric designs of the Caucasus has been registered and codified by the Soviet authorities. In factories throughout the Republics of Armenia, Azerbaijan, Georgia and Daghestan carpets, runners and rugs are made under controlled conditions in rather stereotyped re-interpretations of the old designs. The results demonstrate fairly obviously that the weaver has no creative interest whatsoever in the work he or she is executing: every trace of individuality is squeezed out by the system. Another disadvantage of the new imitation Kazaks and Shirvans is the very wayward colourings often used (an even greater problem with the Daghestan production shown in fig. 517). However, the structure is sound, many of the designs are quite pleasing and, if the hard, synthetic dyes can be softened by washing, many people will think twice before rejecting these goods, for the Russians keep the price artificially low. The only way the layman can tell the difference between Kazaks and Shirvans is that the latter are finer, sometimes much finer. The Shirvan weave is illustrated in fig. 504. Further pieces from this region are illustrated in the section on medallion designs and elsewhere (see index). Zarchereks, zaronims, dozars and narrow runners are all commonly found. A few carpet sizes are made but here the range is very limited. Notes on the finer but single-wefted Daghestans are to be found on p. 210.

514 Kazak
207 × 129 cm, 110,000 TK/m²
(6′ 9″ × 4′ 3″, 71 TK/in.²).

515 Kazak
155 × 104 cm, 96,000 TK/m²
(5′ 1″ × 3′ 5″, 62 TK/in.²).

516 Shirvan
126 × 77 cm, 185,000 TK/m²
(4′ 1″ × 2′ 6″, 120 TK/in.²).

517 Daghestan
280 × 74 cm, 158,000 TK/m²
(9′ 2″ × 2′ 5″, 102 TK/in.²).

514

515

516

517

518

519

520

518, 519 SHIRVAN, QUM

The two extraordinary rugs illustrated here demonstrate once again how the originality and flair of the Caucasian rugs of bygone days simply cannot be captured in modern re-creations. Despite its silk pile and super-fine weave, the Qum rug is far removed from the Shirvan original. As we have seen with other geometric designs produced in floral-weaving areas, it is not technical limitations which prevent the weavers of Qum from making a success of Shirvan designs, it is simply a matter of tradition. Although rugs like this Shirvan were produced under manufacturing conditions, the cultural basis of their production represented the culmination of a centuries old development which enabled a weaver to say – and the beholder to perceive – 'this is how I see it, this subtle balance between postulating bold forms and elegant refined detail is my view of things, and I, the artist, have proved it by the convincing rightness of what I have produced'. In the Qum rug the question of the weaver's expressive intention, of the rightness or otherwise of his artistic composition simply does not arise. At best he can say 'I have executed the design ordered; but it is quite meaningless to me'. The Shirvan design is found in two variants, one as shown here, the other with smaller end-medallions; the Qum is usually made only in the former version.

520 PAKISTAN

Another weaving area that uses geometric motifs is Pakistan. The production is not limited to the standard Bokhara pattern illustrated in figs. 404 and 405, but covers the full range of designs made in all the Turkoman areas, including many variants of the repeating diamond medallion idea illustrated here. Sometimes these very geometric pieces have a markedly Caucasian flavour, but the motifs are almost always of Turkoman origin. As with the Bokhara designs, all sizes are made, in qualities ranging from rather rough (say, 150,000 knots/m²; 96 knots/in.²) to very fine (as much as 500,000 knots/m²; 320 knots/in.²), and in an inexhaustible palette of colours varying from classical Turkoman reds to the most improbable greens and golds.

521 KULA

At this point attention must be drawn to the large manufactured output of Kula in Turkey. There, the only established design tradition these days is that only other

518 Shirvan
182 × 133 cm, 170,000 TK/m²
(6′ 0″ × 4′ 4″, 110 TK/in.²).

519 Qum
92 × 60 cm, 504,000 PK/m²
(3′ 0″ × 1′ 11″, 325 PK/in.²).

520 Pakistan
242 × 90 cm, 305,000 PK/m²
(7′ 11″ × 2′ 11″, 197 PK/in.²).

people's designs are produced, and as they do this rather well, it is very difficult for the layman to recognize the stylistic difference. The geometric style of Kula lends itself readily to Caucasian designs (Turkey is in any case closely linked stylistically and geographically with the Caucasus, and here, too, the Turkoman conquests of the Middle Ages provide an ancient ethnic connection), but any other geometric design may also be found, such as the Yalameh illustrated in fig. 349 or the Qashqai of fig. 447. To distinguish a Kula from a Caucasian is fairly easy: all new Caucasians

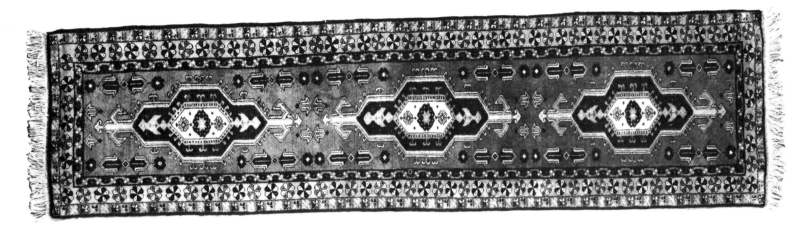

521 Kula
303 × 83 cm, 122,000 TK/m²
(9′ 11″ × 2′ 9″, 79 TK/in.²).

522 Kurdish
226 × 110 cm, 75,000 TK/m²
(7′ 5″ × 3′ 7″, 48 TK/in.²).

have cotton warps and wefts, but Kulas, like almost all Turkish goods, have woollen warps and wefts. The runner illustrated is typical of the style; hundreds of other designs in a like vein are available, drawing on the full range of the potentialities of the Azerbaijan style.

522 KURDISH

Rugs, runners and, above all, kelleyis resembling those of Azerbaijan are often found in eastern Anatolia. As far as weaving styles are concerned, the frontier between Iran and Turkey is, of course, purely arbitrary – the weavers on both sides are Kurds whose design traditions need pay no attention to modern international boundaries. In fact, though, the rugs of the Turkish Kurds are quite different from those of almost all their Persian neighbours. To begin with, they always have woollen warps and two woollen wefts. Secondly, the weave is generally looser, often giving the rugs a rather shaggy appearance. Most obviously, however, the colour style is quite different. The rusty orange tone which is prominent in the kelleyi illustrated in fig. 522 is the most striking feature. Some rugs from this region even have orange warps. The designs themselves however reveal the Azerbaijan connection. The quantities produced are small – as in other parts of Anatolia the production of flat-weaves is much more important – so that the rugs seen in the West usually have considerable individual character. Their appearance is, however, sometimes spoiled by an excessive use of orange.

523–527 ANATOLIA

The little rugs of Anatolia provide a very varied range of permutations of the repeating medallion idea, as the group of five pieces shown here demonstrates. Although for many years Turkey disappeared from view as a supplier of Western markets, until rediscovered by the Germans and Swiss in the 1960s, the age-old traditions of that country once so dominated carpet production that in English, at least, all oriental carpets were called 'Turkey carpets', even if they were made as far away as India. These traditions were, however, preserved intact in the countless peasant weaves to be found throughout Anatolia, and figs. 523–5 show typical examples of the rugs produced for local use while the eyes of the West were turned exclusively towards Persia: 'non-commercial' merchandise in which the weaver's imagination was given free rein. A comparison of the Melas and the Taşpinar with the corresponding pieces of the standardized modern production of these two places (figs. 300 and 538) shows clearly how much character the weaver can put into a rug if she is allowed to do so. The two pieces from Ezineh are examples of that town's current output, which is further illustrated in figs. 542, 543 – soundly made unaffected rugs, perhaps best described as cheap and cheerful. They are about half the price of the shoddy new Shiraz goods and are much to be preferred because, unlike the latter, they do not pretend to express more than technical limitations will allow. Both designs are drawn from the ancient traditions of north-west Anatolia.

523

524

525

526

527

523 Balikeşir
167 × 136 cm, 59,000 TK/m²
(5′ 9″ × 4′ 5″, 38 TK/in.²).

524 Melas
203 × 130 cm, 115,000 TK/m²
(6′ 8″ × 4′ 3″, 74 TK/in.²).

525 Taşpinar
148 × 102 cm, 102,000 TK/m²
(4′ 10″ × 3′ 4″, 66 TK/in.²).

526 Ezineh
126 × 82 cm, 47,000 TK/m²
(4′ 2″ × 2′ 8″, 30 TK/in.²).

527 Ezineh
138 × 89 cm, 72,000 TK/m²
(4′ 6″ × 2′ 11″, 46 TK/in.²).

528 SAMARKAND

Samarkand rugs do not in fact come from Samarkand: just as Bokhara, now the third city of the Uzbek S.S.R., was the market centre for the products of distant Turkoman nomads and gave its name to their rugs, so also Samarkand, the republic's second city, was the trade channel through which East Turkestan goods had to travel to reach the West. Today, East Turkestan is called Sinkiang and forms part of China. The old rugs of Kashgar, Yarkand and Khotan, which were the main producing centres, are traded in Peking, so that they come to be classified as 'old Chinese', but in terms of weave, design and character they form part of the Turkoman or east Persian nomad heritage, as the kelleyi illustrated readily demonstrates. The affinity with the Beshir rug of fig. 165 is striking: perhaps this piece is a corrupt peasant derivative of the Herati design, but as with other pieces which suggest this connection we must always consider the possibility that the corruption is the other way round, i.e. that the conception of this piece reflects an ancient peasant culture upon which the designers of seventeenth-century Khorassan drew when the Herati design evolved. Further notes on Samarkand rugs will be found on pp. 127–8.

529 QUM

Since really fine Shirvans are no longer made, it is not surprising that some enterprising Persian has stepped in to fill the gap by having the designs woven elsewhere. In view of the eclecticism of all Qum designs it should also not surprise us that the source of these goods is Qum. And yet it somehow does seem incongruous, for we think of Qum as a source of absolutely typical floral designs. The outstandingly fine weave and the wide use of silk and mohair are both factors which particularly benefit the floral style; these materials are not necessary for geometric designs. Hence, the result is more showy than artistic. In all art the best results are achieved where the form and the content are in balance, where the artist has used no more and no less of the formal resources at his disposal than are needed to accomplish fully his expressive intent. Where the artist uses more technique than is necessary he becomes a showman, a seeker-after effect, a Meyerbeer, not a Mozart. It would perhaps be too sweeping a generalization to go one step further and claim that a carpet should never be made in a weave that is finer than the design demands, but it is certainly not a bad principle to bear in mind, especially in manufactured carpets. The Qum rug shown here is typical of a substantial output of rugs in Caucasian designs (found also in other fine Persian weaves such as Nain) in which this principle is disregarded. They are all showy in the same manner; they also suffer from the stylistic lapses which often occur when weavers are asked to digest material which is quite foreign to their local tradition. Thus, for example, the podgy four-legged animals at both ends of the ground, which are drawn in the typical Qum realistic style, look quite silly, whereas the strict geometric stylization of old Shirvan rugs produces animal figures of great charm and fantasy.

530

531

532

530–533 KURDISH

Reference has already been made to the boldness of design which is characteristic of the Kurdish tribes in general and of the Kolyai and Kakaberu tribes of western Iran in particular. Often they make up rugs with one single medallion on a fairly plain field, but their particular predilection for the kelleyi format inevitably leads them to repeat their medallions, as in figs. 530 and 533, or to enlarge the medallion's end-pendants to the extent that they themselves effectively become further medallions, as in figs. 531 and 532 (the same idea may be observed in figs. 518 and 519, too). The carpet weaving of the Kolyais, centred around Sonqur between Hamadan and Kermanshah, is more organized; this gives Kolyai rugs a little more elegance, whereas the products of the Kakaberu tribe (more to the north, in Kurdistan proper) are wilder and more uncompromising. Apart from that, the designs of the two groups have much in common and in many cases are interchangeable, but the character of the two types is quite different, owing to features

530 Kolyai
211 × 119 cm, 81,000 TK/m²
(6′ 11″ × 3′ 11″, 52 TK/in.²).

531 Kakaberu
284 × 158 cm, 78,000 TK/m²
(9′ 4″ × 5′ 2″, 50 TK/in.²).

532 Kakaberu
257 × 142 cm, 90,000 TK/m²
(8′ 5″ × 4′ 8″, 58 TK/in.²).

533 Kolyai
250 × 140 cm, 117,000 TK/m²
(8′ 2″ × 4′ 7″, 75 TK/in.²).

534 Viss
215 × 108 cm, 80,000 PK/m²
(7′ 1″ × 3′ 6″, 52 PK/in.²)

535 Kalardasht
254 × 178 cm, 75,000 TK/m²
(8′ 4″ × 5′ 10″, 48 TK/in.²).

of structure and colouring. Both are soundly made, but the Kolyai rugs are single-wefted and generally light in colouring, while the Kakaberus are astoundingly heavy in both weave and appearance. They pack the pile of their rugs into a coarse but immensely solid double-wefted structure, producing one of the most hard-wearing fabrics of the Orient. And they keep the whole of their colour-scheme within the overriding confines of very dark shades of blue and red. Other shades – green, white, gold – are of course used, but the overall effect is completely dominated by the power of the principal dark colours. The weavers have a very cavalier way of handling other people's designs: for example, in fig. 532 the Herati design is wildly distorted in the central medallion, itself a derivative of the Senneh variant of the Herati pattern (cf. fig. 204). What matters, though, is that on everything they touch the Kakaberus imprint their own unmistakable style: they have nothing of the elegance of the Kurdish or other weavers of Shirvan (see fig. 518), but their rugs say, with the same defiance, 'this is the Kakaberu version: take it or leave it'.

Their Kolyai neighbours to the south are not less original in their use of bold, expressive designs, but they are somehow less brutal about it. This lighter touch has much to do with the use of lighter shades of both red and blue, and the wider palette of lighter subsidiary shades which they use, but it is also the result of much more finely drawn lines and more grace in the setting-out of their designs.

534 VISS

The village of Viss in the south of the Arak area (see map, p. 346) occupies an unusual position in the story of carpet design. The weave and colourings clearly proclaim that it is part of the Mahal area, i.e. it makes second-grade Saruq carpets, medium-fine, with a high pile of thick durable yarn. However, the designs of this area are quite different from those of anywhere else in the Saruq region because they have retained an almost fully geometric character while all around have turned to completely floral styles. There is a geometric repeating-boteh design made in small quantities, and the Herati carpet of fig. 221 is also from Viss; but the design for which the village has become universally known is the one shown here. It will be found in every conceivable size and a very wide range of ground colours, both in the Viss original and in the copies made in India, and always in a design form close to the version seen here, with the hexagonal medallion and its diamond-shaped pendants, the great hook motifs at the end of the ground and the steep hooked pyramids reaching from the sides towards the centre.

535 KALARDASHT

This carpet comes from an isolated valley in the Elburz mountains north-east of the Hamadan region. Little is known of the area or its weavers. Old goods, such as were to be found on the market in some quantities ten years ago, but which have now more or less completely disappeared, look as though they are of Luri origin, although they have features in common with both Kurdish and Shah Savan work. Their 'discovery' by Western importers in the late 1960s led to a great upsurge in the production which, regrettably, swept away much of the established traditions of both design and quality, replacing them with the rather bland and not particularly well-made designs of which fig. 535 is an example. A wide range of sizes is made. The main fault with the new Kalardashts is their drabness of basic colouring, which is enlivened but not improved by the addition of a fierce shade of yellow and crude green. The output remains small and the decline in quality has caused Western interest to fade after initial enthusiasm. Only if one finds an old piece will one appreciate what it is that so excited the dealers when the goods were first discovered.

536 KHARAGHAN

In the northern part of the Hamadan region, on the edge of the Shah Savan tribal area, lies the Kharaghan group of villages which produce rugs and runners of all sizes in designs which often look Kurdish-influenced. The single-wefted weave, too, looks to the layman quite like that of Sonqur, although there is less twist to the yarn and the pile is less dense – sometimes rather thin, in fact. The colours are not

536 Kharaghan
152 × 100, 114,000 TK/m²
(5′ 0″ × 3′ 3″, 74 TK/in.²).

so bright and the colour range is less interesting; but there are pieces to be found where almost the only sure distinguishing feature is the size: Kharaghan makes every rug size except the Kolyai kelleyi format. Dark-blue grounds predominate, but red is also found; birds and animals often feature as subsidiary motifs. The correct name for this region is Kharaghan, but sometimes dealers inaccurately call the rugs Shah Savan. The reason for this (as Jenny Housego has established) is that the Shah Savan tribe, as well as being spread through the whole of southern Azerbaijan, also has a clan around Saveh to the east of Kharaghan. This Saveh group weaves many designs which are similar to those of Kharaghan, but their yarn, though fine, is thin and soft, giving a rather spongy feel to the rug, and the dyestuffs used are rather fugitive. The Shah Savan rugs of Saveh have more flair and are more expensive than Kharaghans, but the latter will give better wear. Other designs of both types will be found in figs. 455, 556, 557, 591 and 592.

537 TIBETAN

A slightly anomalous position at the end of this section is occupied by a rug whose design originates in the Chinese cultural sphere; it has no connection with the foregoing illustrations, having a layout which is similar, but only accidentally so. All Chinese designs can be arranged in this layout, and many examples will be found among the old rugs referred to on p. 315; in this section the most appropriate modern piece to illustrate appears to be a rug made by Tibetan refugees living in India and Nepal. For these weavers have preserved the ideals of the old Chinese traditions more than the Chinese themselves have in their new carpets. A number of designs from Nepal are shown in various parts of this book (see index entry 'Tibetan'). All of these have the type of construction described on p. 168, in a weave which may vary from about 70,000 down to as few as 30,000 knots/m² (45 to 20 knots/in.²). As is true of all carpet origins, there are considerable differences between the best categories and the goods produced by weavers whose concern is more with making a quick profit than with sound craftsmanship, but even the coarsest pieces often have a thick pile, using magnificent Himalayan yarn. Indeed, it is one of the marvels of the international carpet trade that the re-generation of the Tibetan carpet has launched on to the market such a large number of excellent rugs, employing outstanding materials, but at very modest prices, and above all, breathing that air of imagination and spontaneity, of commitment on the part of the weaver, which is the *sine qua non* of true folk-art.

537 Tibetan
165 × 89 cm, 44,000 Tibetan knots/m²
(5′ 5″ × 2′ 11″, 28 Tibetan knots/in.²).

3 GEOMETRIC MEDALLION-PLAIN DESIGNS

538 Taşpinar
180 × 102 cm, 145,000 TK/m²
(5′ 11″ × 3′ 4″, 94 TK/in.²).

539 Yahyali
214 × 115 cm, 94,000 TK/m²
(7′ 0″ × 3′ 9″, 61 TK/in.²).

By 'medallion-plain designs' the carpet dealer means those having – in the centre of the carpet – a clearly defined principal motif which is surrounded by a greater or lesser area of plain ground, the whole being framed by a border. The corners of the ground usually have some basically triangular in-filling (often a quarter of the central medallion placed in each corner of the ground), but this is not always so. This category, like all the other arbitrary categories in this book, is not quite watertight, because the 'plain' ground may in fact contain various design elements, and the point at which a plain ground with a few motifs in it becomes a covered ground is vague and undefined. Designs in which the medallion is repeated or so enlarged as to give the effect of a repeating form are included in the previous section (see p. 208).

538–544 ANATOLIA

Turkey is the home of the geometric medallion-plain design, and in the next few pages examples from several villages will be found, all with a marked family resemblance, but all having their own individual traits. They all have a double-wefted all-wool construction. The Yahyali design illustrated in fig. 539 is easily recognizable by its angularity. The colours are also an immediate indicator of the origin – the ground is either deep scarlet or a dull mauvish red, but both are unmistakable. There is almost always a thin line of bright gold – a small but highly distinctive feature – and another or bright green in the subsidiary shades. The wool is of above-average quality, and the weave is finer and tighter than that of most new Turkish village types. The village of Taşpinar (fig. 538) produces a similar design but in a somewhat looser weave and in gaudier colours (a hard bright red is common). A characteristic trait of Taşpinar rugs (but not entirely reliable as a clue to the origin) is the narrow leaf-scroll panel inserted at both ends of the ground before the end borders. Taşpinar is located to the west of Yahyali; between the two is Niğde, which acts as a market centre for both.

A similar but simpler, much coarser (and much cheaper) type of rug is made in Ortaköy (fig. 540). Like the rugs of Ezineh described below, the Ortaköys are mass-produced, but by keeping squarely to the confines of their own style and technical limitations they avoid the pretentious anonymity of Kula and preserve that appealing individuality which characterizes the peasant rugs of Anatolia. Note for example the very simple yet very effective border of fig. 540. The Ortaköy colourings are light and bright – sometimes crude but not necessarily so. The bulk of the production is in sizes with an area of about 2 m² (20 ft²). Yet another variant of this style is made in Kirşehir (not illustrated). Here the weave is finer, which admits a tendency to a floral style which seems uncharacteristic of Anatolia.

With fig. 541 we move right away from the sphere of the new manufactured Anatolians to an example of those richly imaginative and powerfully expressive rugs which spotlight the deep relationship between Anatolia and the Caucasus. Such pieces may be found in many parts of Turkey, from the 'Kazaks' of Kars to the many types unique to the Bergama region. What is striking about Çannakkale is the

539

540

541

542

540 Ortaköy
169 × 109 cm, 57,000 TK/m²
(5′ 6″ × 3′ 7″, 37 TK/in.²).

541 Çannakkale
179 × 132 cm, 49,000 TK/m²
(5′ 10″ × 4′ 4″, 32 TK/in.²).

542 Ezineh
129 × 80 cm, 55,000 TK/m²
(4′ 3″ × 2′ 7″, 35 TK/in.²).

amazingly coarse stitch which suffices to achieve a design of such character and authority. The construction is unlike other Anatolians, having a very large number of wefts between each row of knots, so that the pile is very loose: its function is more decorative than durable. Note also the wide kilim skirts at both ends – a common feature of older Turkish rugs. The squarish format illustrated is typical of this kind of Çannakkale. The design is derived ultimately from the early Turkoman rugs of Anatolia (see pp. 170ff.); the Bergama 'link' in the development is illustrated in fig. 390.

Only a few miles from Çannakkale in north-west Anatolia, but worlds apart in cultural significance, lies the village of Ezineh (figs. 542, 543). However, as has been noted above, there is something to be said in favour of a rug that does not seek to hanker after aspirations it cannot hope to achieve. A comparison of the pieces illustrated in this book (see also figs. 526, 527) – which are typical of many others – reveals that Ezineh is content to present a simplified résumé of the basic elements of the Turkish geometric layout. The structure is like that of many modern Turkish types – all-wool, coarse and double-wefted, with a fairly flat back and low pile. The colourings are very distinctive, for most pieces have only four or five shades: red, light and dark blue, white and camel. The second Ezineh rug shown here (fig. 543) illustrates how much can be achieved from the point of view of design even within the very narrow limits outlined above. The rare idea of repeating the triangular corners of the ground as a frame around the central medallion adds further emphasis to what is already quite a strong motif based on a reciprocating hooked diamond. However, the success of this design lies in the conversion of this dominant rectangle into a hexagon by the light and airy lattice-work pendants – a piece of skilful designing not often found in such cheap rugs.

Of all the new-style goods in large-scale production in Turkey today the Döşemealtis (fig. 544) are the most appealing. They are also among the easiest to recognize. The construction is a variant of the typical Anatolian coarse all-wool style, double-wefted, but with the back only slightly ridged. Note the heavy plaited fringe at one end. The designs are open and well balanced, with latch-hook motifs much in evidence, edging the ground and often the medallions, too. As with the Yagçibedir rugs of Sindirgi (see fig. 577), the subsidiary motifs frequently seem to

543

544

545

be derived from embryonic tree forms. The striking variant of the Herati border, as illustrated here, is unique and unmistakable (although other border designs are occasionally used in Döşemealti, too.) Finally, the colour combinations are highly distinctive: not many shades are used – red, white, blue and green are the dominant colours – but it is their combined effect, enhanced by the use of good lustrous yarn, which makes these rugs so attractive. The deep blue and bottle-green glow brilliantly against the red background, especially when age or modern washing techniques have taken the edge off the sharp white and softened the deep red to rose. The 2 m² (20 ft²) size commonly found in Anatolia is standard here, also, but smaller pieces and narrow runners are also made. Other Döşemealtis are illustrated in figs. 268 and 495.

545 DERBEND

The Derbend and Akhti-Mikrakh rugs illustrated in figs. 470 and 471 are also made in medallion-plain designs. The rug shown here once again spotlights the connections between Anatolia and the Caucasus, as a comparison with figs. 539–44 will confirm. However, there is no possibility of confusion since all Daghestan rugs are single-wefted and have cotton warps and wefts.

546 ARDEBIL

This is an example of the 'old-style' Ardebils referred to on p. 100. It has the densely packed construction, on heavy cotton warps, which is typical of Persian southeastern Azerbaijan. The design, however, reminds us of the original cultural unity of the whole of Azerbaijan, since it is well known to us as a typical pattern of the southern Shirvan district (e.g. Konakend). Unlike some other products of the Ardebil region, which are conscious copies of their northern neighbours, this rug and others like it simply reflect the different lines along which similar designs have developed in northern and southern Azerbaijan since the country's partition 150 years ago. The Persian version is decidedly clumsier and less fluid in its interpretation – the cotton warps alone are enough to ensure this. The border, in particular, entirely lacks the flair of Shirvan examples, but in rugs like these we do not feel these aspects to be faults: the rugs are not inferior, only different, representing

543 Ezineh
123 × 78 cm, 70,000 TK/m²
(4′ 0″ × 2′ 7″, 45 TK/in.²).

544 Döşemealti
197 × 114 cm, 63,000 TK/m²
(6′ 5″ × 3′ 9″, 41 TK/in.²).

545 Daghestan
171 × 107 cm, 150,000 TK/m²
(5′ 7″ × 3′ 6″, 97 TK/in.²).

546 Ardebil
203 × 129 cm, 116,000 TK/m²
(6′ 8″ × 4′ 3″, 75 TK/in.²).

546

547 Indian Heriz
201 × 142 cm, 79,000 PK/m²
(6′ 7″ × 4′ 8″, 51 PK/in.²).

sturdy, hard-wearing peasant products imbued with the independent spirit of the remote mountains in which they are woven.

547 INDIAN HERIZ

At this point is seems appropriate to draw attention to the fact that it is always possible for a weaver to produce a medallion-plain design by taking a medallion/all-over style and leaving out the motifs of the ground; this practice is widely used in Iran, especially in areas with some manufacturing tradition, and the results can be quite striking. The carpet shown is, however, not Persian but one of the many versions of the Heriz design woven in India (see also fig. 601). Limitations of space make it impossible to illustrate the many medallion-plain designs produced by this method throughout the Orient: the reader must make his own mental somersault when faced with this kind of carpet. The Persian designs which follow are all limited to medallion-plain designs from places where such designs are the natural and normal style.

548 BEHBEHAN

This Luri rug is from the Behbehan area, but it is rather untypical of the goods usually found in that market on account of the lightness of its colour-composition and the fact that it is in a regular dozar size. What is typical of its Luri origin is the extraordinary self-assurance of the design – another of those pieces of elemental expressiveness which so marks the tribal products of Persia. Note here, too, the hooked diamond as a subsidiary motif. For general notes on Behbehan see fig. 482.

549 KURDISH

After the Turks the most noted producers of bold geometric designs are the Kurds. We have reason to refer many times to the great treasury of designs woven in the Kurdish area of western Iran, from Kermanshah in the south to Lake Urmia in the north and from the vicinity of Hamadan in the east right across to the Iraqi frontier and beyond. Within this large region many different tribes are settled and wide variations of style are found. Each tribe and type has its own characteristic designs and colours, but it is often possible to see a family resemblance amongst all the Kurdish types and there is also a measure of straightforward exchanging of designs from one type to another (the Kolyai rug in Bijar design in fig. 202 is a clear example). In assessing the origin of a Kurdish piece one must bear this in

548 Luri
194 × 141 cm, 53,000 TK/m²
(6′ 5″ × 4′ 7″, 34 TK/in.²).

549 Kurdish
246 × 148 cm, 125,000 TK/m²
(8′ 1″ × 4′ 10″, 81 TK/in.²).

548

549

mind and consider the structural features of the various types, and not just the elements of the design.

The carpet trade employs almost exclusively five names only for the very wide range of products of Persian Kurdistan: Senneh, for the fine rugs of that town, which is accurate; Bijar, for village or town manufactured carpets from a huge region, which is accurate in general but often very vague; Kakaberu for the dark and heavy rugs of a tribe of this name near Senneh; Kolyai (the name of a tribe) or Sonqur (the name of the market town) for many different types of manufactured or home-produced single-wefted rugs from a large area; and Senjabi (another tribal name) for several not precisely defined types from the south of the region, reaching down into Luristan. Some of these descriptions correspond only loosely with the true places of origin of the rugs, or are used so vaguely as to be confusing. The name Kolyai, in particular, is often bandied about quite indiscriminately for almost any rug produced west of Hamadan. The fact is, of course, that there are many rugs the real origin of which we just do not know. We must not forget that not all the Kurdish tribes produce carpets on a regular basis: a catalogue of the tribes of Kurdistan contains a host of names which the carpet trade has never heard of. The piece shown in fig. 549 is double-wefted like a Kakaberu, and has woollen warps like an old Bijar, the light colours commonly found in Kolyais and the bold geometric style of the Senjabis. Its short kelleyi format is typical of many Kurdish village weaves. Most dealers would call it a Bijar because of its powerful design and magnificent colours and construction; but this is a misnomer, or at least it is certainly not the same sort of Bijar as the pieces shown in fig. 195 or fig. 762. It was probably produced by one of the many smaller tribes of Kurdistan and is an example of the endless diversity of the geometric designs of this area.

550–553 KOLYAI

The bold, angular medallions of the rugs illustrated are popular with Kurdish weavers in many areas, as well as with tribes like the Shah Savan whose designs are derived from Kurdish models. All three modern pieces shown are examples of the village production of the Kolyai tribe around Sonqur, who are the biggest rug producers among the Kurds. (Examples of the Kolyai manufactured production are illustrated in figs. 461 and 498.) The Kolyais use a cotton warp and weft and a medium-fine single-wefted construction. The yarn used for the pile has a fairly high twist, so that the knots often produce a rather knobbly effect on the back of the rug. The pile is of medium length and quite dense and, since the price is moderate, these hard-wearing rugs are very popular. The colours, like the designs, are bold and bright; this means that many of the pieces encountered are made with crude, cheap dyestuffs, but by and large the Kolyais are well coloured, sometimes still using vegetable dyes; some very attractive greens are especially noteworthy. Only one basic size is made: the short kelleyi, i.e. 120–160 cm (4′ 0″–5′ 3″) wide and 220–280 cm (7′ 9″–9′ 3″) long – and this is one of the easiest points to remember in assessing a rug's place of origin.

Figure 550 reveals a certain affinity with the Hamadan village rugs woven to the east of Kurdistan: the lustrous yarn and deep-blue background are typical of the south-west Hamadan area, and so is the 'rope' motif in the border (see fig. 588). However, the boldness of the design and the sparse decoration with rather dismembered subsidiary motifs are typical Kolyai features.

In fig. 551 we see one of the most famous Kurdish designs of all, known as 'Takht-e-Jamshid'. 'Takht' means throne or seat of government; Jamshid was the fourth ruler of the world in the Persian legend of the creation and is considered the patron of arts and crafts. The name Takht-e-Jamshid is used colloquially in Persia to indicate the palace of Darius at Persepolis; why it is used for the design illustrated is not clear. A further puzzle is the use of elements of the design in old Ladik rugs (see fig. 292). The same design, in more sombre colours, is woven by the Kakaberu tribe. It is most unusual in that the central panel does not strike one as being a medallion but the eye is drawn rather to the zig-zag structure and the ends of the rug. The colours are as striking as the design – the medallion is always red (sometimes quite flaming), the ends always dark blue or black. The colours, as in many

550 Kolyai
223 × 140 cm, 95,000 TK/m²
(7′ 4″ × 4′ 7″, 61 TK/in.²).

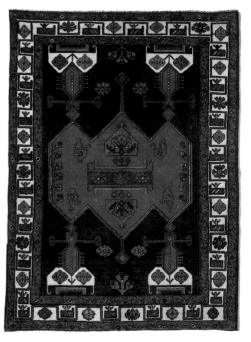

551 Kolyai
243 × 161 cm, 119,000 TK/m²
(8′ 0″ × 5′ 3″, 77 TK/in.²).

552

553

552 Heriz, eighteenth century,
160 × 140 cm, 141,000 ᴛᴋ/m²
(5′ 3″ × 4′ 7″, 91 ᴛᴋ/in.²).
A clear succession of carpets now in museums
proves that the motifs in the ground and corners are
derived from the dragons seen in figs. 749 and 750.

553 Kolyai
225 × 158 cm, 92,000 ᴛᴋ/m²
(7′ 5″ × 5′ 2″, 59 ᴛᴋ/in.²).

Kolyai rugs, are usually full of abrashes (streaks), but most people see these as an asset rather than a fault in the strong Kurdish colourings. This rug is, for a Kolyai, unusually short in relation to its width; as is noted elsewhere, there are exceptions to all the rules about oriental carpets.

Figure 553 shows a design encountered in many parts of north-west Iran and in the Caucasus. The Kurdish connection always springs to mind – fig. 549, for example, can be seen as a fiercely geometric variant, and its influence is felt in fig. 531, as well – but it is also used in areas where Kurdish influence is less easy to prove. One of the most famous versions is found in the nineteenth-century Ferahans, from which another well-known variant is perhaps derived: the 'clock-face' pattern of Tafrish (fig. 555). There are affinities with this design to be seen in the rugs of Kharaghan (figs. 536, 556 and 557) and in the related rugs of the Shah Savan of Saveh. Perhaps this is the connecting link: Ferahan, Tafrish and Kharaghan are all contiguous with the Shah Savan area; but whether the Shah Savan had the design from the Kurds or vice versa it is impossible to say. Probably the design can be traced back to the north-west Persian dragon designs of the sixteenth or seventeenth centuries. The large hooked motifs seem, like those of figs. 487 and 488 (Qashqai), related to the elements in early Heriz carpets (fig. 552) which are clearly derived from the geometricized dragon motifs of this early group.

554 QUM

This is the design that has everything! Qum is, alas, the *nouveau riche* among carpet towns and treads the tightrope between abundant imaginative invention and that excess which is the keynote of bad taste. The basic layout in this all-silk piece reflects the Qum vogue for 'Caucasian' styles, but it also has some of the flavour of certain old Saruq/Ferahan medallion-plain designs (cf. also fig. 553). The medallion and corners are, however, filled partly with botehs, partly with Herati motifs; the five medallions of the Qashqai *hebatlu* design (see fig. 595) add a southern splash, but the octagons themselves contain the *hashtguli* motif used in Senneh (see fig. 132). The elaborate Tabriz or Saruq-style 'teapot' border suits the Herati pattern, but its delicate style is quite out of keeping with the marked geometric elements of the design. Being made of silk, this piece would sell at a very high price; but it is hard to relate the price to any aesthetic value, and this example serves only to emphasize the fact that when considering carpets as an investment one cannot dispense with the advice of an established dealer reputed for his experience and good taste.

555 TAFRISH

One of the villages in the Hamadan group making single-wefted rugs in an unchanged traditional style is Tafrish, whose goods are instantly recognizable by the shape of the medallion. The village is situated just beyond the Ferahan region to the east, not far from Saveh and the Shah Savan area (see map, p. 346). The wool and colourings used in the modern production are reminiscent of the latter. Rudbar, with its Ferahan associations (see fig. 208) is also very close. The medallion, often called 'clock-face' from its clear division into segments (although there are always sixteen segments, not twelve) normally appears on a plain light-red ground; the dark-blue ground of fig. 555 is rather unusual. Dark and medium blue and brown-red are the most striking subsidiary colours, but there is also some cream, orange and green. Cream ground rugs are also encountered occasionally. The special shape of the medallion has given rise to considerable speculation as to its symbolic meaning. Among the possible explanations we find our old friend the sun-bird (see p. 208) and also the idea that the medallion represents the sun itself with radiating sunbeams as a symbol of the Zoroastrian (Parsee) religion. The weave is one of the finest of the Hamadan area and the pile is clipped fairly close. Quite a number of outstanding semi-antique rugs are still available on the market, mostly in dozar size, which used to make up the bulk of the production. Amongst the current output smaller rugs are also found, but there are no runners, and carpet sizes are very rare.

556, 557 KHARAGHAN

Two more rugs from the Kharaghan district in the north-east Hamadan village region serve to emphasize the diversity to be found in the peasant rugs of Iran, even

554 Qum
175 × 120 cm, 555,000 PK/m²
(5′ 9″ × 3′ 11″, 358 PK/in.²).

555 Tafrish
206 × 136 cm, 179,000 TK/m²
(6′ 9″ × 4′ 5″, 115 TK/in.²).

556

557

556 Kharaghan
147 × 102 cm, 99,000 TK/m²
(4′ 10″ × 3′ 4″, 64 TK/in.²).

557 Kharaghan
150 × 94 cm, 78,000 TK/m²
(4′ 11″ × 3′ 1″, 50 TK/in.²).

558 Vordoveh
219 × 127 cm, 96,000 TK/m²
(7′ 2″ × 4′ 2″, 62 TK/in.²).

within the stylistic limits of one small group of villages. A general note on the Kharaghan district appears on p. 237. It is worth listing here the details of design and colouring in the rugs illustrated, which are the dealer's clues to a rug's origin. They include: the dominant dark blue and red; the limited use of other shades, including a little gold; the blue and white broken lines (fig. 557); the bird figures; the 'dragon'-hook motifs (see also fig. 552); the heavy pendants to the medallions; the zig-zag edging of the ground (fig. 556). All these features will, of course, be found in rugs from other origins; but when an expert sees them all together in a rug which also has cotton warps, brown cotton wefts, a single-wefted construction, regular proportions in the zaronim size, reasonably thick medium-quality yarn and a pattern in the weave which he recognizes as typical of the north-east Hamadan region, then he knows for certain that the piece comes from Kharaghan.

558 VORDOVEH

This design is one of the easiest to recognize in the whole of the Orient. The village of Vordoveh belongs to the Tuisarkan group (see p. 259); the dominant medallion is reminiscent of the neighbouring Kurdish areas; but what gives the origin away is the camel-coloured ground. Another distinctive feature is the use of a very noticeable mid-green shade as one of the subsidiary colours. Of course, any Vordoveh weaver can at any time produce a red-ground version of the typical design style, and in this case one has simply to bear in mind the style itself. Camel grounds are, however, the traditional style, and these account for most of the production. The weave and structure are the same as in good-quality Tuisarkans. Note the hooked pendants of the medallion – a reminder of the proximity of Tuisarkan to the Kurdish region.

559 SIRJAND

There have already been many occasions in this book to refer to the Afshari design range; now is the moment to introduce the principal design of the Sirjand region, which completely dominates the production there. The most interesting feature is the idea, mentioned elsewhere, of a medallion – or rather three repeating medallions – within another medallion. The latch hooks on the inner diamond-shaped medallions are typical of much Afshari work (e.g. fig. 496) and remind us also of the considerable web of inter-relationships between most of the tribal rugs of Persia. For the rest this Sirjand design is characterized by classical restraint in its use of simple geometric motifs in the form of stars and rosettes. The colours are always based on a combination of light red with dark or medium blue, plus white and small amounts of other shades. The clarity and balance of this design often makes one think of the Caucasus; but there is no risk of confusion since the structure is quite different – ridged backed, coarse and robust, with cotton warps and pink cotton wefts in new Sirjands, all wool in old Caucasians, neat and only slightly ridged with all-white cotton warps and wefts in new Kazaks and Shirvans (see figs. 514, 515 and 571–3). A variant of this design is made in Shahr Babak, but in the weave and colourings of that region (see fig. 496). Sirjands in this design are made only in the typical sizes of the area – squarish large zaronims and dozars.

560–562 SIRJAND

The design seen in fig. 560 is not an easy one to identify because of the attempt, made in a region that traditionally has a fully geometric style, to introduce curvilinear elements. It is the influence of neighbouring Kerman that inspires the villagers of the Afshar region to produce, for example, the flower bouquets in the corners of this rug (the *gol farang* design in fig. 707 shows a similar influence). The only really typical Sirjand feature of the design is the diamond motif with the 'latch hooks' at the centre of the medallion. For the rest it is the structure (the pink wefts, for example) and the colours – the typical light red, heavy dark blue and strong medium blue – that reveal the origin.

Among the simpler designs of the Sirjand region, the five-medallion layout shown in fig. 561 is fairly common. The medallions themselves seem to be distant relations of the Herati design, but certainly in a rather debased form, which we see here. Note the same centre to the four outer medallions as appears in the preceding example.

Although it is not obvious from some variants, the rug shown in fig. 562 illustrates a vase-and-flower-spray design which harks back once again to the style established in south-east Persia in the seventeenth century. The embryonic Herati pattern in the medallion reminds us of the same period and of the links between the vase idea and the Herati design. The medallion itself is, of course, the same as the one used in the previous example, and the characteristic Sirjand 'latch-hook' diamond appears at the centre. The structure, colouring and sizes made are the same as with all Sirjand goods, as described on p. 111, but a comparison with fig. 399 (26) reminds us that the Afshars of Sirjand are of Turkoman descent.

559 Sirjand Afshari
248 × 158 cm, 112,000 PK/m²
(8′ 2″ × 5′ 2″, 72 PK/in.²).

560

561

562

563 BORUJIRD

The dark colourings employed by the Borujird group of villages, in the southernmost part of the Hamadan area, often cause their rugs to be mistaken for Kharaghan goods. The angularity of some Borujird designs, like the present one, contributes to this error. Generally, however, it is not too difficult to tell them apart, once one has seen a few examples of each, since all Borujirds have the dark-blue-dominated flavour of all the southern Hamadan origins – Malayir, Nenej, Tuisarkan, Nehavend. They also have a rough back, usually with a grey or brown weft, and an uneven surface to the pile, which, however, consists of very lustrous yarn (another feature

560 Sirjand Afshari
175 × 136 cm, 82,000 PK/m²
(5′ 9″ × 4′ 5″, 53 PK/in.²).

561 Sirjand Afshari
166 × 133 cm, 112,000 PK/m²
(5′ 5″ × 4′ 4″, 72 PK/in.²).

562 Sirjand Afshari
219 × 167 cm, 97,000 PK/m²
(7′ 2″ × 5′ 6″, 63 PK/in.²).

563 Borujird
158 × 110 cm, 61,000 TK/m²
(5′ 2″ × 3′ 7″, 39 TK/in.²).

564 Tibetan (Nepal)
190 × 125 cm, 65,000 Tibetan knots/m²
(6′ 3″ × 4′ 1″, 42 Tibetan knots/in.²).

typical of Malayir, Tuisarkan etc.). For further notes on Borujird and the neighbouring village of Oshturinan, cf. fig. 462.

564–567 TIBETAN

The introduction of curvilinear motifs into carpets which often have an essentially geometric style means that designs from the Chinese cultural sphere do not always fit easily into the categories used in this book. This is particularly true of the two west-Chinese rug-producing areas, Tibet and Sinkiang. European scholars, who are usually out of sympathy with the Chinese carpet art on account of its export-oriented cosmopolitan nature, have simply refused to come to grips with the stylistic and cultural-historical problems which this group of designs poses. The Chinese influence on Tibet and East Turkestan is treated as an aberration, and the products of China proper are dismissed as being practically irrelevant to the history of carpet weaving, since China 'adopted the art from the West in the seventeenth century at the earliest and continued to treat it as alien to their culture', This is not good enough. We now know that carpet weaving was practised in China at least as early as AD 700 (see p. 341); and we must also accept that the weavers of Mongolia, East Turkestan and Tibet responded to Chinese commercial influence and later to Chinese rule in a manner which decisively affected their design styles.

There is firm evidence of an ancient weaving craft in these Chinese 'fringe' areas. M. S. Dimand illustrates thirteenth-century Mongolian rugs depicted in Chinese paintings; and Hans Bidder, in his magnificent book on East Turkestan, proves conclusively that rugs were woven there by the Persian and Turkish inhabitants as early as the first century AD, if not before. It is likely that rugs were woven in Tibet in early times, too. Chinese textiles found in the Pazyryk tombs prove that cultural contacts between China and other parts of Asia were probably as old as the art of carpet weaving itself. The Great Wall was built in the third century BC to keep the Mongols out; but since then there have been several periods when the 'Middle Kingdom' extended its power to the borders of India and Persia. The final incorporation of China into the Mongol Empire was accomplished by Jinghis Khan's grandson, Kublai Khan, who founded the Mongol Dynasty which ruled until the accession of the first emperor of the Ming Dynasty in 1368. At least from this period onwards the rugs of Mongolia, East Turkestan and Tibet reflected Chinese influence; and as the Chinese Empire gradually expanded over the succeeding centuries this influence became ever more dominant.

In truth there is some difficulty in distinguishing the many different categories of Chinese goods, since there is a kind of universal validity of their designs which is not found in the culture of the western half of Asia. One of the problems the students of old Chinese rugs encounters is that the weave of many different areas and of many different production periods may be identical – as indeed it still is today. Whereas in Iran one can always distinguish the products of different towns from their weave, however similar someone may have tried to make them in design and colouring, in China one cannot. One can only tell the various categories of goods apart, not their precise origins. Similarly, with the designs, there is a great deal of interchange between all the different areas, so that it comes as no surprise to encounter an old design from East Turkestan used in the production of present-day Tibetan refugees in Nepal (e.g. fig. 564). The three medallions, or güls, are said by Hans Bidder to have religious significance (the Tibetan refugees are strict Buddhists). In his book *Carpets from East Turkestan* he writes (pp. 53f.):

> The '*Triple Medallion*' pattern originated, in my opinion, from the religious art of Gandhara-Buddhism which inspired all the arts and crafts in Khotan during the first millennium of our chronology. As a result of the campaigns of Alexander the Great, who strove to fuse the Greek and Asian spirits, there arose from this meeting of two worlds a culture and religious art which spread from Gandhara in north-west India over the whole of Asia, and which was not stemmed until 1,000 years later by the advance of Islam. The three medallions – of which the central one is often accentuated either by its greater size or heavier ornamentation, or by a yellow instead of a blue ground – represent the three lotus seats on which in the Buddhist temples of old Yotkan (the name for old Khotan) the

statues of Buddha and two Bodhisattvas, flanking him on either side, were seated. Nothing would be more natural than that the pattern must have originated from the three lotus seats or pedestals on the altar and the altar cloth, which in Khotan would have been replaced by a carpet, the more so since the 'Gül' in its single and double forms was already connected with religious conceptions.

The progression of the triple medallion pattern can be traced further from Sir Aurel Stein's collection of frescoes and relief fragments from 7th- and 8th-century Buddhist sanctuaries in the Khotan and Chira-Domoko (east of Khotan) oases; also from A. von Le Coq's abundant finds of wall paintings and Manichean miniature fragments of the same period. Within the framework of its rich religious art Gandhara-Buddhism brought pictorial and sculpted depictions of the Buddha, Bodhisattvas and other holy beings, and also the Lotus pedestal. In order to create an appropriate symbol for the Buddhist allegory of a spiritual rebirth from the Lotus of Knowledge, as the Buddha had formulated it, the Buddhist artists transformed the lotus into a pedestal and showed the Sublime One sitting or standing on the opened crown of the blossom. This symbolized the sublime purity of the Buddha who, like the lotus blossom, had risen from the mud above the sea of physical rebirth darkened with suffering and sin. This is the later Buddhist interpretation of an earlier Hindu allegory in which Indira, wife of Vishnu, arose from the blue lotus blossom.

In both ancient Indian and Buddhist thought red signified – apart from the fiery element of the sun – the portentous world of the senses: Samsara. This would then provide an explanation for the fact that red is always the background colour for the three blue medallions. Blue was for the Buddhists the symbol of spiritualization, and earlier, of the night.

565 Tibetan (Nepal)
180 × 122 cm, 52,000 Tibetan knots/m²
(5′ 11″ × 4′ 0″, 33 Tibetan knots/in.²).

a   b   c   d

566 The development of the swastika motif (from specimens of ancient pottery in the British Museum). The four examples shown are from Samarra, Arpachiyah and elsewhere in Mesopotamia, and date from 4500–3500 BC: (a) representation of four horned animals around a central square, possibly representing a pool; (b) the same motif further stylized; (c, d) forms of the swastika possibly derived from (b).

In fig. 565 note the use of the swastika motif in the border; this symbol, found throughout the Orient, is associated with a host of symbolic overtones, especially in India and China. As a carpet border design, it can be regarded as a natural development of the geometric meander border pattern ('key border') used in ancient Greece (figs. 61 and 95), and perhaps the swastika reached China through the agency of Alexander the Great. To the Indian the pattern has from early times been regarded as a sign of auspicious augury. In China the swastika symbolizes happiness, and when multiplied, as in carpet borders, it expresses a wish for 'ten thousandfold happiness' (Lorentz). The Chinese character *wan*, meaning 10,000, is sometimes written in the traditional swastika shape.

4 GEOMETRIC MEDALLION/ALL-OVER DESIGNS

567 Chinese, late nineteenth century
186 × 243 cm, 60,000 PK/m²
(6′ 1″ × 8′ 0″, 39 PK/in.²).

568 Nehavend/Mishin region
230 × 156 cm, 135,000 TK/m²
(7′ 6″ × 5′ 1″, 87 TK/in.²).

This group includes much of the village production of Iran, having one pronounced geometric medallion, as in the preceding group, but with the ground covered with a regular or irregular pattern of small motifs; and rugs from sundry other sources which use dominant medallion designs whose starkness is softened by the inclusion of a repeating pattern in the ground.

567 CHINA

It is difficult to say whether Chinese designs are rectilinear or curvilinear. With their new production the Chinese seem to have opted for a generally floral style; but with old Chinese goods the question itself seems somehow inappropriate, for elements of both design categories are commonly found in one and the same carpet. Carpets of the type illustrated here are often labelled 'Pao-Tu'. This is an unhelpful description. Pao-Tu is the chief town of the province of Suiyuan in Inner Mongolia, and was one of the many collecting centres for carpets made outside China proper. Another such centre was Ning Hsia, which is also a name much quoted in the trade, but as Lorentz clearly shows, the output of Ning Hsia itself was tiny, whereas the whole of northern China proper – the vast provinces of Kansu, Shensi, Shansi, Chihli (Hopei) and Shantung – has been engaged in carpet weaving for a century or two at least. To describe the huge quantities of old rugs in general as Pao-Tu or Ning Hsia borders on the ridiculous. The difficulty is that since none of the production centres has identifiable individual features, the only general description we are left with for most of the goods is 'old Chinese', which is quite galling to the carpet man brought up on western Asiatic rugs, the origin of which can often be determined with absolute precision. Lorentz reserves the name Pao-Tu for the picture rugs of the type shown in figs. 382–4. The types he describes as Kansu and Suiyuan are also illustrated in this book (figs. 719 – a modern copy – and 713). For the rest he simply uses the word Chinese, and in the absence of further evidence of source it behoves us to do the same. The origins of weaving in China, though very ancient, are shrouded in mystery (cf. p. 341), but it is clear that by the late nineteenth century a massive export-oriented production was under way. The rugs and carpets woven between 1900 and 1950 are still available in large quantities in carpet shops in the West. The supply from China itself began to dwindle in the early 1970s and prices rocketed, especially for larger sizes. Among goods still readily to be found, dark blue predominates as a ground shade, and more pieces are available in the size 120 × 60 cm (4′ 0″ × 2′ 0″) than in any other.

The subject of Chinese carpets is quite specialized but unfortunately very few scholars have had the opportunity of acquiring much detailed knowledge of it, and very little will be found in print, in carpet books or elsewhere (Lorentz is the glorious exception, see bibliography). From the point of view of design recognition the problem is less serious since the Chinese style is widely known, unmistakable, and little more is needed in this book than to illustrate the principal types. Within each type there are of course thousands of designs; but the distinctive elements all have the same family features. One thing almost all old Chinese goods have in common

568

569 Sinkiang
250 × 156 cm, 122,000 PK/m²
(8′ 2″ × 5′ 1″, 79 PK/in.²).

570 Sinkiang
212 × 98 cm, 125,000 PK/m²
(6′ 11″ × 3′ 2″, 81 PK/in.²).

is the same basic structure: very thin cotton warps, often cut off short so that there is no kilim and practically no fringe; two quite thin cotton wefts, giving a flat back to the rug, with very little ribbing; and a thick pile of splendid wool, although the density and length of the pile does of course vary according to the age of the rug and the use it has had. The fringe is often at the narrow ends, as one would expect, but it is also quite common to find pieces with the fringe on what would normally be thought of as the sides, as in the piece shown here. Several features of the carpet illustrated in fig. 567 are typical: the swastika border (which may also take a similarly geometric form without strictly incorporating this ancient symbol of good luck); the not quite accurate circular medallion (with no outline – a feature of Chinese designing rarely found elsewhere); the strictly formal flower lattice-work of the ground; and the colour-plan, which is as restrained and formal as the design, being based on six shades only: dark blue, light blue, gold, buff, ivory and peach. For the modern use of similar motifs, see figs. 459 and 570.

569, 570 SINKIANG
The first of these rugs is a modern Sinkiang piece which shows a clear relationship with the old carpet from the same area seen in fig. 528. It is in the rugs with such a clearly defined connection with the past culture of East Turkestan that this modern development is most successful. The output of this most westerly province of China is now substantial and the variations of design, sizes and colours is endless, but they all have the same general style and colourings revealed by the illustrations in the various sections of this book (see index). The general note on Sinkiang rugs is on p. 108.

A similarly traditional design from East Turkestan is used in the second example, the flattened circular medallion being a common feature in old Khotans. The connection with the Tibetan rug of fig. 564 is also noteworthy. Indeed, the present example demonstrates admirably the fusion of Chinese and Turkoman elements in the East Turkestan style. The outer borders represent a geometric stylization of the Chinese wave and cloud forms seen also in fig. 379, which, according to Bidder, were introduced to Turkestan by the Buddhists (cf. also fig. 564); but the circular güls in the design and the latch-hook motifs are clear evidence of the Turkoman connection.

571–573 KAZAK
The three Kazak rugs illustrated are further examples of the new production referred to in the section on repeating medallion designs (see p. 230). They are all characteristic of the countless permutations that are possible using the ancient motifs of the Caucasus. Note the very wide use of the latch-hook motifs and, in figs. 572 and 573, the idea of inserting repeating medallions within a larger medallion filling almost the whole of the ground of the rug. The very distinctive form of this medallion in fig. 573 is often seen in other Azerbaijan goods, too, including modern Russian Shirvans and Meshkin and other Persian runners. The finesse with which the design is drawn and the skilful and exact execution make this one of the most successful of the new Kazak range. An old rug with this design is illustrated in fig. 14; a comparison of it with fig. 573 illuminates the differences between old and new Caucasian goods mentioned on p. 211.

574, 575 SHAHR BABAK
In truth it is rather artificial to separate all the Afshar production into 'Sirjands' and 'Shahr Babaks' (plus fringe places like Dahaj, Niriz, and Rafsinjan). The tribes cover a wide area in which many different villages have their own distinctive style. However, within this wide area there are two quite densely concentrated groups of villages, for which the market towns are Shahr Babak in the north and Sirjand in the south; and there is a very marked difference between the styles of the two areas, Shahr Babaks being fine and softly coloured, Sirjands coarse and bright. It is this distinction which lies behind the trade's separation of the area into two parts. However, problems of identification arise with rugs made in other parts of the region, such as the village of Pariz, which is about equidistant from both market

571

572

573

574

575

571 Kazak
194 × 131 cm, 115,000 TK/m²
(6′ 4″ × 4′ 3″, 74 PK/in.²).

572 Kazak
149 × 99 cm, 120,000 TK/m²
(4′ 11″ × 3′ 3″, 77 TK/in.²).

573 Kazak
138 × 87 cm, 144,000 TK/m²
(4′ 6″ × 2′ 10″, 93 TK/in.²).

574 Shahr Babak
191 × 131 cm, 209,000 PK/m²
(6′ 3″ × 4′ 4″, 135 PK/in.²).

575 Shahr Babak
191 × 140 cm, 191,000 PK/m²
(6′ 3″ × 4′ 7″, 123 PK/in.²).

centres and whose goods seem to have a foot in both camps, having a fine weave, though not so fine as Shahr Babak, and bright colours, though not so bright as Sirjand. Furthermore, Jenny Housego, for one, has asserted that by no means all the tribes of Kerman province are genuine Afshars in any case, which makes the validity of the carpet trade's general classification even more suspect. All the rugs described in this book as Shahr Babak were at least bought there and it must thus be left to a more competent authority to offer a more accurate categorization. The best known of all Shahr Babak Afshar designs is probably the one shown in fig. 152. That rug has many typical Shahr Babak features – cotton warps and wefts, very fine weave (over 200,000 knots/m²; 130 knots/in.²), close-clipped, rather soft pile, a rich dull brownish red (the most tell-tale feature of all Shahr Babaks) and a rich

576 Behbehan
252 × 144 cm, 70,000 TK/m²
(8′ 3″ × 4′ 9″, 45 TK/in.²).

palette of other colours, sparingly used. The shape of the medallions is very characteristic; so are the botehs and the many zig-zag outlines to the medallions; the border design is found in Ferahan and Bakhtiari carpets, but the form employed in fig. 152 is very common in Shahr Babak, as fig. 574 will confirm. However, within the wealth of designs still to be found in the Shahr Babak area, figs. 574 and 575 are also just as characteristic, fig. 574 showing yet another variant of the repeating hooked-diamond idea and yet another form of the boteh motif, while fig. 575 includes the tree motif and many little bird figures tucked away in the background in a manner absolutely typical of the origin. Only rug sizes are made and, of these, dozars are most common; however, the rugs are made in dimensions both larger and smaller than average for the standard types, so that in the end more or less every size from about 80 × 50 cm (2′ 8″ × 1′ 8″) to 220 × 160 cm (7′ 3″ × 5′ 3″) may be found. The price of Shahr Babaks has risen sharply in recent years; but anyone seeking an example of that ideal structure in a Persian carpet which is often heard of but these days rarely encountered – the combination of tight weave and flexible handle, sound construction and elegant appearance – should seek out one of the many outstanding Shahr Babak rugs still readily to be found, for in view of their originality and fine workmanship they still seem undervalued.

576 BEHBEHAN LURI

While many carpets are named after the village where they are made or the people who make them, some are known simply by the place in which they are marketed; often simply because we do not know precisely where the rugs are made or because it suits the convenience of wholesalers to group goods according to the town where they were bought. So it is with Luri rugs. The market centres are Shiraz, Khorramabad, Behbehan and Isfahan. Of these, Behbehan, in particular, covers goods in a wide variety of styles: all clearly of one family, but equally clearly from many different and no doubt widely dispersed weaving centres. While the Behbehan of fig. 444 has something of the flavour of the Luri kilims marketed in Shiraz, fig. 576 has much more affinity with the Owlad rugs of Naghun (see figs. 446 and 484, and map p. 346). It is not, however, a Naghun but from some other village in the Zagros mountains, the inhospitable region into which the Lurs, centuries – or even millennia – ago, perhaps escaped the warlike pressures of Babylon to the east or migrating Iranians and Turks to the north and west. For further notes on Behbehan see index. Note in this rug the use of black goat-hair warps and the wide colourful kilim at both ends.

577 YAGÇIBEDIR

The origin of this rug is unmistakable when one puts together all the following elements: woollen warp and weft, fine weave, close-clipped pile of fine lustrous yarn (clipped almost to the bone in some cases); dark blue (almost black) ground

577 Yagçibedir
184 × 102 cm, 95,000 TK/m²
(6′ 0″ × 3′ 4″, 61 TK/in.²).

in most pieces, but also some cream grounds; skeletal hexagonal medallion, leaving the ground and the medallion of the same colour; red or rust leaf and tree motifs in the medallion, splendid fine subsidiary motifs in the corners; and a large number of narrow geometric borders. The only sizes made are: 100 × 60 cm (3′ 3″ × 2′ 0″), narrow runners up to 300 × 50–60 cm (10′ 0″ × 1′ 9″–2′ 0″), typical Turkish small seçcadehs (around 180 × 120 cm; 6′ 0″ × 4′ 0″). These are the features of Yagçibedir (the name traditionally used in the carpet trade to describe the rugs of Sindirgi in north-west Anatolia). The design style has something of a Luri feel about it, and the colours and structure remind one of the Beluchis, but only the Yagçibedirs of western Anatolia have precisely the flavour of the rug illustrated here. Yagçibedirs, indeed, always have this flavour: the thousands of pieces woven each year all include some variant of the same design. To see how similar and yet how varied they are, cf. also fig. 457. The Yagçibedir colours vary according to the method of washing used. Unwashed, the rugs have a fierce red, which, against the blackish blue, is not very popular in Western markets. Washed in Turkey, the red is softened, or may be bleached to an attractive silvery grey, but the best colours are obtained by the London wash, which produces beautiful rosy-rust shades which are neither too red nor too pale.

578 Khorramabad
207 × 152 cm, 48,000 TK/m²
(6′ 9″ × 5′ 0″, 31 TK/in.²).

578 KHORRAMABAD

Attention has already been drawn to the dark and often rather unattractive rugs from that part of Luristan that abuts the Kurdish and Hamadan area to the north and the Iraqi frontier to the west. Considering how roughly coloured these rugs often are, there is a surprisingly large range of designs, which frequently seem to owe something to the influence of their Kurdish neighbours. The bold, angular medallion shown here is typical – compare it with the Kurdish designs in figs. 549 and 553. In case of doubt about the origin, the structure reveals all (cf. fig. 483). Note the break in the border design near the bottom of the rug on both sides. Although it is hard for us to imagine how a weaver following the line of the border row by row from the bottom of the rug upwards could make such a mistake, there is in fact no question of its revealing, as a suspicious buyer might think, a piece of sharp practice on the part of a dealer who might have cut up two damaged rugs to make one complete one. In all hand-made carpets, and especially in tribal rugs, design slips of this kind are quite common. To deny that they are weaving errors would be unrealistic, but what is strictly an error in craft is not necessarily a fault in art, and for many buyers the mystery of how a weaver could stop the border in one place and start it again in quite another will increase rather than detract from the rug's appeal.

579 Kakaberu
263 × 164 cm, 112,000 TK/m²
(8′ 7″ × 5′ 4″, 72 TK/in.²).

579 KAKABERU

Not all the rugs of the Kurdish Kakaberu tribe have the wild disregard for balance and harmony of design seen in figs. 131 and 532. Nor do they lose their underlying feeling of strength and self-assertion when the motifs and proportions are as well ordered as in this example, for the visual interest is sustained by the felicitious idea of enclosing each medallion in a second, larger one, from the centre of the rug right out to the edge of the ground. The tree motifs and sundry subsidiary elements in the ground add life to the corners and the largest outer medallion. Note also the unusual border, in which a geometric variant of the Herati border is embellished with what look like peacocks, although the location of the fan-tails in some of the motifs suggests other interpretations. The structure, sizes and colourings are as described on p. 63.

580–589 HAMADAN

The city of Hamadan is one of the oldest of the Iranian plateau; known to the Assyrians as Agamtana, its origins go back to the second millennium BC. The Medes made it their capital (Hangmatana or Agbatana) and after the incorporation of the Median Empire into that of Kourosh (Cyrus) the town became the summer residence of the Achaemenid kings. After the conquests of Alexander the Great the Greek name Ekbatana was used. The town's strategic position on the route to

Baghdad from the north and east brought much suffering to the population in the course of the Seljuq and Mongol invasions and again during the interminable wars between the Safavids and Ottomans. The region was occupied many times by Turki-speaking invaders and today the language of the surrounding villages is dominated by Turkic dialects. The modern city is a thriving commercial centre with a new university, and of particular importance to the carpet industry since it serves as the market centre for hundreds of villages in the surrounding plain and as the base for buyers who cover a wide area of western Iran – the Kurdish areas around Bijar, Senneh, Sonqur and Kermanshah, the Luri centre of Khorramabad, the Borujird and Serabend region, the Malayir valley and Arak, the centre for Saruq carpets, as well as the whole of the Hamadan area proper as far east as Saveh and north to Zenjan. There is also a small production in the town itself. The Hamadan village region has one unifying and unmistakable characteristic: all its products (with only the rarest of exceptions) are single-wefted, and woven with the Turkish knot on cotton warps and wefts. They are also generally relatively coarse and in many cases quite cheap. A few villages make carpets but rugs predominate, with one or two areas specializing in runners also. There are other single-wefted rug origins, of course, but not many: Kolyai, Senneh, Bakhtiar, Karaja, Daghestan, Pakistan and India (also a few old Chinese), and most of these have very distinctive features which make identification easy. Lacking these, a single-wefted rug is almost certainly a Hamadan. The range of designs made in this large area can be broken down into three basic types which are fairly easy to group geographically. As befits a straightforward peasant production, Hamadan goods have uncomplicated geometric designs. These predominate in the villages which run in a large arc from the north-west of the region through the north and the whole of the west down to the south-west. This style was, however, supplanted long ago in the south and east of the Hamadan area by the Herati design – *mahi*, as the locals call it. And sixty years ago the so-called 'American Saruq' floral design spread like wild-fire from Arak in the south-east and made substantial inroads into the areas of geometric production.

580 ZENJAN

The rug shown illustrates what everyone recognizes as the typical style of the geometric Hamadan village rugs. The small town of Zenjan, about halfway along the road from Tehran to Tabriz, marks the northern boundary of the Hamadan area, and is indeed the collecting centre for other goods from the north as well as the single-wefted Hamadan rugs. Details of the different types will be found on p. 90. The Hamadan rugs of Zenjan are brash when new and often too thin; but older pieces often have very attractive colours, among which light blue and a sparing use of orange establish a colour-style which is easily recognized. Black (generally quite rare in Persian rugs) is often used in place of dark blue and the red palette also includes a brownish-red shade not common in other parts of the Hamadan region. Note the dismembered Herati motifs in the ground and the medallion-within-medallion idea. Dozars are the most common size.

581 QOLTUQ

Qoltuqs, in simple terms, are double-wefted Zenjans. The village of Qoltuq lies to the west of Zenjan at the point where the single-wefted structure of the Hamadan region gives way to the double-wefted work of Azerbaijan; also, it is adjacent to the area which makes the Zenjan Bijar types illustrated in figs. 203 and 248. The weave is clearly of the Azerbaijan type, often reminding one of some of the rugs marketed in Ardebil, but the design, as in this example, is firmly in the style of the Hamadan area. The colour combination illustrated is typical of that of the single-wefted Zenjan rugs described above, but other designs are also found with more emphasis on other shades. A greater use of green is common in some pieces and here, too, a particularly distinctive feature is the wide use of black instead of dark blue. Qoltuqs, like the single-wefted Zenjans, tend to be rather thin – as in some other double-wefted constructions, the weight often seems to be all in the back – but soundly made pieces in a fine weave can be very attractive.

580 Zenjan
189 × 125 cm, 178,000 TK/m²
(6′ 2″ × 4′ 1″, 115 TK/in.²).

581

582

583

582 BIDGENEH

Bidgeneh (sometimes spelt Badeganeh) is a village south-west of Zenjan, near Qoltuq, in the group which specializes in fine Bijar-type designs in a double-wefted construction. The weave, as in the present rug, can be very fine and the structure very tight, giving an outstanding result at a considerably lower price than one would have to pay for a Bijar of equal stitch. The reason for this lies surely in the stiffness, even gawkiness, of design which marks the style of this area. This can be seen in fig. 203, in which the Herati design is used, and it is equally evident in the piece shown here; note how many lines of the design run vertically from end to end of the rug. This inhibits the feeling of mellifluous flow that one would sense in a Bijar. Note, by the way, that the border is the same as in the Shahr Babak Afshar rug shown in fig. 152. It is occasionally used in other parts of Persia, too, but the comparison inevitably reminds us that Afshars formerly lived in the area around Bidgeneh. The small output of this village is made almost entirely in dozar size.

583 KHAMSEH

Khamseh is the name of an administrative district south of Zenjan; as applied to Hamadan rugs, the name has nothing to do with the Khamseh Confederation, a group of rug-weaving tribes near Shiraz. Khamsehs are among the cheapest, most basic rugs of the Hamadan village area. The design illustrated here is, of course, based on the Herati pattern, but not all Khamseh rugs are in this style. More distinctive is the shape of the medallion and its hooked pendants. In colouring, the Khamsehs often resemble Zenjan goods, but the general appearance is less imaginative. As in many Hamadan villages, dozars make up the bulk of the production.

584 KHARAGHAN

Contiguous with Khamseh to the south-east lies the district of Kharaghan. Here there is a noticeable change in style. Firstly, the colours are much darker and, secondly, the designs are rather bolder. The more common type has a completely open ground, as in fig. 557, but a medallion/all-over style sometimes appears. The rug illustrated is in a rather finer weave than is usual for the area, but the basic character is typical. For general notes on Kharaghan see p. 237.

581 Qoltuq
194 × 124 cm, 125,000 TK/m²
(6′ 4″ × 4′ 1″, 81 TK/in.²).

582 Bidgeneh
219 × 138 cm, 394,000 TK/m²
(7′ 2″ × 4′ 6″, 254 TK/in.²).

583 Khamseh
193 × 133 cm, 100,000 PK/m²
(6′ 4″ × 4′ 4″, 65 PK/in.²).

584 Kharaghan
198 × 131 cm, 127,000 TK/m²
(6′ 6″ × 4′ 3″, 82 TK/in.²).

585 Kemereh
195 × 137 cm, 105,000 TK/m²
(6′ 5″ × 4′ 6″, 68 TK/in.²).

586 Nehavend
220 × 141 cm, 130,000 TK/m²
(7′ 2″ × 4′ 7″, 84 TK/in.²).

585 KEMEREH

As is noted below (cf. p. 282), the villages of the Kemereh district are not really part of the Hamadan region: they represent a pocket of single-wefted weaving in an otherwise double-wefted area. The connection with Saruqs appears in the rosy-red colourings and the American Saruq influence on the designs. Lilihans, which belong to this group, are often woven entirely in the American Saruq style (see fig. 638); in the rug shown here the stiff flower sprays arising from the medallion seem to represent a stylized peasant derivative of the idea. A very useful clue to recognition of Kemereh rugs is the shape of the medallion – the same in the present example as in the Herati-pattern piece shown in fig. 216. Here again dozar sizes predominate.

586 NEHAVEND

An interesting characteristic of the whole Hamadan region is that the changes of style from one village to the next are rarely abrupt: there always exists a link, in the form of the typical features which are shared, to be set against the other features which are contrasted. However, in the transition from one geographical area to the next it is a different feature which changes: village A may have thick, dark rugs, B will be thin and dark, C thin and light with angular designs, D thin and light with floral designs, E thick and bright with floral designs, etc. One can trace the progressive changes in design in the same way as one can follow the physical geography, or the subtle and gradual changes of dialect, or the changes in farming and crops throughout any country. That is one reason why we speak of the carpet folk-art as an expression of the people as a whole: their carpet styles are as characteristic as their dialects. In the Hamadan region this sometimes makes recognition difficult: there are hundreds of villages and the changes in weave and design from one to the other are gradual. It is inevitable that some pieces seem to belong half to one area and half to another. Borujird goods, from the south-west of the region (cf. figs. 129 and 563), have fine wool, deep pile and very dark colours, the white warps on the back of the rug being starkly contrasted against the dark knots and dark wefts; on seeing these characteristics in a Nehavend rug, one may well be tempted to call it a Borujird, for these are the features which are shared by the two areas. However, Nehavend has a special design and style of its own, as in the example illustrated. In fact the design is a kind of clumsy geometric version of the American Saruq design (see pp. 280ff.), but it is so thoroughly reconstituted that it may be seen as an independent design in its own right. A particularly noteworthy feature is the border, in which the flower groups break through into the ground of the rug – a rarely used and instantly recognizable feature. Other important features are: the sizes –

almost the whole production consists of very large, narrowish dozars, up to 4 m² (43 ft²) in area and rarely less than 3 m² (32 ft²); a few rare zaronims, wide runners and the occasional small carpet are also found. The structure is finer than that of Borujird and the wool even silkier, with the sort of strong twist that is visible on the back of the knot – a connecting link with the Kurds, whose area begins immediately to the west of Nehavend. The colours of new Nehavends are rather strong, but the rather sparing use of white avoids the 'busy' effect seen in other new Hamadan rugs. Most Nehavends, unlike the present example, are dark blue, but the red ground seen here appears from time to time.

587, 568 USHVAN/MISHIN-MALAYIR
Within the Nehavend area, there is one village, Ushvan, which – while making rugs in the same sizes and in the same quality – employs a rather different design, as illustrated in fig. 587. The first thing that strikes one is the different border – Ushvans never have the overspill of flower-sprays into the ground which is such an obvious feature in Nehavends, and the whole design layout, with the large hexagonal centrepiece and the cream corners, is also distinctive. In other respects, the Ushvans clearly belong to the Nehavend region. Moving away from the centre of the region, we begin to encounter other designs. One type – half-Nehavend, half-Malayir – is called Mishin-Malayir: these rugs are single-wefted, with some of the flavour of Malayir, but they are generally more geometric in design, sometimes reminding one of Nehavend, sometimes of Taimeh (see fig. 220). Figure 568 shows another type from this region, having more of the design style of Tuisarkan (see fig. 588), while retaining the construction and colours of Nehavend. Apart from the great dominant medallion, there are three very distinctive features of this design: the white 'cock's-comb' motif that outlines the medallion and reappears in the corners; the unusual combination of a medium-blue medallion on a dark-blue ground; and the khaki corners. Large dozars are the only size made in this type.

588 TUISARKAN
The reader will notice that the style of the whole area of Borujird, Nehavend, Malayir and Nenej is marked by a predominance of dark-blue grounds. The same feature is found in Tuisarkan, but here there is a stylistic change: brighter colours are used as well, often including some unpleasant bright greens and orange. The quality is a little less fine than Nehavend, and in particular the pile is much thinner, although the general quality is still above the Hamadan average. One village of the group, Vordoveh, makes the unusual type shown in fig. 558, but otherwise the bulk of the production is in designs closely related to the Tuisarkan example shown here. Superficially, the design might be confused with some of the Nehavend types, but there are many points to enable us to tell them apart: Tuisarkan is less long and narrow in format and much thinner in pile; the cock's-comb or saw-tooth edging to the medallion and corners, and the 'rope' design in the border (see also fig. 653) are unmistakable features of Tuisarkans; and Nehavend never goes in for the jazziness of colour mentioned above. A wide range of rug sizes is made in Tuisarkan, all in Persian standard proportions: pushtis, zarchereks, zaronims, dozars. Runners and carpets are not unknown, but are very rare. Note that before the Second World War Tuisarkan had a small manufactured output with a double-wefted construction.

589 SENNEH
The elegance and finesse of Senneh rugs is superbly and inimitably described by A. C. Edwards in *The Persian Carpet*, the standard English monograph on the subject. The key feature he emphasizes is the subtlety of design, colour and structure which distinguishes the fine rugs of the capital of Kurdistan from the peasant products of the surrounding villages. In this book, however, we may see the Senneh style *within* the context of the Kurdish and West Hamadan area. A comparison with the Nehavend/Kolyai area (see figs. 530–3 and 550–3) serves to underline the fact that within this whole region one of the keys to success lies in the brilliantly skilful manipulation of large blocks of colour. Many Western buyers in search of carpets have pastel shades in mind, or 'decorator' colours – golds, peach and rust

587 Ushvan
232 × 145 cm, 122,000 TK/m²
(7′ 7″ × 4′ 9″, 79 TK/in.²).

588 Tuisarkan
210 × 145 cm, 125,000 TK/m²
(6′ 10″ × 4′ 9″, 81 TK/in.²).

589 Senneh
209 × 146 cm, 223,000 TK/m²
(6′ 10″ × 4′ 9″, 144 TK/in.²).

590 Baba Haidar
212 × 152 cm, 69,000 TK/m²
(6′ 11″ × 5′ 0″, 45 TK/in.²).

589

590

tones, browns, greens, and the wide spectrum of pale blue and lilac (suggested no doubt by the colour-schemes of other home textiles). They then find themselves confronted with the blunt dominance of dark blue and red in the vast majority of Persian carpets and receive a shock from which they sometimes never recover. The immense success of 'gold Afghans', new Chinese rugs made to order in Western colours, Indian Mirs in all shades of the rainbow, Taba Tabai Tabrizes and the like is built on the importers' awareness of the resistance on the part of many buyers to the Persian villagers' uncompromising adherence to traditional colour schemes. However, in spite of all the skill and ingenuity devoted to such market-oriented articles, they can never match the expressive strength achieved in the combinations of blue and red used by village weavers throughout Iran and much of the rest of the Orient, too. Part of the secret lies in the fact that dark indigo blue – the colour the Western housewife likes least in her home – is far and away the best foil for most of the other colours of the spectrum. Another factor contributing to the strength of the colour scheme in the west-Persian rugs enumerated above is its restraint, its simplicity: red and ivory on dark blue sums up 90% of the surface area of many rugs of this region. In the case of the Senneh rug illustrated the idea is developed further, the dark blue being used to set off the huge block of ivory and the piquancy of the overall effect being heightened by the strong medium blue of the medallion and border (fig. 550, another Kurdish product, has a similar colour combination); note also the use of a 'French' design border. For general notes on Senneh rugs see p. 61.

590 BABA HAIDAR

It can sometimes be quite difficult for the layman to distinguish Hamadan rugs from Bakhtiars. Of course, all the double-wefted Bakhtiars are clearly recognizable, because Hamadans are always single-wefted; also, the single-wefted Bakhtiars in panel designs are not in doubt, because the panel design is not made in any of the Hamadan villages. The difficulty arises with single-wefted rugs with medallion designs, such as the Baba Haidar rug illustrated here. Baba Haidar is a village in the west of the Bakhtiari province, near the Luri areas, with a substantial output in the design shown: one encounters it most commonly in carpet sizes (especially 300 × 200 cm; 10′ 0″ × 6′ 6″), in which case two medallions are included, but dozars with one medallion are not unusual. For the most part there is no confusion with Hamadan rugs because Baba Haidars usually have a coarse double-wefted construction, a weave somewhat reminiscent of Viss (see fig. 534), but in the dozar

591

592

591 Kerdar
193 × 127 cm, 130,000 TK/m²
(6′ 4″ × 4′ 2″, 84 TK/in.²).

592 Shah Savan
207 × 136 cm, 91,000 TK/m²
(6′ 9″ × 4′ 5″, 59 TK/in.²).

size single-wefted pieces are also made. In the rug illustrated note the border, which is just as distinctive a feature of its origin as is the shape of the medallion. The colours are generally untypical of Bakhtiar goods, showing more Luri influence in the deep red which predominates. There is also a large amount of dark blue and sometimes medium blue.

591–593 NOBERAN, SHAH SAVAN, KAKABERU

Just to the east of the Kharaghan area there are three villages – Kerdar, Noberan and Maslaghan – which weave one particular design that is easy to remember because of the 'lightning' pattern around the edges of the medallion and corners. The elongated shape of the medallion and the lattice of flowers or stars in the corners are further distinguishing features (fig. 591). The weave is single-wefted and shows the clear connection with the Kharaghan area (see p. 246). The rugs are known variously by the names of all three villages. The dozar is the most common size, but zaronims also occur. As with other designs used in the Kharaghan area, the same type is also made nearer to Saveh (i.e. still further east) by the Shah Savan tribe. Figure 592 shows a typical Shah Savan example of the design, which is plainly different from the Kerdar version, but sometimes the differences in design are not so clear-cut, and then one must rely on one's feeling for colour and the handle of the goods to distinguish one from another (see p. 237). A third area producing the same 'lightning' design is that of the Kurdish Kakaberu tribe, near Senneh. Here there is no problem of identification since Kakaberus are all double-wefted, as well as being very heavy both in weight and colouring; also, as with other Kurdish goods, another clue is to be found in the long and narrow kelleyi format.

This design is also found in Taleghan, a small, remote valley north of Saveh in the Elburz mountains, the last Persian limb of the Caucasus which curls around the southern shores of the Caspian Sea. Taleghan is the source of high-quality single-wefted goods in a range of designs suggesting Shah Savan or Luri influence, but the rugs in the 'lightning' design are mass-produced and are all as alike as two peas. A dominant feature is their dark-blue/light-blue colour scheme.

593 Kakaberu
269 × 141 cm, 131,000 TK/m²
(8′ 10″ × 4′ 7″, 85 TK/in.²).

594 SHIRAZ

It has been noted that the very complex mixture of tribes in Fars province is reflected in the wide variety of goods found on the Shiraz market. The nomadic Lurs and Qashqais have generally kept their independent styles, but the settled tribes have the same kind of mixture of designs as one finds in Azerbaijan and the

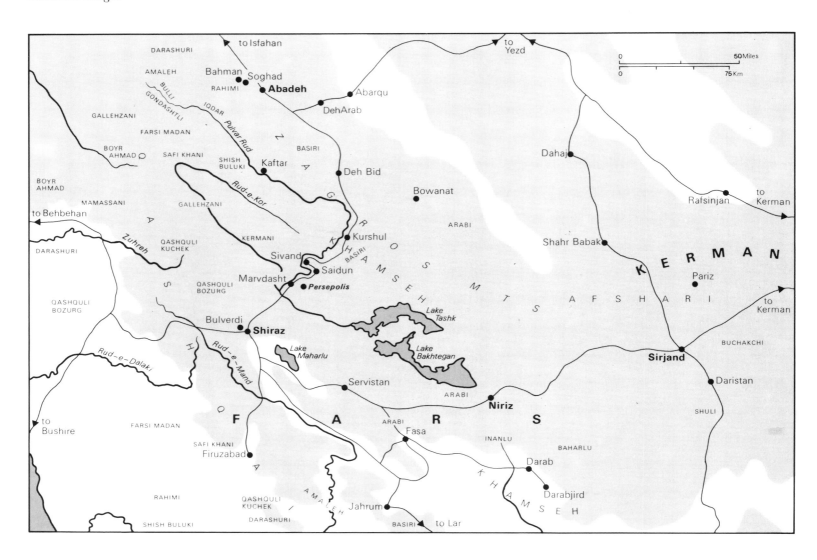

Map of the Qashqai and Afshari weaving areas; names appearing twice in the Qashqai area are those of nomadic tribes which migrate between summer and winter quarters.

594 Shiraz
155 × 117 cm, 88,000 TK/m²
(5′ 1″ × 3′ 10″, 57 TK/in.²).

Caucasus (detailed notes on the racial make-up of the region will be found in Jenny Housego's excellent *Tribal Rugs*, and in *The Persian Carpet* by A. C. Edwards). In the carpets from this area there are thus thousands of design variants and many surprises. The structure is very similar throughout the region – woollen or goat-hair warps, woollen wefts (usually two but often more) – and a quite thick woollen pile. Cotton warps are used in one category of fine Qashqai carpets and in the Afshar-style rugs of Niriz, but nowhere else in the region. The selvedge very often has the 'barber's-pole' type of very decorative whipping, sometimes with bunches of wool in various shades hanging out down both sides. Although the designs vary greatly, the bulk of the production keeps to the basic style of the Shiraz rug illustrated, with one or more medium-sized medallions, triangular corners and simple geometric borders. What generates the enormous appeal of Shiraz rugs is the myriad of small motifs which fill the ground: these may be tiny or elaborate, including birds, dogs and other – imaginary – animals, as well as all kinds of stylized plant forms, trees, flowers, stars and geometric spangles of every description. One of the main keys to the typical Shiraz style is the colouring, which is generally rich and dark: not gloomy, but not light and airy, either. The majority of pieces have red grounds – quite a deep madder red which, with age, turns into a fine shade of brown – but blue-ground rugs are also found. The main secondary colours are medium blue, green, white, orange and gold. The standards of dyeing are very variable, and streaks and changes of colour are common. The blues in particular may often be streaked with black and grey. A range of certain set sizes is made: meteri (rather more than a square metre or yard in area, and longer and narrower than the normal Persian zarcherek), largish zaronims, largish dozars, dozaronimi (about 240 × 150 cm; 7′ 9″ × 5′ 0″), and kelleguis, a designation which means carpet sizes in general (not long and narrow pieces as elsewhere in Persia). Some runners are found, but they are usually inferior in quality. Pieces over 9 m² (100 ft²)

in area are rare. Prices vary considerably and some sizes cost more per square metre than other sizes of the same quality. The range of qualities made is very great; some pieces seem to contain more cows' hair than sheep's wool, but there are also large numbers of really good rugs to be found, with an honest construction and lovely wool. Generally, Shiraz goods are fairly loose in construction and not especially hard-wearing: it is their richness and warmth, both of colour and design, that earns them their popularity.

595, 596 QASHQAI

Amongst the Shiraz weaves, the group of nomadic tribes known as the Qashqai stand out as the best. Their weave is finer and firmer than the Shiraz average, with a tighter ridged-back construction and shorter pile. Really old Qashqais, which one sometimes encounters, are miracles of weaving and colouring skill, but even today excellent Qashqai goods, both new and oldish, are still available in a considerable range of designs. The one shown in fig. 595, called *hebatlu*, with the five Turkoman-göl-type motifs in white, is the most common. (Hebatlu is the name of one of the smaller Qashqai tribes.) The border of this rug is also very common in Qashqai goods, as too are the many tree and plant forms in the ground. The medallion shape, whether single as in this rug, or multiple as in figs. 487 or 488, is shared with other goods of the Shiraz area. In fact the distinction between 'Shiraz' and 'Qashqai' is vague. The names of some of the individual tribes and indeed their approximate locations and migration routes are fairly well known, but few dealers can offer precise attributions of origin to the Qashqai rugs and for the most part the name is used simply to indicate any Shiraz rug of above-average

595 Qashqai
250 × 189 cm, 120,000 PK/m²
(8′ 2″ × 6′ 2″, 77 PK/in.²).

596 Qashqai
216 × 148 cm, 135,000 PK/m²
7′ 1″ × 4′ 10″, 87 PK/in.²).

595

596

597 Abadeh
201 × 145 cm, 163,000 PK/m²
(6′ 7″ × 4′ 9″, 105 PK/in.²).

quality. This is a great pity since the Qashqai are the most important of the Turkic tribes in Iran, and a proper documentation of their carpet designs would be a valuable contribution to anthropology. It should be added, though, that the Qashqai are a political confederation of tribes and their ethnic character has been changed by their acceptance within the confederation of a number of other tribes of Luri, Arab and Persian origin. It is, thus, for example, no longer true that the Qashqai use only the Turkish knot.

The blue-ground rug of fig. 596 illustrates another typical Qashqai design; blue is less common as a ground-shade than red. Sizes around 250 × 150 cm (8′ 0″ × 5′ 0″) are common, but all sizes – ranging in area from 2 m² to 6 m² (20–65 ft²) – are found, as well as a huge range of bags and tent and animal trappings of every kind.

597 ABADEH

About halfway along the road from Shiraz to Isfahan, and on the north-eastern edge of the Qashqai area, lies the town of Abadeh, the source of a variant of the Qashqai *hebatlu* design, as illustrated here. In the past Abadeh rugs had rather a different character – a kind of Arab weave more akin to Bowanat goods (see fig. 494), or Bahman, the name of one of the Arab tribes and of a village not far from Abadeh. Now, however, Abadeh rugs have developed a style entirely their own and in no way comparable with the Qashqai origin of the design. The weave is fairly fine and the woollen pile, on cotton warps and wefts, clipped quite thin. This alone is enough to distinguish Abadehs from Qashqais, for Qashqai goods normally have wool or goat-hair warps, but the treatment of the design is also quite distinctive: the layout with the small central medallion within a large hexagonal field, the strange stiffness of the tiny secondary motifs (the birds and animals, stars and rosettes are always larger in Qashqai and Shiraz rugs), the tree stem and branches which form an axis along the length of the rug, the rather floral (often semi-curvilinear) concept of the border, the pyramidal motif of the outermost guard – these are all features not otherwise encountered in Fars Province. The colour-range is great: bright-red grounds with corners of medium-to-dark blue are the most common, but one also finds blue, gold, light green and cream as ground colours. The main border, which is usually white, contains quite a lot of green in the leaf motifs. Most rug sizes are made, generally larger than the Persian average – the pushtis, for example, run to about 105 × 65 cm (3′ 6″ × 2′ 2″), and dozars are often 150 cm (5′ 0″) wide. Small square carpets and other carpet sizes up to 6 m² (65 ft²) in area are quite common, but that is the maximum size. Abadeh is one of those places (like Senneh) where, inexplicably, the price per square metre of any given size is by tradition higher than that of the size below. The design illustrated accounts for the vast bulk of the Abadeh output, but two others are included in this book (figs. 235 and 271). The design of the present example can also be made in medallion-plain form by the simple omission of the secondary motifs (see fig. 547). It is in this form that the *hebatlu* design is used in Niriz, another small town of the Shiraz region where the Arab tribes influence the designs. Niriz rugs are, however, as much Afshari in style as Arab, the weave, in particular, being reminiscent of Sirjand, with the use of cotton warps and two pink cotton wefts.

598 RUMANIAN

Although for centuries the Balkan countries formed part of the Turkish Empire, they have no carpet design tradition of their own. The famous museum pieces of Transylvania seem to have been made in Anatolia and it is only since the Second World War that the governments of Rumania, Bulgaria, Yugoslavia and Albania have organized production of a range of copies of Persian designs. They are sold in the West under a variety of names – Macedonian, Bessarabian, Dacian, Transylvanian, Sibiu, Arad and many more. The originators and market leaders are the Rumanians, who have a substantial output in a variety of standard grades and styles. The biggest production is in the quality illustrated here, that is a double-wefted construction with about 110,000 Persian knots/m² (72 knots/in.²). In this density, the geometric designs tend to be the most successful. They are mostly not close copies of Persian originals but re-interpretations of the styles of certain areas, often reminiscent of Tabriz, where there is a similar tradition of copying designs from other places. The design and colouring work is clearly a professional job and the materials used and workmanship are usually of a high standard. The main objection to them is that they look machine-made. There is, of course, no question of this: like all the carpets illustrated in this book, they are woven entirely by hand; but the mechanical treatment of the designs and the standardized accuracy of the weaving result in the same stiffness of appearance that is characteristic of machine-woven carpets in Persian designs. In the 'Bucureşti' quality illustrated there are some forty or fifty designs, made in practically every carpet, runner and rug size commonly found in the Orient.

599 MEIMEH

One of the most distinctive designs woven in Iran today is that of Joshaqan, a village high in the mountains north of Isfahan. Grote-Hasenbalg demonstrates that the design is a direct descendant of the vase carpets of south-east Persia (see figs. 739, 747 and 765 for this connection). There is a dispute among scholars as to the antiquity of carpet weaving in Joshaqan. It is universally accepted that Nadir Shah in about 1730 transported leading weavers from Kerman and Khorassan (Herat?) to the Isfahan region. In so doing he virtually destroyed the carpet art of east and south-east Persia, but laid the foundations for the flowering of weaving that occurred in central and western Persia in the nineteenth century. Grote-Hasenbalg illustrates under the generic name of 'so-called Joshaqans' several carpets which clearly originated in various central and west Persian areas and which equally clearly document the transfer thither of the whole gamut of east Persian all-over designs. The dispute arises over the importance of Joshaqan before this. Arthur Upham Pope, author of the monumental *Masterpieces of Persian Art*, ascribes the original vase carpets themselves, and much else besides, to the looms of Joshaqan in the sixteenth and seventeenth centuries. Later writers have simply followed Pope's attribution, but others have questioned it. Edwards, in particular, argues that the complex designs of the sixteenth century were quite beyond the resources of remote mountain villages. This is not to deny the importance or antiquity of the weaving tradition of Joshaqan; but the vase carpets are clearly the work of town manufactories. Pope cites an inscription on a silk rug from the mausoleum of Shah Abbas II (died 1674) which reads 'the work of the master Nimat Allah of Joshaqan'. This is probably the clue to the error: we know that Shah Abbas I had founded a Court Manufactory in Isfahan some eighty years before; it would be perfectly natural for a famous provincial weaver to have the opportunity of working in such an establishment, but proudly to proclaim his origin in a commission for the Shah's mausoleum. Thus Pope's 'Joshaqan' silk rug was probably woven not in Joshaqan, but in Isfahan by a Joshaqan weaver.

After the transfer of the panel variant of the vase design to Joshaqan in the eighteenth century, a style was established which has been woven in the area ever since. Joshaqan rugs themselves are fairly coarse peasant products (see fig. 7); but the bulk of the goods seen in the West today come from a string of small towns and villages down in the valley, on the road to Isfahan. These include Meimeh, Vazvan, Khosrowabad and Morcha Khurt, all names which one encounters in carpet shops, the last named being spelt in a dozen different ways (see p. 40). Some of the goods produced in this area are made in a very fine weave indeed, and the best include natural dyestuffs. The design as illustrated in fig. 599 is the standard version, on which there are surprisingly few variants. Sometimes the medallion is omitted, and occasionally a geometric framework is superimposed on the ground, but the flower-sprays always have the symmetrical forms shown here and are always arranged in diagonal rows. The border is distinctive: it is a variant of the Herati border, but the angular form used in Meimeh is not found elsewhere. In the bulk of the production the grounds are red, but dark blue, light blue and just occasionally cream are also found. Most standard Persian sizes are made, from small mats and squares upwards. The design is sometimes found in dozar sizes from the Hamadan or Arak areas, and a particular variant of it is made in Kashan (see fig. 600) and Qum (fig. 730).

598 Rumanian 'Bucureşti'
256 × 186 cm, 110,000 PK/m²
(8′ 5″ × 6′ 1″, 71 PK/in.²).

599 Meimeh
348 × 240 cm, 320,000 PK/m²
(11′ 5″ × 7′ 10″, 206 PK/in.²).

600 Kashan
215 × 138 cm, 325,000 PK/m²
(7′ 1″ × 4′ 6″, 210 PK/in.²).

600 KASHAN

The fine forty-year-old Kashan rug illustrated might seem at first glance to be a blue-ground Meimeh. In fact it is entirely characteristic of a certain type of Kashan, made mainly in dozar sizes and usually on a blue or red ground. Apart from tell-tale details in the design work, such as the 'blackberry-chain' of the guards, which is an almost indispensable element in Kashan rugs, the feature which confirms the origin is the colour scheme. Colour-printing cannot convey the nuances that make it possible to tell a Kashan from a Meimeh at a glance, without any need to study the weave, which also reveals distinct differences (quite apart from the fact that Kashans of this type are appreciably finer than most Meimehs). However, colour differences are quite easy to pick up if one can examine a few pieces: the red shade, in particular, is much lighter and brighter, more vermilion, in Meimeh than in oldish Kashans, where the red is either deep and brownish or decidedly mauvish. The design itself is a manufactured development of the Joshaqan design – Kashan is scarcely any further from Joshaqan than Meimeh is (see map, p. 346). Kashan also makes another design derived from the same idea but incorporating a vase at the base of a prayer-mihrab. Figure 307 illustrates an Agra copy of this Kashan-vase Joshaqan style.

601 HERIZ

A single illustration is enough to establish the character of Heriz, one of the most important of all the carpet-producing regions of Iran, with a huge output (especially of medium and large carpet sizes), and a reputation for durability surpassed only by that of Bijar. There are in fact dozens, if not hundreds, of villages in the Heriz region, and each has its own individual features – Georovan makes quite cheap, coarse carpets, Bilverdi a single-wefted structure, Sharabian a stiff floral version which looks like a coarse Tabriz, Ahar another floral type which is as stiff as a board, Mehrivan a bright, regular fresh-looking style (and also a pattern of oak-leaves without a medallion), Bakhskaish an elaborate and finely balanced medallion version packed with interesting detail – but they are all unmistakably variants of the design illustrated here. For the sake of comprehensiveness the Ahar and all-over Mehrivan types are illustrated in their relevant sections – see figs. 693 and 464. The amazing thing is that for all the thousands of carpets produced, all in one basic design, one never sees two exactly alike: each piece is made individually by villagers working from no more than a snippet of material or a drawing giving only a general indication of the required style. So the whole design comes from the weaver's head as she goes along: the principal guide is the local tradition. The most obvious feature is the dominant central medallion, which is often so large as to fill the ground almost completely; the bold corner motifs, related to the central medallion but not exact quarters of it, are another. Perhaps the most typical element, however, is the very individual treatment of the oak-leaves and other plant-forms in the ground. The colouring is an important guide to origin with Heriz goods. The dominant factor is the rosy brown shade which is obtained from the madder plant and is still used today in the best of the new production. This rosy brown shade often has streaks or abrashes, which may or may not be attractive (usually it is a question of degree). What is certainly not an asset is the fact that the dark blue often has ugly grey or black streaks. Other important colours are a light or medium pink, made by toning down madder with lactic acid (the same process as is used to produce the *dughi* rose in Saruq and Bijar carpets); a dark brown-red (making three different rose-red shades in all, a feature rarely found elsewhere); medium and dark green – these, too, often produced by natural dyes; light blue; ivory; and a striking shade of khaki-gold. Not many border designs are used – 90% or more of the production has either the design shown here or the oak-leaf and rosette design shown in fig. 76. The construction is very massive – heavy cotton warps and wefts, with a dense pile of thick, hard-wearing wool. Thus, although its weave is coarse, the Heriz is a very good carpet: nowhere else do carpets as coarse as this have such a good construction or so much individuality of design or colouring. For most of the 1960s, prices remained steady, but in the early 1970s the weavers of Heriz realized how undervalued their carpets were and prices rose suddenly and

601

sharply. One result of this has been that the weavers of Bhadohi in India have jumped in to fill the gap and there is now a large output in Heriz designs from India (as well as others from Rumania). Some of these modern copies are of good quality, and one, at least, from India is so well made that many experts have to look very closely to establish that it is not Persian; but most of the copies have a long way to go – in respect of both colouring and materials – before they can claim to be considered reasonable replacements for the cheap Heriz goods, or can match the variety of design and the expressiveness that are to be found in the spontaneous Persian production.

602 MUSHKABAD

Mushkabad was the principal city of the Ferahan/Arak region until it was destroyed early in the nineteenth century. The ruins still stand near Arak (previously called Sultanabad), which was built to replace it. The name Mushkabad was adopted at the beginning of the twentieth century to describe the lowest of the standard grades of Saruq goods (see also p. 286). Thus, Mushkabads were produced in many different villages and made in a variety of styles in carpet and rug sizes. Nowadays the name is little used for cheap Saruqs, for many Mushkabads had a thin pile and gave poor wear, so that a carpet with any pretension to durability automatically came to be called a Mahal (the second grade of Saruqs). Today the name Mushkabad is mostly used for rugs of the type illustrated here, which is from Sar Cheshmeh. The weave in this case is about twice as fine as that of the Saruq-Mushkabads, but the pile is usually still rather thin. At first glance they look like Hamadan village rugs, but this impression will be corrected by an inspection of the back, which reveals a double-wefted construction. The colour of the wefts is usually a distinctive medium blue. The appeal of Mushkabad rugs lies in their unaffected

602

601 Heriz
340 × 240 cm, 115,000 TK/m²
(11′ 2″ × 7′ 10″, 74 TK/in.²).

602 Mushkabad
194 × 130 cm, 102,000 PK/m²
(6′ 4″ × 4′ 3″, 66 PK/in.²).

267

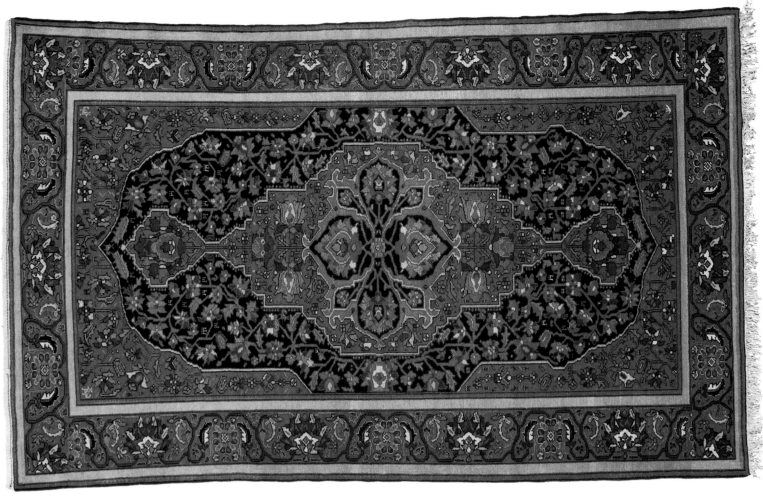

603

604

603 Ferahan
207 × 135 cm, 173,000 TK/m²
(6′ 9″ × 4′ 5″, 112 TK/in.²).

604 Saruq
147 × 102 cm, 238,000 PK/m²
(4′ 10″ × 3′ 4″, 154 PK/in.²).

geometric style and in the pleasing colourings, which are very often derived from natural dyes.

603, 604 SARUQ/FERAHAN

These rugs are nineteenth-century pieces which illustrate something of the magnificent style of the Saruq and Ferahan area before the advent of the American Saruq design. Many pieces of oustanding quality and in superb colours are still to be found in specialist carpet shops, usually at very high prices; and the same kind of design may be copied from time to time in manufactured new goods of the Arak region. The decisive feature which characterizes the style is the integration of curvilinear and rectilinear elements in the design – the same stylistic point which is noted with regard to Bijar carpets and some of the best Bakhtiars, and which suggests a manufacturing arrangement where the weaver is given an indication of what is required, but is then left to use his or her own imagination in the interpretation and execution of the design.

It is worth pondering at this point the way values change in the assessment of Persian carpets. A. C. Edwards, reviewing the early years of the renewal of carpet production in Persia (the period 1880–1920), was clearly out of sympathy with this stylistic mixture of curvilinear and rectilinear elements. He suggests that the Kashans and Saruqs were clumsy and deficient in design or execution and remained so until graph-paper scale drawings were introduced and the village weavers had mastered their use. Today we see manufactured carpets of all origins accurately worked to precise graph-paper drawings and lament the soulless anonymity consequent upon the separation of the functions of designer and weaver; and, looking at the pieces produced by Mohtasham in Kashan (cf. fig. 680) and by the weavers of figs. 603 and 604, we long for a return to a form of manufacture in which the weaver exercises as much influence on the design as he did in those days.

V Floral designs

1 FLORAL MEDALLION/ALL-OVER DESIGNS

605 Stucco roundels from the Sassanid capital, Ctesiphon, *c.* AD 600. This pre-Islamic Persian design style is absent from carpets of the Mongol period; it re-emerged in those of the late fifteenth century. Staatliche Museen, Berlin.

606 Kerman
400 × 292 cm, 312,000 PK/m²
(13′ 1″ × 9′ 7″, 201 PK/in.²).

The development of floral designs in Persian carpets is one of the most tantalizing matters that the carpet historian has to deal with, for the simple reason that we possess no actual examples of what preceded them. Whereas the history of the Turkish carpet can be traced from before 1300 right through to the present day, in the case of Persia we have, suddenly, in the sixteenth century, an unparalleled abundance of magnificent floral carpets, unquestionably the climax of a mighty tradition; and nothing, not a single shred, of earlier date.

That curvilinear weaving techniques – and design concepts – were known long before is proved by the Pazyryk carpet (fig. 56). The 'Spring of Chosroes' (see p. 144) must have incorporated curvilinear patterns, even if it was a kilim; the tapestries of sixth to tenth century Egypt retain curvilinear elements; the curvilinear styles of the Sassanid Persian Empire (fig. 605) lived on, and the thirteenth-century tilework from Kashan (figs. 305 and 670) shows that even at this date the fully-fledged arabesque was readily available to Persian designers. Of carpets our only evidence is the portrayal of their use and patterns in other art-forms, especially painting; and all the available evidence indicates that until the late fifteenth century the carpet designers knew nothing of curvilinear forms. The traditional theory is that curvilinear – i.e. naturalistic – patterns were suppressed by the advent of Sunni Islam, but this is not convincing. Not least of the arguments against the idea that Safavid floral designs reflect the Persian Shi'ite revolt against geometric stylization is the fact that at exactly the same time the court manufactories in Cairo and Bursa of the Sunni Ottoman Empire participated in the same floral-design renaissance. A more likely explanation for the dourness of fourteenth- and fifteenth-century Persian carpets is the suppression of Persian art resulting from the cultural shock of the Turkoman and Mongol invasions.

It is ethnographically perhaps not strictly correct to speak of the Mongols and the Turkomans in one breath, since they seem to represent two separate groups within the Uralic/Altaic racial family. However, they were certainly related groups, and in many cases they rode together. There is some dispute among experts, for example, as to whether Timur was a Mongol or a Turkoman. For the carpet student this is immaterial. What matters is that the Aryan world suffered three massive waves of invasions by Uralic/Altaic peoples. The first was Turkish and Turkoman, the second Mongol and the third probably a mixture of both. Together, they all caused a much greater rupture than did, for example, the Norman conquest of England at about the same period. The Turks and Mongols brought into the world of the Iranian and other Indo-European peoples a culture which was alien in every respect. The invasions of the Seljuq Turks are described on p. 128. Even more devastating were the campaigns of Jinghis Khan. As a young man he had gained fame for his daring raids from his Mongolian homelands against the Chinese Empire. The scope and success of these 'strike, plunder and retire' enterprises constantly increased, to the point where the Mongols posed a serious threat to the very existence of the Chinese state. In 1206, when he was about fifty, Jinghis was elected Khan, or paramount chief, of all the Mongols. He was in the midst of

606

607

608

609

607 The wedding of Humay and Humayun, miniature by Junaid Nakkash, 1396. British Museum.

608 Medallion design from a Herat manuscript, 1410. This elaborate style was widely used in carpet design, but not until at least a century later; it reveals strong Chinese influence. Calouste Gulbenkian Foundation.

609 A fifteenth-century Nepalese mandala. Charles Grant Ellis (*Textile Museum Journal*, Dec. 1974) suggests a link between this Buddhist cult diagram and the medallions of the Mamluk carpets of fifteenth-century Cairo; Bidder also argues strongly in favour of a connection between this and the carpet patterns of East Turkestan. Cleveland Museum of Art.

preparations for the final conquest of China in 1219 when the members of a Mongolian trade delegation to the Muslim state of Khwarezm, Jinghis Khan's nearest western neighbour, were murdered. The Khan sent an ambassador to Sultan Muhammad to demand justice. The ruler of Khwarezm was injudicious enough to have the envoy beheaded and send his retinue home minus their beards; this insult was to unleash a tempest such as Asia had never known. The Great Khan postponed his conquest of China and turned his army westwards. His fury was not abated for five years, during which the whole of western Asia was pillaged. Town after town was burnt to the ground, the inhabitants massacred, their treasures plundered; perhaps worst of all was the wholesale destruction of the irrigation systems on which so many of the cities in this semi-desert region were totally dependent for their survival. It is said, for example, that Bokhara languished for 600 years after the silting up of the water supply system as a result of Jinghis Khan's depredations.

When he attacked Persia, Jinghis Khan was an old man, having devoted most of his life to his campaigns within Mongolia and against China; after his death in 1227 the Mongols spent almost thirty years consolidating their power. Then Jinghis Khan's two grandsons, Kublai and Hulagu, were given the task of completing the conquest of East and West and of uniting the two into one great empire. Hulagu's main objective was the capital of the Islamic world, Baghdad, which he captured in 1258, slaughtering nearly a million inhabitants in the aftermath. In reaching this goal he had gradually subdued the whole of northern and western Persia, Hamadan having fallen in 1256. It is from this period that the predominance of Turkish as the vernacular of north-west Persia must be dated; and it was Hulagu's campaigns that led to the settlement of the Borchalu, Karagöslu and other Turkic or Mongol tribes in the area. Indeed, an Arabic manuscript of the fourteenth century refers to Persia simply as the 'land of the Turks', which – although it strikes us as odd today – indicates just how much Persia as a cultural entity had become submerged by that time. Meanwhile, Hulagu's elder brother had destroyed the last remnants of the Sung dynasty in China and transferred the capital of the Mongol Empire to Peking. The rulers of Persia, their capital now established in Tabriz, became Buddhists and with this the suppression of Persian art was complete. Two centuries would pass before the submerged Persian style reasserted itself.

However, a Chinese sage had told Jinghis Khan: 'You can conquer an empire on horseback, but you cannot govern it on horseback.'; in other words, to rule the empire the Mongols needed an administrative structure. They had none of their own devising, and were obliged to adapt and build on what they found in the territories they had conquered. And thus the process of fusion and assimilation began. The Mongols became Muslims in 1295, and in the fourteenth century, under Hulagu's successors, known as the Il-Khanid dynasty, Persian culture began to recover, but a third wave of Uralic/Altaic culture was yet to come, sweeping across western Asia in the wake of Timur (see p. 79). Thus, when Timur's son Shah Rukh began in earnest the reconstruction of the culture which his forefathers had shattered, the basis from which he started was Turkoman, Mongol and Chinese, not Persian.

We know something of what thirteenth-century Turkoman rugs looked like thanks to the finds in the Ala-ad-Din Mosque at Konya (fig. 388). The style of Mongol rugs of the same era is known to us through a group of Chinese paintings (reproduced in M. S. Dimand's *Oriental Rugs in the Metropolitan Museum of Art*). They have a similarly abstract style, although they often have a dominant central motif. This is a feature which is absent from the rugs depicted in Persian paintings from the period of Mongol/Turkoman rule. These paintings, mostly in the form of book illuminations and illustrations, and known simply as miniatures, are at once our best source of information about the carpets and also, as far as we can guess, the stylistic guide for the carpet designers themselves. Figures 608, 615, 742, 743 and 733 show examples of how the ideas of the book-decorators were translated

610 Buddhist 'cloud-collar' mandala. The central circle is seen as a hole in the sky through which the soul can escape into Heaven. Royal Ontario Museum, Toronto.

611 Chinese cloud-collar. The symbolic robes of Chinese emperors were crowned with a collar of this kind, which also represented the gateway to Heaven. Cammann asserts that this shape is at the root of representations of the sun-bird, the guardian of the gate to Paradise. Victoria and Albert Museum, London.

612 The ceremonial tent of the Emperor Chien Lung (after an eighteenth-century French engraving); the cloud-collar emphasizes the Emperor's embodiment of supernatural forces.

613 Cloud-collars used on Turkoman yurts (after Bidder). The opening in the top of the yurt is a smoke-hole; the cloud-collar is used as external decoration, and there can be little doubt that both the hole and collar also have a symbolic meaning.

610

611

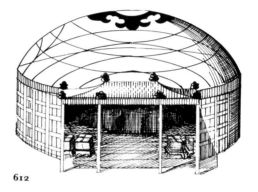

612

613

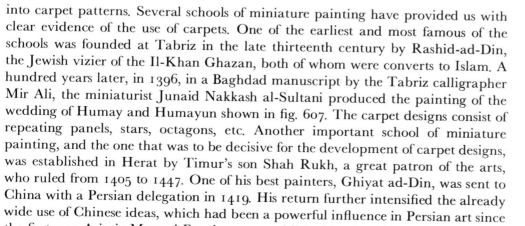

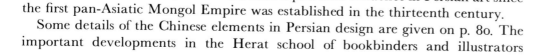

into carpet patterns. Several schools of miniature painting have provided us with clear evidence of the use of carpets. One of the earliest and most famous of the schools was founded at Tabriz in the late thirteenth century by Rashid-ad-Din, the Jewish vizier of the Il-Khan Ghazan, both of whom were converts to Islam. A hundred years later, in 1396, in a Baghdad manuscript by the Tabriz calligrapher Mir Ali, the miniaturist Junaid Nakkash al-Sultani produced the painting of the wedding of Humay and Humayun shown in fig. 607. The carpet designs consist of repeating panels, stars, octagons, etc. Another important school of miniature painting, and the one that was to be decisive for the development of carpet designs, was established in Herat by Timur's son Shah Rukh, a great patron of the arts, who ruled from 1405 to 1447. One of his best painters, Ghiyat ad-Din, was sent to China with a Persian delegation in 1419. His return further intensified the already wide use of Chinese ideas, which had been a powerful influence in Persian art since the first pan-Asiatic Mongol Empire was established in the thirteenth century.

Some details of the Chinese elements in Persian design are given on p. 80. The important developments in the Herat school of bookbinders and illustrators

614 Mamluk rug, Cairo, *c.* 1500.
The connection between Turkoman design
elements and the Mamluk carpets has been pointed
out on p. 176. Here another connection is revealed.
The central medallion and general layout of
Mamluk carpets often offer striking parallels to the
cloud-collar and other features of the mandala.

615 Binding of an illuminated manuscript of the
Herat school, 1482/3.

involved two key factors: the introduction of the medallion as the centre-piece of
the design, and the abandonment of strictly geometric line-work in favour of free-
flowing curvilinear patterns. It remains a puzzle that it took so long for these
influences to reach the world of carpet design. The development of the elaborate
medallion (fig. 608), inspired, perhaps, by the Buddhist mandala patterns, had
taken place in Herat even before Ghiyat's visit to China. By 1440 the designers of
bookbindings had produced fully-fledged 'medallion and corner' designs similar
to the one illustrated in fig. 733. Shah Rukh's sons, Baisunghur Mirza and Ibrahim
Sultan, devoted much of their energy to twin academies of the art of the book in
Herat and Shiraz. Baisunghur imported a group of leading illustrators from Tabriz
who laid the foundations for the supreme flowering of the Herat school in the second
half of the fifteenth century. Figure 615 illustrates a painted binding of 1483 with a
medallion and a close-covered ground. Technical mastery in the drawing of this
sort of pattern was an essential prerequisite for the production of carpets like the
Ardebil (fig. 702). What cannot at present be explained is why another fifty years
had to elapse before these ideas were used by carpet designers. For in the time of
Shah Rukh, while book artists and miniaturists were producing work such as the
examples shown in figs. 608 and 743, the carpets shown in paintings of the period
remain strictly in the geometric style, some like fig. 741, others showing close links
with Turkoman rugs of the so-called Holbein type (compare figs. 616 and 394).
The explanation is not that the carpet art was insignificant. The phenomenal
wealth of carpets dating from the early sixteenth century itself presupposes a
flourishing industry in the fifteenth. Also, the large number of carpets depicted in
manuscripts from many centres (as far apart as Baghdad and Bokhara) confirms
that production throughout the fifteenth century must have been substantial.
The high esteem in which carpets were held may also be judged from the fact that
in many depictions of them in miniature paintings people do not sit or walk on
them directly: some further cover is spread over the carpets to protect them. A. C.
Edwards rightly draws attention to the fact that the floral and medallion designs
could only have been woven from graph-paper scale-drawings; but this, too, does
not explain their late introduction, for schools of art as advanced as those of Herat
and Tabriz could surely have produced the drawings had they been needed. The
carpets must have remained in geometric all-over styles because that was the way
people wanted them, but we cannot say why.

The first sign of a change of style appears *c.* 1480. A rug depicted in a Shiraz
manuscript of Shi'ite inspiration still has the narrow geometric border of earlier
pieces, but the ground has a repeating pattern of curvilinear cloud-bands (cf.
p. 43). In 1485 the greatest Herat master, Bihzad, produced a painting showing a
carpet with a full medallion/all-over design (fig. 617), and in 1488 the same painter
included in another miniature a floral compartment rug (see fig. 744).

During this same period the Tabriz school regained some of its earlier importance.
Following the check to the expansion of the Ottoman Empire after the defeat of
Bayazid the Thunderbolt by Timur at the battle of Ankara in 1402, the Turkomans
of eastern Anatolia, Mesopotamia and Azerbaijan established an independent
state, with Tabriz as their capital. The ruling clan were called the Kara Koyunlu
('Black Sheep'), after the emblem on their banners. In the decoration of the Blue
Mosque, built at Tabriz by Jahan Shah (ruled 1437–67), the same kind of curvilinear motifs are used as in the book illustrations of Herat. The Kara Koyunlu
were ousted in 1469 by the Ak Koyunlu Turkomans ('White Sheep'), who, by the
end of the century, had extended their power over much of central and southern
Persia. The rugs in use at the court of Uzun Hasan, who ruled Tabriz until 1478,
are described in enthusiastic language by contemporary reports.

Several carpets which have come down to us and which have squarish central
medallions, stiff and hesitant floral scroll-work in the ground and rather heavy,
curvilinear but angular borders, are assigned by some scholars to the workshops of
Tabriz at the end of the fifteenth century; fig. 179 is one such example. However,
the real flowering of Persian carpets begins with the Safavid dynasty. Sheikh
Ismail, closely related to the Ak Koyunlu Turkomans, swept to power as their successor in 1501 and quickly established his authority over the whole of Persia. After

the capture of Herat in 1510, Bihzad and other artists were transferred to Tabriz, and from this period onwards the floral style in carpet design was firmly established.

Eastern Persia, as explained on pp. 324f., seems to have led the field in the production of all-over floral designs (see also p. 80), while the medallion style appears to be associated more with the court designers, Bihzad and his successor, Sultan Muhammad. For a long time the medallion carpets continued to have an uncertainty of execution that the products of the Herat tradition had overcome. Even such masterpieces as the Ardebil and Chelsea carpets contain weaving errors and distortions which show that the weavers had not yet totally mastered the reading of scale drawings. Unlike the weavers of today, who produce carpets many times over from the same drawings, the weavers of the sixteenth century had, after all, to get it right first time; but if they lack the maturity revealed in carpets like the one shown in fig. 178, the grandeur of their conception and the boldness of their layout has secured the pieces in the medallion/all-over style a lasting place in the public mind as *the* typical Persian carpet.

For the classification adopted in this book the floral style presents a certain problem: it is easy to convert a medallion/all-over design to a completely all-over one by leaving out the medallion; and into a medallion-plain by leaving out the design of the ground. A few examples of this are shown in the preceding chapter on geometric designs; with floral designs – and manufacturing traditions – it is much more common. The reader must therefore be prepared for a few mental somersaults to take account of this. Another important factor is that in a manufactory every design can be woven and there are countless thousands of variants on every style employed; one must therefore be able to recognize the typical features of each style in whatever design they may crop up. Unless otherwise noted all floral designs are on a double-wefted structure and all have cotton warps and wefts.

616 Another episode in the story of Humay and Humayun (cf. fig. 607): a scene depicted in an illuminated manuscript painted in Herat, 1428. The design of the ground pattern of the carpet depicted has clear affinities with that of the Turkoman rugs of Anatolia, and decoration on mosques of the Mongol era in Herat include many variants of the carpet's border design; see photographs published in the *Afghanistan Journal* (1980/1).

617 Detail of a page from the *Khamseh* of Amir Khusrau Dihlavi, painted by Bihzad, Herat 1485: 'The Birth of Majnun'.

618–627 ISFAHAN

The spiritual home of the floral medallion is probably Isfahan. It was here that Shah Abbas established his court in 1595; here that the magnificent mosques are adorned with brilliant blue and gold tiles that inspired the patterns for the covered grounds of floral carpets; here that to this day the most 'classical' Persian carpet designs are woven. Finer pieces may be made in Nain, but most carpet experts would agree that of today's production the carpets of Isfahan are the best.

618 The dome of the Shah Mosque, Isfahan.

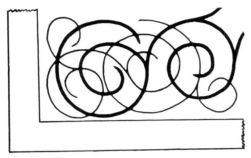

619

620

619 Islimis correctly developed.

620 Faulty elaboration of islimis.

621 Isfahan
154×105 cm, 350,000 PK/m²
(5′ 0″ × 3′ 3″, 226 PK/in.²).

Many different grades are made, in an area embracing not only Isfahan itself but also the surrounding villages and small towns within a radius of about 15 miles. Some of the output in this large area is pretty coarse and thin and not worthy of the name of Isfahan; it is of course correspondingly cheap, and cheapness should not be a buyer's prime consideration in Isfahan. The standard good-quality village Isfahan is represented by the rug shown in fig. 621, which comes from the village of Habibabad to the north. It has about 350,000 knots/m² (226 knots/in.²) and a fairly short but tight pile. The weave is difficult to distinguish from that of Kashan and Tabriz but there is a small clue in that the fine cotton wefts often have slubs in them, so that by following the line of the weft (which is usually pale blue) on the back of the rug one will see spots at irregular intervals where it widens out a little and then immediately drops back to its original thickness. This gives the Isfahan weave a certain fluidity which distinguishes it from the more regular weaves of Tabriz and Kashan. Nonetheless this is a rather intangible difference and there are other features which are more readily discernible. To tell an Isfahan from a Tabriz is easy: Tabriz always uses the Turkish knot and Isfahan the Persian. Kashan also uses the Persian knot, and here it is the design and colours which provide the clues.

The most striking feature of many Isfahan designs is the roundness of the medallion and its subdivision into eight or sixteen (or even 32 or 64) elaborate segments like a compass rose or a star (see figs. 624 and 629). This is one of the features the carpets share with the designs of the mosques (cf. fig. 623). The second important point is the clear and well-ordered layout of the motifs of the ground – leaves and flowers usually called 'Shah Abbas palmettes', which are stylizations from Chinese lotus or paeony patterns (see figs. 2, 176 and 177). These are all borne on tendrils or stalks called 'islimis', which in a well-designed rug arise from the ends or sides of the medallion or its pendants and unfurl over the ground in a perfectly balanced and finely graduated stem-and-branch layout. Much skill is devoted by the Isfahan designers to maintaining the symmetry and avoiding the pitfall – often not achieved elsewhere – of allowing the flow of the islimis to be interrupted by dead-ends or to have to turn back on itself. In finer (and larger) pieces the possibilities of elaboration of subsidiary islimis, and the crossing and re-crossing of the principal stems, are endless. This is another feature which carpets share with the mosques, as fig. 618 illustrates. In some Isfahans (e.g. figs. 624 and 777) the islimis are very prominent. In others, such as fig. 622, their light colouring causes them to fade into the background; in this piece attention focuses on the wealth of lancet leaves, cloudbands and other motifs taken from sixteenth-century designs.

An important element of the Isfahan style, which fig. 621 exemplifies, is the coloration, with its emphasis on light and medium blue, cream and vermilion. Of

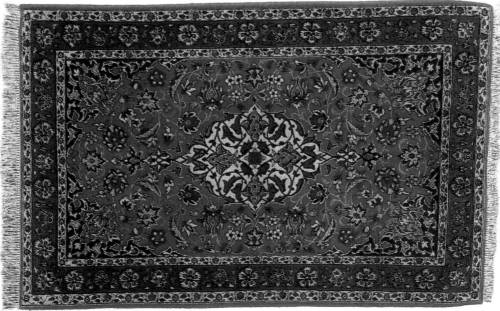

621

course, all other shades are used as well, but the dominant impression is of subtly balanced light-to-medium shades, without crude juxtapositions or some of the excruciating shades used in Qum or Arak, for example.

Some of the new Isfahans nevertheless look horrible to Western eyes, especially if they contain too much white, which tends to produce a 'busy' and dazzling effect. The Persians love this showiness, which extends from the decoration of parts of the mosques to patterns on such simple things as ashtrays and the like, for which the silversmiths and other metal-workers of the Isfahan bazaar are famous – but to Western eyes it seems gaudy, until the white softens to cream, the new red mellows to a rosy brown and the underlying harmony of the basic colour-scheme asserts itself. The Isfahan rug shown in fig. 624 is of this type, often called Serafian after one of the manufacturers who made this style popular. The stitch may reach a million knots/m² (650 knots/in.²), which is the finest woven there today. It was adopted in Isfahan not so very many years ago in competition with Nain, which had been the finest Persian weave until then. The finest Isfahans are usually woven

622

623

624

622 Isfahan
358 × 262 cm, 620,000 PK/m²
(11′ 9″ × 8′ 7″, 400 PK/in.²).

623 The Shah Mosque, Isfahan: interior (after Pope).

624 Isfahan
236 × 150 cm, 815,000 PK/m²
(7′ 9″ × 4′ 11″, 526 PK/in.²).

on silk warps (which is one of the features to distinguish them from Nains). To begin with, Serafians were made with all-wool pile (again, different from Nain), but in recent times Isfahans have appeared with some motifs woven in silk as well. One characteristic feature of this grade of Isfahan is the small panel added at the end of the rug to incorporate the weaver's signature, and often the Iranian flag, too.

Between the two grades illustrated in figs. 619 and 623 a considerable range and diversity is found in Isfahan goods, especially in carpets with between 350,000 and 500,000 knots/m^2 (226–322 knots/in.^{2}). The circular medallion (fig. 624, also fig. 629) is the most common type, but the possibilities are boundless, as may be judged from figs. 625–7.

In view of the relatively organized nature of the Isfahan production it is surprising that the range of sizes made is so limited. Pushtis and zaroquarts are found only in small quantities and in the finest grade; long and narrow rugs like kharaks and mossuls are practically non-existent, as also are runners. So the only rug sizes in regular production are zaronims and dozars, the latter exceptionally large – $3\frac{1}{2}$–4 m^2 (35–43 ft^2) in area, as in fig. 623. The dozars are much more expensive per square metre than zaronims. In carpet sizes, pieces with an area of 4 or 6 m^2 (43–65 ft^2) are more common, but all sizes are available.

628 NAIN

Nain is a small town, east of Isfahan on the edge of the great desert, almost halfway between Isfahan and Yezd. Nain rugs, however, are woven over a huge area stretching from the vicinity of Isfahan right out into the Kavir-e-Lut – the vast desert that accounts for some 15% of the whole land area of Iran – where, at the oasis of Bia-banak, the finest rugs are made. The carpet production in Nain is fairly recent; none existed during the great classical era, the town then being famous for other fine textiles. It was when this industry began to decline in the 1920s that the manufacturers of Nain switched to carpets. At first they made medium-fine goods in rather stiff designs that look sometimes like fine Bakhtiars, sometimes like fine Yezds, with rich blue and brown-red colourings. Since the Second World War, however, they have settled on an unmistakable superfine style of their own. The traditional medallion shape is similar to that of Isfahan, but the layout of the ground is different with a less clear articulation and often an effect more akin to 'mille fleurs'. All the outlines of the design are in silk; the rest of the pile is wool, the warps and wefts cotton, but the most obvious characteristic of Nain is the colouring, which is dominated by light or dark blue and cream or mushroom. All other colours are used, but mostly very sparingly; some pieces have red or gold grounds, but these are rare. Red, in general, is noticeable by its absence. The overall effect of the colouring is restrained, not to say decidedly cool. All sizes are made, although the price is so high that few dealers hold stocks of carpet sizes. The stitch ranges from a minimum of 500,000 knots/m^2 (322 knots/in.^{2}) up to over double that figure. A few other designs are made, usually of a semi-pictorial nature (see fig. 264), but some all-over pieces are found, as also are rugs with the sort of imitation geometric designs alluded to in the note on Qum on p. 234.

629 KHAMARIAH

Isfahan (along with Kerman, Kashan and Arak) has long been the source of inspiration for carpet designers in India, especially for the old Indo-Persian designs that were produced in both Kashmir and the Bhadohi/Mirzapur region for many years before the great surge of interest in Indian carpets in the 1970s, details of which will be found on p. 305. The design of fig. 629 is woven in Kashmir in a stitch in excess of 500,000 knots/m^2 (322 knots/in.^{2}), usually in rug or small carpet sizes. Nothing approaching this fineness was produced in Khamariah before 1980, but the original from which the Kashmir version was developed is one of the very few Persian designs woven there during the period after the Second World War when practically the whole production of the region was switched to French designs destined for the British and North American markets. It is a tribute to the Indian designers' skill that the essential character of the Isfahan style is preserved in this copy despite its relatively coarse weave.

625 Medallion from a small extra-fine Isfahan mat.

626 Medallion based on bird motifs from a new superfine Isfahan zaronim woven with *kork* wool and silk.

627 Medallion from a classical Isfahan rug; 500,000 PK/m^2 (323 PK/in.^{2}).

628

629

628 Nain
262 × 152 cm, 700,000 PK/m²
(8′ 7″ × 5′ 0″, 452 PK/in.²).

629 Khamariah
365 × 275 cm, 218,000 PK/m²
(12′ 0″ × 9′ 0″, 141 PK/in.²).

630–633 BAKHTIARI
The finest Bakhtiar rugs are made in Chahal Shotur, a small village just west of
Shahr Kurd, the capital of the Chahar Mahal va Bakhtiari province; and in other
villages between Shahr Kurd and Isfahan. They are sometimes called 'Bibibaff',
i.e. 'woman's weave' or 'grandmother's weave' because of the fineness of the work.

630 Farah Dumbeh
210 × 135 cm, 175,000 TK/m²
(6′ 11″ × 4′ 5″, 113 TK/in.²).

There are many different designs, some strongly reminiscent of the Isfahan style, others having much more of the typical flavour of the Bakhtiar panel designs. They all have a kind of sturdy *unflowing*, *unflowery* character which is derived from the fact that the Bakhtiar weave is really a geometric one. The group illustrated shows four of the types with central medallions which are clearly influenced by the style of neighbouring Isfahan. Of these the most geometric is that from Farah Dumbeh, a village in the south of the province making unusually fine single-wefted carpets. The yarn used is fine but rather soft (this is unusual in Bakhtiar goods) and the designs have a certain busy angularity which is not often successful. A deep, slightly maroony shade of red is typical, often used in combination with a lighter variant of the same shade, as in the example shown, where the medallion is dark red on a lighter red ground. A problem with Fara Dumbeh goods is that the colours are prone to bleeding.

The other three rugs of this group are double-wefted. The two from Shahr Kurd both have typical eight- and sixteen-point Isfahan medallions, but both rugs are clearly village products woven without an elaborately drawn graph-paper design. The first of these, for example, makes no attempt to reproduce the Isfahan 'islimis', and if the weaver of the second was trying to do so she has failed. Both rugs are, however, extremely appealing, partly because of their very unpretentiousness, partly because of their immense robustness. Many great carpets are made in this region which draw on the medallion-and-corners layouts of the manufactories without losing the spontaneity and primitive warmth of the traditional village carpet. The colours are one of their glories, with rich combinations of natural dye-stuffs – e.g. glowing madder red, leafy greens, gold and medium indigo – put together with that instinctive sureness of touch of the Persian villager, which the clever colorists of the town manufactories can rarely match. The rugs of Chahal Shotur are the most elaborate of the whole Bakhtiar group, sometimes, indeed, too elaborate; but here, too, it is the colourings and the magnificent robustness of the rugs which set them in a class apart. In all the above-mentioned villages the only rug size made is the dozar, but carpets are found in all sizes from 4 m² (43 ft²) to over 20 m² (235 ft²). The finer double-wefted Bakhtiars are, regrettably, all very expensive, the same sort of price as, for example, the very much finer Bijar rugs shown in figs. 195, 761 and 762.

The American Saruq

We come now to one of the great abortions of oriental carpet design, which is the direct responsibility of buyers and manufacturers for the North American market: namely the total corruption and irretrievable elimination of the ancient design traditions of the Saruq/Ferahan region. Strangely, very little is known about this phenomenon: we do not even know where the rugs displaced by the American Saruq were made. For an area of nineteenth- and early twentieth-century carpet art of such great significance as that of the Ferahan carpet, it is amazing that no scholar has published any detailed study of the region. The goods are still available from specialist dealers in old rugs; the names used for them in the trade are Saruq, Ferahan and Malayir, which are interchanged more or less at will. Both single- and double-wefted types exist (the former mainly in Herati design), as they still do today in this region, which embraces most of the area north and west of Arak, which at that time was called Sultanabad. Three examples of the double-wefted style are included in this book (see figs. 120, 603 and 604): a comparison of these three illustrations reveals that what they have in common is a strangely geometric interpretation of basically curvilinear designs – something like some of today's fine Bakhtiar styles. The old Ferahans were as fine as Bijars, occasionally much finer, but with a different construction. They had a close-clipped and tightly packed pile of fine yarn, giving a handle as hard as leather.

By contrast, over 90% of the Arak region's production before the First World War was in the cheaper grades known as Mushkabads and Mahals, counting 50,000 to 100,000 knots/m² (32–64 knots/in.²). The export of carpets from Sultanabad had begun in the 1870s, when Tabriz merchants started buying used pieces from the

631 Shahr Kurd
220 × 152 cm, 115,000 TK/m²
(7′ 2″ × 5′ 0″, 74 TK/in.²).

632

633

villagers and shipping them to Istanbul; from there, via the entrepôt trade, they reached the European and American markets. In 1883 an Anglo-Swiss company, Ziegler and Co., established the first foreign office in Sultanabad and began to supplement local purchases with direct manufacturing. By the beginning of the twentieth century this enterprise had become big business, and other European and American companies began to establish themselves in the region. One of the European buyers working in the area before the First World War was A. C. Edwards, who gives a detailed account of the development in *The Persian Carpet*. The effects of the war posed a serious threat to the Sultanabad manufactories, but American buying of the Saruq grade (180,000–240,000 knots/m² or 116–154 knots/in.²), increased, although the thin pile, the angular medallion designs and the predominantly blue grounds were not really to their liking. In the early 1920s Mr S. Tyriakian, the local representative of K. S. Taushandjian of New York, produced a pattern that perfectly suited the American demand for thick-piled carpets in an all-over style: a sort of imitation Axminster design – just simple sprays of inconsequential flowers strewn more or less at random all over the carpet. America wanted large carpets (120 ft² and above) – always popular with weavers the world over; America was rich, untroubled by the economic depression that made Old World buyers choosy, and as long as the pile was thick and the dyestuffs good it did not matter how clumsily the design was executed. The word soon spread around the weaving villages north of Arak and within a few years the weaving traditions of the Saruq area were gone for ever. Not only the Saruq region but a large part of

632 Shahr Kurd
217 × 147 cm, 150,000 TK/m²
(7′ 1″ × 4′ 10″, 97 TK/in.²).

633 Chahal Shotur
216 × 146 cm, 205,000 TK/m²
(7′ 1″ × 4′ 9″, 132 TK/in.²).

634 American Saruq
218 × 111 cm, 330,000 PK/m²
(7′ 2″ × 3′ 8″, 213 PK/in.²).

635 American Saruq
199 × 133 cm, 235,000 PK/m²
(6′ 6″ × 4′ 4″, 152 PK/in.²).

the Hamadan area adopted the design and in many cases have used it ever since. In some villages, in the course of time, the main elements of the design were digested and became fused with the local style, so that a properly thought-out variant of the design was developed (e.g. Borchalu). Certainly, each region that adopted the design gave it its own special imprint, but nothing that has been produced in this design anywhere can begin to compensate for what was sacrificed to produce it.

Nowadays the Americans have grown tired of these carpets and now export them for re-sale in Europe, principally Germany. A carpet buyer from southern Germany told the author a few years ago about an American aunt of his who used a large carpet (over 240 ft²) of this type as floor-covering in her garage – 'to wipe her shoes off before she went through into the house'. Since old carpets from almost every other source have almost disappeared from the market, these 'American Saruqs' find a ready sale in some quarters, for there are many people who will buy anything old on the principle that, however ugly it may be, it is sure to be better than something new. The superior materials used mean that the carpets are mostly still in good condition and, thanks to the use of natural dyestuffs, they largely retain attractive colours, although the American wash was not always beneficial (see Edwards, p. 142). Buyers should beware of extravagant claims made about the age of such carpets. Although the origins of the style may go back to before the First World War, it was certainly not until the 1920s that they were exported in any quantity. Hence, claims that an American Saruq is 'antique' or 'nineteenth-century' are likely to be wishful thinking on the part of the dealer or his customers (the latter are as much to blame: thousands of people who own brand-new carpets bought them only because they induced the dealer to let them think they were semi-antiques – any piece that looks beautiful when you say it is old tends to become only half as attractive if you call it new).

634, 635 AMERICAN SARUQ

The first of these rugs illustrates a typical version of the American Saruq design, which made up the bulk of the production; this rug would be about fifty years old. Although Saruq weavers were not used to handling a proper curvilinear style, they gradually mastered the technique and in some cases produced the kind of elaborate and finely balanced design illustrated in the second example; this dates from perhaps the 1930s.

636 KERMAN

This kind of fine-weave American style was also made for a time in Kashan, Kerman and Qazvin. The Kashans and Qazvins are very difficult to distinguish from the Saruqs, but the Kermans have a different flavour, being at once more colourful and more elegant and delicate than the Saruqs. We show here a typical above-average Kerman piece made about fifty years ago in a style which, albeit in a sadly debased form, has persisted in the 'bazaar' grade to this day.

637 AMERICAN SARUQ

The design is still produced in Saruq carpets today, although in a stitch and colouring which bear little resemblance to those of fifty years ago. The knot-count is around 180,000/m² (116/in.²), the colours almost always consist of a red ground with dark-blue border and various subsidiary shades, often including some unpleasant light blues, oranges and turquoise greens. Most sizes are made, from small pushtis up to quite large oversize carpets. The type is quite easy to recognize since it is the only Persian version of the American Saruq design currently made in a double-wefted construction.

638 LILIHAN

South of Arak there is a small area called the Kemereh, of which the main town is Lilihan, which is Armenian. Since the products of this region are single-wefted they are for convenience classed among the Hamadan village goods, although the area is in fact quite a long way from Hamadan and its rugs belong, in design and colouring, to the Saruq group; also, they are often woven with the Persian knot.

636

637

636 Kerman
317 × 183 cm, 325,000 PK/m²
(10′ 5″ × 6′ 0″, 210 PK/in.²).

637 American Saruq
149 × 103 cm, 180,000 PK/m²
(4′ 11″ × 3′ 4″, 116 PK/in.²).

Although Lilihan rugs in other designs do exist (for a Herati pattern see, for example, fig. 213), the American Saruq design so dominates the production to this day that for many people it is as the 'Lilihan design' that it is known at all. Lilihan has its own distinctive form of the design, as illustrated here. The spidery medallion and the many flower-sprays of the ground are its outstanding feature. It is usually made on a light red ground (the same kind of madder-oriented shade as is common in Saruq carpets), with some particularly unpleasant shades of bright green and light turquoise blue. These colours are however, usually produced by poor-quality dyestuffs and often fade very quickly, so that twenty- to thirty-year-old Lilihans can be quite attractive. The quality is good – with quite a fine weave and a thick pile. Pink wefts are common – a helpful clue to identification. Most rug sizes are made, and some carpets, including unusual dimensions like 220 × 180 cm (7′ 3″ × 5′ 9″). Lilihan carpets are sometimes called 'Armenibaff', i.e. 'woven by Armenians', especially when the precise origin is uncertain; but the name Armenibaff is given to carpets from other Armenian areas, too, for example some of the Bakhtiar types.

639 BORCHALU

Of all the American Saruqs the version which has perhaps been most transformed is that of the Borchalu tribe, who live in a rather inaccessible valley in the mountains east of Hamadan and north-west of the village of Saruq. The Borchalus are a Mongol clan who formed part of the forces of Jinghis Khan's successor, Hulagu, who consolidated the Mongol grip on north-west Persia in the mid-thirteenth century. They also settled in a village of the same name in the Kazak area; the piece illustrated in fig. 17 features a design frequently found in old Borchalu Kazaks. There is today no connection between the two groups. The most important villages of the Hamadan Borchalu group are Khumajin, Kumbazan, Simavor and Melajird, but the rugs are almost always known simply as Borchalu. Leaving aside certain supergrade articles like old Enjilas rugs (see fig. 214), Borchalus are among the best rugs of the Hamadan region. As can be seen from the piece illustrated, the design has been digested and re-thought to give balance, symmetry and a sense of flow among the flower-sprays. The colours are light and harmonious once the rug has

638 Lilihan
195 × 158 cm, 130,000 PK/m²
(6′ 5″ × 5′ 2″, 84 PK/in.²).

639 Borchalu
210 × 145 cm, 120,000 TK/m²
(6′ 11″ × 4′ 9″, 77 TK/in.²).

640 Darjezine (fine grade)
124 × 77 cm, 200,000 TK/m²
(4′ 1″ × 2′ 6″, 129 TK/in.²).

639

640

acquired a little patina, although like all Hamadans they can be a trifle hard when the rug is new. Red grounds are the most common, but cream (as in the piece illustrated) and dark blue are also found. The single-wefted weave is fine and the pile thick. There is not much of a range of sizes to be found: the most common are dozars and carpets 4 m² (43 ft²) in area although zaronims are also fairly easy to find; just occasionally one comes across a mossul (200 × 100 cm – 6′ 6″ × 3′ 3″ – or a little larger), and with that the list of sizes is complete. The same region produces a considerable output in the Herati design (see fig. 208). Although the Borchalu area has a recognizable independent existence as a carpet origin, it is – in its weave – in effect a sub-division of the Ferahan (meaning by this the actual administrative district of this name, which lies immediately to the east of the Borchalu region, and not the vague, undefined area called Ferahan by collectors of old rugs). Both the Herati design and an almost identical version of the American Saruq design are made in Ferahan. The weave of the two areas is almost identical, too, so that the differences between them become rather intangible. The best clue is the shade of red used – light and clear in Borchalus, dark and brownish in Ferahans, which sometimes gives the whole rug a rather gloomy appearance. In the floral design both Borchalu and Ferahan rugs may be found with the Persian knot, the use of which reflects the proximity of the Saruq area.

641 Darjezine (standard grade)
256 × 69 cm, 65,000 TK/m²
(8′ 5″ × 2′ 3″, 42 TK/in.²).

640, 641 DARJEZINE

To the north of the Borchalu region, not far from the Hamadan-Tehran road, lies the village of Darjezine, the centre of a biggish producing area with a huge output of rugs and strips. The standard grade, illustrated here, is coarse, using a singularly undistinguished version of the American Saruq design. However, the wool used is sound and the goods sell well because of the low price and the shortage of small rugs and narrow runners in general. The same area also produces – at very high prices – a much finer grade of goods, also single-wefted, the best of which are superbly woven. The designs are reminiscent of Jozan (see fig. 653) or Tuisarkan (fig. 588), but the rugs may be distinguished from the Jozan goods by the weave and from the Tuisarkans by the much denser pile and wider range of colours. The rug illustrated, representing the cream of the production of a large manufacturing area, demonstrates the stultifying effect that fifty years of American Saruq production has had on the designers of the region. A comparison with some of the designs that can be achieved with a similar knot-count (e.g. figs. 220, 275, 313) reveals the pattern of this rug to be disjointed, inconsequential and utterly boring. One can only lament the waste of the exceptional weaving skills employed in its execution.

642, 643 MEHRIBAN

The northernmost outpost of the American Saruq 'bulge' is Mehriban, an administrative district north of Hamadan incorporating a large number of villages whose individual names are never used in the carpet trade. The area (not to be confused with the Mehrivan of Azerbaijan – see p. 206) is contiguous with the Kurdish region and the rugs have several features in common with the Kurdish products. There are two distinct types of Mehriban, both single-wefted: the older style, which is more geometric, like the second piece shown here, in which dozars, wide runners and kelleyis predominate, and the newer style, as in the first example, best known for long, narrow runners and carpets. This newer type of Hamadan Mehriban is based on the American Saruq style and seems to have begun as a kind of superior Darjezine. Many other designs also exist in the new-style production, some of them being further developments of the American style, others quite different, including for example geometric, slightly Caucasian-looking patterns. The quality is good: fine, thick yarn with great natural lustre, combined with a fine weave. The yarn has a high twist, which gives the back of the rug a knobbly effect. The most common ground colour is dark blue, but a whole range of other shades is readily available – red, cream, gold and light blue in particular; some very unpleasant subsidiary shades of green are used, but in the main the overall colour effects are better than in most new Hamadans. In runners a strangely limited range of sizes is made. The width is usually about 80–90 cm (2′ 6″–3′ 0″), although pieces 100 cm (3′ 3″) wide are also found. The lengths made are 200–250 cm (6′ 6″–8′ 0″) and from 430 cm (14′ 0″) upwards; there is hardly any production in lengths between 250 and 430 cm (8′ 0″ and 14′ 0″). In addition to the runners there is a considerable output of carpets, mostly in largish sizes (intended for the American market), and also a few dozars. The latter are usually in the medallion-plain style, while the former may have plain or covered grounds – an example is shown in fig. 729. Mehriban runners are quite finely woven for single-wefted goods and their price is high; that of carpets is even higher.

642 Mehriban
242 × 86 cm, 133,000 TK/m²
(7′ 11″ × 2′ 10″, 86 TK/in.²).

643 Mehriban
326 × 97 cm, 90,000 TK/m²
(10′ 8″ × 3′ 2″, 58 TK/in.²).

644 KABUTRAHANG

To the south of the Mehriban region is a group of villages centred on Kabutrahang which for long has made nothing but goods in the American Saruq style, mainly in American standard sizes (12′ 0″ × 9′ 0″ and larger). The quality is coarse and

644 Kabutrahang
367 × 267 cm, 72,000 TK/m²
(12′ 0″ × 8′ 9″, 46 TK/in.²).

rough but the pile is very thick. Red grounds are the most common. The design, as illustrated, is almost identical to that of some of the Mehriban carpets but is easily distinguished from these neighbours by the much lower quality. Like all Hamadan village products, Kabutrahangs are single-wefted. The backs of the carpets have a knobbly effect similar to that found in Mehriban carpets, but the knobbles are looser and bigger. The colours are unremittingly strident.

645–648 SARUQ

Saruq, also spelt Sarouk and Sarough, is a village south of the Borchalu region and east of Malayir in central Persia. In view of the impact of the Turkoman invasions between AD 1000 and 1400, it is a reasonable guess that the village is connected with the Turkoman tribe of the same name; but from the point of view of carpet design there is not the faintest resemblance. Furthermore, Saruq carpets do not generally come from the village of Saruq but from a very large region centred on the old provincial capital, Arak (previously called Sultanabad). When Western importers began organizing the manufacture of carpets in the area in the late nineteenth century they found that Saruq village produced rugs of exceptional quality, and hence the name was quickly universally adopted to indicate high-quality goods wherever in the region they were made, just as all fine Kermans were called Lavers. The second grade of Saruqs was dubbed Mahal (no-one knows quite why), while the cheapest grade was named after Mushkabad, which is north-east of Arak on the road to Qum. Today the names Mahal and Mushkabad are not much used and more attention is paid to the names of the actual producing villages, such as Ghiassabad, north of Arak on the edge of the Ferahan area, and Mahallat, south of Arak and in the direction of Kashan. The name that is still universally used is, however, Saruq; this designation thus covers quite a wide range of types (see index for a complete list).

Figure 645 illustrates a style manufactured in the town of Arak and in the surrounding villages, including Ghiassabad, and often referred to as Saruq Afshan (i.e. all-over), although the description could just as appropriately be used for almost any other design made in the area. The pile is usually thick, the weave medium-fine and outstandingly neat, with a well balanced construction. A striking feature is the rosy-red ground shade, which in the best pieces is derived from madder root, called *ronas* in Farsi. The light blue of the medallion and guards in fig. 645 is very typical; so also is an unpleasant turquoise green which is often used in the subsidiary shades. The bulk of the production in this style is in quite large carpet sizes and on red or rose grounds, but dozars and smaller carpets are also found, and so are dark-blue or cream grounds. A finer grade, encountered mainly in rug sizes, is illustrated in the Ghiassabad rug of fig. 646. The coloration is strikingly different,

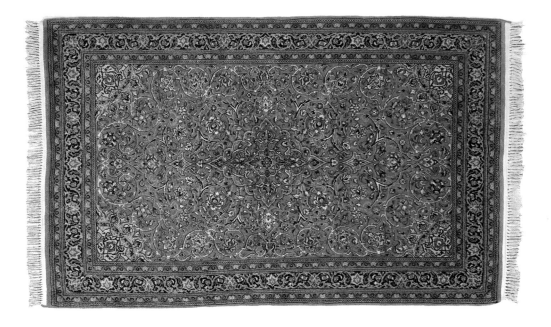

645 Saruq
207 × 136 cm, 250,000 PK/m²
(6′ 9″ × 4′ 5″, 161 PK/in.²).

646

647

648

drawing attention to a certain similarity of style between Saruq and Qum. There are indeed occasions when it is difficult to tell these two origins apart, and there are other towns, like Saveh and Gulpaigan, which are somewhere between the two in character, making identification even more difficult. However, a comparison with fig. 691 reveals that the Saruq version of the design is more definite and solid in delineation – one might say more masculine in conception. The final arbiters in cases of doubt are the weave and construction: the Saruq weave is neater and 'squarer' and the pile is much thicker. Modern woollen Qums are more often found with parts of the pile in silk, which is an easy distinguishing feature, but Qums with an all-wool pile can also be recognized from the thinner pile and more irregular weave.

Figure 647 illustrates a rug from Qazvin, a town located a long way north of Arak, on the road from Tehran to Zenjan; it no longer produces carpets, but between the two World Wars there was a small output closely related in style to the Saruqs. Only experts can tell them apart; the main clue is a certain fuzziness in the overall appearance. From the point of view of design classification, they clearly belong to the Saruq group. Some features of the rug illustrated, such as the style of the vases in the ground, the flower-clusters in the border and the broad 'picked' edging to the medallion and corners, remind one more of manufactured Malayir rugs than of Saruq. Here, too, problems of identification can arise, since the western edge of the Saruq area spills over into the Malayir region. Since Malayirs have the Turkish knot a definite origin can be established; but sometimes the knot is the only apparent difference. Fig. 648 illustrates a rug of this type. If it were single-wefted we should have no hesitation in assigning it to the same area as figs. 654 and 655; but being double-wefted and made with the Persian knot, albeit coarse, it is called a Saruq.

649–652 NORTHERN INDIA

This group of three pieces from northern India illustrates the importance of Saruq as a source of many of the designs now made in India and Pakistan. Other styles manufactured there are clearly derived from Kashan, Isfahan or Kerman, and others again simply have a general 'central Persian' flavour. Of the three 'Indo-Saruqs' shown, fig. 649 is the best: by any standards, it is exceptionally well done,

646 Saruq
207 × 134 cm, 388,000 PK/m²
(6′ 9″ × 4′ 5″, 250 PK/in.²).

647 Qazvin
188 × 137 cm, 422,000 TK/m²
(6′ 2″ × 4′ 6″, 272 TK/in.²).

648 Saruq
210 × 130 cm, 184,000 PK/m²
(6′ 11″ × 4′ 3″, 119 PK/in.²).

649 Kashmir
178 × 126 cm, 395,000 PK/m²
(5′ 10″ × 4′ 1″, 255 PK/in.²).

650

651

650 Kashmir
220 × 153 cm, 340,000 pk/m²
(7′ 2″ × 5′ 0″, 219 pk/in.²).

651 Agra
191 × 122 cm, 260,000 pk/m²
(6′ 3″ × 4′ 0″, 168 pk/in.²).

652 An Agra carpet (left) showing typical skimpy
design work, compared with a much more detailed
Persian treatment of similar motifs, even with a
coarser weave. Agra detail shows an area of approx.
60 × 20 cm, 270,000 knots/m²
(2′ 0″ × 8″, 174 knots/in.²); Persian detail
approx. 76 × 24 cm, 205,000 knots/m²
(2′ 6″ × 10″, 132 knots/in.²).

652

with an elaborate and richly coloured design. It is also finely woven, with a very
firm construction: there is no trace here of 'jufti' weaving – what in India is called
'langri', i.e. a lame woman, an expressive epithet for the malpractice, so common
in Kashmir, of tying a knot over three or four warps (fig. 35) instead of over two.
Figure 650 exhibits a certain stiffness, which may, however, perhaps be derived not
from its origin but from the use in the ground of the flower sprays employed in the
American Saruq design. As with the previous example, however, the quality and
colourings are excellent – far better than much of the new production of Persia, and
much cheaper.

The rug from Agra illustrates a different category: a single-wefted double-
weave production using a wide range of rather anonymous central Persian designs
in a fine stitch. Regrettably, these rugs have all the hallmarks of inferior workmanship which are often associated with double-weave merchandise, especially in
India. They are not too difficult to recognize: the thin yarn and flabby quality, the
complete absence of a ridged back and the far higher knot count along the warp
than is found across the width of the rug – features which are completely foreign to
the traditions of central Persia – along with the unlikely and unbalanced colour
combinations (an excessive use of yellow and rust is a common fault, and the blues
are often badly dyed as well) reinforce the impression of rootlessness produced by
the designs and point to an Indian origin. The designs themselves sometimes have
a certain panache (see fig. 283, for example), but more often they are far less
imaginative than the fineness of stitch would entitle us to expect, as fig. 652
demonstrates. In all three Indian types shown here a wide range of carpet and rug
sizes is available; runners, on the other hand, are rare.

653–655 JOZAN, MALAYIR
One of the most interesting types of rug from the Saruq region – yet independent
of it – comes from a group of villages between Hamadan and Arak, near the town

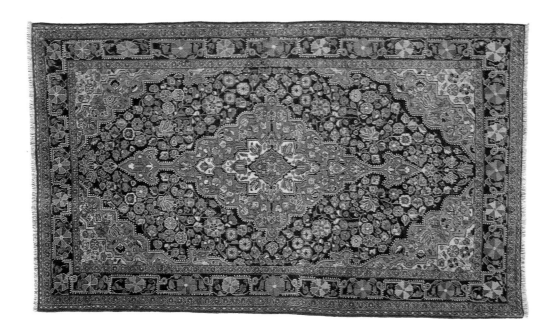

653 Jozan
211 × 132 cm, 230,000 TK/m²
(6′ 11″ × 4′ 4″, 148 TK/in.²).

of Malayir. The best rugs of the group come from Jozan and this name is often used for rugs of the whole area, but the biggest production is from Malayir itself. Note that the geometric-design Taimeh (see fig. 220) also belongs in this group. The modern Malayir design often has something of the American Saruq style about it, but the best pieces draw on the older traditions of the Saruq and Ferahan region, whose elements, however, are digested and transformed into a distinctive and finely balanced style which is pure Malayir. The production is mainly in dozar sizes, although zaronims and pushtis (but no other sizes) are also found. The most common ground shade is dark blue, but red and cream are also made. There is always a medallion of roughly the shape illustrated here, and always the same distribution of flowers around it; the differences between one piece and another, apart from matters of colouring, are a matter of spacing and of the degree of geometricity in the design. Some pieces tend to look rather rigid and lack the fluidity which characterizes Saruq. Others may, on the other hand, be confused with Saruq, for the square-looking neat weave is very similar; Malayirs, however, always have the Turkish knot, Saruqs the Persian. Note the kind of white dotted coping around the medallion and the rope-loop effect of the main border pattern. This is also used in other parts of the Hamadan region and is referred to in the notes on Tuisarkan, Darjezine and Kolyai rugs. Note also that this rope-loop effect is quite different from the one mentioned in the Qum rug shown in fig. 691.

As a carpet name, Malayir is used mainly for double-wefted Saruq-type pieces, as illustrated in fig. 653. The town is, however, also the collecting centre for many villages to the north and west, and some to the south, which produce goods in the typical single-wefted construction of the Hamadan area. One of these, Mishin, with a rather geometric design, is known by its own name, but the rest are simply called 'Malayir single-wefted'. The two rugs shown here are typically debased peasant forms of the classical styles of the area; the first comes from the south-west of Malayir, with elements of Borujird and Nehavend in its style, while the second shows some affinity with the Borchalu or Ferahan region to the north-east. Figure 654 is amazingly clumsy, considering the unusually fine weave. The outlines of the medallion and the corner-pieces, for example, are inordinately unimaginative; the design of the corners is a mere jumble; and the border, for a rug of this size and stitch, is a disgrace to the weaver. And yet the rug will fetch quite a high price: it has a strength both of construction and of expression which outweighs its lack of technical elegance; and it has the tremendous glowing colours that result from the use of natural dyestuffs and fine yarn, still prevalent in the area west of Malayir. The dark-blue ground is streaky but provides an intense foil to the rich combination of gold, light green and 'dughi' rose (madder red softened by lactic acid). Not so the rug in fig. 655, which is more typical of the cheaper Malayir village rugs. The design

654 Malayir area
201 × 140 cm, 185,000 TK/m²
(6′ 7″ × 4′ 7″, 119 TK/in.²).

655 Malayir
230 × 145 cm, 90,000 TK/m²
(7′ 6″ × 4′ 9″, 58 TK/in.²).

itself is a debased form of the American Saruq with only a distant connection with the double-wefted Malayir types. The clumsy flower-sprays, the gaps and distortions which occur from the centre of the medallion upwards, the feeble concept of the medallion and the inconsequential, disjointed border are all symptoms of the average village weaver's inability to cope with the complex graph-paper drawings which are necessary for the successful execution of floral designs. The rug shown here has a red ground; blue is also quite common. The blue (here used in the medallion and border) has a very dead look to it, with grey streaks and a blackishness which is an indication of bad dyeing habits; also the red is neither soft nor brilliant, so that the whole rug appears drab. Generally only dozar and zaronim sizes are found in this area.

656–661 MESHED

Meshed, the capital of Khorassan province, has a very large number of manufacturers, some with only a couple of looms, others with substantial output. They all work around one essentially similar style (as shown here) with a dark-blue sixteen-point medallion, dark-blue border, dark-blue corners and a red ground filled with large Shah Abbas motifs on a framework of fairly well ordered islimis. Some typical Meshed medallions are illustrated in figs. 658, 660 and 661. The medallion may also be oval; and the ground motifs rather more like sprays of flowers than Shah Abbas palmettes. There is also a tradition – which is always quite easy in a manufacturing town – of weaving in the style of other areas, especially Kerman (see fig. 668) or Yezd; but it is usually easy to identify a Meshed by certain elements of structure and colouring. The latter in particular can make Mesheds unpopular: the heavy dark-blue medallions, the large amount of dark blue in the corners and the wide dark-blue border give the carpet a very heavy, Victorian look; the red is also on the dark side. Meshed used to be known in particular for its rather mauvy red, but partly because of resistance to this shade in Europe, but also – and no doubt mainly – because of the huge increase in the cost of the natural dyestuff, cochineal, previously used to produce it, the Meshed manufacturers have now largely switched to a shade which is less blue, but still fairly dark. The manufacturing palette of subsidiary shades is very wide, but the quantities of each colour used are small and the overall effect is dominated by the principal red and blue, even though some of the secondary colours may be very sharp. Mesheds have the reputation of not being very hard-wearing, owing to the soft yarn said to be used in their manufacture, or to a weakening of the yarn in the dyeing process. In the author's experience this criticism is exaggerated: some Mesheds are certainly not hard-wearing – but the same can be said of some goods from more or less every carpet origin of the Orient. In fact, the basic Meshed structure is perfectly sound: a ridged-back construction based on medium weight warps with one thick and one thin weft supporting a medium-length pile that is reasonably well packed. Fine carpets from Meshed are very rare; most of the output has 160,000 to 200,000 knots/m² (104–130 knots/in.²), the better goods coming from the town itself and a generally lower grade from the surrounding villages, but when a superfine Meshed does appear it can look quite magnificent. Not many rugs are made, and those that are tend to be of poor quality, but all carpet sizes are found, usually in standard metric measurements – 300 × 200 cm (10′ 0″ × 6′ 6″), 350 × 250 cm (11′ 6″ × 8′ 0″), 400 × 300 cm (13′ 0″ × 10′ 0″) etc., but including squarish shapes like 300 × 250 cm (10′ 0″ × 8′ 0″) and 300 × 300 cm (10′ 0″ × 10′ 0″), as well as large oversizes. All Meshed carpets bear the weaver's or manufacturer's signature, as illustrated in fig. 51.

Meshed carpets are also made in several towns of Khorassan province, such as Nishapur, Tabas, etc., but except to a few local experts they are not individually distinguishable. However, there is one Meshed village which has a distinctive style of its own, and that is Mahavallat, near Kashmar. In fact the products of this village are often among the best Meshed carpets of all. Apart from the general Meshed style, Mahavallat weaves two individual designs (figs. 657 and 659). The first is a design also made in Meshed itself, but in a somewhat coarser quality; the Mahavallat weave is finer, stiffer and firmer than that of Meshed, having something of the character of neighbouring Kashmar. The carpets are indeed sometimes rather

656 Meshed
354 × 259 cm, 165,000 PK/m²
(11′ 7″ × 8′ 6″, 106 PK/in.²).

657 Mahavallat (detail);
full size 393 × 307 cm, 216,000 PK/m²
(12′ 11″ × 10′ 1″, 139 PK/in.²).

658 Meshed medallion.

659 Mahavallat medallion.
This is used in carpets that have a ground filled with long spiralling flower racemes.

660 Meshed medallion.

661 Meshed medallion.

656

657

658

659

660

661

662 Moud
297 × 200 cm, 280,000 PK/m²
(9′ 9″ × 6′ 7″, 181 PK/in.²).

663 Kashmar
350 × 247 cm, 192,000 PK/m²
(11′ 6″ × 8′ 1″, 124 PK/in.²).

too stiff – the weight being in the back (i.e. the warps and wefts) and not enough body in the pile. Otherwise Mahavallats are very similar to Mesheds.

662 MOUD

The finest carpets of Khorassan come from the Birjand region, which specializes in the Herati design (see figs. 168 and 230), but many other styles are also made (e.g. fig. 341). The example shown here is particularly associated with the village of Moud, just south-east of Birjand. The easiest way to recognize a Moud is not in fact from the design – which is of the standard central Persian medallion-and-islimi style – but from the weave. The stitch is very fine, double-wefted, but owing to a peculiarity of the structure the back is often covered with white specks of warp showing through, so that at first glance one might think it to be a fine single-wefted type, perhaps from Senneh. The fabric tends to be rather thin, but sells well enough because it is so fine in relation to the price. Dark blue and red are the most common ground colours, but dark green (rare in Persia, since it is the holy colour of the Prophet), plus light blue and cream, are also found. A style similar to the carpet illustrated is made in Birjand itself, and also in the eastern Khorassan village of Dorukhsh. As with other places in Khorassan, rug sizes are rare and tend to be of inferior quality.

663 KASHMAR

The town of Kashmar just south of Meshed produces a number of different designs, with a particular predilection at present for imitation Kashans, which are made for the Persian home market rather than for export. Fig. 366 illustrates the design most often thought of as the traditional Kashmar style; the present example shows what is in essence the same style relieved of the exuberant, not to say wild, pictorial elements. In both the colours are an unmistakable guide: the ground is almost always dark blue, the border light blue or beige; there are many subsidiary colours, many of them light in tone, giving a rich but not heavy overall effect. Carpets with cream or buff grounds are occasionally found, but these are rare. Note the huge, rolling, convoluted border, which in both examples bursts its own bounds, with several motifs breaking through the guards into both the ground of the carpet and the outer edge. This is a common feature of Kerman carpets and is also found in Mesheds, while in Kashmar it is absolutely standard; it is rarely found elsewhere. The weave is like that of Meshed, but as fine and neat as Kerman (and with a certain resemblance to Birjand, too), but the structure is different from all three, being tight, firm, fairly flexible (i.e. the warps and wefts are not excessively heavy) and with a short to medium pile.

606, 664–667 KERMAN

Kerman is thought of today as the home of the medallion-plain design, but medallion all-overs are also made, like the one illustrated here. The reason for the preference for medallion-plains is, regrettably, that this style offers the weaver the maximum opportunity to cheat: the plain area, where the weaver does not have to think about the pattern, can be completed very quickly, and if she misses out the odd knot here and there, who will notice? A more detailed note on this problem will be found on p. 322. Clearly, with patterned grounds the weaver is obliged to take more trouble, so for the buyer they represent a certain safeguard against the worst of the malpractices mentioned there. In other respects Kermans have much to recommend them, especially those from the specialist manufacturers who produce the better grades, like the pieces shown in figs. 347 and 606: the whole production is rather export-oriented and thus less influenced by the vagaries of taste in the Persian home market and by the interest shown by oil-rich buyers which has pushed prices of other Persian carpets to phenomenal levels. And if the demands of importers in London and New York for quality control have not succeeded in preventing the practice of looped weaving (the Persian 'knot' used in oriental carpets is not a knot at all in the strict English sense of the word: the wool is twisted around the warp strings, crossed and pulled tight; the deficiency in Kerman is that the wool is not crossed, merely threaded around the warp strings in the shape of a U or W),

664

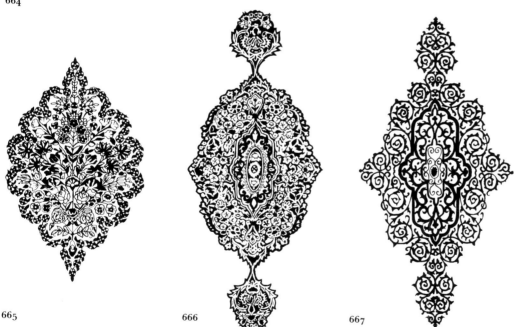

665   666   667

664 Kerman
243 × 153 cm, 385,000 PK/m²
(8′ 0″ × 5′ 0″, 248 PK/in.²).

665 Medallion from a fine-quality Kerman; in the exuberance of their floral elaboration, Kerman goods surpass all other Persian origins. This medallion, like that of fig. 667, shows French influence in its layout and in the treatment of the flowers. Cf. fig. 709.

666 Kerman medallion.

667 Kerman medallion.

it has at least been possible for them to insist on classical designs, good materials, sound dyestuffs, etc. There are three main manufactured grades woven in Kerman, known as 70/35, 80/40 and 100/50; in these the first figure represents the number of warp strings, the second the number of pairs of wefts per *gireh*; the equivalent knot-counts are 250,000, 325,000 and 510,000/m² (160, 210 and 330/in.²) respectively. There is also a considerable output of 'bazaar' goods in lower grades, mainly in the style of fig. 735. In manufactured Kermans a very wide range of designs may be found, the only connecting feature being their strongly floral nature. Another feature which aids identification is the predominance of pastel colourings and the wide range of subtle ground shades – light blue, medium blue, sand, camel, light

668

669

668 Meshed (detail);
full size 340 × 250 cm, 168,000 PK/m²
(11′ 2″ × 8′ 2″, 108 PK/in.²).

669 Yezd (detail);
full size 483 × 333 cm, 310,000 PK/m²
(15′ 10″ × 10′ 11″, 200 PK/in.²).

rose, dark green, medium green, grey-green – the palette is endless. Some manufacturers still make wide use of natural dyestuffs: the red is particularly recognizable, being cochineal-based and therefore rather bluish or plum-like (unlike central- and west-Persian goods, in which madder-reds all tend towards orange or brown). The weave is very regular and neat: on examining the back one sees clean straight ridges along the length of the carpet but the lines of the weave across the width are hardly discernible. Fifty years ago Kerman carpets were all clipped quite thin, but today they are among the thickest goods made in Persia, largely owing to pressure from the North American market, which still absorbs a large part of the production. Both carpet and rug sizes are made, but the latter are mainly restricted to the cheaper 'bazaar' grades, i.e. goods produced by individual weavers for sale in the bazaar, without the supervision – and quality control – of the manufactories.

668 MESHED
One of the traditions throughout Khorassan province is to make carpets in the style of Kerman. A typical example of this procedure, from Meshed, is illustrated here. The broken border and many details of design are faithfully copied: the vase of flowers in the corners, for example, is an instantly recognizable Kerman trait, yet the carpet is unmistakably a Meshed. Not only is the weave more uneven than in Kerman, and the coarser weave does not allow a proper *mille fleurs* effect in the ground; but above all it is the colouring which is the crucial factor, especially the dominant contrast of red and very dark blue, and the mauvishness of the red shade, both in itself and in the combinations employed. Kerman-style Meshed goods are found in the same sizes and have the same general characteristics as the normal Mesheds described elsewhere in this book.

669 YEZD
The carpet production of the small town of Yezd, on the edge of the desert between Kerman and Nain, probably best known as a centre of the ancient religion of the Zoroastrians (Parsees), was not started until early in the present century. The guiding influence in structure, design and colouring was Kerman, and to this day it is this influence which is the key to the identification of Yezd carpets. The main difference is that the weave of the bulk of the production is coarser, but the pile is more even (in more recent production, at least: older Yezds are often unbelievably thin) and the designs are less florid. But the most obvious difference is that although there is a family resemblance in the colourings caused by the use of cochineal for the reds, the range of colours is much more restricted in Yezd: cream, beige, red and blue predominate, and there is little sign of the rich palette of the light and medium shades of green and blue, the sand and the gold, which distinguish Kerman.

Finally, Yezd is a more honest weave, not (yet) afflicted by the blight of the looped pile. All sizes are made, but large carpets are less common. The design illustrated shows the typical Kerman influence seen in older carpets, but in the last few years the production in this kind of traditional type has fallen off, the weavers preferring to make 'Kashans' for the Persian home market.

670–682 KASHAN

The town of Kashan, which lies between Qum and Isfahan on the old caravan route which skirts the Great Desert (the new main road runs through Meimeh, to the west), has been famous for its outstanding handicrafts for almost 800 years. Exquisite ceramic bowls unearthed in the excavations at Rayy, near Tehran, document the supreme skills of the potters of Kashan at the beginning of the thirteenth century. It is thought that it is they who discovered, *c.* 1200, the important technical innovation of underglaze painting. Silk textiles from Rayy, in a style similar to the pottery, could also be from Kashan. Like Rayy, the town was destroyed by Jinghis Khan in 1224, but, unlike Rayy, was rebuilt and regained its leading place in the art of ceramics. Figs. 305 and 670 illustrate the achievements of the Kashan craftsmen in the later thirteenth century. In the late 1530s Kashan's fame as a textile centre led to the commissioning of the master-weaver Maqsud by Shah Tahmasp to produce one of the greatest Persian carpets of all time, the Ardebil carpet (see p. 31 and fig. 702). Whether the carpet was actually woven in Kashan is uncertain, but there was undoubtedly a major carpet manufactory in operation there later in the sixteenth century. After the destruction of the Safavid dynasty by the Afghans in 1722, weaving in Kashan seems to have dropped to a low ebb, as elsewhere in Persia, and it was not until the late nineteenth century that it revived. However, the standards set by the weavers of Kashan between 1900 and 1950, the balance they achieved between all the elements of structure, colour and design – that ideal unity of form and content – have established Kashan in many people's minds as the home of the very best in carpet weaving.

In carpet sizes one particular design came to dominate the production; one may say that in recent years it has become over-dominant, but this pre-eminence is itself a testimony to the excellence of the design. It is shown in figs. 671 and 679. There are of course countless variants on the one basic style, but they all have the same essential features, which are perhaps best illustrated by comparison with the basic Meshed style shown in fig. 656. The Meshed carpet, it must be said, is very skilfully designed; but the Kashan is just that little bit more subtle, more elegant and finely conceived all along the line. For example, although in the Kashan carpet the medallion, corners and border are all dark blue, this shade does not dominate the colouring to the excessive extent that it does in the Meshed piece. The judicious use of ivory and the lighter shades of the subsidiary motifs contribute to the better colour-balance of Kashan; and of course the finer weave permits much greater delicacy of both drawing and colouring throughout. Indeed, one of the key factors in the recognition of Kashan carpets is the discreet richness of the colouring: a large number of warm subsidiary shades is drawn from right across the spectrum without any sense of imbalance or the garish flamboyance that marks richly coloured rugs of other origins such as Qum or Tabriz. This design is instantly recognizable from the shape of the medallion: the little spikes and the rectangular corner-turns in the outline of the medallion are features that are absolutely characteristic of the Kashan 'handwriting'. In fig. 671 the weave is 38 knots per *gireh* of $6\frac{1}{2}$ cm (340,000/m^2; 220/in.^{2}). Much of the older production has a nominal knot-count of 40 per *gireh* (almost 380,000/m^2; 246/in.^{2}), but in practice the count was often nearer 36. Persian (and not only) Persian weavers rarely take these matters very literally. Despite the widespread use of the design of fig. 671 many other outstanding carpets were produced and may still be found today, although at prices which reflect both their intrinsic excellence and the fact that by the late 1960s the production of this grade had practically ceased. Fig. 672 illustrates the wealth of invention to be found in fine Kashans, especially in the large sizes commonly found. Note the rich differentiation of motifs in the floral detail which distinguishes Kashan from Kerman, where the equally fine floral detail is more homogeneous. In fig. 673 we see a most

670 Part of a set of thirteenth-century Kashan tiles. Louvre, Paris.

671

672

671 Kashan
400 × 292 cm, 340,000 PK/m²
(13′ 1″ × 9′ 7″, 219 PK/in.²).

672 Kashan
405 × 296 cm, 370,000 PK/m²
(13′ 3″ × 9′ 8″, 239 PK/in.²).

clearly drawn example of the standard design in the rare size known as the long kharak, and with the rarely found cream ground. Fig. 674 is an older piece, probably pre-1920, woven with a silk pile. It is included here to illustrate the point made on p. 275 that with sufficient knowledge of the essential characteristics of any place producing manufactured goods in floral designs, one can usually identify the origin of rarer pieces on the basis of stylistic associations. Fig. 675 is in the classical style that was widely used in rug sizes in Kashan between 1930 and 1950, with the dark blue that was the most common ground shade then; the amount of light blue in this rug is slightly unusual. Fig. 676 is typical of the best wool Kashans in current production. It lacks some of the subtlety of colour of older examples, and the shape of the medallion is somewhat awkward, but the well thought out flow of the design, the attention to detail and the careful colour balance are all preserved. This carpet has the advantage of being in a size readily acceptable to European buyers. By contrast,

673 Kashan
165 × 65 cm, 319,000 PK/m²
(5′ 5″ × 2′ 1″, 206 PK/in.²).

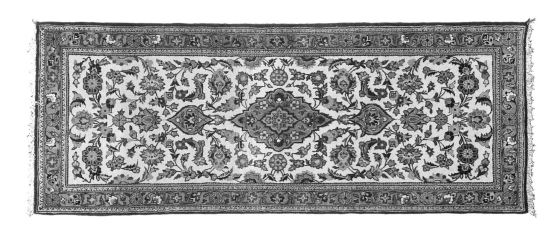

674

674 Kashan (silk)
198 × 130 cm, 395,000 PK/m²
(6′ 6″ × 4′ 3″, 255 PK/in.²).

675 Kashan
206 × 128 cm, 348,000 PK/m²
(6′ 9″ × 4′ 2″, 225 PK/in.²).

676 Kashan
308 × 200 cm, 260,000 PK/m²
(10′ 1″ × 6′ 7″, 168 PK/in.²).

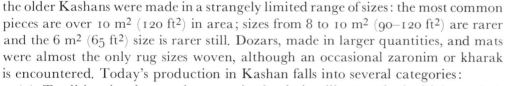

675

676

the older Kashans were made in a strangely limited range of sizes: the most common pieces are over 10 m² (120 ft²) in area; sizes from 8 to 10 m² (90–120 ft²) are rarer and the 6 m² (65 ft²) size is rarer still. Dozars, made in larger quantities, and mats were almost the only rug sizes woven, although an occasional zaronim or kharak is encountered. Today's production in Kashan falls into several categories:

(1) Traditional red-ground carpets in the design illustrated: the highest stitch woven at present in woollen carpets is about 33 per *gireh* (about 260,000/m²; 168/in.²). On a visit to Kashan in March 1977 the author saw many pieces with as few as 26 knots per *gireh* (less than 160,000/m²; 104/in.²) – too few for the design to preserve any of the finesse which makes the great Kashan carpets beautiful.

(2) The same style woven in other towns. The Kashan-style carpet has (like the Nain, for example) always been woven over a rather large area of central Persia. It is said that some of the best old Kashans came from Ardistan, which is some 75 miles away. Today, however, the area is even greater: there is a big production of 'Kashans' in Kashmar, and some of the most reliable pieces are actually made in Yezd.

(3) The new Persian-style Kashans, rather sterile cream-ground pieces in all-over designs (see fig. 778). These goods have little appeal in Europe and are not much exported.

677

678

679 680 681 682

(4) Traditional-design rugs in *kork*. This is a new and welcome development. Properly speaking, *kork* is the fine sub-pelt of the goat, i.e. mohair, but in the carpet trade the word sometimes embraces other superfine animal hairs and high-grade worsted wool. *Kork*, in the form of imported Australian merino wool, was used for the best Kashans in the nineteenth and early twentieth century, but since the Second World War its use has been rare. The recent re-introduction of the Kork-Kashan seems to have been inspired by the success of the Kork-Qum (see p. 303), rather than by any desire to emulate the traditions of the nineteenth century, but it is no less welcome for that. These pieces are extremely fine and are priced accordingly. At present the production is limited mainly to dozars, but carpet sizes will no doubt follow.

In the 1970s Kashan carpets enjoyed a special vogue on the Persian home market, which pushed the prices of new Kashans out of reach of many Western buyers. This led not only to the production of the Yezd-Kashans mentioned above but to a number of Kashan copies being made elsewhere: two notable examples are shown in figs. 677 and 678. The Egyptian copy is particularly well done; though not cheap, it succeeds in capturing much of the detail of the original. Carpets were produced in Egypt in the classical era and before (see figs. 65 and 614), but after the destruction of the Mamluk Empire by the Ottomans in 1517 the production gradually died out. It was re-started in the 1930s but remained insignificant until the oil crisis of 1974 created the boom conditions in Persia which inflated the prices of fine carpets beyond the reach of most Western buyers. Today the Egyptian production in Persian designs is still small, but there are several manufacturers weaving a range of qualities between about 150,000 and 400,000 knots/m^2 (96 to 258 knots/in.^{2}). Their standards are extremely variable, but the best are excellent. Some of the finest pieces are all silk. Although Kashan designs predominate, the range includes examples from all the finer Persian origins. The Kashmar version of the Kashan style is more cumbersome than the Egyptian, but is perhaps more interesting in that it represents not so much a direct copy as a new departure 'in the style of Kashan' from a centre of production which has, and will no doubt maintain, an independent character of its own.

683 BIJAR

As can be seen from several pages in this book, there exists in floral manufactured rugs from central Persia – Isfahan, Kashan, Qum and Arak – a considerable interchange of design ideas, so that the design alone is often not enough to identify the origin. Bijar, too, must be added to this list, since this Kurdish centre, famous for a more bucolic product, usually in Herati design, than is associated with Kashan or

677 Egyptian 'Kashan'
291 × 200 cm, 360,000 PK/m^2
(9′ 6″ × 6′ 7″, 232 PK/in.^{2}).

678 Kashmar in Kashan style
307 × 204 cm, 193,000 PK/m^2
(10′ 0″ × 6′ 8″, 125 PK/in.^{2}).

679 The standard Kashan medallion, as used in figs. 671, 673 and 677.

680 Medallion from a Mohtasham carpet (Mohtasham was the most famous Kashan master-weaver of the end of the nineteenth century). Although the fame of the Kashan carpet reaches back to Safavid times (see fig. 177), it was Mohtasham who established the standards of excellence that have marked the Kashan production of the twentieth century. The medallion shown here is a forerunner of fig. 679.

681 Mohtasham medallion.
Most of Mohtasham's output was marked by a considerably more rectilinear style than is used in Kashan today. One of his most famous designs is illustrated in figs. 686 and 692.

682 Kashan medallion.
The rich curvilinearity of the medallions in figs. 672, 674 and 721 is supplemented by the many variant forms of fig. 679, as exemplified here.

683 Bijar
215 × 133 cm, 290,000 TK/m^2
(7′ 0″ × 4′ 4″, 187 TK/in.^{2}).

684 Veramin
153 × 108 cm, 354,000 PK/m²
(5′ 0″ × 3′ 6″, 228 PK/in.²).

Isfahan, also produces goods (especially in rug sizes) in which the floral elaboration is close in style to that of the town manufactories. The surest key to identification in such cases is the structure: Bijars always have the Turkish knot, the others mentioned above all use the Persian; and Bijars always have a density and thickness of handle which the central Persian manufactories avoid (not always to their advantage). There are in addition stylistic differences which are easily recognizable. The medallion shapes illustrated in figs. 671–83 are all typical of their respective origins. Also, Kashans generally have greater panache than Bijars: compare the skimpy Herati border in fig. 683, which is typical of Bijar, with the inventive development of the same idea in Kashan (fig. 676). Compare, too, the treatment of the corners of the ground: again the same idea is used, but the Kashan version is drawn with a much greater sense of balance and proportion. The self-assurance and superb construction of Bijar rugs are present in the example shown here, but they are less effective than in the stronger, less florid designs shown elsewhere in this book.

684 VERAMIN

Veramin, a small town near Tehran with both Luri and Kurdish elements in its population, is best known for the repeating Mina Khani, Herati and other patterns illustrated in figs. 757–59. Just one medallion design is made now and again, in zaronim and dozar sizes. The colours are normally as they appear in the example illustrated, but sometimes the red has a much more mauvish tinge. The construction is the same as in the all-over Veramin carpets – fine, tight weave using excellent silky wool on cotton warps and wefts (the weave sometimes looks scrappy and irregular on the back of the rug, but this does not impair the quality). The rug shown here has, separating the guards, the dark-brown lines which are one of the typical subtle clues to the recognition of Veramins.

685–688 TABRIZ

The city of Tabriz, huddled on the edge of the Caucasus mountains, undoubtedly has by far the biggest range of designs and qualities of any manufacturing town in the whole of the Orient, which is anything but an advantage as far as this book is concerned! The author well remembers a case some ten years ago when a Swedish importer presented the following problem: we have an enquiry from a customer who has a short Sarab runner of a rather unusual type and is looking for another piece to match it exactly. The solution was: have a copy made in Tabriz, for there they can make anything; and they did. Hence, from the point of view of design there is

685 Tabriz
197 × 141 cm, 245,000 TK/m²
(6′ 5″ × 4′ 7″, 158 TK/in.²).

little information which can be offered which is entirely reliable. In fact, however, Tabriz goods are surprisingly easy to identify by other features. These are best ascertained from studying a few specimens, illustrated here. Several points stand out: (1) the remarkable thinness of the yarn – except in the finest carpets, even where the pile is quite long the carpet seems to lack body or feels as though the weight is 'all in the back'; (2) the extraordinary precision, squareness and regularity of the weave, induced partly, no doubt, by the use of a small metal hook in tying the knots; (3) the regularity of the knot itself – the Turkish knot, as used in Tabriz, is more symmetrical than the Persian; and (4) an exceptionally wide range of colours, many of them often rather strong and not well balanced. The Tabriz designs also have a marked regularity: indeed they often appear stiff and mechanical, lacking both the spontaneity of peasant-weave Turkish knot carpets like Bijar and the warmth and flow of manufactured designs from Kashan or Isfahan, which use the Persian knot. We should remember that when Rumanian carpets are described as having a 'machine-made' appearance, most Rumanians are in fact copies of Tabriz designs and the original itself looks 'machine-made'.

In Tabriz all sizes are made, and in all qualities, ranging from carpets which even today retail at less than the Rumanians to pieces priced five and ten times higher and sometimes more. The production area includes not only Tabriz itself but also the neighbouring towns of Marand and Khoi and many surrounding villages. One of the most common designs in a standard medium-grade stitch is the one illustrated in fig. 686. This is the same design as in the Qum rug of fig. 692 – a nineteenth-century design made famous by the leading Kashan manufacturer Mohtasham; it is no longer made in Kashan. In Tabriz carpets it has a certain gawkiness, which is a characteristic element of the Tabriz style. It is of course considerably more geometric than the flowing style of modern Kashans, but this is a reflection of a local tendency that goes back hundreds of years: Azerbaijan has always been the home of the geometric style. Grote-Hasenbalg illustrates two fascinating examples (his figs. 44 and 65) of how, in the early sixteenth century, Azerbaijan was still keeping to the strict style while in the east (his fig. 66) the Mongol influence was bringing about the floral revolution referred to on p. 79.

Stiffness of layout is evident in figs. 686 and 687, too, especially in the former, which, despite its higher knot-count, is extremely clumsy. There is a clear stylistic affinity with fig. 688, but the details of the design are both badly drawn and badly executed in fig. 686. There are, of course, good and bad carpets produced in every weaving centre of the Orient, but the clumsiness referred to above is almost the

686 Tabriz
264 × 175 cm, 220,000 TK/m²
(8′ 8″ × 5′ 9″, 142 TK/in.²).

687 Tabriz
294 × 201 cm, 175,000 TK/m²
(9′ 8″ × 6′ 7″, 113 TK/in.²).

688 Tabriz
295 × 198 cm, 340,000 TK/m²
(9′ 8″ × 6′ 6″, 219 TK/in.²).

hallmark of modern Tabriz. The willingness to tolerate a 'botched job' may be sensed in the hunting rug of fig. 364 and in the Taba Tabai carpets referred to on p. 320. Perhaps it is a sign of a lack of taste or discrimination. Even in the fine carpet illustrated in fig. 688 there is a lack of grace and harmony: the fronds edging the medallion are simply overdone and the motifs of the ground not only seem to belong stylistically to a different carpet, they are cramped in themselves and jerky in their layout.

689 KAYSERI

Apart from the fine natural-silk rugs described on p. 129 and the coarse artificial-silk production referred to on p. 127, Kayseri in Turkey also produces manufactured carpets with a wool pile on cotton warps in a range of designs, the most common of which are prayer-rug designs similar to that seen in fig. 289 and the Tabriz-style medallion-all-over design shown here. Carpets and rugs are produced, but not over about 7 m² (75 ft²) in area. The weave is like a medium-fine Tabriz, but the construction is less sturdy than that of Tabriz – warps and wefts are thinner and the yarn used in the pile is rather brittle and dry. However, the price is considerably lower than for Tabriz carpets of equal fineness, and the colours are usually

689 Kayseri
219 × 152 cm, 180,000 TK/m²
(7′ 2″ × 5′ 0″, 116 TK/in.²).

better balanced. Here, too, the Taba Tabai type of pastel shades predominate (cf. fig. 731), including some weird choices of ground colours (such as sickly greyish blue-green). The designs are mostly characterized by their highly involuted detail. The shape of the medallion in fig. 689 is very typical, as are also the 'shark's teeth' used as an edging for so many of the motifs.

690 HEREKE

If some Kayseri goods must be counted among the most slovenly in modern Turkish production, others must be numbered among the best pieces woven in that country today, for, within the output of this largest of Anatolian carpet-weaving centres, there is a small production of fine natural-silk rugs in the style of Hereke. Of the two, Hereke (fig. 690) has by far the larger production, and the best Herekes are finer than the best Kayseris, but with many pieces it is difficult to distinguish between the two; stylistically they certainly belong together. As with manufactured goods from elsewhere, the number of designs available is very large, the more so in this case since the stupendous price of what is, in the case of Hereke at least, certainly the most sumptuous and finest rug produced anywhere in the world today leads to a heavy demand for small pieces, so that although the total yardage produced may be limited the actual number of individual pieces woven is quite considerable. Prayer designs of the types shown in figs. 289 and 301 predominate in both the Hereke and Kayseri production, but there is still a sizable output of small pieces in the medallion style shown here.

691, 692 QUM

The city of Qum, for centuries a centre of pilgrimage and religious fanaticism, has also, since the Second World War, become an important market for carpets from villages in a large area, reaching as far as Ravand in the south and Saveh in the west (to the east there is only desert). Although the wide-ranging designs woven are generally gaudy and lacking in taste, it is a pleasure to note that the actual quality of the output has constantly been improved over the past fifteen years: there are not many towns in Persia of which this can be said. In the early 1960s the production (which began in the late 1930s) consisted mainly of medium-fine wool-pile rugs on cotton warps, but from the earliest period in the Qum production some weavers had produced rugs in which certain parts of the design were highlighted in silk (i.e. whole motifs were woven in silk, not just the outlines, as in Nain). In about 1967 this idea suddenly seized the imagination of weavers and buyers alike, and within a few years the part-silk Qum came to dominate the entire production. At about this time the weavers began to make all-silk rugs in a much finer stitch and very soon even the part-silk woollen rug had also been eclipsed. A demand for the latter persisted, and so a super-grade part-silk emerged, finer in stitch than the original part-silks (but less fine than the 100% silks) and using *kork* (mohair or other super-fine yarn) instead of sheep's wool. Today these two super-grade types – the all-silks and the part-silk *korks* – account for the vast majority of the production. The most common size made is the dozar, but other rug sizes are found, especially in the all-silk production. Carpets in 4 m², 6 m² and 7 m² (43, 65 and 80 ft²) sizes are fairly common; anything larger is rare.

An enormous range of designs is made: boteh, tree, hunting and panel designs and several others are illustrated in this book (see index). All of these are equally 'typical', and so are the two types shown here. It is to matters of detail that one must refer in trying to distinguish Qums from Kashans, Isfahans and Saruqs (they cannot be confused with Tabriz rugs because Qums have the Persian knot). In fig. 691 (cf. also the Saruq of fig. 646) one would note the following points: the rope-loop ribbon which separates the ground of the rug from the corners; the almost circular flowers in the corners; the cramped layout of the ground, which has neither the balance of the islimis seen in fig. 623 nor the easy poise of the motifs in the ground of fig. 671 – but which is still elegant in a way that the ground of the Kayseri shown in fig. 689 is not; and the shape and internal layout of the medallion. All these are features which are characteristic of Qum (but not necessarily only of Qum). In both rugs the border is taken from that of the old Mohtasham Kashans; note the

690 Hereke
91 × 61 cm, 540,000 TK/m²
(3′ 0″ × 2′ 0″, 348 TK/in.²).

691 Qum (silk)
217 × 142 cm, 485,000 PK/m²
(7′ 1″ × 4′ 8″, 313 PK/in.²).

692 Qum (silk)
227 × 138 cm, 620,000 PK/m²
(7′ 5″ × 4′ 6″, 400 PK/in.²).

691

692

straightforward repetition of a series of motifs without the alternation and inter-linking which is a feature of border designs derived from the Herati border. Fig. 692 reminds us strongly of the essential eclecticism of Qum designs. The weeping willows in the corners and the medallion are part of the standard design of Mohtasham, while the panel framework of the ground and the flower-sprays within them are clearly inspired by old Joshaqan carpets (see fig. 730).

The palette of colours used in Qum is as rich as the range of designs: one finds, in addition to bright-red and dark-blue grounds, light blue, light green, mushroom, rose and gold. Some pieces have a very strong combination of contrasting colours, others a more pastel effect. Qum rugs often succeed very well when 'antique washed' (i.e. when the bright colours have been toned down by a subtle washing process), but they are also made new in 'antique washed' shades. The latter, however, are usually either drab or hard and jarring: they are never as harmonious as the shades contained in a rug that has mellowed with age or been antique washed from what were originally strong colours.

With all this variety, the reader may feel that Qum rugs are likely to be difficult to identify, but in fact it is usually fairly easy, not only because their colours betray their origin, but also because almost nowhere else makes either all-silk or *kork/* part-silk rugs in this kind of design.

693 AHAR

The small town of Ahar, north of Tabriz, belongs to the Heriz group, but is the odd-man-out among Heriz carpets because its design is curvilinear. It is not really possible for a coarse peasant weave like this to produce a proper curvilinear design, and the use of a big clumsy medallion often reminds one of the some of the coarser curvilinear Bakhtiars (see fig. 631, for example), where the same difficulty arises. However, there is something courageous about the way the villagers of Ahar cope with the technical limitations; and the carpet's appeal is further enhanced by the unbelievably stiff and tightly packed back of the piece, which gives the whole structure a feeling of immense strength and durability. The colours are very similar to those of the rest of the Heriz area, perhaps a little lighter overall, for there is quite a lot of yellow and white used in Ahar, and the red tends more to light madder than to the deep chestnut encountered in some parts of the region. Only a few rug sizes, mostly squarish, some runners and largish carpets (7·5 m² – 80 ft² – upwards) are made. The border shown in fig. 693 is characteristic of Ahar and is rarely used

693 Ahar
362 × 265 cm, 77,000 TK/m²
(11′ 10″ × 8′ 8″, 50 TK/in.²).

elsewhere in the Heriz area, but most Ahars feature the border design shown in fig. 76.

694–696 KASHMIR

The weaving tradition of Kashmir goes back at least to the sixteenth century, and may be considerably older, having its roots in the very close cultural links between Persia and northern India following the incorporation of both of them into the Mongol Empire. Today the name Kashmir is used rather loosely to describe carpets from a very wide area of Pakistan and India, as well as Kashmir proper – a usage which is not entirely unjustified since the Lahore carpets of Shah Jahan's time were woven in the Punjab, and other centres like Agra are just as much a part of the weaving tradition as Kashmir itself. However, with the ever-increasing importance of the Indian sub-continent as a source of carpets woven in Persian designs, it would be better for more emphasis to be placed on the individuality of the different regions. A very rough grouping, in ascending order of fineness listed, would be:

(1) Ellore (Elluru), in the south, a source of wild, rough carpets, some in Gebbeh-type designs, some so jumbled as to be beyond description.

(2) Bhadohi, north-west of Benares in the Ganges valley, the source of huge quantities of cheap goods, often of wretched quality, mainly in geometric designs, and of some better grades, overlapping with:

(3) Mirzapur, Khamariah and Gopiganj, west and south of Benares: cheap-to-medium grade (mostly in the 100,000 to 200,000 knots/m² – 65–130 knots/in.² – range), some geometric, some floral.

(4) Agra, on the Jumna, south-east of Delhi: medium grade (*c.* 200,000 knots/m²; 130 knots/in.²) in both single- and double-wefted constructions, mainly curvilinear.

(5) Jaipur, west of Delhi, in Rajasthan: fine single-wefted double-weave goods in Caucasian designs.

(6) Lahore in the Punjab (in Pakistan), the home of two distinct types – single-wefted designs in Turkoman and Caucasian style, and double-wefted Kashan and Saruq types; all these are also woven in many other centres throughout Pakistan.

(7) Amritsar, also in the Punjab, but in India – making fine Persian designs, mainly dating from the sixteenth and seventeenth centuries.

694 Kashmir
186 × 121 cm, 455,000 PK/m²
(6′ 1″ × 3′ 11″, 294 PK/in.²).

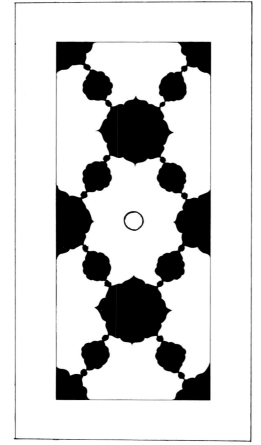

695 The layout of the 'Chelsea' carpet.

696 Kashmir
415 × 324 cm, 563,000 PK/m²
(13′ 7″ × 10′ 7″, 363 PK/in.²).

(8) Srinagar, in Kashmir, has a small output of superfine carpets, often exceeding 500,000 knots/m² (322 knots/in.²), in wool, silk and part-silk, in a wide range of (mainly older) Persian designs.

The above list includes all the most important centres of production in the late 1970s, but there are many others (Shahjahanpur, Gwalior, for example) and as the demand for Indian carpets grows new weaving areas are opening up all the time.

Leaving aside the very ancient origin of the art of carpet weaving in India, some of the above types, such as the carpets of Amritsar or Agra, are as traditional as the carpets of Nain or Yezd, while others, like the better grades made in the Mirzapur area, are as recent as *kork* Qums or Ardebils in the Herati design. Those purists who believe that only nomadic rugs are *real* oriental carpets, or who go even further and suggest that the most genuine carpets are those made by Turkic peoples and not by the Persians at all, will scarcely acknowledge the existence of the carpet-making art in India, and certainly regard it as a debased form, devoid of any artistic value. In any wider view of the matter, however, the carpets stand up well to comparisons with Persian goods. The worst are no worse than the worst of Persia (except that the European buyer never sees the worst carpets from Persia, because there even the most abysmal rubbish is relatively expensive, whereas the rubbish from Bhadohi is really quite cheap). Further, the best carpets from India are very sound in all technical respects – in fact, usually better woven than the average new Persian. What one cannot get from India is *old* carpets – pieces that have been in use in people's homes for thirty or forty years and have thus acquired that mellowness of colour that is so prized in the West. This is where Persia scores – but at a price! Illustrations of various Indian designs will be found in this book (see index).

Figure 694 illustrates a design that is made in both Amritsar and Srinagar in an all-wool or part-silk pile. It is inspired by the style of Kerman, which is a consequence of the interchange of designs among many weaving centres by companies like the OCM group, who played a dominant role in oriental carpet manufacturing in the inter-war years when the Kashmir production as we know it today was becoming established. A lot of romantic nonsense is talked about the design traditions of the East. We can see from Afshar rugs (e.g. fig. 273) and Beshirs (e.g. fig. 429) that nomadic tribesmen as are as adept as any at adapting other people's designs. What could be more natural then, than that manufacturers with production units, for example, in Tabriz, Hamadan, Kerman and Amritsar should use the same design in all these places if they thought that the output could be sold at a profit. If the job was done properly the resulting carpets were not the same, of course, for each area imparted its own stylistic imprint to the end-product. Hence a Kashmir rug in a design first thought of in Kerman will still look like a Kashmir, and a Tabriz rug in the same design will look different from both. Attention has been drawn to this phenomenon with regard to the Mesheriki carpets of Arak and Tabriz, a perfect example of a manufacturer on the highest level copying his own design in a second manufactory once it has proved successful in the first. This is standard practice in manufacturing; it was true in the case of the manufactured Caucasian rugs of the nineteenth century (the most prized of today's 'folk-art' carpets), and it will have been the case in seventeenth-century Kerman – and no doubt in tenth-century Isfahan, for that matter, if we had the evidence to prove it.

The design shown in fig. 695 is adapted from that of one of the most famous carpets in the world, the 'Chelsea' carpet, produced in Persia in the time of Shah Tahmasp and now hanging in the Victoria and Albert Museum, London. The adaptation consists in the use of only half of the original design (see fig. 695): the Chelsea carpet represents a garden with, at its centre, a small white pond containing fishes. The dark-blue medallions, seen as an excerpt from an infinitely repeating pattern, overlie the garden like part of a huge lattice-work. Looking at the design from a different standpoint, one may interpret the two principal medallions as arising from the great vases which are supported by dragons and lions on either side of the pond. Modern versions of this design set one of the blue medallions at the centre, and this creates an overall effect entirely different from that of the original, the reason for the adaptation being, of course, that there is no demand today for carpets in the exceptionally long and narrow format which the original layout

696

697 Lahore
210 × 137 cm, 390,000 PK/m²
(6′ 11″ × 4′ 6″, 252 PK/in.²).

698 Peking
diameter 185 cm, 90,000 PK/m²
(6′ 1″, 58 PK/in.²).

requires. The version illustrated in fig. 695 is produced in Kashmir, usually only in quite large sizes (around 14 m²; 150 ft²), in a stitch of well over 500,000 knots/m² (322 knots/in.²). This represents the peak of Kashmir production, with magnificent workmanship and well-balanced colours. The weaving is carried out under controlled conditions which largely prevent the use of the *langri* knot, which is woven over four warp strings instead of two. This malpractice is common in the Kashmir rugs of the bazaar grade and results in carpets with only half the body to be found in the best pieces from the organized manufactories.

697 LAHORE

Figure 697 illustrates one of the oldest-established of the fine Persian designs woven in the Punjab and other parts of northern Pakistan. Its use there reflects the strong influence exercised by Kerman on the early development of what is now a carpet-weaving boom in this area, embodying many features of the elaborate floral style of the Laver-Kerman production. The rug shown, with 16 × 16 knots to the inch, is characteristic of hundreds of designs which we lack space to illustrate here. With industrialization and political changes in Iran forcing up the price of fine rugs, Pakistan is fast becoming the world's principal source for this kind of merchandise. At present the main production is in dozar sizes, other rug and small carpet sizes being rare and large carpet sizes almost non-existent. Great care is needed in checking the three faults which plague the Pakistani (and Indian Kashmir) production, namely the prevalence of thin yarn; the use of the so-called *langri* knot – which together give an 'empty' weave, lacking in body and durability; and the wide use of poor dyestuffs, resulting especially in a dark blue tending to mauve or streaked with grey-black. However, where these faults are avoided the fine rugs of the Punjab offer very good value for money.

698 CHINESE 'PEKING'

To Western eyes this is undoubtedly the most easily recognized of all oriental carpet designs because of its use of the – universally known – traditional Chinese motifs. All-over carpets and medallion-plains are also made, but the most common layout for new Chinese carpets is the one shown here – a basically circular medallion, fairly floral but perhaps also containing Chinese animal motifs – bats, dragons, dogs, phoenixes – or stylized symbols derived from the Chinese character for long life; with a number of further motifs arranged symmetrically over the ground – usually involving flower-sprays, vases or other motifs such as writing desks or paint brushes, which were used to depict human accomplishments in eighteenth-century Chinese art. As new designs are being produced all the time in several parts of China, the range of possibilities around this basic schema is very great indeed. The category illustrated here is called Peking, but the production centres include most of the major cities of eastern China, such as Tientsin and Shanghai, and many others about which little is known. Every conceivable colour combination – including such outlandish ideas as a black ground with red border, or pale-lilac ground with purple border – is used, and all sizes are made. China is one of the few origins to produce circular carpets without limitation, although the buyer may be surprised to find that, in arriving at a selling price based on a carpet's area, the dealer calculates the area of the circle as if the carpet were square. This may seem unfair, but it is normal practice; there is, after all, quite a lot of work involved in executing a circular shape on a weaving structure which is, by its very nature, essentially square – to say nothing of the technical problem of getting the fringe to go all the way round. For a note on the structure of new Chinese carpets see p. 32.

699 CHINESE 'AUBUSSON'

Most of the 'Aubusson' designs used by the Chinese are medallion-plains (see fig. 705), but there is no design that the Chinese will not make if asked. The example shown is derived from an eighteenth-century French original. What the Chinese bring to its execution is a technical skill in both weave and coloration that is unmatched anywhere else, whether in the Orient or in Europe. Note that the leaf pattern used to cover the open ground is not woven in a different colour, but is

699

700

carved, self-tone, after the pile has been finished. For all the reservations one may have about the showiness of their taste, the vulgarity of their eclecticism, the fact remains that the Chinese are incomparably skilled in the art of putting together a sound carpet. The 'l'art pour l'art' objectivist view (as set out in Wagner's *Die Meistersinger*; see p. 39) has been taken very much to heart by the Chinese. One may not like the results but within the parameters of their own aesthetic concepts the carpets the Chinese produce are magnificent.

700 BIJAR

The influence of French carpet design on the carpets of the East is illustrated mainly on pp. 314–5, but there is one example of foreign influence on Persian art which must be illustrated here, following the Chinese version of a French design, and that is the Rose Bijar. The use of the bouquet of roses, which is the striking feature of the design, dates back to the very beginning of the European-inspired revival of Persian carpet weaving in the nineteenth century. Variant forms of the design are found in Ferahan carpets which are certainly at least a hundred years old. Whatever the origin of the tradition, in the case of Bijar the foreign element has been completely absorbed into the local style and yet remains a feature sufficiently striking to focus one's attention on it wherever it appears. The colours, as illustrated here, are an indispensable factor: the combination of medium and deep rose with light green is unmistakable. Notice on this rug two other unmistakable feature of Bijar: the broad ribbon-contour of the medallion and the overbraiding of the kilim, between the end of the rug and the fringe.

699 Chinese Aubusson
365×273 cm, 90,000 PK/m²
($12'$ $0'' \times 8'$ $11''$, 58 PK/in.²).

700 Bijar
86×70 cm, 260,000 TK/m²
($2'$ $10'' \times 2'$ $3''$, 168 TK/in.²).

2 FLORAL MEDALLION-PLAIN DESIGNS

701 Kashan
208 × 135 cm, 320,000 PK/m²
(6′ 10″ × 4′ 5″, 206 PK/in.²).

The section of this book devoted to geometric designs illustrates how easy it is to convert a medallion/all-over to a medallion-plain by the simple expedient of leaving out the design of the ground. With floral designs this is common practice and, although no such pieces of the Safavid period have come down to us, their being depicted in early miniatures proves that the concept is as old as the medallion designs themselves.

701 KASHAN

The more common type of Kashan rug features the covered ground illustrated in fig. 675, but versions of the design with the ground detail omitted have always been made. The distinctive medallion shape again gives away the origin – here slightly more rounded than in fig. 679. Note the superb colour-balance and the serene lightness of the coloration, despite the use of dark blue as the principal shade for medallion, corners and border. Both the guards used here are very typical of Kashan. In other respects all the general comments made about Kashan rugs elsewhere in this book also apply here.

702, 703 KASHMIR

The Kashmir versions of the Ardebil design (figs. 702, 703) illustrate how the medallion-plain layout is arrived at. The design is that used in two of the most magnificent products of Safavid Persia – the Sheikh Safi or Ardebil carpets. Their origin is obscure, despite the inscription they contain (see p. 31). They were made as a pair by order of Shah Tahmasp in memory of the Ardebil Sheikh who, at the beginning of the fourteenth century, founded the Shi'a convent which was to become the power-base from which Sheikh Ismail set out to found the Safavid dynasty in 1501. Modern scholars have noted that at the time of the carpets' production (1539/40) Ardebil itself possessed no building large enough to house them, but they are assumed to be identical to the carpets in the mosque at Ardebil described by a British traveller in 1843. In 1887 the mosque was in need of urgent repair, the costs of which were defrayed by the sale of the carpets, which by then were seriously damaged, to Ziegler and Co., who in turn sold them to a London company who spent four years converting the pair of damaged pieces into one complete one and one very large fragment. The complete one was bought for the Victoria and Albert Museum by public subscription; the fragment found its way to the Los Angeles County Museum. Most experts ascribe the carpets to Tabriz, which Shah Ismail had made his capital in 1502. The fact that the master-weaver Maqsud mentions his home town, Kashan, in the inscription suggests not that the carpets were woven in Kashan but that he was working somewhere else at the time. (Cf. Nimat Allah of Joshaqan, p. 265). But A. C. Edwards has raised the objection that Azerbaijan was overrun by the Turks in the 1530s. None of the scholars who confidently attribute the Sheikh Safi carpets to Tabriz has yet answered this objection. According to P. M. Sykes' history of Persia, Tabriz was occupied by Suleiman the Magnificent in 1534 and again in 1538. The two Ardebil carpets each measured 11·50 × 5·34 m

702 Kashmir
220 × 134 cm, 448,000 PK/m²
(7′ 2″ × 4′ 5″, 289 PK/in.²).

703 Kashmir
157 × 93 cm, 448,000 PK/m²
(5′ 2″ × 3′ 1″, 289 PK/in.²).

(38′ 0″ × 17′ 6″), with about 32,000,000 knots each; thus allowing seven weavers per loom for each carpet, producing 8,000 knots per day each (the stitch of over 500,000 knots/m² – 322 knots/in.² – would hardly allow more and quite possibly much less), the weaving time required, on the basis of a six-day working week, would have been 95 weeks. However, a considerable addition to this figure would be needed for the preparation of the loom drawings, the warping of the loom, the dyeing of the yarn, the interruption of work during religious festivals etc., so that the total production time for each carpet must have been at least two and a half years. Whether the two pieces were woven consecutively or concurrently we cannot now tell, but if the Turks were in Tabriz in 1538 and the carpets were produced by the beginning of 1540 the weaving cannot have been carried out there. This is the kind of difficulty which makes a definite attribution of origin practically impossible for almost all the Safavid carpets.

The design of the ground of the carpet is foreshadowed in the bookbinding illustrated in fig. 615; the pattern of the medallion may be seen in several miniatures of the 1480s and 1490s, and may also be related to the Kashan tiles shown in fig. 670; the medallion layout also harks back to the Turkoman cloud-collar and sky-door ideas illustrated in fig. 613; and the border conception is derived from the ideas shown in figs. 743 and 744. The design may thus be seen as a fusion and exemplary summary of some of the most important concepts developed by the Herat designers before their transfer to the Safavid court. Adaptations of it are woven today (on many different ground colours) in most manufacturing centres in Iran (a simplified red-ground version from Meshed is quite common, for example), and an excellent cream-ground version is made in Pakistan.

The Kashmir version seen in fig. 702 keeps fairly close to the blue-ground original, the principal adaptation, apart from the use of a green ground, being the conversion of the proportions of the original to sizes commonly used in Western homes; fig. 703 shows the same design, also woven in Kashmir, mainly in rug sizes. Here the whole of the ground design is eliminated, producing an effect totally different while using essentially the same design. This version is made in many different ground colours.

704 KHAMARIAH ('RAJBIK')

A vast, sprawling village on the Ganges near Mirzapur, Khamariah Bazaar is the home of several manufacturers producing Indian carpets in French designs. The designs were introduced there in the 1930s and 1940s, almost completely eclipsing the Persian and Turkish designs which had hitherto been the traditional style woven there. Today it is the French designs which are called 'traditional' (as opposed to the finer Persian types, which have been woven in this part of India only since the early 1970s).

The description 'French' needs some qualification: the original ideas for this style came from the Aubusson and Savonnerie carpet factories of seventeenth- and eighteenth-century France (a tradition still continued at the factory in the Avenue des Gobelins in Paris, a visit to which is a 'must' for any carpet-lover travelling to that city), but the versions made in India and China today are rather re-interpretations of the basic design concept than actual copies. The design usually consists of an elaborate floral medallion with more floral motifs in the corners and border. The treatment of flowers is quite different from that employed in Persia: there are no outlines and the leaves and petals are handled much more naturalistically, with subtle and sometimes very skilful shading effects (an Indian 'Aubusson' may have as many as thirty shades, whereas a Persian carpet rarely has more than twelve, and the tribal types often have as few as six). Also, the flowers are usually done up in garlands, with bands and ribbons rounding off what is basically an asymmetrical arrangement, whereas the stylized flowers of Persian carpets are usually arranged in sprays or purely abstract symmetrical patterns.

Within this framework endless variations are possible, including all-over designs and medallion/all-overs, but the medallion-plain type predominates. Every conceivable ground colour – from white to black via yellow and purple, as well as traditional oriental shades – and every conceivable size can be found, in a very large

704 Khamariah ('Rajbik')
365 × 275 cm, 51,000 PK/m²
(12′ 0″ × 9′ 0″, 33 PK/in.²).

range of qualities. These fall into three main grades: unwashed handspun, unwashed millspun and washed millspun. Unlike in Persia, where the best yarn always used to be handspun, in India it is often the most inferior wool that is spun by hand. It is brittle and short-stapled and hence handspun carpets shed their wool pile heavily and will be hard-wearing only if the pile is densely packed. There is no lower price-limit in India: if one customer wants a carpet 10% cheaper than normal, he can have it, and if a competitor wants it 20% cheaper he can have it, too. At each step there is, of course, a corresponding reduction in quality; less yarn, looser weaving, jute instead of cotton for the wefts, one-ply yarn instead of two-ply, corner cutting and use of inferior materials of every kind – and the lower one gets the worse the problem becomes. For in a good carpet costing, say £1,000 (or its equivalent), with high weaving costs, the raw materials will probably have cost about £160, whereas in a good piece in a coarser stitch costing, say, £400, the cost of raw materials will represent perhaps £130 – not much less, because in any good carpet one needs 3–4 kg/m^2 (5–8 lb/yd^2) of good yarn, which leaves little leeway for price-cutting. If, however, one takes a carpet of similar size that sells for only £150, the raw materials cannot be worth more than £60, and this can only be achieved by radical sacrifice of quality or quantity of yarn, or both. If one goes even lower, as is certainly possible with Bhadohi goods, it is unlikely that any form of quality materials will be found at all.

The second category of Khamariah goods – unwashed carpets made from millspun yarn – embraces the majority of merchandise in French designs sold in Europe. The third type, the washed goods, in the upper price range, includes most of the carpets in Persian designs and a small output in French designs, the greater part of which is sold in North America, the European demand for this type being fulfilled by Chinese exports.

Almost all goods in French designs, from both China and India, have one feature in common – the designs are 'carved', that is the outline of each colour or design element is incised by hand after the carpet has been woven, giving an effect of embossing throughout the pile surface. This carving process is a corollary of the naturalistic style previously referred to: in Persia coloured areas are separated by an outline in a different shade, while in India and China the outlines are replaced by the embossing.

705 Chinese Aubusson
274 × 183 cm, 90,000 PK/m^2
(9′ 0″ × 6′ 0″, 58 PK/in.^{2}).

705, 706 CHINESE 'AUBUSSON' AND 'PEKING'

The same style of French design that is woven in the Khamariah area is also produced over the full range of qualities of the new Chinese carpets (fig. 705). These are generally superior to the Indian goods, being mainly in the washed category – and also more expensive. The range of qualities produced in China is outlined on p. 32. The design principles for the Chinese 'Aubussons' or 'Esthetics' are the same as those described above for the Indian versions.

The 'Peking' designs (fig. 706) are produced in essentially the same manner but introduce more classically Chinese motifs. Among the great assets of Chinese carpets are their colours. As Lorentz repeatedly stresses, Chinese rugs must be seen as works of art, not as technical achievements. Fineness of weave, miracles of intricacy and symmetry in interlaced arabesques, the brilliant juxtaposition of many contrasting colours – all these essentially technical features which are so important in Persian carpets have no place in Chinese art; nor have the strict conventions and traditions observed in the carpets of the whole of western Asia. Chinese fantasy runs free in the art of carpet weaving, not only in the choice of motifs but also in the use of colour, with the result that China offers many carpets in splendid and imaginative colours and combinations which would be unthinkable in Persia. This characteristic may take on many forms, from the startling effect achieved simply by the association of two shades of the same colour (fig. 713), to the equally striking, but quite different, impact of the subtle shades seen in fig. 706.

707–711 THE 'GOL FARANG'

The vogue for French-style designs in oriental carpets began as a nineteenth-century phenomenon. The development is not at all documented, although it has

706 Chinese 'Peking'
diameter 245 cm, 90,000 PK/m^2
(8′ 0″, 58 PK/in.^{2}).

707

708

709

708 Sirjand
169 × 130 cm, 156,000 PK/m²
(5′ 6″ × 4′ 3″, 101 PK/in.²).

709 Senneh
51 × 80 cm, 219,000 TK/m²
(1′ 8″ × 2′ 7″, 141 TK/in.²).

707 Fethiyeh
180 × 109 cm, 53,000 TK/m²
(5′ 11″ × 3′ 7″, 34 TK/in.²).

710 Kerman (detail);
medallion from a square carpet
(325,000 PK/m²; 210 PK/in.²).

been suggested that the originators of the idea were the interior decorators of fashionable St Petersburg society who demanded French-style carpets from their Caucasian suppliers to match the Empire-style furniture then in fashion. Something of this nature seems a very likely explanation, although some of the French designs of Kerman seem to have had more to do with the introduction of the same design styles in India and China in the 1930s. Fig. 707 illustrates a Turkish rug which has the same general appearance as the Caucasian pieces in this style, which today are little more than oddities. In Sirjand this style is not in regular production but Afshar pieces like the one shown in fig. 708 are found from time to time. They have a rather appealing geometric cast to the motifs copied from early carpets of the Kerman manufactories. In the case of Senneh (fig. 709) the use of the 'gol farang' – foreign flower, as it was called – was more significant, as it was also in Bijar (see fig. 700). The rug illustrated here is a *vagireh*, a sample mat used as a guide in some areas in place of a paper loom-drawing.

Of the group illustrated here it is the Kerman which comes closest to the original French style, being, of course, a detailed copy executed by a skilful designer. The carpet was produced by the manufacturer who is also responsible for such widely differing styles as the armorial rug of fig. 367, the 'Chosroes' carpet of fig. 347 and the vase design of fig. 773. Anyone who has had experience of the laborious process of preparing design drawings in India can only wonder at the ease with which master-designers in towns like Kerman can draw and colour any design idea the manufacturer may wish to use, be it a typical example of the area's current style, a re-interpretation of an antique carpet or a completely new development inspired by a foreign tradition. In the past, only the work of such artists was accepted as 'art' in oriental carpets; today the pendulum has swung the other way and scholarly attention is focused almost exclusively on the 'spontaneous' folk art of peasants and nomads. It is no doubt right to redress the balance in this way and give the village tradition the attention it deserves, but we now seem to be reaching the point at which the undoubted skill of great designers is being entirely neglected. This distorted view is the more regrettable inasmuch as many of the most prized 'folk' carpets are themselves certainly the products of the manufacturing tradition – much of the best work of the Caucasus, for example, falls into this category, and there is good reason to suppose that the idea of manufacturing hand-made carpets goes back at least as far as the Pazyryk carpet (see p. 35). Whatever problems we may encounter, therefore, in the modern production of Kerman (and other Persian manufacturing towns) we should nevertheless acknowledge that from the point of view of design and colour they still frequently achieve an artistic standard rarely equalled and certainly not surpassed anywhere in the Orient today. The design shown in fig. 710 is one of several made in Kerman in the French style in a wide range of colours and a variety of carpet sizes.

The Bakhtiari rug shown in fig. 711 is, of course, a panel design and, strictly speaking, belongs in the appropriate section of this book. However, it is included here so as to keep all the Persian versions of the *gol farang* together. It is fascinating to see two different treatments of the same idea within one rug. The border and the red panels keep to what one might call the 'impressionist' interpretation of the French style, such as is used also in the border of the Senneh rug in fig. 589, but the white panels show much more strongly the imprint of Persian peasant interpretations of the idea, such as are seen in the Sirjand rug of fig. 708 and the not at all French-looking Feridan Bakhtiar of fig. 336. Many variants of the design are woven in the Bakhtiar region especially in Farah Dumbeh; the best guide to their origin is often the colour, as shown in fig. 711, of which we may say that every shade employed is typically Bakhtiar.

711 Bakhtiar
300 × 219 cm, 104,000 TK/m²
(9′ 10″ × 7′ 2″, 67 TK/in.²).

712 TIBETAN

Another rug showing the influence of the French style is this Tibetan piece. This is an example of the modern production of Tibet itself, the French flavour to the design being derived presumably from China. These Lhasa products are cheaper than the best of the Tibetan refugee carpets, but they are also rather stereotyped in appearance and, although finely woven, they rarely have the firmness of handle found with the goods described on p. 168. The successful pieces are those in which design and colourings reveal the positive individuality of Tibet's ancient cultural tradition, with the foreign influences kept in the background. Note in the rug illustrated the bat motif, symbolic of good luck, which is used quite often in carpet designs. As in the case of several other Chinese symbols, the origin of what may seem a puzzling association of ideas is simply that in Chinese the words 'good luck' and 'bat' have the same sound.

713–718 OLD CHINESE

A large quantity of old Chinese rugs has come on to Western markets in the past twenty years, and even today an early twentieth-century Chinese rug is probably easier to find than a piece of similar age from any other origin. Compared with other oriental rugs, they are surprisingly cheap, and since they are no longer made their price is certain to rise with the passage of time. From the point of view of a dealer trying to buy a balanced stock, they have the disadvantage that they are nearly all dark blue, and nearly all measure about 4′ 0″ × 2′ 0″. Other sizes exist, as figs. 717 and 718 demonstrate, but they are scarcer (the larger the size, the scarcer they become). For the retail customer who only wants one carpet the predominance of dark blue need not be an obstacle. The blue in question, which varies from a deep royal blue to an almost black midnight-blue, has enormous expressive intensity and is unquestionably the best background colour there is to show off the simple elegance of the design and the other colours.

Figure 713, however, illustrates a piece from Inner Mongolia – this is the type of small dark-blue rug which is most commonly available among old Chinese goods; note that, apart from the four white dots around the eyes of the dragons, only two shades are used in the whole rug – light and dark blue. This simplicity is underlined by the naivety of the design – the dragons made up of leaves (or are they wisps

712 Lhasa
183 × 119 cm, 72,000 Tibetan knots/m²
(6′ 0″ × 3′ 11″, 46 Tibetan knots/in.²).

713

714   715

716

717   718

713 Old Suiyuan
129 × 66 cm, 84,000 PK/m²
(4′ 3″ × 2′ 2″, 54 PK/in.²).
The 'foliage' dragons are surprisingly reminiscent of
the Mongol arabesques seen in fig. 742.

714–6 Medallions from old Chinese carpets.

717 Old Chinese
338 × 279 cm, 72,000 PK/m²
(11′ 1″ × 9′ 2″, 46 PK/in.²).

718 Old Peking
350 × 275 cm, 80,000 PK/m²
(11′ 6″ × 9′ 0″, 52 PK/in.²).

of clouds?) surrounded by a few symbolic motifs: there is nothing to it, and yet the eye will be arrested by the never-ending line of the 'knot of destiny' and by the compelling intricacy of the fret-work border just as much as by a highly-coloured Persian floral elaboration. Some of the infinite range of possibilities at the disposal of Chinese designers are illustrated in three carpet medallions (figs. 714–6); these examples are all taken from pieces that were produced in the early years of the twentieth century.

Figure 718 shows a carpet made in Peking or Tientsin after the collapse of the Chinese Empire in 1911. Under the Republic increased foreign influence in the political sphere is reflected also in the carpet designs which led up to the establishment of the New Chinese style, mainly by American importers, in the 1920s. This

719

example is typical of a class of goods of this era showing the influence of the Art Deco Movement. The intertwining of abstract and pictorial motifs is a feature of Chinese art of all periods.

719 PEKING 'ANTIQUE FINISHED'

Just as the old Chinese carpets ranged in style from completely covered grounds, such as fig. 458 to very open ones like fig. 713, so also do the modern pieces made in imitation of them which are sold as 'antique-finished' Pekings: a typical example of the open-ground style is shown here. Its characteristics are the same as those described on p. 123. Note the combination of the strictly geometric inner guards with flower-motifs which are semi-curvilinear in some cases and completely curvilinear in others.

720

720 TIBETAN

The rugs and carpets made by Tibetan refugees in Nepal and northern India preserve the traditional characteristics of Chinese peasant weaving, but with an individual flavour which makes it quite easy to distinguish them from the products of pre-Communist China. A general note on the structure and types to be found in this, the most original of all the modern developments in the world of oriental carpets, will be found on pp. 168 and 237. Note here the same combination of the floral and geometric treatment that was alluded to in respect of fig. 719; another noteworthy feature is the neat idea of using four dragons to form a medallion – this is just one of the many typically felicitous, simple ideas that the Tibetan weavers use to such great effect.

721 SABZEVAR

As is noted elsewhere, the names and distinguishing features of the various towns in Iran that produce Meshed-style carpets are little known outside the Meshed bazaar. One of the exceptions is the town of Sabzevar. It is the pendants of the medallion and the semi-plain field that give this design its individuality, though in other respects Sabzevar carpets have much in common with Meshed. The weave is a little different – Sabzevars are usually thinner and are often finer – but the only other feature the layman is likely to notice is that the general coloration is lighter. Rather more light blue and cream are used, and hence one is less conscious of the overpowering presence of dark blue that characterizes Meshed carpets; this applies not only to the design illustrated, but also to the other designs in the Meshed tradition woven in Sabzevar. The design shown here is made almost exclusively on red grounds. As with Meshed goods, the bulk of the production is in carpets in standard metric sizes.

722–724 SARUQ, QUM

The three pieces illustrated spotlight the problems that can arise in identifying manufactured pieces from Central Persia. All three have medallions set in a plain

721

719 Peking 'Antique Finished'
183 × 91 cm, 81,000 PK/m²
(6′ 0″ × 3′ 0″, 52 PK/in.²).

720 Tibetan
164 × 88 cm, 48,000 Tibetan knots/m²
(5′ 4″ × 2′ 10″, 31 Tibetan knots/in.²).

721 Sabzevar (detail);
full size 299 × 198 cm, 240,000 PK/m²
(9′ 9″ × 6′ 6″, 155 PK/in.²).

ground, the edges or corners of which are decorated with an elaborate garland of flowers; to a trained eye, however, there is no difficulty in identifying the two different origins. Firstly, the medallion shapes are distinctive, the first two of Saruq, the other of Qum. It is quite common for a certain class of Saruq medallions to have, as in fig. 722, a fairly small centrepiece surrounded by a rather filigree-style arrangement of sprays of flowers, while the medallion of fig. 723 has a certain stolidness, a kind of compact firmness which would be untypical in a Qum. Secondly, the garland of flowers around the edge of the ground in fig. 722 is laid out in a manner not found elsewhere, and the corner-pieces of fig. 723 are also characteristic of Saruq. The Qum piece introduces a slightly geometric, Caucasian style (see figs. 519 and 529) which is rarely used in Saruqs. The Saruq main borders are easily recognized; one can sometimes determine a carpet's origin simply by the way the classical Herati-derivative border is handled, as may be judged from a comparison of the borders of Kashan (figs. 671 ff.), Meshed (fig. 656) and the Saruq borders here.

There are, of course, other features, too, which the expert will recognize. For instance, the distinctive shade of red which the Saruq dyers obtain from madder-root, or the particular square neatness of the Saruq weave. Saruqs are also always thicker than Qums, so that even where an old Qum has mellowed into the same sort of rose-red shade as is used in Saruq the thinner handle will still reveal the origin. Another little clue is that in Qum rugs there is often a full fringe at one end only (see fig. 28). This feature is found in several areas apart from Qum, but Saruq is not one of them. It arises from the fact that when the rug is finished the warp strings are cut along the top of the rug but not at the bottom: the warp strings at the bottom are wound around the bottom bar of the loom during weaving, and when the rug is finished the bar is simply drawn out leaving an uncut looped-ended kilim strip. This finish is found on both woollen and silk-pile goods.

722 Saruq
237 × 228 cm, 235,000 PK/m²
(7′ 9″ × 7′ 6″, 152 PK/in.²).

723 Saruq
197 × 130 cm, 260,000 PK/m²
(6′ 6″ × 4′ 3″, 168 PK/in.²).

724 Qum
213 × 137 cm, 380,000 PK/m²
(7′ 0″ × 4′ 6″, 245 PK/in.²).

722

723

724

725

726

727

725, 726 PAKISTAN

Several references have already been made to the fine rugs woven in increasing numbers in Pakistan. These two pieces are typical of the production in medallion-plain designs derived originally from classical Persian centres: the first is in the style of Qum or Isfahan, and the second could come from either Kerman or Arak. As with other types from India and Pakistan illustrated elsewhere, the quality may vary considerably. The bulk of the production lies between nominal counts of 14×14 and 20×20 knots per inch, i.e. 300,000–620,000 knots/m². In addition to this significant variation in stitch there are also great differences in workmanship and colourings, but the best Lahore pieces can certainly hold their own against the modern production of Qum and Kerman and may, indeed, eclipse the latter in view of the price difference. For many years rug sizes only (especially dozars) were made, but recently some carpet sizes have appeared. These are still very limited in numbers, but in the course of time the range will no doubt increase.

727 AGRA

This typical American Saruq-style design has been used in Agra in northern India for generations. The quality of this category is standardized on a double-wefted ridged-back structure with a squarish knot, not unlike Saruq but less fine, with rather under 200,000 knots/m² (130 knots/in.²). The best pieces are good value for money, but one has to be selective. The yarn used varies considerably from fine quality wool imported from Australia to scrap material from the spinning mills of India. The colours also vary from tolerably harmonious to downright garish, often impossible to improve even by skilled washing. The bulk of the production in this style is in quite large carpet sizes; few pieces under 300×200 cm ($10'\ 0'' \times 6'\ 6''$) are made.

728 HAMADAN

The town manufactory in Hamadan was set up in 1912 by A. C. Edwards of the OCM group, and for notes on how the weave came to be established the reader is referred to Edwards' own account in *The Persian Carpet*. The manufactory was nationalized by the Persians over forty years ago and today produces the fine weaves and over-ornate designs much loved in the Middle East but rarely sold in the West. In its heyday, however, Hamadan produced a huge quantity of goods,

725 Lahore
186×126 cm, 460,000 PK/m²
($6'\ 1'' \times 4'\ 2''$, 297 PK/in.²).

726 Lahore
210×132 cm, 405,000 PK/m²
($6'\ 11'' \times 4'\ 4''$, 261 PK/in.²).

727 Agra
360×246 cm, 198,000 PK/m²
($11'\ 9'' \times 8'\ 1''$, 128 PK/in.²).

728 Hamadan Town (detail);
full size 250 × 164 cm, 165,000 TK/m²
(8′ 2″ × 5′ 4″, 106 TK/in.²).

729 Mehriban
221 × 133 cm, 90,000 TK/m²
(7′ 3″ × 4′ 4″, 58 TK/in.²).

many examples of which still appear on Western markets as semi-antiques. There is a certain rootlessness about the style of these older pieces: sometimes they can be mistaken for Kerman, sometimes even for Meshed; often they look like Saruqs (the simple solution is to check the knot, which in Hamadan is always Turkish, whereas all Saruqs and Kermans, and most Mesheds, use the Persian knot). The designers of Hamadan, egged on by their European masters, were always keen to try something new (though generally keeping to ideas derived from genuinely Persian traditions and resisting the temptation to switch everything to the American Saruq style). Sometimes the new ideas worked, sometimes they had only limited appeal. The open border effect used in the present illustration, for example, which originated in Kashan, is a neat way of ringing the changes but has never been adopted in other Persian manufacturing centres.

729 MEHRIBAN
One or two of the American Saruq types woven in the Hamadan area are made in medallion-plain versions. They resemble the modern Saruq style shown in fig. 722 more than they do the American style of the 1920s. They are easy to distinguish from Saruq itself because Saruqs are double-wefted whereas Mehribans, Lilihans and the other Hamadan medallion-plain types are single-wefted; distinguishing a Mehriban from, say, a Lilihan is less easy, however. One has to go by the characteristics of weave and coloration described on pp. 283 and 285. The Mehriban design shown here is made in dozar and carpet sizes, especially large carpets, on red, blue or cream grounds. Note the boteh motifs in the border – the boteh is a common subsidiary item in Mehriban goods. A coarser and altogether clumsier version of this style is made in Kabutrahang, a village to the south of Mehriban (see fig. 644). Another origin of the northern Hamadan area should also be mentioned here, namely Bahar. This small town lies between Hamadan itself and the Mehriban district and makes carpets which seem to have associations with both: the weave is normally double-wefted, like Hamadan town, but is sometimes single-wefted like Mehriban; the designs, too, have something of the flavour of both neighbours, pieces in a style similar to the rug illustrated here being particularly common; other Bahar rugs have designs reminiscent of fig. 640.

730 QUM
Qum's general eclecticism and the particular penchant for geometric designs are demonstrated by this rug, for this piece is based on the old Joshaqan pattern (see fig. 599). This rug, which should also be compared with the Kashan shown in fig. 600, remains unmistakably Qum, however, being at once too chic and too elaborate and bombastic to have come from anywhere in the Joshaqan/Meimeh group of villages. The structural features (including the looped fringe at one end) are as described above (figs. 691 and 724).

731 TABRIZ (TABA TABAI)
The listing in the index reveals the immense diversity of styles found in Tabriz. In recent years, however, a substantial part of the production has come to be dominated by the type of carpet shown here. Taba Tabai is the name of a manufacturer who some years ago introduced a new and highly distinctive style. A particular emphasis was placed on pastel shades, and much use is made of the burnt orange shade seen in the ground of fig. 731, which was strongly in demand in the United States for much of the 1970s. The design work is not particularly distinguished, but the Taba Tabai carpets had found a colour style not used elsewhere (the nearest competitor being Kerman). The Taba Tabai was immensely successful in the medium price range and rapidly swept the market but, as often happens in Persia with this kind of success story, the price rose and the quality dropped. The style was quickly taken up by imitators, however, and the Taba Tabai remains a competitive carpet. Regrettably, the construction is often far from sound: the particular weakness to look for when checking the quality is that the density of the construction is very uneven – one finds six inches (in the length of the carpet) of tightly packed pile and then suddenly half an inch of very loose weaving with no body at all. This can play

730

731

732

havoc with the wearing quality. A large range of carpet and rug sizes is made, in many different pastel shades and some more strongly coloured styles. A particular shade of pale green is commonly used, which, once seen, is an easy feature by which to recognize this type. Another distinctive clue is the tooth-pattern which edges the outer guard.

732 ALBANIA

The Balkan states that until 1918 formed part of the Ottoman Empire did not acquire the carpet-weaving tradition that centuries of Turkish domination might have led us to expect. The whole production of Eastern Europe has been set up since the Second World War by Communist governments. The most recent newcomer to the field is Albania, where a limited range of Persian designs is made. There is as yet no 'typical' Albanian style – whereas all the carpets from neighbouring Rumania have a recognizable stylistic similarity, in Albania several different designs are woven which have few, if any, features in common. One is illustrated here and another which is widely made is an all-over version (on a deep-green ground) of the Meimeh design seen in fig. 599. The weaving quality and materials are excellent and the colourings harmonious, reminding one of the many excellent machine-made copies of oriental carpets made by continental carpet manufacturers, but superior to these in execution.

733, 734 KERMAN

The rug shown in fig. 734 has features which hark back to the sixteenth-century connections between designs used for carpets and bookbindings, and is indeed still called Khorani for this reason. A typical binding from Herat is illustrated in fig. 733. Apart from the strikingly simple basic layout, there are several unusual features of the design-work in fig. 734, which to some extent reflect the French influence which was strong in Kerman in the late 1950s. Note, for example, the rococo effect of the scrolling leaves and flowers in the corners of the ground, or the filigree decoration of the edge of the medallion. Note also that the main border breaks into the guards, and that the border itself is based on repeating cartouches – Kerman is one of the few manufacturing centres to have overcome completely the problem of dependence on the Herati-border derivatives used elsewhere. There are many versions of this design made in Kerman (and Yezd, too), using every conceivable ground shade. As with other export-oriented manufacturing areas, all sizes are possible, but the design seems to work best on carpets not over about 6 m² (65 ft²)

730 Qum
209 × 140 cm, 250,000 PK/m²
(6′ 10″ × 4′ 7″, 161 PK/in.²).

731 Tabriz: Taba Tabai
187 × 140 cm, 177,000 TK/m²
(6′ 1″ × 4′ 7″, 114 TK/in.²).

732 Albania
399 × 295 cm, 240,000 PK/m²
(13′ 1″ × 9′ 8″, 155 PK/in.²).

733 Persian bookbinding, Herat, 1440.
Cleveland Museum of Art.

734 Kerman Khorani
240 × 168 cm, 325,000 PK or loops/m²
(7′ 10″ × 5′ 6″, 210 PK or loops/in.²).

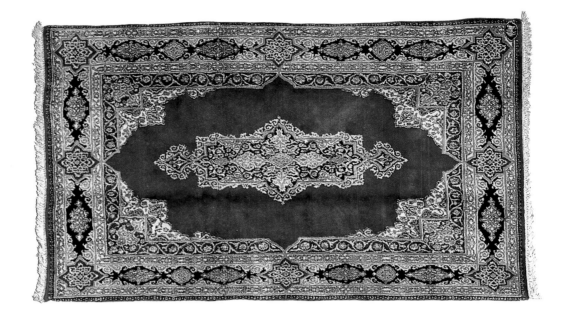

in area. The pile, which, as explained elsewhere, is looped rather than knotted, is usually long and quite well-packed, but one needs to look carefully at the density of the open ground section. If the carpet seems to lack body here or shows a notice-able change of density between the ground and the border it is likely that the weaver has cheated by leaving out alternate threads in the ground. Among other risks associated with plain-ground carpets, streaks may be more pronounced, for exam-ple, and if a warp-string should break and be knotted together again this knot can be incorporated into the pile of the carpet, which on a plain ground may produce the effect of pitting or speckling. All these faults are avoidable, however, and in well-dyed pieces the ground produces a most striking effect.

735 KERMAN

The main production in Kerman, known simply as 'bazaar goods', is in the design shown here, destined mainly for the North American market, but quite often sold in Europe, too. Many pastel shades and some strong ground colours are used; almost all sizes and shapes are available, including squares and circles (the latter being almost unknown in Persia, though readily available from India and China). Again it is the romantic treatment of the flowers which makes the design easily recognizable, along with the choice of basically pastel colours. Many Kermans include flower sprays along the edge of the ground which recall those of the Saruq, fig. 722, but one can never mistake a Saruq for a Kerman, since, apart from the obvious difference in weave, the use of cochineal-based (i.e. bluish) reds in Kerman and madder-based (i.e. brownish) reds in Saruqs produces a totally different style of colouring.

Regrettably, the quality is also an unmistakable clue to the Kerman origin: the stitch is coarsest and the use of simple loops instead of knots is at its worst in the American-style bazaar production; and the difference in pile density between the patterned border and plain ground is often so marked that one almost feels as if one is going down a step when walking from one to the other. This is no doubt connected with the fact that the weavers of Kerman are paid no more than those of some parts of India, whereas, when the author visited Kerman in 1977, the rate in Birjand (in Khorassan province to the north) was about 40% higher, while the weavers in Meshed were earning almost three times as much. This difference in earnings means that Kermans are relatively cheap: one can over-exaggerate the problems of looped weaving – after all, if the carpet is tightly woven the loops are not likely to fall out; and Kerman has by no means a monopoly of bad weaving practices. Therefore, if one likes the Kerman style, and can find a piece with a solid

735 Kerman: American style
165 × 98 cm, 200,000 PK or loops/m²
(5′ 5″ × 3′ 2″, 129 PK or loops/in.²).

736 Yezd
318 × 203 cm, 216,000 PK/m²
(10′ 5″ × 6′ 8″, 139 PK/in.²).

construction and good pile density, it will certainly prove cheaper than any other manufactured Persian carpet of equal fineness.

736 YEZD

The designs of Yezd are often thought of as variants of the Kerman style, which is no doubt correct, since Kerman designers have provided many loom-drawings used in Yezd in the past thirty years. But there are certain features which enable one to tell the difference and confirm a distinctive Yezd style independent of Kerman. The colourings play an important part, for Yezd carpets mostly keep much closer to the basic scheme of red, blue and white which is the hallmark of nearly all the carpet origins of Persia, and indulge much less in the pastel and other imaginative combinations common in Kerman. This example also illustrates some typical differences of design. The vases and flower-garlands in the corners could easily be from a Kerman carpet; but the borders and above all the over-elaborate medallion are more florid than in typical Kerman goods, while the tooth-like leaves decorating the straight edges of the extended corners introduce a note of stiffness which a Kerman designer would have avoided. More examples of the Yezd design style are shown in figs. 669 and 767.

737 BIJAR

One thinks of Bijar as the home of close-covered designs, with or without medallions, but the region covered by the name Bijar is quite large, and includes most of the fine and many of the coarse double-wefted carpets of Kurdistan. Some of the Bijar tribal names are also encountered – Gerus, Helvai, Afshar Bijar, for example; such names are rarely used correctly, though a description such as 'Gerus' or 'Afshar' may well help to make a rug sound more exclusive. Within the output of this wide range of tribes there is of course a huge wealth of different designs, particularly as the Bijar production is carried out on a semi-organized village manufacturing basis. When medallion-plain designs are made they are usually, as shown here, strikingly effective. Somehow one senses all the power and vibrant energy of those close-covered geometric pieces, enhanced by the tremendous impact of the boldness and simplicity of the medallion-plain style. The secret perhaps lies in the Kurds' unerring sense of colour, that instinctive ability to set strong colours cheek by jowl without any sense of disharmony or imbalance. The design shown here – a variant of the Rose Bijar illustrated in fig. 700 – uses this skill to magnificent effect, the madder-red ground glowing within the dark-blue frame and providing an admirable foil to the shades of light blue, yellow and rose used in the medallion and corners.

737 Bijar
256 × 162 cm, 255,000 TK/m²
(8′ 5″ × 5′ 4″, 165 TK/in.²).

3 FLORAL ALL-OVER DESIGNS

738 Floral Herat carpet, sixteenth century;
765 × 300 cm, 322,000 PK/m²
(25′ 1″ × 9′ 10″, 208 PK/in.²).
Metropolitan Museum of Art, New York
(Gift of Joseph V. McMullan, 1959).

739 Vase carpet, sixteenth century,
269 × 174 cm, 343,000 PK/m²
(8′ 10″ × 5′ 8″, 221 PK/in.²).
Thyssen-Bornemisza Collection, Lugano.

There are two main types of all-over curvilinear designs: those whose layout is infinitely repeating and those which revolve around a centre-point which is implied but usually not represented. There are inevitably limits to the range that can be encompassed by these two types because in the curvilinear style the basic design element is the stylized flower and 'all-over floral' can therefore only mean repeating flowers. The flowers and the relative sizes of the various motifs may be varied, but the design is bound to keep coming back to the same basic scheme. This is not to belittle the concept as such: some all-over floral designs have a classical simplicity and restraint which to many people is preferable to the medallion style but is yet combined with a fluidity and warmth that cannot be matched by geometric pieces in all-over patterns.

Any consideration of this design category must begin with Bihzad and the Herat school of painting. We saw in the first section of this chapter how the weavers of eastern Persia threw off the shackles of the rigid Turkoman style to create floral forms; and in the second section of the chapter on Universal Designs how the Herat floral style was developed into the Herati pattern. We must now look again at the Herat floral style and the companion group, the vase carpets. The transfer of Bihzad and other artists to Tabriz in 1510 did not mean the end of the Herat design school; apart from the fact that the royal court continued to draw on Herat (and may, indeed, have founded a Court Manufactory there), other artists of a new generation were available to continue the traditions of the fifteenth century. At this point, however, we encounter the problem that with very few exceptions we do not know for certain either when or where any of the classic carpets of the sixteenth century were produced. Eastern Persia, the province of Khorassan, which is huge today and was perhaps double the size at that time, reaching as far as Merv and Balkh, with Herat as its capital, contained many towns and villages which are possible sources for the rugs illustrated in the Herat and Bokhara miniatures of the fourteenth and fifteenth centuries, for the Herat floral carpets of the sixteenth and seventeenth centuries and for the goods in the Herati pattern of the seventeenth century onwards. Whether Herat itself produced carpets is not known: the name Herat is used in the following pages to denote all the carpets of Khorassan, wherever they were made. The vase carpets are attributed by most scholars to Kerman (Dimand favours Isfahan, however); but here, too, there is no definite evidence. As to dating, the vase carpets (e.g. fig. 739) are often ascribed to the first half of the sixteenth century, the floral Herat carpets (e.g. fig. 738) to the late sixteenth and early seventeenth centuries. If this is so, what, we may ask, was woven in Herat between 1480 and 1580? Is it not more likely that the perfectly judged and harmonious carpets like those shown in figs. 179, 270 and 738 were woven in the reigns of Shah Ismail and/or Shah Tahmasp as the immediate successors of the Herat school of bookbinding, while the weavers of central and western Persia were occupied with the magnificent but daunting new development of the medallion carpets? A few tantalizing carpet fragments employ in the border the compartment scheme seen in a miniature of 1485 (fig. 744), while the ground seems to be part of a layout

739

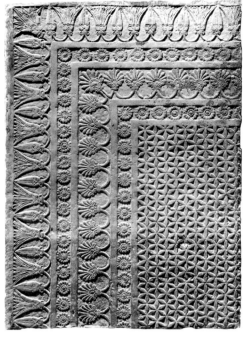

740

74¹

741

74²

743

744

740 Stone panel (detail) with carpet pattern, from the Palace of Ashurbanipal at Nineveh, seventh century BC. British Museum.

741 Carpet depicted in an east Persian miniature of the Timurid School, 1439.

742 Page from a Koran illuminated in Hamadan in 1313, during the Mongol period.

743 Frontispiece from the *Khamsa* by Nizami, a manuscript illuminated in 1442. British Library.

744 Detail of a miniature by Qasim 'Ali, 1485, showing the mystic and theologian, Khwaja 'Abd Allah Ansari, with four disciples.

like that of the sixteenth-century carpet shown in fig. 738. One such fragment (fig. 745) was recently described by Sotheby's as 'early seventeenth century'; but in what respects would it differ if it had been woven between 1490 and 1520?

The origins of both the Herat and the vase styles can be traced in early miniatures. The oldest all-over curvilinear carpet pattern is to be seen in one of the Nineveh stone 'carpets' (fig. 740; cf. also fig. 56). A similar pattern was still in use in Persia in the early fifteenth century, as may be seen from the carpet depicted in fig. 741. An important variant of this layout is illustrated in fig. 742, which is a page from a copy of the Koran illuminated in 1313 in Hamadan for the Il-Khan Oljeitü. The interlocking circles form compartments which are filled with abstract floral ornaments similar to those seen in fig. 670. This idea was further developed by the book designers (fig. 743) and taken up 175 years later by the carpet designers to produce

745

746

747

a number of schemes in which circular and other curved forms overlie one another to produce a layout consisting of compartments in different colours. This layout is shown in fig. 744, and has come down to us in the form of the compartment and cartouche borders of figs. 745 and 92, and in a small sub-group of the vase carpets of which fig. 764 is an example. Two other vase-design sub-groups also divide the field of the carpet into compartments, as illustrated in figs. 746, 765 and 768. Kühnel describes these compartment vase carpets as forerunners of the free-flowing style illustrated in fig. 739. They are supplemented by yet another variant, as shown in fig. 747. It is no longer possible to piece together a dependable chronology for these five variant forms of vase designs, nor indeed to show precisely how they are related; but there are many derivatives of them in the designs woven in the Orient today. Other classical vase carpets are shown in figs. 170, 183, 184, 270 and 766.

748 CHAHAL SHOTUR

A fascinating version of a vase design is seen in this Bakhtiar carpet; it is in a style particularly associated with the village of Bain but woven also in Chahal Shotur (cf. also p. 148). We have already seen how the Bakhtiar panel designs are derived

745 Fragment of an east Persian carpet, sixteenth century; 450,000 PK/m² (290 PK/in.²). WHER Collection.

746 Fragment of a vase carpet with panel layout, sixteenth century.
Victoria and Albert Museum, London.

747 Vase design, early seventeenth century (detail); here, the compartments have been transformed into repeating medallions.
Victoria and Albert Museum, London.

748 Chahal Shotur
305 × 198 cm, 185,000 TK/m²
(10′ 0″ × 6′ 6″, 119 TK/in.²).

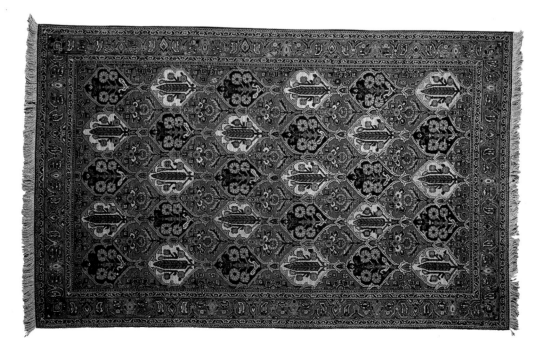

749 Early Caucasian dragon carpet, attributed to Kuba, late sixteenth century, 350 × 195 cm, 125,000 TK/m² (11′ 6″ × 6′ 5″, 81 TK/in.²). Victoria and Albert Museum, London.

750 Dragon carpet, seventeenth century; 213 × 184 cm, 155,000 TK/m² (6′ 11″ × 6′ 0″, 100 TK/in.²). Victoria and Albert Museum, London.

from the vase carpets through the intermediary of the seventeenth- and eighteenth-century garden carpets. Here we can see that the Bakhtiar lozenge-panel variant is also derived from the vase design, but by a more direct route. Other diagonal-panel derivatives are illustrated in figs. 335 and 711. Hans Bidder has drawn attention to the connection between the Khotan tree design (fig. 238) and the vase carpets. This introduces a considerably perplexing element, since the vase and tree designs of East Turkestan can be proved to be 2,000 years old and seem, indeed, related to the 'heraldic' image portrayed in fig. 237.

749, 750 DRAGON CARPETS

Another mysterious, but most important, group associated with the vase carpets is that of the Caucasian dragon carpets; although the oldest known examples are already quite corrupt in form, they seem to be derived directly from the type shown in fig. 746, but how the design found its way from southern Persia to Kuba, the presumed origin of the Caucasian pieces, is not known. Perhaps it had something to do with one of the many ruthless transportations of tribes undertaken by Shah Abbas I at the beginning of the seventeenth century. The reason for the introduction of dragon motifs into some of the panels is also not known. No animals appear in the vase carpets; several Herat carpets show leopards attacking deer in forms (cf. fig. 178, also fig. 175) which are brought to mind by the stylized shapes in some of the panels of dragon carpets, but such a connection may be fortuitous. Sometimes the dragons appear to be accompanied by phoenixes, which may indicate a connection with the Turkoman animal rugs like fig. 174. Carpets in dragon designs are still produced in the Caucasus today, in the category of Armenian goods sold as Erivan (see fig. 513). Fig. 750 is particularly interesting for the stylistic pointers it contains towards the Chelabi rug of fig. 469. 'Eagle Kazak' rugs often feature a broad white-ribbon motif which suggests a dragon, and there are other elements, including colouring, which seem to connect them with fig. 750.

751, 752 THE BEGINNINGS OF THE HERAT FLORAL STYLE

Herat carpets in the designs shown in figs. 178, 185–7, 189, 190, 738 and 745 were frequently depicted in seventeenth-century European paintings, and this is no doubt the reason why it has been contended that these designs were woven later than the vase carpets. The Herat floral style is, however, also foreshadowed in early miniature paintings; one of the earliest examples of a carpet with curvilinear elements depicted in an extant Persian miniature dates from *c.* 1480 – it occurs in a manuscript (originally consisting of 685 folios) in the Museum of Decorative Arts, Tehran, recounting the 'Adventures of 'Ali bin Abi Talib' – and the carpet on which 'Ali is shown seated (taking a meal out of doors) has a ground consisting of an all-over pattern of cloud-bands (cf. figs. 66, 175). Another Persian miniature – painted by Bihzad only a few years later (fig. 751) – shows the basic layout of the Herat floral design fully developed. M. S. Dimand and others have illustrated in considerable detail how the characteristic motifs used to clothe this layout were developed in Herat in the fifteenth century. Attention may also be drawn to the pattern of a silk caftan made for the Ottoman Sultan Bayazid II between 1481 and 1512 (fig. 752); this incorporates many motifs used in both the vase carpets and the Herat carpets. The caftan is the earliest extant textile of major importance that contains important features of both designs. Two carpets depicted in an illuminated manuscript dated 1494 (reproduced in F. R. Martin's classic collection on pl. 94 and in Arthur Upham Pope's *Survey of Persian Art*, V, p. 882, in colour) shed important light on the development of all-over curvilinear design techniques. One includes the geometric pattern seen in fig. 616 at the height of its elaboration; the other shows the same design converted into curvilinear form (the elements of both patterns are shown in fig. 398g, h).

753, 754 THE 'HARSHANG' DESIGN

The transfer of weavers from East and South Persia to central and western districts which occurred in the early eighteenth century led to the creation of an important semi-geometric north-west Persian version of the Herat design known as the

753

754

751

752

751 Detail of a miniature, 'Sultan Husain Mirza in a Garden', painted by Bihzad, Herat, *c.* 1485. Gulistan Museum, Tehran.

752 Silk caftan of Sultan Bayazid II (r. 1481–1512). Topkapi Seray Museum, Istanbul.

753 Detail of a Joshaqan carpet with *harshang* design, eighteenth century; full size 269 × 198 cm, 105,000 PK/m² (8′ 10″ × 6′ 6″, 68 PK/in.²). Victoria and Albert Museum, London.

754 Joshaqan: detail of a carpet with design derived from the Herat floral style, eighteenth century; full size 391 × 200 cm, 167,000 PK/m² (12′ 10″ × 6′ 7″, 108 PK/in.²). Victoria and Albert Museum, London.

harshang design. *Harshang* means crab: the name originated, like the name *mahi* (for the Herati pattern), among weavers or dealers who read their own interpretation into a design taken over from an alien tradition. This design was widely used in the Karabagh region of the Caucasus in the nineteenth century and may be found today in places as far apart as Rumania and India (fig. 763). Many other *harshang* designs are woven today; some are illustrated in the following pages; another example may be seen in fig. 462. Figures 447 and 464 may also be related. Among other geometric derivatives of the Herat floral group mention must be made of fig. 754. This *harshang* variant is usually attributed to eighteenth-century Joshaqan, but some other central Persian origin is also possible. The design forms the basis of the style used today in Reihan (fig. 467), while the particular shape of the framework may be found in both the Saruq and Meimeh areas.

755–759 THE MINA KHANI DESIGN.

In the sixteenth century the Herat carpets were always composed symmetrically around an implied centre-point, whereas the vase carpets were built up as an asymmetrical progression of endless and endlessly variable repeats. They thus represent the two categories of all-over floral designs alluded to at the beginning of this section. However, in the eighteenth century (or earlier) both types were changed. The vase designs were organized into symmetrical lattice-patterns, some

755

756

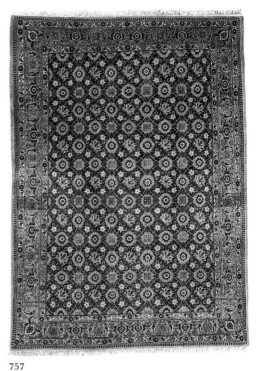

757

755 Detail of an eighteenth-century carpet in Mina Khani design; full size 348 × 175 cm, 124,000 PK/m² (11′ 5″ × 5′ 9″, 80 PK/in.²).
Victoria and Albert Museum, London.

756 Mina Khani carpet from Khamariah, India; 275 × 230 cm, 78,000 PK/m² (9′ 0″ × 7′ 6″, 50 PK/in.²).
The design is derived from a north-west Persian Kurdish rug in a style similar to that found in the old 'tribal' Veramin rugs.

757 Veramin
303 × 210 cm, 310,000 PK/m² (9′ 11″ × 6′ 11″, 200 PK/in.²).

including a dominant medallion, while the Herat design was developed into two different small repeating patterns capable of being used independently of any implied centre-point in the carpet. One of these is the Herati pattern, discussed and illustrated in detail in chapter III. The other, involving a fusion of the vase and Herat styles, is called the Mina Khani design. The origin of the name is obscure. Cammann's suggestion that it may be a corruption of *aina khaneh*, meaning 'hall of mirrors', may be the answer. Fig. 755 shows an early form of the design, from an eighteenth-century 'Joshaqan', which spotlights its relationship to the Herati pattern. A geometric version, woven today in India in the Bhadohi/Mirzapur area of the Ganges valley is shown in fig. 756, a Beluch version may be seen in fig. 434 and a Beshir variant in fig. 429. The most common modern version is the one illustrated in fig. 757, from Veramin in central Persia. It should be noted that there are two distinct types of carpet from Veramin. One has a markedly Luri character: the carpets usually have blue grounds and are mostly long and narrow, with a geometric version of the Mina Khani design; they are woven by both Luri and Kurdish groups around the town. The output is small and the rare pieces one encounters are mainly old goods, often in excellent colours and with the kind of intensity noted in blue-ground tribal rugs elsewhere. The second type, illustrated in figs. 757–9, is made in the town itself. The Mina Khani design dominates the production; it is woven on cotton warps in a very fine stitch. Medium and dark blue, and madder-red grounds predominate, but cream grounds are also found. The range of sizes is severely limited: in general only pushtis, zaronims, dozars and carpets around 320 × 210 cm (10′ 6″ × 7′ 0″) are made, but just occasionally a carpet 10 m² (110 ft²) in area is found. Prices are high, too high for many people in view of the simplicity of the design, but the standard of weaving and the quality of the (natural) dyestuffs, even today, compare favourably with those of many other expensive Persian carpets from elsewhere.

Veramin also makes other variants of the Herat and vase design derivatives. A piece in the Herati pattern is shown in fig. 232; two other Veramins appear in figs. 758 and 759. In the first of these the vase design has lost its vases, but the 'cloud-band' lilies and the richly ornate palmettes remain, the latter flanked here by pairs of pheasants (cf. also fig. 764). The design seems related to another vase-carpet derivative, the Zil-i-Sultan design (fig. 271). Note the use of light blue as a ground shade. Fig. 759 shows a Veramin version of the *harshang* ('crab') design (cf. fig. 753). The characteristics of weave and colouring and the sizes available for both these pieces are the same as those noted for fig. 757.

758

759

760

760 NENEJ

The same 'crab' design is made in the village of Nenej, on the edge of the Malayir/ Ferahan area; old carpets from this place are usually called Malayirs. This version of the vase design spread to the whole of central and north-west Persia in the same way as the Mina Khani and Herati designs did and it may be encountered in several of the Hamadan village areas that produce carpet sizes. In Nenej there is a substantial output today: medium-fine, single-wefted on cotton warps, using (like all Hamadan village production) the Turkish knot. Here, as with the old Mina Khani rugs, this all-over floral design betrays geometric origins in the version as executed in Nenej. Most of the output is in large carpet sizes (9 m² – 100 ft² – and over) with dark-blue grounds; but some smaller carpets and rugs, and some red grounds are also found. Rugs tend to be on the large side, like the dozar illustrated. The wool is thick and of very high quality; the price, alas, is correspondingly high, a good average piece costing more than, for example, a comparable grade from Meshed, which is not only 50% finer but double-wefted into the bargain.

761, 762 BIJAR

Further variants of the floral all-over 'crab' design with geometric overtones are found in Bijar. From the practical point of view it is not surprising that peasant weavers working in a geometric tradition who have a hankering after the curvilinear style should produce all-over designs. To create a piece like the medallion-Isfahan of fig. 623 a great deal of detailed design work on graph paper is required, and this is certainly beyond the resources of most village enterprises; also, once the design is drawn the weaver has to learn a full quarter of the whole carpet in order to execute it. However, the two designs shown here are easier to manage: once the weaver has mastered the principal repeating design unit the battle is half won.

Of the two Bijars shown, the design of fig. 761 is the more common. In the piece illustrated here it is fascinating to note the retention of fully fledged Chinese cloud-bands and properly drawn lotus-flower palmettes. Introduced into Persian carpet design nearly 500 years ago, they reached the Kurdish areas of north-west Persia some 250 years ago. This is what we mean by tradition! Of course the design here is distorted; for a Bijar the weave is on the coarse side and there is the typical matter of peasant weavers' being unable quite to cope with the intricacies of curvilinear designs. Note the braiding at both ends, a typical clue to the Bijar origin; and the inclusion of French-style roses (cf. figs. 103 and 709) in both the ground and the border. Fig. 762 successfully accomplishes the difficult task of constructing a

758 Veramin
258 × 151 cm, 411,000 PK/m²
(8′ 5″ × 4′ 11″, 265 PK/in.²).

759 Veramin
193 × 140 cm, 330,000 PK/m²
(6′ 4″ × 4′ 7″, 213 PK/in.²).

760 Nenej
208 × 155 cm, 110,000 TK/m²
(6′ 10″ × 5′ 1″, 71 TK/in.²).

761 Bijar (detail);
full size 204 × 132 cm, 230,000 TK/m²
(6′ 8″ × 4′ 4″, 148 TK/in.²).

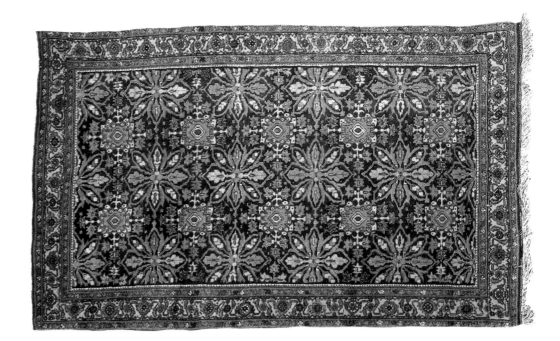

design simply from repeating medallions. This is Bijar at its best: no attempt is made at an intricate layout of interdependent elements, simply the positive juxta-position of richly coloured abstract forms. What is convincing is the self-assurance of this juxtaposition and its rightness. The eight-pointed rosette is also found in other forms in Bijar goods: it may appear at the centre of the medallion (fig. 195) and is also used in an enlarged form in the coarser Bijar weaves. Several more elab-orate variants of vase and Herat designs are woven in carpet sizes in the finest Afshar Bijar quality: they always exhibit the characteristic combination of essential respect for the court manufactory style and an earthy, peasant approach to its realization.

763 MIRZAPUR

The *harshang* carpet shown in fig. 753 and its nineteenth-century Karabagh variants form the basis of designs in a similar vein made today in both India and Rumania. In both countries the design works well because the knot-count used to reproduce it suits its essentially geometric style but is just fine enough to introduce a trace of the curvilinear to prevent a feeling of rigidity.

764–766 KASHMIR, TABRIZ

Three of the original forms of vase-carpet designs are shown in this group of twentieth-century copies. The first represents a Kashmir carpet of the old school, that is, a piece based on an antique original, the design having been woven in Kashmir since the modern industry was set up in the 1920s. The original may be seen in the Österreichisches Museum für angewandte Kunst in Vienna; it is illustrated in Sarre and Trenkwald's famous masterwork known simply as the Vienna Book, which is, indeed, the source for many modern copies of antique designs throughout the Orient. The design is closely related to that of the carpet shown in fig. 744. The Kashmir carpet is woven in very small numbers in a stitch of over 600,000 knots/m² (388 knots/in.²) and represents one of the very best examples of the Kashmir weaving art.

Another variant of the Kerman vase style splits the ground of the carpet into more or less diamond-shaped panels, the plant stems arising out of the vases or palmettes being fixed in diagonal lines to produce the basic framework. This is the scheme underlying the layout of fig. 746; it also forms the basis for fig. 765. The carpet shown is from Tabriz, but closely follows the original design known to us through many fragments in museums throughout the world. Modern copies are made in several places, notably in Agra, where it is woven in a double-wefted construction with 185,000 knots/m² (120 knots/in.²), and in Srinagar, where

764

764 Kashmir
298 × 252 cm, 610,000 PK/m²
(9′ 9″ × 8′ 3″, 394 PK/in.²).

765 Tabriz
285 × 195 cm, 360,000 TK/m²
(9′ 4″ × 6′ 5″, 232 TK/in.²).

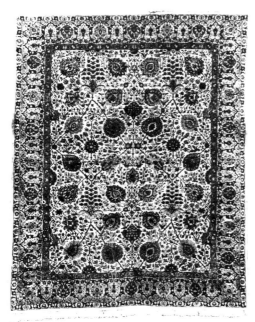

765

magnificent pieces up to 15 m² (165 ft²) in area are produced, with a knot-count of over 600,000/m² (388 knots/in.²). For all the effort put into the design it is very difficult to bring off, owing to problems of colour-distribution. The carpet is not usually made with a purely symmetrical layout of colours in the panels, but lacking this, the different intensity of the shades used can give the overall appearance an unbalanced air. The dark-blue panels, in particular, may stick out like a sore thumb. Another problem arises with the actual choice of shades for the panels: large blocks of pastel colours are difficult to judge successfully, and an injudicious shake of the dye-master's hand can result in a sickly shade that will ruin the whole colour-composition. The compensation is that where these problems are overcome (as in fig. 765) the stiffly archaic quality of the design produces a unique and stimulating effect.

The original forms of the straightforward all-over vase design vary considerably, as a comparison of figs. 183, 270 and 739 will confirm. In some cases, perhaps the oldest examples, the forms of the motifs are noticeably more rounded; indeed, the first carpets (figs. 184 and 170) reproduced by Charles Grant Ellis in his analysis of the vase carpets in the *Textile Museum Journal* (December 1968) contain several elements which remind one of fig. 752. This feature is seen in fig. 766, a manufactured Tabriz carpet of the 1930s. The strength and richness of carpets of this kind, which were produced by several companies in Tabriz under European control, serve to remind us that a carpet cannot be judged inferior simply because it is a copy:

766 Tabriz
345 × 270 cm, 250,000 TK/m²
(11′ 4″ × 8′ 10″, 161 TK/in.²).

imaginative use of the design material at the weaver's disposal is as sure a key to success today as it was in the sixteenth century, wherever that design may have originated.

767–770 YEZD, KERMAN

In contrast to the group of central Persian carpets seen in figs. 774–78, in which all-over designs are often created simply by leaving out the central medallion of a medallion/all-over carpet, Yezd and Kerman – both in the south of the country – produce a number of designs directly or indirectly related to the vase carpets and conceived from the beginning as repeating patterns. This is perhaps a result of the fact that their production is mainly export-oriented and Western furnishing styles have always created a demand for carpets without a dominant centrepiece. One way of achieving this effect is to base the design on repeating medallions. This is not easy to bring off: there are problems of colour-balance, of the relative size of the medallions, and of how to link the motifs together. The solution shown in fig. 767 was devised in Kerman, where the design was drawn, but this carpet's style became known through the production of a Yezd manufacturer. It was one of the first designs to be used in India in the new production of Persian designs that emerged

767 Khamariah Yezd
235 × 180 cm, 214,000 PK/m²
(7′ 8″ × 8′ 11″, 138 PK/in.²).

768 Kerman (detail);
full size 365 × 271 cm, 328,000 PK/m²
(12′ 0″ × 8′ 11″; 212 PK/in.²).

769 Drawing for a Kerman carpet,
full size 400 × 300 cm
(13′ 1″ × 9′ 10″)

770 Kerman (detail);
full size 298 × 190 cm, 457,000 PK/m²
(9′ 9″ × 6′ 3″, 295 PK/in.²).

767

768

769

770

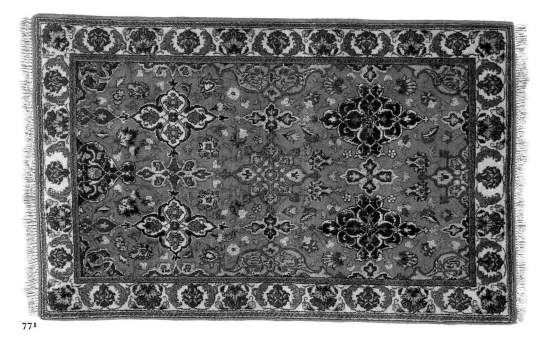

771

772

in the Khamariah district in the 1970s; the carpet illustrated was woven in Khamariah in 1976. The key to the success of the design is the conversion of the leaf framework of fig. 746 into a lattice-pattern which can be superimposed on a single-coloured ground. This eliminates the problem of colour balance noted with regard to fig. 765 and gives coherence to the whole layout. The 'medallions' then simply become the centre-motifs of a repeating lattice-work of lozenges. The design seen in fig. 768 may be thought of as a further graceful variant of figs. 762 and 767, while fig. 769 shows an adaptation (also used in Meshed) of the cartouche-style of early miniatures (cf. fig. 744). The complex design of fig. 770 is more closely related than the others to the original vase carpets and at the same time underlines the connection with the garden design concept.

771, 772 TABRIZ, QUM

Although the manufacturing towns of central and northern Persia tend to favour derivatives of the Herat design for their all-over carpets, they all weave repeating-medallion designs as well; two examples are illustrated here. Both clearly show the influence of fig. 747. The Tabriz version reflects the manufacturing style of the inter-war years when this simple, but well balanced, design was woven in a number of centres and was much copied. Note the green shades, which are a useful clue to the recognition of Tabriz goods. In the Qum piece the designer has sought to add interest by borrowing *Zirhaki* motifs from Tabriz (see figs. 281 and 366). The design, however, owes its success to the balance between the medallions and to the finely judged richness of the palmette and leaf motifs.

773 KERMAN

A simple derivative of the vase carpets consists of the repetition, without interlinking, of individual motifs. This idea was much used in the Moghul carpets of India, which were strongly influenced by the designs of south and east Persia in the sixteenth and seventeenth centuries. Several famous carpets, for example, have plant motifs, like those of figs. 180 and 181, distributed freely across the ground. The Zil-i-Sultan from Abadeh (fig. 271) uses the same principle, retaining the vases of the original conception. Another centre basing patterns on repeating vases is Kerman (fig. 773). The prominent and distinctive flower vases used there have been noted in respect of figs. 273 and 736; here they come into their own as the principal feature of the design.

774 MESHED

This carpet illustrates clearly how a medallion/all-over design with 'Shah Abbas' palmettes can be converted into a completely all-over style by the elimination of

771 Tabriz
118×77 cm, 322,000 TK/m²
(3′ 10″×2′ 6″, 208 TK/in.²).

772 Qum
214×316 cm, 510,000 PK/m²
(7′ 0″×4′ 6″, 329 PK/in.²).

773 Kerman
247×157 cm, 325,000 PK or loops/m²
(8′ 1″×5′ 2″, 210 PK or loops/in.²).

773

the medallion and corners. The tiny centre motif, which is absent in the genuinely all-over designs shown in the preceding pages, provides the key. This piece otherwise has all the same features as a medallion Meshed, and the colours, sizes, quality etc. are as noted on p. 290. This principle, which is derived from the Herat floral carpets (figs. 178 and 738), is used in all the centres of fine manufactured production in Iran – Isfahan, Kashan, Qum, Tabriz and so on.

775–777 ISFAHAN

Many highly qualified experts, invited to comment on fig. 775, were puzzled as to its origin. The author heard the following assessments: 'Qum, because of the ground colour and design'; 'Saruq, because of the handle'; 'Tabriz, because of the stiff squareness of the weave'; 'Isfahan, because of the colour-combination of the border'. In the author's judgement the last suggestion is the most convincing: in this case, although the final arbiter is supposed to be the weave, none of the experts was sure enough of this aspect to be able to depend on it. However, there is something definitely Isfahan-ish about the border; if it were a little more greenish, no doubt several experts would plump for Tabriz, despite the use of the Persian knot (Tabriz uses almost – but not quite – exclusively the Turkish knot), but this light grey-blue background, combined with the medium blues and the other shades of the secondary colours, is strongly reminiscent of the Isfahan village production (Nejafabad, for example). The problems of attribution of origin can sometimes be very great, and can have serious consequences, especially where contentious legal issues are at stake. People may have to pay considerable sums for expert opinions for assessments and valuations and are understandably concerned if they then discover that it is by no means certain that any one expert's assessment is reliable, or worse: that it really is only a matter of opinion; however, the public must not expect more than is reasonable. Whereas art experts can obtain the grounding they need in schools of fine art throughout the world, and serious scholars can reach an extremely high level of knowledge through the research facilities these institutions provide, the carpet expert has no such facilities. The only way anyone can acquire the vast amount of detailed knowledge a carpet expert needs is through the trade, and thus it is almost inevitable that almost every expert is a trader, whose knowledge and experience is bound to be coloured – and limited – by what he can sell; but even leaving aside this serious reservation, the very nature of carpets itself means that most stated facts on the subject are at best no more than considered opinions and

776 Isfahan
213 × 157 cm, 820,000 PK/m²
(7′ 0″ × 5′ 2″, 529 PK/in.²).

at worst no more than inspired guesses. One cannot be definite about an article which is affected by so many indeterminate factors. Even basic definitions of origin are vague: for example, if Tibetan refugees make carpets in Kathmandu, Nepal, we still call them Tibetans. Yet another factor affecting identification is the fact that carpet weaving is still a living art and is thus constantly changing. The established style of any area is not something rigid and sterile but a 'language' which is constantly evolving.

In some places the pace of change in recent years has been breathtaking: thus, in the Bhadohi area of India the two biggest manufacturers in 1973 had between them about five Persian designs in regular production in no more than three different weaves. Only five years later the same two manufacturers were weaving well over a hundred designs in at least twelve different weaves, with projects in hand to treble this programme by the early 1980s, by which time a myriad of smaller manufacturers had produced well over a thousand different designs in at least thirty different constructions. No expert can keep himself fully informed about this kind of development, and in many cases could hardly be blamed not only for mistaking an Isfahan for a Qum (or a Kayseri for a Hereke), but even for failing to spot much more fundamental differences in the face of the complexity of origins now on the market.

The domes of the Isfahan mosques provide the carpet designers of that city with constant inspiration for elaborate arabesque patterns. It is perhaps here that the Herat carpet design is woven with most variety today, not in slavish imitations but in adaptations of the original layout incorporating the typical palmettes and other motifs of modern Isfahan. Note (fig. 777) the skilful introduction of birds into parts of the design and the suggestion of a skeletal medallion shape around which the layout revolves. Isfahans of this type often have a cream ground. As is noted elsewhere, the designers of Isfahan are not limited to the style shown in fig. 777. The basic islimi layout can be adapted in many ways to produce a diversity of style. In fig. 776 the designer has used the floral Herat idea rather in the way indicated in fig. 172, setting a large elaborate Herati motif at the centre of the carpet as though it were a medallion.

778 KASHAN

The design layout employed in fig. 777 provides the basis of a style which has been made in Kashan in recent years and sold very successfully on the Persian

777 Isfahan
235 × 152 cm, 420,000 PK/m²
(7′ 8″ × 5′ 0″, 271 PK/in.²).

home market. These new all-over Kashans are marked by a very cool colour-scheme – an unusual feature for Kashan – and as a result are not much imported by Western buyers. Occasionally, however, one comes across pieces with a little more warmth, like the present one. Kashans of this type are always fine and expensive, and usually in large sizes; but the identical style is also available from Kashmar, still in very good quality, but at appreciably lower prices. For a general note on Kashmar Kashans see fig. 678.

779, 780 HEREKE
From the very beginning of its production in the late nineteenth century Hereke has concentrated on designs based closely on classical sixteenth-century originals. The exceptionally fine weave (a million knots/m² – 650 knots/in.² – is not at all rare) permits the reproduction of almost any design without restriction. Even in

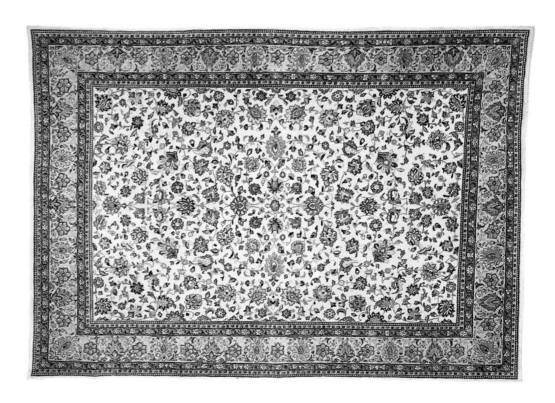

778 Kashan
408 × 302 cm, 310,000 PK/m²
(13′ 4″ × 9′ 11″, 200 PK/in.²).

very small pieces the Hereke designer can indulge his fantasy more or less at will. Even so, there is a considerable difference between the most and the least successful pieces, as a comparison of figs. 779 and 780 reveals. There is an expressive strength to fig. 779 which is quite lacking in fig. 780. The lines followed by the islimis in the latter rug are gawky as well as unimaginative, while the rigid central axis serves to emphasize the dullness of the symmetry and a certain insipidness in the overall conception. The border, too, is a hopeless jumble. In fig. 779, however, the design is carefully worked out to produce a balanced and harmonious composition containing an amazing amount of elaborate detail in such a small size. Both rugs illustrated are of silk with metal thread, that is, certain motifs are treated in kilim weave with gold or silver metal wefts.

781, 782 KHORASSAN

The Meshed rug illustrated, although not a particularly attractive piece, is included here because it illustrates a characteristic stiffness one encounters in Meshed (and in Khorassan generally) when designers there depart from the firmly established 'Shah Abbas' designs which the province typically produces. Here an attempt has been made to use the layout of the sixteenth-century vase carpets, but with motifs drawn by modern designers trying perhaps to be original but also bearing in mind the principles that make a design easy to weave (and therefore quick and profitable to produce). The attempt fails because the motifs are not interesting enough in themselves, because the layout is too rigid, and because the colour-distribution produces a 'busy' and unharmonious effect. Once again the enormous importance of tradition in the Orient is emphasized: just as fig. 777, for example, illustrates what can be achieved by adhering to tradition, this example demonstrates the risks involved in departing from it.

A very much more successful piece of modern designing is illustrated in fig. 782. Like the splendid Meshed boteh design of fig. 161, this piece reveals skills among Khorassan designers which are often neglected by Western buyers. Inspired perhaps by European demand for muted shades – 'autumn colours' – the artist has evolved out of the Mina Khani design a new pattern which has the classic combination of richness and restraint which is so often at the heart of a successful Persian carpet. This carpet is an interesting specimen for the historian, too, for it illustrates the same kind of development out of the Mina Khani design as may also be seen in that design's development out of the Herati pattern (see fig. 755).

779 Hereke
136 × 99 cm, 950,000 TK/m²
(4′ 5″ × 3′ 3″, 613 TK/in.²).

780 Hereke
147 × 97 cm, 780,000 TK/m²
(4′ 10″ × 3′ 2″, 503 TK/in.²).

781 Meshed
230 × 136 cm, 140,000 PK/m²
(7′ 6″ × 4′ 5″, 90 PK/in.²).

782 Kashmar (detail);
full size 342 × 248 cm, 230,000 PK/m²
(11′ 2″ × 8′ 2″, 148 PK/in.²).

780

781

782

783 Saruq
198 × 142 cm, 189,000 PK/m²
(6′ 6″ × 4′ 8″, 122 PK/in.²).

783 SARUQ

This is a Saruq rug in the so-called Mustaufi design, which is named after a nine-teenth-century Persian prime minister. In essence it may be thought of as a stiff degenerate variant of the vase-and-islimi style, with *gol farang* (see fig. 700 and pp. 313f.) flowers within the dominant wreath motifs. The oldest forms of the design are found in Ferahan carpets, but it may be seen today in pieces of all origins from Birjand to Ardebil; in all production centres it must be counted a rare design. Note that the border as illustrated here is a simple precursor of the one used by Mohta-sham of Kashan (see figs. 691 and 692).

784 KAIMURI

One of the finer designs woven in the Ganges valley in India, at the foot of the Kaimur Hills, is derived from a Ferahan carpet of the early years of the twentieth century, at which time European and American manufacturers in Sultanabad were introducing new elements into the traditional Saruq style (see also p. 280). What makes this carpet interesting is the juxtaposition of the clumsy bold banana-leaf motifs and the string of elegant floral motifs, which clearly reveal the Malayir/Saruq village area as the origin. In re-interpreting the design the Indian weavers have separated out the various constituent elements and re-synthesized them in many different combinations. The results may not have the patina or indeed the flair of the seventy-year-old Ferahan original, but they are certainly superior to any American Saruq made in Persia today – and only a fraction of the price. All sizes are made and several ground colours are found.

785 CHINESE 'FLORAL'

The simplest and yet in some ways the most appealing of the new Chinese carpets is just called 'floral'. The characteristic feature of the design is a spray of flowers in two corners of the carpet. The embossed leaf pattern seen in the piece illustrated is an 'extra' which is often omitted. The appeal of these rugs lies in their simplicity – the expressive keystone of Chinese art – behind which however lie impressive technical skills in the realistic designing and execution of the flower motifs. Nowhere else in the Orient, for example, can the weavers reproduce the colour-shading within the leaves and petals which we tend to take for granted in Chinese goods. As with other new Chinese carpets, all sizes are available and there is no limit whatsoever to the range of shades that can be ordered.

784 Kaimuri Ferahan
291 × 200 cm, 220,000 PK/m²
(9′ 6″ × 6′ 7″, 142 PK/in.²).

785 Chinese floral
300 × 200 cm, 90,000 PK/m²
(9′ 10″ × 6′ 7″, 58 PK/in.²).

784

785

786

787

786–788 OLD CHINESE

Scholars now believe the art of carpet knotting in China to be much older than was previously accepted. Carpet designs have long been known to us through the 67 floral-pattern rugs from eighth-century China which are still preserved in the Imperial Treasury of Shosoin in Japan. These pieces are in fact felt rugs with the designs sewn on. However, evidence of the production of pile carpets is contained in a remarkable poem by Po-Chu-i (772–847). In it the poet laments the extravagant waste of silk used to produce a carpet for the hall of the concubines in the Imperial palace. The carpet is said to have measured thirty metres square and needed a hundred men to carry it. It is described as being so thick that the dancer's feet sink into it at every step. In view of this description, the conclusion seems inescapable that the piece in question was a knotted pile carpet. The poem says of the design only that it was delicate; fig. 786, which illustrates one of the felts, may perhaps indicate the general style. Many centuries lie between the Shosoin felts and the earliest preserved pile carpets from China, but the idea of an all-over floral style like that of fig. 787 is still preserved in the piece shown in fig. 176, which dates from the seventeenth century. Old pieces from the first half of the twentieth century are to be found in a huge range of all-over floral styles. Fig. 786 illustrates a typical example, revealing that same semi-geometric flavour noted with regard to other rugs of this origin (see fig. 567, for example). Here, as in so many cases, the ground is dark blue; the expressive power lies in the restraint of both design and colouring, through which the Chinese artist secures that same certainty of being right that was remarked in respect of fig. 699; however, there is no element of stiffness in this work – the changing shades of blue on the deep rich ground are alone enough to prevent that. Moreover, the whole is also lifted by the powerful border, with those great muscular geometric blocks embracing the delicate flower motifs like some Nureyev lifting a graceful Fonteyn above the stage with effortless ease. For good measure there is a jester in the corners, too: a different motif in each one, just in case you thought the rest of the design was entirely symmetrical.

The same ideas are to be found in the new Chinese 'antique finished' production (fig. 788) – without the problem of everything being on a dark-blue ground, without the problem that carpet-size pieces are so scarce that prices are astronomical, and without Nureyev and Fonteyn, too. Like most modern manufactured imitations of an ancient style, they lack the courage that imbues the originals with vitality. The carpet shown here illustrates how nicely everything is done in new Chinese carpets: sound construction, well executed design, skilfully balanced colours. What is missing is that elusive element of spontaneity and individuality of expression that turns craft into art.

788

786 Suiyuan(?)
206 × 135 cm, 88,000 PK/m²
(6′ 9″ × 4′ 5″, 58 PK/in.²).

787 Chinese felt rug, eighth century.

788 Peking 'Antique Finished'
297 × 192 cm, 87,000 PK/m²
(9′ 9″ × 6′ 3″, 56 PK/in.²).

SELECT BIBLIOGRAPHY

There are many excellent books about oriental carpets, and many more that are more notable for their authors' ignorance or for their fanciful sales talk. I have drawn on the following books, sometimes quite heavily (and I readily acknowledge my debt to the authors):

Bode, Wilhelm von, and Kühnel, Ernst, *Antique Rugs from the Near East* (trans. Charles Grant Ellis), 4th revised ed., London 1970. A short, but illuminating account of classical carpets.

Dimand, M. S., *Oriental Rugs in the Metropolitan Museum of Art*, New York 1973; includes a chapter on Chinese carpets by Jean Mailey. The best historical survey of the classical period.

Edwards, A. Cecil, *The Persian Carpet: a survey of the carpet-weaving industry of Persia*, London 1953. An indispensable study of the carpets of the period 1880–1950, by a man intimately involved in their manufacture and distribution.

Erdmann, Kurt, *The History of the Early Turkish Carpet* (trans. Robert Pinner), London 1977;

—, *Oriental Carpets: an account of their history* (trans. Charles Grant Ellis), London 1976;

—, *Siebenhundert Jahre Orientteppich: zu seiner Geschichte und Erforschung* (ed. Hanna Erdmann), Herford 1966.
Stimulating surveys of early carpets and their history.

Grote-Hasenbalg, Werner, *Der Orientteppich: seine Geschichte und seine Kultur*, Berlin 1922. The most penetrating study of the cultural background and importance of oriental carpets before 1900.

Housego, Jenny, *Tribal Rugs. An Introduction to the Weaving of the Tribes of Iran*, London 1978. The best little book on Persian nomadic goods.

Iten-Maritz, J., *Enzyklopädie des Orientteppichs*, Herford 1977. The most comprehensive general compendium yet published.

The following are all outstanding monographs on their respective areas:

Bidder, H., *Carpets from East Turkestan known as Khotan, Samarkand and Kansu Carpets*, Tübingen and London 1964;

Denwood, P., *The Tibetan Carpet*, Warminster 1974;

Iten-Maritz, J., *Turkish Carpets*, Fribourg 1977;

Loges, Werner, *Turkoman Tribal Rugs*, London 1980;

Lorentz, H. A., *A View of Chinese Rugs from the seventeenth to the twentieth century*, London and Boston, Mass., 1972;

Schürmann, Ulrich, *Central-Asian Rugs*, Frankfurt/Main and London 1969;

—, *Caucasian Rugs*, Frankfurt/Main, Accokeek, Md, and Basingstoke 1974. Both deal with eighteenth- and nineteenth-century rugs.

(1)

(2)

(3)

(4)

For map references see general index. In addition to the historical items on this page, the maps included in this volume are:

northern India and eastern Persia in the late sixteenth century – p. 83;
northern Afghanistan – p. 175;
the Kurdish and Luri weaving area – p. 212;
the Qashqai and Afshari weaving area – p. 262;
Turkey – p. 344;
central and eastern Asia – p. 344;
Pakistan and northern India – p. 344;
Azerbaijan and the Caucasus – p. 345;
western Persia – p. 346;
the Khorassan region – p. 347.

Notes on the historical maps

The maps on this page show (with appropriate land areas shaded) the extent of:

(1) the Persian Empire under Darius I, *c*. 500 BC;
(2) the Arab Empire by AD 750; (3) western and central Asia in the thirteenth century, showing Mongol influence from the east; (4) western and central Asia, *c*. 1550, showing the Ottoman, Safavid and Moghul Empires.

(1) Among the earliest Indo-European tribes to occupy the area of present-day Iran were probably the Kurds (Kassite Babylon, 1800–1200 BC) and Lurs (Elamite Susa, 1200 BC). Urartu (ninth–eighth centuries) and Armenia (sixth century onwards) – both occupying a similar region centred on Van – were also occupied by Indo-Europeans. The Medes and Persians (of the Iranian eastern branch of the Indo-European group) seem to have entered the Iranian plateau in about the fourteenth century BC, moving from the north-east along the shores of the Caspian; they reached the Zagros mountains by *c*. 850 BC. The early powers of Urartu, Assyria, Babylon and Elam had fallen to the Medes by 600 BC; however, in the sixth century the Median Empire itself succumbed to the great Achaemenian rulers Kourosh II (Cyrus the Great), Darius I and Xerxes. The Persian Empire fell to Alexander the Great in 330 BC and was incorporated into the Greek Empire. After the breakdown of Greek rule the Parthians established a realm in Persia which was hardly less extensive, and this was followed by the spread of the Sassanid Empire which, at its peak in the sixth century AD, ruled the whole of the area shown, except Egypt, Syria and Anatolia.

(2) From the first, the Muslim leaders were soldier-priests and within a few years of the Prophet's death the Arab armies had conquered most of western Asia. A century later, they had reached the limits shown here. Ctesiphon fell to the Arabs in 637 and the power of the Sassanids was destroyed at the battle of Nehavend in 641. The Arab armies were small and fast-moving, leaving garrisons rather than colonists; hence their influence on Persian ethnography and culture was small (in parts of Iran, however, pockets of tribes of Arab origin remain to this day). The Arab capital, Baghdad, was built opposite the ruins of Ctesiphon.

(3) By the middle of the thirteenth century Jinghis Khan, his son Chagatai and his grandsons Hulagu and Kublai Khan had established control over an empire stretching from eastern Europe to Korea. The Mongols had been preceded as invaders in western and central Asia by the Turks, who occupied West Turkestan in 552 and the Tarim Basin by 650. From the end of the tenth century onwards, the Seljuq Turks pushed westwards, conquering Persia in 1043 and capturing the Islamic capital, Baghdad, in 1055. The Turkoman tribes entered Anatolia in 1071 and founded the Empire of the Seljuqs of Rum (capital Konya, 1071–1276). The invasions of Timur between 1378 and 1402 strengthened the Mongol and Turkoman hold on Iran.

(4) The fourteenth and fifteenth centuries saw the rise of the Ottoman Empire in western Anatolia and the Balkans. By 1453 (fall of Constantinople) the whole of western Anatolia was in Ottoman hands, while the Kara Koyunlu Turkomans controlled eastern Anatolia and western Persia. In the early years of the sixteenth century two new empires were established – Moghul India and Safavid Persia. From 1514 until 1732 Mesopotamia, western Iran and the Caucasus were disputed between the Ottomans and Safavids (Persia finally secured western Iran and most of the Caucasus, while Turkey held Mesopotamia and most of Armenia). In the east, too, the frontier fluctuated, much of Afghanistan being disputed between India and Persia (it was only in 1857 that Herat was finally established as part of Afghanistan).

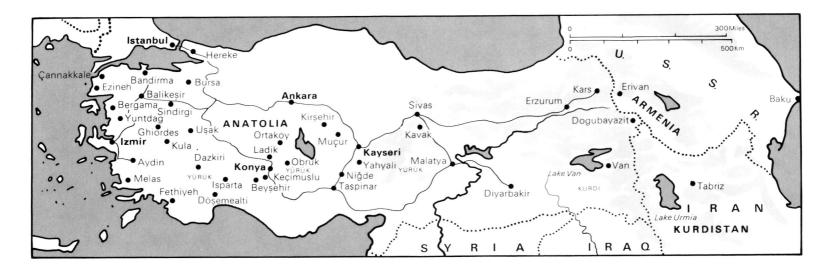

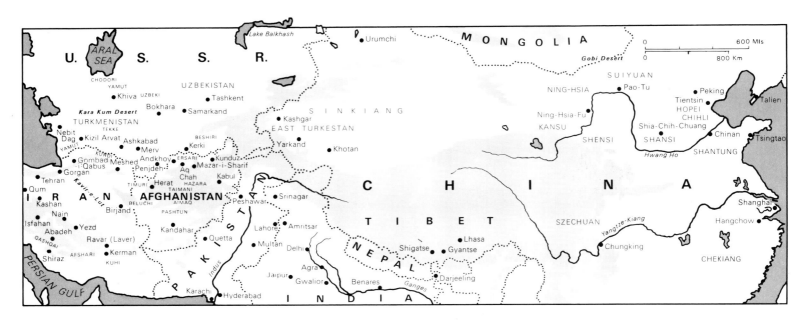

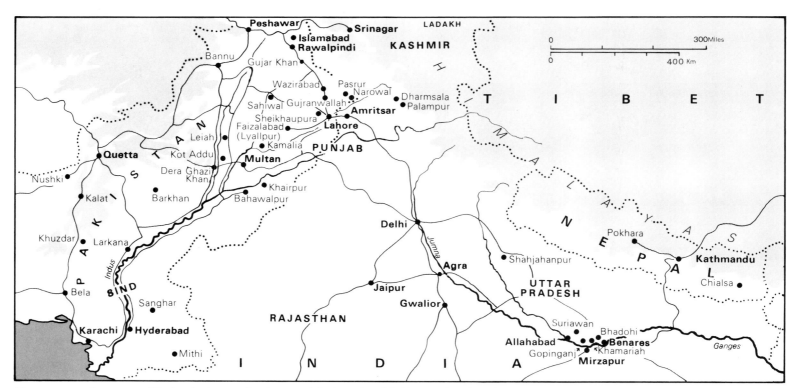

The carpet-weaving centres of Turkey (top), central and eastern Asia (centre) and Pakistan and northern India.

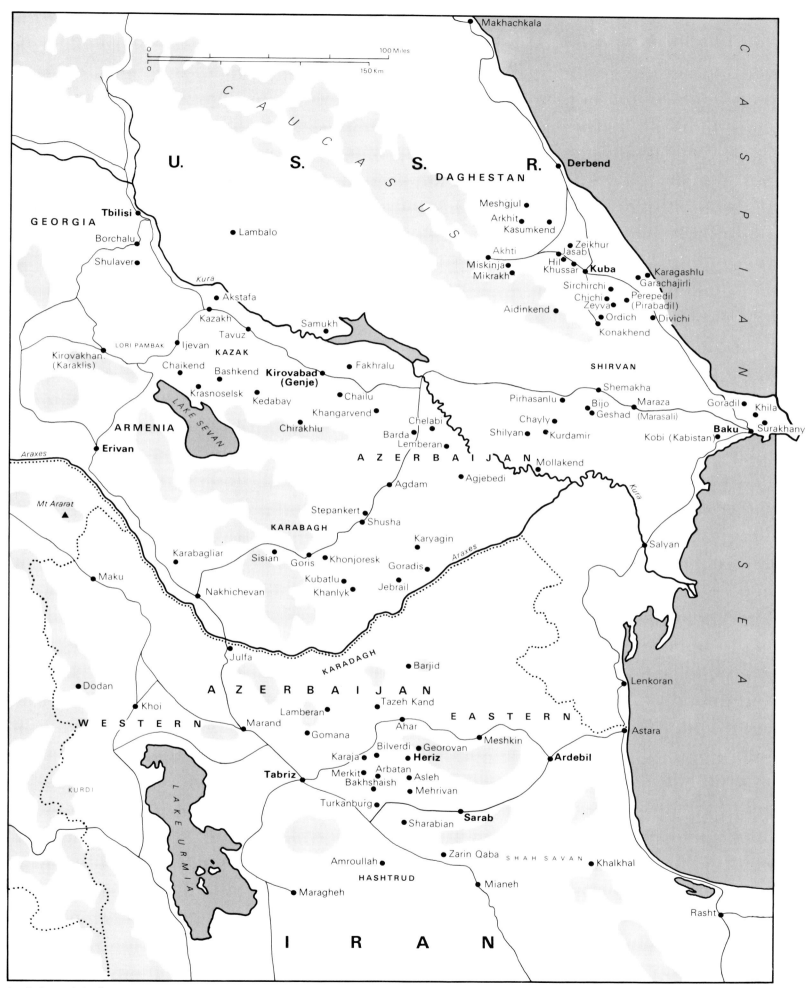

Azerbaijan and the Caucasus.

Western Persia.

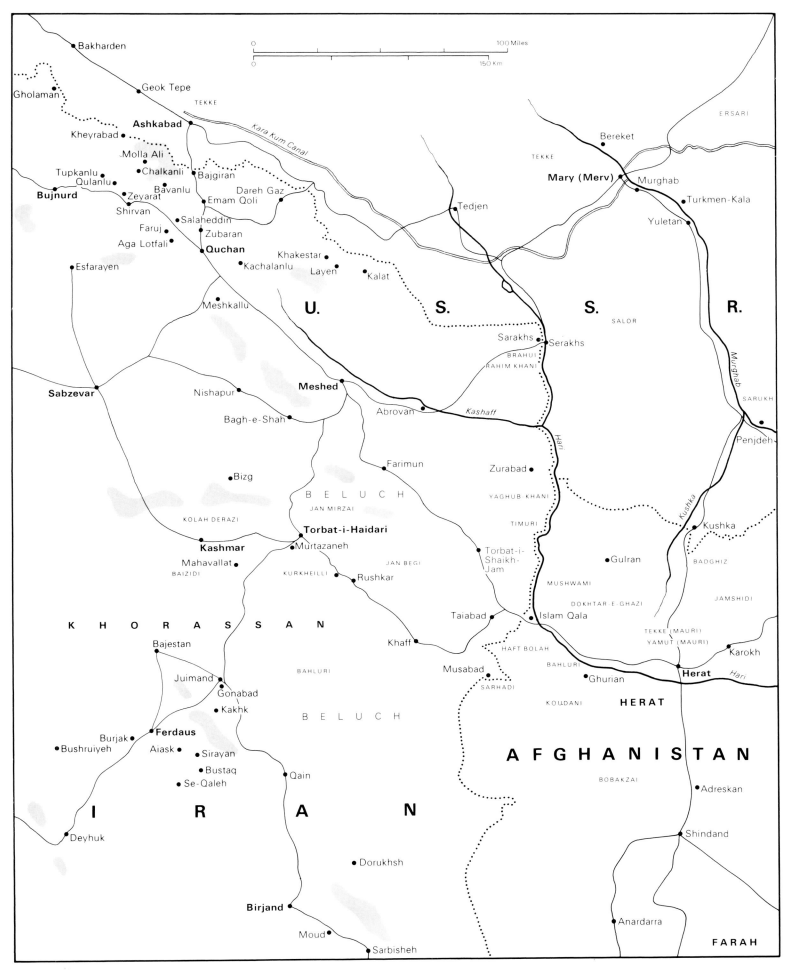

The Khorassan region.

INDEX OF CARPET ORIGINS ILLUSTRATED

All numbers refer to illustrations. For illustrations of objects other than carpets see general index under the following headings: architectural features; artefacts; bookbindings; mandalas; miniature paintings; paintings; textiles.

GENERAL INDEX

For general categories (e.g. border designs, prayer rugs) see table of contents on pp. 5, 6; references to carpets illustrated will be found in the separate index on p. 348. For notes on spellings used, see p. 40; in the case of Chinese place names the new official version in the roman alphabet (as used by the Chinese authorities) is shown in parentheses in each entry as required (e.g. Peking = Beijing). Tribal areas and almost all place names mentioned in this book are included in one or other of the maps; numbers printed in italic refer to the page on which the relevant map appears. In addition to individual entries for historical personages and events and references listed under names of countries, general entries are included under 'history' and 'Persian history'.